GROUP SUPPORT SYSTEMS

GROUP SUPPORT SYSTEMS

New Perspectives

EDITORS

LEONARD M. JESSUP
California State University, San Marcos

JOSEPH S. VALACICH
Indiana University

Macmillan Publishing Company
New York

Maxwell Macmillan Canada
Toronto

Maxwell Macmillan International
New York   Oxford   Singapore   Sydney

Editor: Charles E. Stewart, Jr.
Production Supervisor: Publication Services, Inc.
Production Manager: Aliza Greenblatt

This book was set in Helvetica and Garamond by Publication Services, Inc. and was printed and bound by R. R. Donnelley & Sons.

Copyright © 1993 by Macmillan Publishing Company,
a division of Macmillan, Inc.

Printed in the United States of America

All rights reserved. No part of this book may be reproduced or transmitted in any form or by any means, electronic or mechanical, including photocopying, recording, or any information storage and retrieval system, without permission in writing from the Publisher.

Macmillan Publishing Company
866 Third Avenue, New York, New York 10022

Macmillan Publishing Company is part
of the Maxwell Communication Group of Companies.

Maxwell Macmillan Canada, Inc.
1200 Eglinton Avenue East
Suite 200
Don Mills, Ontario M3C 3N1

Library of Congress Cataloging-in-Publication Data
Group support systems: new perspectives / Leonard M. Jessup, Joseph
    S. Valacich, editors.
      p.   cm.
    Includes bibliographical references and index.
    ISBN 0-02-360625-8
     1. Work groups—Data processing.   2. Decision-making, Group—Data
processing. 3. Decision support systems. I. Jessup, Leonard M.,
1961- . II. Valacich, Joseph S., 1959-
HD66.G754   1992
658.4'036—dc20   92-11495
                                             CIP

Printing: 1 2 3 4 5 6 7   Year: 3 4 5 6 7 8

*To our families, colleagues, and students
for their ideas, support, and understanding
in helping us to complete this book*

Preface

The increasing numbers of papers and presentations on Group Support Systems (GSS) at conferences, in academic research journals, and in the popular press attest to the rapid pace of GSS research and development. This research is fueled by the growing awareness within organizations that groups are essential, that group work is often unproductive, and that several forms of computer-based technology are now available to support group work. Because GSS research is growing quickly, and because GSS research is very much an interdisciplinary science, our strategy is to provide an integrated guiding book on GSS. The primary objective of this book is to present a set of focused readings on several interrelated GSS issues so that researchers, graduate students, and practitioners will have a foundation for GSS research.

To present the most complete coverage of GSS, we asked those researchers who are active in particular research areas to contribute specific, relevant chapters for this collection. This process resulted in the book's division into four sections: (1) GSS overview, (2) research issues in GSS, (3) issues in GSS design, development, use, and management, (4) bridging GSS to other disciplines—and a final chapter in which we present relevant conclusions, implications, and challenges.

In the overview section, we begin in Chapter 1 with a discussion of the nature of technological development generally, and, in particular, the nature of GSS research. In the second chapter, Gerald Wagner, Bye Wynne, and Brian Mennecke provide a tour of various GSS research programs and facilities. After this initial overview section, we turn to a discussion of relevant GSS research issues.

In the research issues section, Brent Gallupe and Alan Dennis first provide a review of prior relevant empirical GSS research. The next two chapters focus on theoretical issues; in the fourth chapter, Joseph McGrath and Andrea Hollingshead discuss the research issues involved in the development and use of various systems in terms of information, work, interaction processes, task outcomes, and user-subjective experiences. In Chapter 5, Gerardine DeSanctis discusses five theories underlying GSS research, presents the assumptions and weaknesses of these perspectives, and argues for a shift in the theoretical foundation of GSS research. Chapter 6, by Ilze Zigurs, is the last chapter in the research section. This chapter covers many relevant methodological and measurement issues in GSS research.

The third section of the book focuses less on research and more on issues in the design, development, use, and management of GSS, although the chapters in this section are heavily influenced by relevant GSS research. Chapter 7, by Jay Nunamaker and his colleagues, provides a fitting transition between the section on research issues and the third section. Nunamaker et al. integrate the laboratory and field environments through a discussion of their experiences and research with GSS at the University of Arizona. In Chapter 8, Robert Bostrom, Robert Anson, and Vikki Clawson provide a foundation for those researchers interested in understanding and investigating facilitation in GSS environments. In Chapter 9, Richard Polley and Philip Stone, guided by research in facility design and social psychology, raise questions regarding the design of GSS facilities and offer suggestions for effective GSS facilities design. Similar design suggestions are offered in Chapter 10; in this chapter, Paul Gray, Munir Mandiwalla, Lorne Olfman, and John Satzinger explore the issues involved in GSS interface design. In Chapter 11, Jeffrey Hoffer and Joseph Valacich discuss organizational memory issues in GSS and suggest implications of managing group memory. In Chapter 12, the final chapter of this section, Karl Weick and David Meader discuss the effects that use of GSS has on our abilities to make sense of our environment, a critical first step to solving problems and make decisions.

In the last major section of the book we attempt to create bridges between GSS and other research disciplines. First, in Chapter 13, we work with George Huber to build links between GSS research and the "macro" perspective of organizational theory. In this chapter we present a theory of the effects of GSS on an organization's nature and decisions. In the following chapter, Chapter 14, Terry Connolly discusses the tendency for GSS to enhance or mitigate some decision-making heuristics and biases in order to integrate GSS research and the more "micro" perspective of decision behavior theory. In Chapter 15, M. Scott Poole builds links between GSS and communication theory, using the constructs of media differences, group communication, argumentation and reasoning, and rhetoric as the linking pins. In Chapter 16, the final chapter in this section, Joy Egbert demonstrates how GSS can be used for purposes other than those primarily intended by GSS designers. She presents relevant research on computer-assisted language learning and shows how GSS can be used to assist in the language-learning process.

We finish with a final chapter in which we offer conclusions, a discussion of relevant implications, and a set of future directions for GSS research and development. To assist researchers in the area, we also include on page 345 a detailed author index and in Chapter 2 a facility index.

We intend this book to be primarily a scholarly book for those interested in GSS or other related research areas. However, we believe that this book is relevant and important to those who design or develop GSS, to those who purchase, rent, or use GSS, and to those who manage GSS use. We suspect that heaviest use of this book will be for direct research purposes (at university, governmental, and corporate sites) in the GSS area and in graduate seminars on GSS. Other uses include advanced undergraduate courses on GSS and de-

Preface

cision support systems, relevant graduate and undergraduate classes in other academic departments (e.g., courses in departments of education, management, psychology, social psychology, etc.), and corporate and governmental training courses on GSS.

As this book is a study of technologies for collaborative work, so was the writing of this book a collaborative endeavor. This book was truly a shared work between the two editors. As editors we shared equally in the creation and production of this book. It is unfortunate for one of us that the other had the good fortune (a last name beginning with the letter *J*) that let him be listed first in the alphabetical listing of names for editorship of the book. We thank the chapter writers for their hard work in producing excellent chapters in a very short amount of time. Working with these people was very easy, very fun, and very productive. We would also like to thank our families, namely Joy, Jackie, and Jordan, and our colleagues and students at our respective universities, California State University, San Marcos, and Indiana University, for providing the support and resources necessary to make this work possible.

Trademarks

We would like to acknowledge the systems and developers that are referenced throughout this book. Each of these developers holds a registered trademark and/or other legal right of ownership to their system. The systems discussed most extensively in this book include Bridge Toolkit (Softbridge Incorporated), Claremont Group Support Environment (The Claremont Graduate School), Comments (Indiana University), Computer Aided Meeting (University of Minnesota), Coordinator (Action Technologies Incorporated), DECAID1 (University of Minnesota), Electronic Information Exchange System (New Jersey Institute of Technology), GroupSystems (Ventana Corporation), Lotus 1-2-3 and Lotus Notes (Lotus Development Corporation), Mindsight (Execucom Systems), NewWave (Hewlett-Packard Company), OptionFinder (Option Technologies Incorporated), PLEXSYS (University of Arizona), Software Aided Meeting Management (University of Minnesota), Software Aided Group Environment (National University of Singapore), TeamFocus (IBM Corporation), THINX (Bell Atlantic Corporation), Virtual Classroom (New Jersey Institute of Technology), VisionQuest (Collaborative Technologies Corporation), and WINDOWS (Microsoft Corporation).

L. M. J.
J. S. V.

Contents

PART I
INTRODUCTION AND OVERVIEW OF GROUP SUPPORT SYSTEMS — 1

1 On the Study of Group Support Systems: An Introduction to Group Support System Research and Development — 3
Leonard M. Jessup, Joseph S. Valacich

    Introduction — 3
    Research on and Development of GSS — 5

2 Group Support Systems Facilities and Software — 8
Gerald R. Wagner, Bayard E. Wynne, Brian E. Mennecke

    Introduction — 8
    The EMS Framework (or Efficiency-R-Us) — 9
    Adaptive Structuration Theory (AST) (Give-N-Take) — 10
    In the Middle — 11
    The Rest of the World — 12
    Capsule Descriptions of Nine GSS Research Sites — 13
        University of Arizona — 13
        University of Minnesota — 16
        University of Georgia — 18
        Indiana University — 20
        New Jersey Institute of Technology — 22
        Queen's University — 24
        University of Michigan — 26
        The Claremont Graduate School — 28
        University of Hohenheim — 30
    Conclusion — 33
    Appendix: GSS Research Facilities — 33

PART II
RESEARCH ISSUES IN GROUP SUPPORT SYSTEMS   57

3 A History of Group Support Systems Empirical Research: Lessons Learned and Future Directions   59
Alan R. Dennis, R. Brent Gallupe

Introduction	59
Research Review	61
Roots	61
Initial Explorations	62
Early Experiments	64
Field Studies	66
In-Depth Studies	68
Parallelism	69
Anonymity	69
Group Size	70
Process Structuring	70
Group Development and Studies Over Time	72
What We Know and What We Don't	73
Summary of Findings	73
Implications	75
Future Research	76

4 Putting the "Group" Back in Group Support Systems: Some Theoretical Issues About Dynamic Processes in Groups with Technological Enhancements   78
Joseph E. McGrath, Andrea B. Hollingshead

Introduction	78
Systems for Technological Enhancements of Work in Groups	79
GCSS: Technologies for the Group's Internal Communication	80
GXSS: Technologies for the Group's External Communication	85
GISS: Technologies for the Group's Information Base	86
GPSS: Technologies for the Group's Performance Processes	88
Groups, Tasks, and Electronic Support Systems	89
Group and Member Characteristics	90
Task Types	90
Task Types, Communication Media, and Information Richness	91
The Task/Media Fit Hypothesis	92
Group Support Systems from a Group Theory Perspective	93
Concluding Comments	95

5 Shifting Foundations in Group Support System Research   97
Gerardine DeSanctis

Introduction   97
The Role of GSS in Organizations   98
    GSS as Tool: Individualism   98
    GSS as Product: Collectivism   100
Assumptions and Theories of GSS as Organizational Change
   Mechanisms   101
    Competing Theories for GSS Research   103
    Missing Elements in Existing Theory   107
    Shifting Foundations   109
Conclusion   111

6 Methodological and Measurement Issues in Group Support Systems Research   112
Ilze Zigurs

Introduction   112
A Framework for Research Methods   112
Choosing An Appropriate Research Method   114
Method Issues Within GSS Research   115
    Role of Reference Disciplines   115
    The Dependent Variable   116
    Development of Measurement Instruments   117
    The Problem of Appropriate Comparisons   118
    The Unit of Analysis   119
    Data Issues Within GSS Research   120
    Recommendations and Conclusions   120

PART III
ISSUES IN THE DESIGN, DEVELOPMENT, USE, AND MANAGEMENT OF GROUP SUPPORT SYSTEMS   123

7 Group Support Systems Research: Experience from the Lab and Field   125
J. F. Nunamaker Jr., Alan R. Dennis, Joseph S. Valacich, Douglas R. Vogel, Joey F. George

Introduction   125
Theoretical Foundations   126
    Research on Process Gains and Losses   126
    Mechanisms for Process Gains and Losses   128

Group Support Systems Design 133
    Meeting Leader/Facilitator 134
    Software Toolkit 134
Group Support Systems in Practice 136
    Task Structure 137
    Task Support 138
    Process Structure 138
    Process Support 140
Conclusion 145

8 Group Facilitation and Group Support Systems   146
Robert P. Bostrom, Robert Anson, Vikki K. Clawson

Introduction 146
Meeting Model 148
    What is a Meeting? 148
    Facilitation Activities by Meeting Stage 150
Review of Prior Research Literature 152
    Meeting Research 152
    Group Dynamics/Process Interventions Research 153
    GSS Research 155
    Summary of Research 156
A Meeting Facilitation Framework 156
    Overview 156
    Facilitation Targets 158
    Facilitation Sources 159
    Facilitation Functions 160
    Structure 160
    Support 161
Future Research Issues 162
    Introduction 162
    A Theoretical Perspective of Facilitation 162
    Is a Facilitator Necessary in GSS Environments? 163
    Facilitating in Different GSS Environments 164
    Developing Facilitation Skills 166
    Future Research Summary 167
Conclusion 168

9 Flexspace: Making Room for Collaborative Work   169
Richard B. Polley, Philip J. Stone

Introduction 169
Time and Space 170

	GSS Facilities: A Critique	170
	Some Mistaken Premises of Collaborative Work	179
	Flexspace Designs for Collaborative Work	185
	A Vanguard Case: Off-Site Training Centers	186
	Implications of Flexspace for Future Research on Groups	188
	Concluding Comments	189
	Appendix A: Questions for a Structured Interview on Flexspace	189
	A. The Team	189
	B. On-Site Facilities and Computer Support	190
	C. Coordination with Other Teams and External Members	191
	D. Off-Site Facilities and Computer Support	191

10   The User Interface in Group Support Systems   192
Paul Gray, Munir Mandviwalla, Lorne Olfman, John Satzinger

Introduction	192
The Interface in a Group Support System	193
Issues in Design	194
Issue 1: The Design of the "Public Screen(s)"	194
Issue 2: The Interaction Between the Public Screen and the Individual Screen	196
Issue 3: The Design of the Individual Workstation in the Group Environment	197
Issue 4: Interaction Among Participants	199
Issue 5: Cognitive Style	200
Issue 6: Cultural Differences	200
Issue 7. Content Specific to the Meeting	201
Issue 8. Information Input and Output	202
Example: The CGS Environment (CGSE)	205
Background	205
The User Environment	206
Personal	210
Summary and Conclusions	210
Needed Research	211
Conclusions	213

11   Group Memory in Group Support Systems: A Foundation for Design   214
Jeffrey A. Hoffer, Joseph S. Valacich

Introduction	214
Overview of Organizational Learning and Memory	216

Organizational Learning	218
Organizational Memory	219
Group Decision Making and the Role of Group Memory	221
Common Organizational Information	222
Relevant External Information	222
Education of New Group Members	222
Session Continuity Support	222
Response to Change	223
Group Coordination and Work Flow Management	223
Support for Distributed Groups	223
Creation of a Group and Organizational Memory	224
Support for the Design of Group Memory	224
The Relationship of Database Management to Group Memory Management	224
Database System Limitations for Group Memory Management	228
Summary and Conclusions	229

12 Sensemaking and Group Support Systems — 230
Karl E. Weick, David K. Meader

Introduction	230
Sensemaking in Equivocal Contexts	231
Activities of Sensemaking	235
Sensemaking in Meetings	236
Action	237
Triangulation	241
Unaided Triangulation	242
Affiliation	243
Deliberation	246
Contextualization	249
Conclusion	251

PART IV
BRIDGING GROUP SUPPORT SYSTEM APPLICATION AND RESEARCH TO OTHER DISCIPLINES — 253

13 A Theory of the Effects of Group Support Systems on an Organization's Nature and Decisions — 255
George P. Huber, Joseph S. Valacich, Leonard M. Jessup

Introduction	255
The Nature of GSS	256
Toward a Conceptual Theory	257

	The Theory	257
	Summary and Recommendations	268
14	**Behavioral Decision Theory and Group Support Systems**	**270**
	Terry Connolly	
	Introduction	270
	Decision Behavior Research	271
	Idea Generation	272
	Hindsight and Overconfidence	274
	Externalizing Judgments and Policy Capturing	277
	Conclusions	280
15	**Communication Theory and Group Support Systems**	**281**
	M. Scott Poole, Michele H. Jackson	
	Introduction	281
	Communication Media Research	282
	Communication Processes in Group Decision Making	285
	Rationality and Argumentation	289
	Rhetorical Approaches	291
	Conclusion	293
16	**Group Support Systems for Computer Assisted Language Learning: Of Evolution, Purpose, and Real-Time Interaction**	**294**
	Joy Egbert	
	Introduction	294
	A Framework for Looking at Computers and the ESL Classroom	295
	Learning Strategies for Optimal Language	296
	Strategy #1 Provide Opportunities for Learners to Interact	296
	Strategy #2 Provide an Authentic Audience and Opportunities to Negotiate Meaning	297
	Strategy #3 Create/Use Authentic Tasks	298
	Strategy #4 Promote Exposure to and Production of Varied and Creative Language	298
	Strategy #5 Provide Learners Opportunities to Formulate Ideas and Thoughts	299
	Strategy #6 Promote Intentional Cognition	299
	Strategy #7 Create an Atmosphere with Optimal Stress/Anxiety	300
	Strategy #8 Create a Learner-Centered Classroom	301
	Summary of Step One	301

        Examining Computers as Material for Supporting Strategies   302
            Stand-Alone Programs   304
            Networks   305
        Exploring New Technologies   306
            Interaction in Real Time   306
            Group Support Systems   308
        Future Research   309
        Summary   310

17 Future Directions and Challenges in the Evolution of Group Support Systems   311
    Leonard M. Jessup, Joseph S. Valacich

    Introduction   311
        GSS in the Next Century: Anything, Anytime, Anywhere   312
        GSS Scenario 1: "Any Time/Any Place"   313
        GSS Scenario 2: "Orchestrated Workflow"   314
        GSS Scenario 3: "Virtual Team Rooms"   315
        GSS Scenario 4: "Culture Bridging"   316
        GSS Scenario 5: "Just-in-Time Learning"   316
        GSS Scenario 6: "Window to Anywhere"   317
    Conclusion   317

References   319

Contributors   345

Index   357

PART I

INTRODUCTION AND OVERVIEW OF GROUP SUPPORT SYSTEMS

CHAPTER 1

On the Study of Group Support Systems: An Introduction to Group Support System Research and Development

Leonard M. Jessup
California State University, San Marcos

Joseph S. Valacich
Indiana University

INTRODUCTION

History suggests that, for us to understand any new technology, we have to move beyond traditional notions of what we did without the technology. We must think in novel ways about how we will use the new technology and about the effects that the technology might have on us. The use of the technology may change things. Take, for example, some familiar technologies that had great effects on us personally and socially in our organizations and in society; these technologies forced us to think differently about how we do things. The invention of the clock drastically changed our measurement and use of time. The discovery and harnessing of electricity led to the development of artificial light and enabled us to extend the day and change our use of it. The invention of the telegraph and telephone altered markedly the nature of communication. The invention of the compass and the telescope dramatically changed travel and our understanding and use of the planet. The microscope radically altered our understanding and treatment of the human body. The printing press and movable type fundamentally changed communication and the transference of knowledge (see Boorstin, 1985, for a wonderful discussion of these discoveries and inventions and their effects on us). We could not have easily imagined the uses and outcomes of these new technologies based on our experiences without the technologies.

More broadly, the development of the "technologies" of geography and cartography, astronomy, anatomy, mathematics, and physics, to name a few, radically altered the way we think about our world. In many instances these technologies—discoveries, inventions, sciences—helped us to do things better, faster, more accurately, more easily, more safely, more efficiently, and more precisely. More important, these technologies often brought radical, fundamental change to our lives, to what we can do and to how we think about things, often in ways we could not have previously imagined. Alternatively, in some cases these new technologies created side effects, new problems and new ethical dilemmas for us to deal with. For example, Rifkin (1987) argued that the invention of the clock, and the subsequent changes in our notion and use of time, has had tremendous adverse effects on us.

Similarly, the introduction of new computer-based information system technologies for organizations requires that we think of new ways of communicating, new ways of working, and it requires that we not limit ourselves to traditional notions of what we can do or what we have done. Our expectations of what we will do with these systems are inherently simplistic and constrained. Our forecasts are inevitably constrained by traditional notions of what we did previously in similar situations without the technology. For example, with the introduction of a new computer-based loan application data base, loan processors or loan officers can easily see that the new system will enable them to process loan applications faster. It is not as easy for them to see that the new system might enable them to do the process better, with better control over information, with enhanced security capabilities, and with greater probability of accepting sound applicants and rejecting risky applications. The new system may also enable them to better understand the cycles and patterns of their work processes so that they can, perhaps, better monitor, control, or even completely change the process in ways that enable them to do their jobs better. Shosana Zuboff (1984) referred to this way of thinking about new technologies as "informating," as opposed to "automating."

The advent of Group Support Systems (GSS) is no different. It is easy to envision some of the simple logistical efficiencies afforded by GSS—a GSS enables many people to speak and listen at once during a meeting. However, it is also now possible that, as a result of the advent of the GSS, our notions of the effective size of workgroups are obsolete. Our propositions about effective group size are based on antiquated assumptions of group process. The relationship between group size and group effectiveness and efficiency is changing with the advent of technology; it is now possible that, with GSS, large groups can be as efficient as small groups. Similarly, we cannot be bound by traditional notions of groups as static entities in time and place; our assumptions about the possibilities for interaction no longer fit. The technology makes possible "virtual" groups that can span time and space effectively and efficiently. Furthermore, we should explore potential negative effects. For example, we may find that over time a GSS depersonalizes group members to such an extent that group performance diminishes or group members ultimately reject the technology.

With GSS, as with any technology, we must open our minds to new possibilities and new problems. We should think critically about how we might use the system and about the effects that the system might have on work, relationships, management, and organization. What influence will GSS have, with what repercussions, consequences, implications, bringing about what changes? How, when, and why will this technology be adopted and used? What does this mean for the way that we work together and socialize at work, for the way we manage work, for the way we structure, organize, plan, and control? Asking and answering these types of questions will help us to better understand GSS, and this inquiry will provide more useful answers than the data provided by traditional information systems feasibility analyses, such as cost-benefit analysis.

GSS research is beginning to take us in this direction of inquiry. This approach to research is vital to our understanding the possibilities and limits of GSS, and to our ability to harness the real power of the technology while minimizing or avoiding the dysfunctional aspects. The proper question guiding this book is not "what will GSS do for us?" but rather, "what will GSS do to us?" or "what will we do with GSS?"

RESEARCH ON AND DEVELOPMENT OF GSS

It is difficult to even begin to ask what effects GSS will have or how they will be used because the term Group Support System is somewhat nebulous. Indeed, there are marked differences from one GSS to the next. By "Group Support System" we mean computer-based information systems used to support intellectual collaborative work. The general domain of this book is the GSS environment in which the technology is used to aid goal-directed group work. An easy way to envision the scope of this book is to think of the type of work that takes place in a meeting. Therefore, our focus is not necessarily on electronic mail and other, more general communication technologies. This does not, however, preclude the discussion of several important concepts such as group member proximity, media differences, and other such issues common to all group work environments. In Johansen's (1988) terminology, the primary focus of this book is on the same time/same place GSS dimension (Figure 1.1). This choice was made because much of the GSS research, to date, has focused on the same time and place dimension and there is a growing need for a focused set of readings

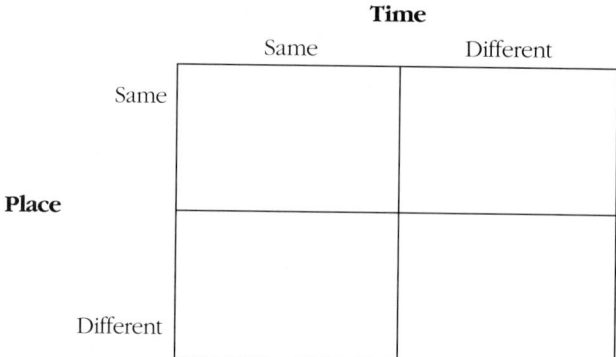

FIGURE 1.1 Time and place dimensions in which technology may be used to support group work.

to present what we "currently know and don't know." However, because of the obvious interrelationships to other dimensions of GSS, the discussions in many chapters are clearly relevant to these other time/place dimensions, and in fact, in many instances these relationships are discussed directly.

Because there are so many variants of GSS throughout the time/place dimensions, GSS research has been conducted under a complex rubric of names. For example, relevant GSS research is conducted under the names Group Decision Support Systems, Electronic Meeting Systems, Computer-Supported Collaborative Work, Computer-Mediated Communication Systems, and Group Negotiation Support Systems. The issues discussed in this book are relevant to research conducted in each of these areas. Similarly, the issues discussed in this book have relevance to the development and use of technologies known by such names as groupware, electronic boardrooms, electronic mail, and computer-conferencing software packages.

The diversity in types of GSS research conducted is mirrored by the diversity of GSS researchers. An analysis of papers concerning GSS research presented at the past few meetings of the Hawaii International Conference on System Sciences (HICSS), which is quickly becoming a popular forum for GSS research, reveals rapid growth in GSS research. At HICSS, GSS research is now presented by many different participating researchers, representing many different institutions and disciplines. At present, GSS research and development of one form or another is conducted at over 30 different universities throughout the United States and many more throughout the world, and many of these universities have at least one GSS facility. GSS research and development is also being conducted in nearly as many nonuniversity private and public organizations. For example, in one corporation, International Business Machines, there are over approximately 30 GSS facilities, with many more planned for development. There are now at least a half dozen true GSS software products available, with

Chapter 1 On the Study of Group Support Systems

an additional 20 or more different "groupware" software products—packages focusing on the more generic tasks of E-mail, group scheduling, and document sharing—now available on the market.

The proliferation of GSS-related products is not surprising given that the technology is so attractive to users seeking products that enable them to work together electronically and utilize the new, sophisticated networking technologies now available. Similarly, the diversity of GSS research is not surprising given that the technology involves research in information systems, organizational behavior and theory, communication, and social psychology. Given the positive response of users in industry and the complex, diverse nature of GSS research, the GSS research area offers problems of relevance, importance, and interest. Indeed, there is a great deal of very interesting, important research being conducted, with many interesting and important questions still unanswered.

Aside from the inherent interest and importance of GSS research, there is good reason for GSS researchers to be excited. As Gary Dickson exclaimed at the most recent Academy of Management Annual Meeting in a session on GSS research, "...this is one of the few areas of information systems research where academicians are leading practitioners in the development of an information system technology." GSS researchers are uniquely positioned to lead a careful, systematic investigation of GSS and their use that will lead to thoughtful, effective use of the technology. Perhaps we can help to forecast some of the effects that the technology will have on us, describe some of the ways that the technology might be used or misused, and suggest some of the possibilities and problems that GSS presents. We suspect that at this point we must feel somewhat like Jacopo and Giovanni de' Dondi, Galileo Galilei, Robert Hooke, and John Harrison did between the years 1344 and 1761, as they each contributed greatly to the development of the mechanical clock—wondering about the possibilities, excited about the prospects, frightened by some of the potential consequences, eager to see development and use grow. The following chapters are offered to GSS researchers, developers, and users to stimulate their imaginations and to guide GSS research, development, and use.

CHAPTER 2

Group Support Systems Facilities and Software

Gerald R. Wagner
Collaborative Technologies Corporation

Bayard E. Wynne
Indiana University

Brian E. Mennecke
Indiana University

INTRODUCTION

The field of computer support for cooperative work is generally agreed to have been identified and championed—if not invented—by Dr. Doug Engelbart. Engelbart has been associated with a variety of institutions such as Stanford University, SRI International, and McDonnel-Douglas. He is currently director of the Bootstrap Institute, which he founded to promote his vision. He has been credited with the invention of now commonplace computing artifacts such as the mouse, windows, hypertext, and personal computing. These achievements came about in the early 1960s, but the results of Engelbart's endeavors were brought to the public eye only in the mid-1970s. Given that Engelbart's objective was—and still is—the augmentation of human intellect, his vision continues to provide a target for sociologists and technologists alike to pursue, and many of his ideas seem as fresh now as they were three decades ago.

The forerunner of all so-called Group Support Systems (GSS), particularly of the kind being investigated in academia, was a system called Mindsight. Mind-

Chapter 2 Group Support Systems Facilities and Software

sight was more than a software product—it was a research project undertaken by Dr. Gerald R. Wagner, a former University of Texas professor. In 1975, Wagner founded a successful decision support system (DSS) software company called Execucom. He then went on to investigate the possibilities of using computer systems to support group idea generation, elaboration, analysis, synthesis, and decision making. Mindsight included a well-furnished conference room replete with a conference table that included recessed computer terminals capable of displaying graphics, a color projector with a public screen, and decor to promote group discussions. Adjacent to the conference room was a room that allowed a social psychologist to observe meetings via a one-way mirror. Mindsight was developed in the late 1970s and was far ahead of its time. Indeed, the basic configuration of Mindsight has provided the inspiration for "Planning" or "Decision" laboratories in scores of university labs, including those at the University of Arizona. In combination, Engelbart's vision and Wagner's implementation of Mindsight are themselves the root of GSS and CSCW development. Building on this early work, a number of researchers at a variety of institutions have subsequently focused their attention on deepening our collective understanding of this technology. The purpose of this chapter is to present a survey of these current research efforts in order to provide a perspective on where GSS research currently is positioned.

In many respects, the variety of GSS research centers is pronounced, both in terms of the technologies used to support research and in terms of the research philosophies and theories adopted to provide direction and focus. In order to make this point clear, as we discuss these GSS research organizations, we use the underlying philosophies and theories employed by these institutions as a theme for guiding our discussion. The first to be discussed will be the University of Arizona and the EMS framework. Next, the University of Minnesota and Adaptive Structuration Theory (AST) will be discussed. The third section presents a discussion of those organizations that, to one degree or another, represent institutions exhibiting research thrusts that are, for lack of a better word, "hybrids" of the University of Arizona and the University of Minnesota perspectives. The fourth section will include those organizations that do not fit readily into one of the first three categories. These discussions will be followed by brief descriptions of the nine research sites discussed. Throughout this chapter we would also like you to see that, in spite of the many differences that exist among these various organizations, similarities do exist between these institutions on several levels and that convergence toward a more coherent line of inquiry is perhaps on the horizon.

THE EMS FRAMEWORK (OR EFFICIENCY-R-US)

Dennis and coworkers (1988) proposed a conceptual model of computer-based meeting support systems, that they referred to as the EMS framework. Having come out of the software engineering environment at Arizona, this framework represents a research philosophy grounded in an engineering "worldview." This view encourages methodologies designed to systematically study the framework components in strictly controlled manipulations—manipulations in which the researcher attempts to impose and enforce a structure. An important assumption underlying this framework is that group performance and behavior can be improved by imposing an efficient structure on the group through specific heuristics, processes, and technologies.

To a large degree, the originators of the EMS framework have conducted research that has reflected the EMS framework philosophy. Much of their research effort, both in the laboratory and in the field, has represented leading-edge inquiries designed to systematically fill in the missing components of the EMS framework variables. They have also taken the lead in the design and promotion of state-of-the-art software and facilities. In many ways, Arizona represents a model GSS research and development center in which both cutting-edge research and software design are combined to set the pace in GSS research.

ADAPTIVE STRUCTURATION THEORY (AST) (GIVE-N-TAKE)

Researchers from the University of Minnesota, most notably M. Scott Poole and Gerardine DeSanctis, advanced the AST theory. This theory suggests that the GSS technology is not an object that is necessarily adopted in an equivalent manner across all groups, but is appropriated by each group uniquely. This implies that it is not the technology that becomes the independent variable of interest in the study of human behavior, but rather the manner or pattern of use made of that technology. (See Chapter 15 for a more complete description of AST.) The focus of research that is based on this theory is to understand how and whether the group interacts with, changes, or adopts the technology. Implicit in this theory is the idea that structure does not need to be and, in fact, should not be imposed on the group. Rather, the group should be exposed to the technology and enabled to selectively adopt the technology provided structure.

In many respects, the implications of this theory for research methodology and design run counter to that of the EMS framework. This can be seen when one examines the design of research conducted at the University of Minnesota. Certainly this is not to imply that the research conducted at Minnesota is any less rigorous than that at Arizona. Rather, the difference lies in the goals and outcomes sought from the research. Minnesota often appears to be interested not so much in identifying the most efficient means of implementing a GSS, but instead in identifying how the group reacts to and feels about the experience.

We hope that the discussion to this point makes it clear that both Arizona and Minnesota have significantly contributed to our understanding of GSS in three important ways: in terms of the development and application of theory, in terms of the generation of research, and in terms of software development. However, in many respects, each of these two schools has historically approached these issues differently. Certainly one could argue that as a consequence of this, the institutions are perceived by many people inside and outside of the GSS field as having unique, and perhaps opposing, philosophies and approaches for working with GSS. For example, suppose that both Arizona and Minnesota were considered on a spectrum on which the left end represented GSS research institutions adopting an engineering and system design philosophy and the right end represented GSS research institutions adopting a more traditional social science research philosophy. Clearly many people would perceive that much of Arizona's research efforts lie to the left of center, whereas much of Minnesota's research efforts lie to the right of center.

Does this stereotype accurately describe Arizona and Minnesota today? If one looks at the diversity of both laboratory and field research emanating from both sites, one would clearly have to answer this question negatively! Nevertheless, historically the differences between Arizona and Minnesota have been more pronounced. As a consequence of this heritage, it is likely that Ph.D. graduates from both these programs are likely to carry these differing philosophies to their positions at other research institutions. The next logical question is this: Where do such research institutions fit on the aforementioned spectrum? Let us examine them and see!

IN THE MIDDLE

The University of Georgia and Indiana University both are GSS research institutions that represent hybrids of the Arizona and Minnesota programs. Because these schools include personnel who come out of both the Arizona and the Minnesota heritages, they are likely to represent institutions in which a marriage of the Arizona and Minnesota philosophies will be evident.

The University of Georgia GSS research effort was initiated by Bob Bostrom, a graduate of Minnesota, when he migrated to Georgia from Indiana University in 1988. He was quickly followed by Rick Watson from Minnesota in 1989 and Alan Dennis from Arizona in 1991. This amalgam of personnel truly represents a rich mixture of talent from a variety of schools. It is not clear what direction the Georgia program will take. However, it is likely that having faculty who represent both the Minnesota and Arizona perspectives will benefit this GSS research effort.

The Indiana University GSS research effort was initiated by Bob Bostrom in the early eighties, while he was at Indiana prior to his move to Georgia. In 1986, Bye Wynne, representing both the Minnesota viewpoint and significant industrial and consulting experience, joined the Indiana program as director of the Institute for Research on the Management of Information Systems (IRMIS). Upon Bostrom's departure, Wynne picked up the reins of leadership in GSS research at Indiana. He was joined in this effort in 1988 by Alan Heminger and in 1990 by Joe Valacich, both new graduates from Arizona. As with Georgia then, Indiana's faculty are influenced by both the Arizona and the Minnesota perspectives, and the research that is generated within this environment is likely to benefit from these diverse influences.

Both Georgia and Indiana represent GSS research sites where significant research has been conducted outside of the context of overt influences from Arizona and Minnesota. For instance, Georgia has focused on exploring facilitation and comparing various GSS technologies. Indiana, for its part, has applied the existing theory-base from other disciplines to GSS by exploring issues such as gender composition, group history and development (including team building), spatial decision support systems (related to Geographic Information Systems), equity theory, and theories of persuasion. We have yet to see how these relatively recent changes in personnel will affect the research direction of these schools. Nevertheless, we expect that, as with any group or society, diversity will breed innovation and change and that, as a consequence of this, the future research products generated by these institutions will continue to be important.

THE REST OF THE WORLD

Although the schools discussed so far have significantly influenced GSS research, they are by no means the only institutions displaying a prominent role in this field. Several important research institutions from around the world are playing an important role in exploring the development and use of GSS from perspectives different from those outlined above. Some of these institutions are discussed below.

The New Jersey Institute of Technology (NJIT), under the leadership of Murray Turoff, was one of the first institutions to investigate GSS. Currently, both Turoff and Starr Roxanne Hiltz lead the GSS research effort at NJIT. The Turoff and Hiltz team first explored collaborative computer conferencing systems used for decision making in the mid-1970s. The type of GSS research at NJIT has varied; however, they are most noted for investigating systems that support large groups (50–100) in conferencing and E-mail environments.

The University of Michigan's GSS research program, like the NJIT program, has been investigating facets of GSS technology since the 1970s. Gary and Judy Olsen, the coordinators of Michigan's GSS research effort, have brought together a group of researchers from diverse disciplines such as engineering and computer science, organizational behavior, and political science. This diversity in personnel is manifest in the diversity of research conducted at Michigan. However, a number of these researchers have recently begun to focus their efforts on exploring issues associated with using GSS to support synchronous distributed work.

At Queen's University, Brent Gallupe continues his experimentally focused research in the Queen's Executive Decision Center. Joining him in these efforts are seven associates whose interests range from systems development, through total quality management to organizational behavior. GSS application is studied at Queens in terms of (1) brainstorming, (2) longitudinal development, and (3) group-framing issues.

The Claremont Graduate School began doing GSS research in 1985 after Paul Gray migrated to Claremont from Southern Methodist University, where he had been involved in GSS research from the early eighties. Gray was joined in this research by Lorne Olfman, an Indiana graduate, in 1987. Together, they have been involved in a number of research studies on a diverse set of issues. Much of the focus of Claremont's efforts has been on application development. One unique facet of this involves combining desktop applications with group software in a WINDOWS™ environment.

The University of Hohenheim research program was initiated in 1987 with the construction of the CATeam meeting room, that is, a GSS decision room. The Hohenheim researchers have used this facility as a research environment to explore, among other things, issues related to GSS adoption and usage by multinational organizations, group knowledge development, and distributed meetings. Hohenheim is actively applying GSS technology within the European Community by supporting and coordinating research among researchers from several of the European countries. In addition, like many other GSS sites, Hohenheim is active in GSS software development and in applying existing software in new ways and in different environments.

CAPSULE DESCRIPTIONS OF NINE GSS RESEARCH SITES

University of Arizona

Inception. The heart of the University of Arizona GSS research program, GroupSystems™, evolved from the idea that a phase was needed to assist users and analysts with the determination of system requirements. Much of the early work began in the ISDOS (Information System Design and Optimization System) project at the Case Institute of Technology and later at the University of Michigan (Teichroew & Sayani, 1974). The focus of the ISDOS project was to aid in the definition, development, and maintenance of information systems. ISDOS (and later PLEXSYS: see Konsynski, 1976; Nunamaker et al., 1988) started with the assumption that the system requirements were known or that the individual or group responsible for the system building project was capable of stating the requirements. Through the course of using this process, it became clear that system requirements were not known or could not be easily described by most design teams; hence the need for an initial computer-supported group meeting environment.

Development. Construction of the first GSS room at Arizona began in 1984. Called PlexCenter, it was designed to support group-process tasks such as idea generation, idea organization, voting, and policy formulation. The realization that this PLEXSYS software technology enabled groups to perform many tasks beyond system development (e.g., strategic planning), led to the next phase, which began in 1986 with the establishment of several research projects with IBM. The second GSS facility, the Collaborative Management Room, was opened in 1987. During this phase, the software was very extensively revised and, as a consequence, was renamed GroupSystems™. This software was installed at GSS facilities at more than 36 universities and at more than 12 corporations, including IBM, Dupont, BellSouth, and Greyhound Financial Corporation.

Software. There are many different configurations for GroupSystems™ depending upon whether it is used in electronic meeting room(s) or distributed in individual offices. The general design for the meeting room version of GroupSystems™ builds on three basic concepts: (1) a meeting room, (2) meeting facilitation, and (3) a software toolkit. Although many different meeting room designs have been used, the minimum configuration provides a separate networked microcomputer workstation to each participant, a network server, and another one or two workstations serving as the meeting leader/facilitator's console, which is attached to a large public display screen. The distributed version of GroupSystems™ is similar to the meeting room version, except that group members log into the system from their offices. This version also permits the role of meeting leader to pass from user to user as decided by the group. The GroupSystems™ software toolkit provides tools in five areas: (1) session planning and management, (2) group interaction, (3) organizational memory, (4) individual work, and (5) research data collection. The focus is on tools for group interaction, which fall into four categories: (1) exploration and idea generation, (2) idea organization, (3) prioritization and alternative evaluation, and (4) tools that provide formal methodologies to support policy development and evaluation. The tools may be used in whatever order the group chooses; there is no mandatory order, although many tasks follow a natural order of idea generation, idea synthesis, prioritizing, and exploration of important issues.

Personnel. Jay Nunamaker established the Arizona research program and has continued to lead it as it has evolved over the past decade. In the early 1980s, Benn Konsynski was involved with GroupSystems™ use in the software development process, while Doug Vogel and Joey George have played key roles in more recent years. A number of doctoral students have made significant contributions, including Linda Applegate, Erran Carmel, Bob Daniels, Alan Dennis, Glenda Hayes, Alan Heminger, Bruce Herniter, Ben Martz, Mark Pendergast, Craig Tyran, and Joe Valacich. Research support personnel Kendall Cliff, David Chappell, Bill Saints, and Lee Walker have also played important roles.

Facilities. The first GSS facility to be installed at the University of Arizona, PlexCenter, houses a large U-shaped conference table with 16 computer workstations and a single large screen public display. The facility also contains four breakout rooms equipped with workstations to allow for small group discussions. Software developed to support group work at PlexCenter included idea generation, idea organization, voting and policy formation tools. The second GSS facility, the Collaborative Management Room, was opened in 1987. This facility contains 24 workstations (with space for two people per workstation), gallery seating for observation, and two large-screen public displays. The facility also has numerous other audio and video support technologies (see Nunamaker, Dennis, George, Valacich, & Vogel, 1991 for a detailed description). Four additional facilities are scheduled to open in early 1992. Each of these new facilities addresses a different type of GSS research. One facility is a large group meeting room, with 31 workstations and three public display screens. The second facility is a small group meeting room incorporating telecommunications, notepad technology, wireless LANs, and virtual reality and multimedia technology. The third is a meeting room-to-meeting room teleconferencing facility designed to create the illusion that all participants are in the same room. The fourth facility supports distributed large groups in separate work areas.

Research. Space precludes a complete description of the research studies now in progress as part of the Arizona GSS research program. Several broad areas, each of which have several specific GSS research studies, include distributed GSS, organizational adoption and diffusion, strategic planning, GSS for negotiation, organizational memory, multimedia GSS, enterprise analysis and information system design (e.g., joint application development, or JAD), effects of specific GSS components (e.g., anonymity), facility design, and support for project teams and task forces. They employ three broad methodological approaches: laboratory experiments, field research, and software building (the design, development, and testing of new software tools, techniques, and methodologies). This research program has produced more than 15 doctoral dissertations, dozens of masters projects, and well over 100 academic papers in books, conferences (e.g., HICSS, ICIS) and journals (e.g., *Communications of the ACM, Management Science, Academy of Management Journal, Information Systems Research, MIS Quarterly*).

Curriculum. The Arizona MIS (Management Information Systems) Ph.D. program currently has 40 students, and the Masters program has 110 students. A graduate-level course devoted solely to GSS is offered every year. Group Support Systems are also discussed (and typically used) in many graduate and undergraduate courses each year.

Administrative Use. There is no "typical" type of group that uses the Arizona facilities. While most tend to be relatively large (15–20 members), they have included more than 200 separate large and small corporations, state and federal agencies, nonprofit organizations, political parties and special interest groups, the military, native American tribes, national societies, as well as groups and task forces from the University and MIS department itself, including for example, the Provost and College Deans. In short, any group striving to improve its productivity and communication for the purpose of arriving at a shared vision can benefit from using GroupSystems™.

University of Minnesota

Inception. Brent Gallupe chose in late 1983, to investigate GSS as a doctoral dissertation topic. His advisors, Gerardine DeSanctis and Gary Dickson endorsed this topic. Some thought was given to using an existing product, Mindsight, from Execucom Systems of Austin, Texas. The inadequate computing resources that existed at that location for GSS research dictated that a simple GSS be created instead—one that could be locally supported. This first GSS (at Lakehead University, Canada) had three simple features: idea input and display, ranking, and voting. The first Minnesota GSS, CAM (for, Computer Aided Meeting), was a semiproduction version of the Gallupe prototype GSS that included modest changes that were made at the same time that reengineering for different hardware was completed. This GSS, the forerunner of Software-Aided Meeting Management (SAMM), was first available for use by the end of 1986. From 1985 through 1987, Gallupe and DeSanctis collaborated on a set of early research or "foundation" papers to define directions for the immature field of GSS.

Development. The design team for CAM was interdisciplinary, spanning the Business School's MIS faculty (Dickson and DeSanctis), Scott Poole from the Speech Communications Department, as well as faculty and students from the schools of public policy and of computer science. Rick Watson, an MIS student, played a major role in coding CAM, the early GSS. Ilze Zigurs was a second doctoral student contributor. All published, telling their collective development story at the same time that they made contributions to the developing theories of GSSs. NCR Corporation provided equipment support that enabled the team to move quickly into the development of SAMM as the next generation of CAM. The first edition of SAMM was applied in 1987. The Minnesota team's design departed from the norm in two significant ways. First, other GSSs at the time had a history of seeking efficiency and perhaps effectiveness in group outputs; in addition to doing this, SAMM was designed from the start to put more emphasis upon being friendly, enabling fun, and, in essence, providing process support as opposed to merely imposing externally generated rational structure upon a group. Second, SAMM was designed to give each group member full and equal access to all aspects of the software, rather than giving special control to a group leader, facilitator, or technician.

Software. Minnesota has since implemented GroupSystems™ and SAGE, a Macintosh-based version of SAMM. Minnesota is in the process of making major upgrades and migrations in preparing the next version of SAMM for release. Now it has commercial clients as well as research needs that drive the evolution of SAMM. SAMM is a major installation within the Texaco Company. There it is employed as a distributed GSS (in AIX/370) though WAN/LANs and a mainframe. This contrasts with most GSS installations, which are server/LAN operations. The IRS is also a significant driving applications case for the Minnesota GSS research team. SAMM is installed in research configurations at Marquette University (a distributed, dual channel or mode version), Washington University in St.Louis, and at the National University of Singapore. A major new direction for SAMM is the inclusion of a tool for conflict and negotiation tasks. The other thrust for SAMM has been its specific application for JAD teams. SAMM has been used for JAD teams at Texaco and the State of Minnesota. This is a neat twist since the genealogy of GroupSystems™ stems from the systems requirements extraction process.

Personnel. Minnesota has a very strong GSS research momentum. It is well founded in theory, with special emphasis laid upon Poole and DeSanctis's AST (adaptive structuration theory). The tradition of the Minnesota GSS researchers is a strong flow of ideas. When this is coupled with the more pragmatic implementations of their research tool in industry and government and with the Dickson-led consulting applications that they make with their tool, expectations run high, and properly so. Faculty who have joined the core Minnesota GSS team now include Les Wanninger of the Information and Decision Sciences Department. Wanninger has high-level IS management experience from Pillsbury, Inc., and General Mills, Inc., and is helping with applying SAMM in systems-development settings.

Facilities. Minnesota's GSS installations and research laboratories are housed in the modern Hubert Humphrey Institute on the West Bank of the Main Campus of the Twin Cities University complex. As at the other major GSS universities, there are a number of able students available to staff the various rooms and to facilitate as required for demonstrations and for actual research. Minnesota is constantly in a state of just having upgraded or of being just about to upgrade or migrate the software and/or hardware. As with most universities, Minnesota is not in the software development business. Because of this they have neither the personnel nor the equipment and facilities that might otherwise be expected to be available for use in research and as well as for development.

Research. The research stream at Minnesota has included Gallupe's work on problem finding, Watson's work on consensus decision making, Zigur's work on computer-mediated influence, DeSanctis' work on heuristic decision making, and Poole's work on conflict management. In each of these cases, research has focused on comparing GSS-supported groups with those that are not technologically supported. Strategic planning under communications support versus GSS support was done by Sambamurthy. Billingsly contrasted one-time versus repeated use of GSS for strategic planning. Dickson, DeSanctis, and Zigurs have contributed to another stream of research on perceptions of GSS users relative to operation, interfaces, and introduction to GSS. Minnesota is almost unique among GSS research universities in reporting detailed case studies of GSS applications. The IRS case has been and continues to be reported. In addition, the Texaco case is just coming into its own.

Curriculum. Minnesota uses the various GSSs as *demonstration of concept* vehicles for the students and also uses the GSS as a teaching resource in several M.B.A. courses and research seminars.

Administrative Use. Although the main purpose for the Minnesota GSS (SAMM) is for GSS research, the system is occasionally used within the Business School for applications such as personnel evaluation and selection, project and research planning, and student evaluations.

University of Georgia

Inception. Georgia's team technology research program began within the Department of Management during the summer of 1985 with the receipt of an IBM management of information systems grant. The initial exploration of team technology began when the University of Arizona's software, then PLEXSYS, now GroupSystems™, was obtained by Hugh Watson. Two GSS-oriented faculty were hired for the fall of 1988: Bob Bostrom, to head the GSS research, and David Van Over, to bring his GSS education to bear with Bob's direction. That year was spent developing the infrastructure for the GSS program within the overall framework of the Department's Executive 2000 research program.

Development. Rick Watson, carrying the Minnesota GSS genes, joined the management faculty in 1989 to expand the expertise of the team. The Georgia *conference room of the future* evolved into the "Smart Office," a configuration accommodating a variety of GSS and decision room hardware and software. Georgia researchers committed themselves to understanding three GSS settings: workstations for all group members (e.g., GroupSystems™), keypads for all group members (e.g., OptionFinder), and a workstation for only the facilitator (e.g., COPE). One major focus of the Georgia GSS team is the training of facilitators for meetings with and without GSS technology.

Software. Georgia is rich in GSS software, because of its focus on the evaluation of alternative GSS technologies. It made a major study of OptionFinder for the 3M Meetings Management Institute of Austin, Texas. Georgia also served as the primary beta site for VisionQuest, a GSS developed by Collaborative Technologies Corporation, and a site for PLEXSYS-GroupSystems™. In addition, Georgia has worked with the National University of Singapore in the development of SAGE, a Macintosh-based system modeled on SAMM. Other universities have gained from Georgia's entrepreneurial spirit in collecting GSS software. It has helped in the establishment of University Support programs for OptionFinder and VisionQuest.

Personnel. Georgia has pursued a policy of creating research alliances within and outside the university to broaden the range of expertise it can access. Its faculty have served on dissertation committees at Indiana and Georgia State

University. The OptionFinder study entailed researchers from the Universities of South Florida and Calgary. Research alliances have been forged with groups such as the Center for Creative Leadership and Georgia's Institute of Community and Area Development. In 1991, recently graduated Ph.D.s Alan Dennis (Arizona) and John Satzinger (Claremont) joined Bostrom and Watson. The result is a highly fertile amalgam of investigative skills initially nurtured at major GSS research sites.

Facilities. As mentioned above, Georgia has the "conference room of the future," the Smart Office, as a central facility. Its companion facility, the PC Research Laboratory, is located across the hall. The Smart Office is a state-of-the-art conference room with a high degree of built-in modularity that provides extensive computer-based meeting and presentation support. Unlike many facilities that provide fixed room configurations, the Smart Office modular design approach allows the room to be configured in a variety of formats for face-to-face meetings. In its various configurations, the room will support groups of 10–30 members engaged in a face-to-face meeting. The PC research laboratory is a 20-workstation facility that can accommodate 40 people. This room is used for electronic meetings, training/classroom sessions, and demonstrations. All microcomputers in the two facilities and the department's faculty offices are connected via an IBM Token Ring Network, supported by the Novell Network Operating System. Network gateways are provided to the department's IBM 4381 mainframe computer and other computer resources (networks, mainframes) available at the University of Georgia.

Research. Each research center has developed its own research agenda, that is, its own niche. Given Georgia's facilities and expertise, it has translated its research agenda into a number of research themes and application domains. Research themes focus on issues that are applicable to a variety of team tasks and contexts. Current themes being researched are the following: comparison of GSS technologies, facilitation and leadership in GSS environments, team/group development, team/group creativity, cross-cultural issues, and adoption-diffusion-impacts of GSS technology. For example, the OptionFinder study mentioned above focused on both the comparison and adoption-diffusion-impact themes. Research application domains focus on specialized environments where application-specific technology may be utilized. Georgia has targeted four domains for investigation: systems analysis and design, crisis management, the conference room of the future, and collaborative learning.

Curriculum. Georgia, like all of the other active GSS universities, does not use the environment to deliver content in classes on other subjects. The pedagogical use of GSS to date is limited to case analysis and other forms of vicarious exposure to the GSS technology. The experiences that Georgia has had nonetheless include the following very interesting examples of what may lead to much greater classroom or learning environment application of GSS. All students within the Department of Management are exposed to GSS through classroom demonstrations and experiences. Using GSS to analyze and facilitate case discussions has been experimented with in both MIS and general management courses. GSS technology has also been used to support class group projects, for example, system analysis and design.

Administrative Use. As has been true with the majority of other GSS-active universities, Georgia has been very active in helping the management of various university and business organizational units by means of GSS. GSS is used regularly by the MIS group. Other university applications include strategic planning efforts, support for various committees, faculty selection, curriculum design, organization design, demonstrations for football recruits, and opinion gathering (e.g., course or curriculum evaluation). The Georgia GSS group regularly provides services (e.g., facilities, facilitation, consulting) to a wide variety of organizations on a range of applications. Georgia is one of the few places that a company can visit to see and experience many of the major GSS technologies. The administrative use is expected to continue and to expand as the GSS capabilities become more fully developed and understood.

Indiana University

Inception. Indiana's GSS research site dates from 1984. Their operation started within the Institute for the Study of Developmental Disabilities (ISDD) in its Collaborative Work Laboratory. A combination of ISDD faculty and Indiana Business School faculty (particularly Bob Bostrom) developed software to support small group idea generation, sharing, and analysis.

Development. From this beginning, Indiana's GSS work has had a strong applied orientation, encompassing many field and case studies particularly in the social services arena. The other early subject area of work was in the area of developing systems requirements. In 1986, Bye Wynne joined Indiana's Business School from industry to manage the Institute for Research on the Management of Information Systems (IRMIS). GSS was made a major emphasis for IRMIS. Bostrom and Wynne spent the next year converting ISDD from the use of Indiana's homegrown software into becoming the first university beta site for what was then known as the University of Arizona PLEXSYS system (now known as GroupSystems™).

Software. Indiana's GSS researchers have done the bulk of their GSS work on GroupSystems™. Also installed and actively used at Indiana and/or some of its cooperating research sites are (1) OptionFinder, the keypad technology, (2) VisionQuest, the relatively recent commercial GSS product, and (3) Comments™. Comments™ is GSS research software developed at Indiana specifically to operationalize the anytime-anyplace concepts of GSS. Indiana's GSS researchers utilize a variety of software in order that their findings be comparative and thus apply across rather merely than within GSS technologies.

Personnel. A strong GSS research program has been developed at Indiana. Faculty from Indiana's Speech Communications Department, Pat Andrews and Joe Scudder, have joined with the Decision and Information Systems (D&IS) faculty in this research program. Jeff Hoffer is bringing his database expertise to bear on GSS issues such as the design of group and organizational memories. Bill Perkins provides a DSS perspective to the group support program. D&IS doctoral students continue to provide professional infrastructure for the ISDD laboratory. Alan Heminger and Joe Valacich have been added to the D&IS faculty, as new graduates from the Arizona GSS culture, because of their interests and expertise in the GSS arena. The original ISDD Collaborative Work Lab is directed by researcher Vicki Pappas. Vicki brings both social services knowledge and expertise in the use of the naturalistic inquiry approach to some of the Indiana GSS research.

Facilities. The Collaborative Work Lab is housed at the Institute for the Study of Developmental Disabilities. It consists of a meeting room with workstations in flexible configurations, connected in an Ethernet, and supported by Novell Netware version 3.11. The Lab's portable configuration consists of a portable server and ten 80386SX notebook computers connected via Ethernet and Novell Netware version 3.11. A second GSS facility is now under development within the Business School. Separate and apart from electronic classrooms, this second Indiana University GSS research facility is based upon more advanced technology (Intel 80386 and 80486 central processors) and is appropriate for managerial and executive use of the GSS capabilities. The facility is outfitted with custom furniture for maximum flexibility and thus supports many different space, time, channel, and process variants to facilitate variant designs for both applied and experimental research. From the very outset with the ISDD software, Indiana researchers have treated GSS work as something portable. They "take the lab to the people" simply as a way of broadening their experience and of ensuring greater reality checks on GSS use; this helps to accommodate the Indiana emphasis on the study of intact groups.

Research. Historically, a large percentage of the GSS research has evolved from doctoral dissertations lead by Bye Wynne, Jeff Hoffer, and Bill Perkins, as well as Bob Bostrom and Tawfik Jelassi (with the latter two no longer at Indiana). Abby Foroughi and Beth Jones each did work on negotiation applications of GSS, with Foroughi coupling individual DSS to the shared GSS environment. Bostrom and Wynne, with their student, Jack Fellers, extended the use of GSS into the extraction of knowledge from groups of practicing-knowledge engineers. Rob Anson highlighted the potential major role to be played by the GSS facilitator. Laku Chidambaram opened the laboratory study of GSS group development over a sequence of meetings. Several students have extended these works into a focus upon the use of intact groups; Rick Herschel studies the effects of group gender composition, and Tim Noel studies issues of justice and anonymity. Brian Mennecke is exploring the use of GSS as a means for team development as an objective in itself. Lai Lai Tung is studying nonconsensus group processes in a GSS setting. The Indiana GSS research team is moving heavily into the study of asynchronous, distributed GSS and support for application to adaptive, learning organizations. In this regard, Valacich and Heminger are leading several field studies on the application of GSS in distributed team environments. Valacich is also looking at how GSS technology can be used to support groups making decisions under time pressure. Pappas and her team are investigating the impact of collaborative work systems on the user through a naturalistic paradigm.

Curriculum. Indiana emphasizes the use of GSS in teaching. As a matter of policy, every graduating M.B.A. from Indiana has at least one working experience within a GSS laboratory. These may be for business case development, for example, or for any number of other integrative experiences. Several key information systems courses at all three levels require student utilization of the GSS laboratory. These uses need not be just on class materials or issues, but can be any reasonable activity that has relevance to and motivation for the students involved. Other schools and departments, particularly Education and Recreation, use GSSs for orientation experiences as well as to support a variety of instructional activities.

Administrative Use. ISDD, in depth, the D&IS Department, and a variety of the university administrative units (planning and budgeting in particular) apply the GSS lab to their operating problems. This use has become routine for some units and purposes. Such use is expected to continue and to expand as the GSS capabilities become more fully understood and developed or exploited. A wide variety of local and state agencies as well as for-profit organizations use the group facilities for meetings, to explore the use of the technology, and to better understand how a GSS might be exploited within their environment.

New Jersey Institute of Technology

Inception. The Computerized Conferencing and Communications Center at the New Jersey Institute of Technology (NJIT) was established in 1975 by Murray Turoff, for the purpose of development, application, and assessment of computer-mediated communications systems. The first experimentation with structures and processes to support group decision making within a computer conferencing system began in 1978, under National Science Foundation (NSF) sponsorship.

Development. The initial set of GSS experiments took place on EIES™, the Electronic Information Exchange System, a conferencing system operated as both a research laboratory and as a utility for 1000–2000 members around the world. NSF funds allowed the construction of a high-level language for prototyping special systems and features within EIES. In addition to GSS structures and research, the program has developed and assessed special structures to support scientific research communities (e.g., an online journal, information exchange structures, notebook and report structures for joint authoring) and educational delivery (the Virtual Classroom™). The original EIES operated on only one specific type of minicomputer. Beginning in about 1985, development and assessment began on a new generation, EIES 2, a tailorable and fully distributed system that operates on a variety of UNIX machines. EIES 2 was released to market and replaced EIES in 1991.

Software. Most of the GSS work is done on EIES 2. Any new type of tool can be programmed in a superset of SMALLTALK™ and added as a new kind of "activity," that is, any executable program attached to a text item. For instance, the current program of GSS research is adding activities to support common list building, various forms of rating and voting on items on a list, and a survey or polling activity. The content and appearance of the interface can also be tailored for any particular study. In addition, NJIT hopes to acquire several other "groupware" systems for comparative study. The NJIT emphasis is on "distributed" or asynchronous group support systems; that is, use of the system by people at different times as well as in different locations. Same time/different places or same time/same place conditions are also supported for experimental comparisons.

Personnel. The program is led by Murray Turoff and Starr Roxanne Hiltz. James Whitescarver has been the lead systems programmer for over a decade. Other faculty members and Ph.D. students and staff members are involved as funds and interests allow. For example, in the current NSF-sponsored program of research on distributed group support systems, Scott Poole of Minnesota and Ronald Rice of Rutgers are involved as consultants. NJIT's computer science department plans to add more faculty interested in group support.

Facilities. EIES 2 serves as a "laboratory without walls" that can be accessed from anywhere in the world. Current versions of the system are being run on a variety of machines, including HP minicomputers, a SUN network, and DEC equipment. In addition, there is a very modest "Collaborative Systems Laboratory," with seven machines arranged around a U-Shaped set of tables, for training of subjects or for conducting "decision room" type meetings.

Research. NJIT strives to include a mix of controlled or "laboratory" experiments, field experiments, and field trials. One area of particular interest has been very large groups, of 50–200 members. Ronald Rice did his dissertation (at Stanford) on data from EIES. Other past dissertations include one by Ahmed Bahgat on collaborative online zero-based budgeting and by Usha Rao on hypertext. Currently, Donna Dufner is replicating Minnesota work with preference tasks, Ajaz Rana is working on peer review experiments, Jerry Fjermsted is focusing on equivocality in strategic planning, Enrico Hsu is completing a dissertation on an online collaborative management laboratory, and several other Ph.D. students are in the dissertation proposal stage.

Curriculum. The group support systems research program is closely tied to the joint NJIT/Rutgers Ph.D. program in Management of Information Systems. There is one course regularly offered on Computer-Mediated Communication Systems, plus occasional seminars on special topics. The use of EIES 2 as a Virtual Classroom is built into about a half dozen courses at NJIT in computer science, management, and psychology.

Administrative Use. Used by NJIT's Pre-College Program to coordinate joint programs with secondary schools, not only in New Jersey, but with other schools in locations such as Hawaii and Japan. A wide variety of for-profit and not-for-profit organizations also use the NJIT systems to support their activities.

Queen's University

Inception. The Queen's University Executive Decision Center began operations as the Decision Lab in the School of Business. The Lab was set up by Brent Gallupe in 1986 upon his arrival at Queen's in order to continue a program of GSS research that started with his doctoral dissertation.

Development. The GSS research program at Queen's began with a strong experimental orientation, one it has nurtured and enhanced over the years. The first experimental sessions were conducted with the DECAID1 group software. This software had been developed for Gallupe's dissertation while he was at the University of Minnesota. DECAID1 is still used and supports primarily idea generation and consensus formation tasks. In 1987, the PLEXSYS system from the University of Arizona was installed and a permanent site for the Decision Lab was established in the School of Business. With improvements in hardware and software, and a broadening of orientation from just a research facility to a multipurpose group support facility, the name was changed to the Queen's Executive Decision Center.

Software. The PLEXSYS system (now called GroupSystems™) and DECAID1 are the main group support software used at Queen's. Two additional packages that have been installed are (1) VisionQuest from Collaborative Technologies Corporation, and (2) SAGE, a Macintosh-based system developed at the National

University of Singapore (based on the SAMM system from the University of Minnesota). Queen's also uses individual support software such as Lotus 1-2-3 and Expert Choice in a multiuser, face-to-face meeting mode by using the CloseUp/LAN screen and keyboard sharing software.

Personnel. The research team at the Queen's Executive Decision Center (QEDC) consists of two groups. The first is the technical support group composed of the technical manager, Helen Chiasson, and part-time graduate and undergraduate research assistants. The technical manager is responsible for maintaining all the hardware and software in the Center. The research assistants aid in developing software and facilitating experimental sessions. The second group consists of the research faculty. From the MIS area, Brent Gallupe provides his expertise in conducting group experiments, Jim McKeen brings his interests in MIS steering committees and systems development, and Peter Todd adds his experience with DSS and human-computer interfaces. Bill Cooper, with his organizational behavior background, supplies insights into group process. Ken Wong from the Marketing area provides expertise with the marketing tasks that are frequently used in the experiments. From the Production/Operations area, John Gordon brings an interest in quality circles and total quality management.

Facilities. The current facilities at Queen's consist of a custom-designed modular U-shaped table with 6 groupstations and one facilitator station. The screens have been imbedded in the table to improve the line of sight between group members. Workstations consist of IBM-based processors—the result of a joint study agreement between IBM and Queen's. The file server and facilitator station are IBM PS/2 model 80's, whereas the groupstations are IBM PS/2 model 55's. A ceiling-mounted Sony 3-gun VGA unit is connected to the system to project the public screen. Audio and video recording equipment is installed in the Center when experimental sessions are conducted.

Research. GSS research at the Center is conducted on the basis of research programs. These programs are multiple experiments intended to build a cumulative knowledge of the use of GSS. All the research has been led by Brent Gallupe. The first program, called "A Longitudinal Study into the Use of a GDSS," was a two-year study that used 40 four-to-five-person groups to study the impact of repeated use of a GSS (in this case GroupSystems™). The groups remained intact for the entire two years of the study. The second program, called "A Study into Electronic Brainstorming," is a three-year investigation into the phenomenon of electronic brainstorming. Bill Cooper and a number of undergraduate psychology students have assisted in conducting six experiments involving over 800 subjects. The third program is entitled "Executive Development using a GSS." Four years of data have been collected from use of the Decision Center by participants in the Executive Program at Queen's. The fourth program is just getting underway, primarily through the efforts of Ph.D. student Mary Liz Grise.

This program, entitled "Group Framing and GSS Use," will study the concept of group frames and the impact of GSS use on these frames.

Curriculum. The Center is an integral part of teaching at Queen's. It is used for class teaching (mainly small seminar classes), small group case analysis, and software demonstrations. An example of class teaching is the simulated JAD sessions in the Center using Excelerator in the systems analysis and design course. As previously mentioned, the Center is a prime facility for teaching in the executive programs.

Administrative Use. Committees within the School of Business are the main administrative users of the Center. The Computing Committee, Research Committee, MBA Society, and the MIS Area group are some of the groups that regularly use the Center and its facilities for meetings. Administrative groups from outside the School but within the University, such as the Alumni Board and the Pay Equity Task Force have also used the Center. A number of public and private organizations use the Center for their meetings. A recent example is the Kingston Literacy Foundation, which uses the Center for strategic planning meetings.

University of Michigan

Inception. The University of Michigan has been active in facets of GSS research since the 1970s, being a pioneer in time-sharing, networking, and computer conferencing. More recently during the mid-eighties, the EXPRES project explored multimedia electronic mail as a collaborative tool. In the last few years a number of faculty have come to work in this area, representing a diversity of approaches and projects.

Development. A number of different faculty from across the university have been active in the development of past as well as ongoing GSS research programs. Members of the Electrical Engineering and Computer Science (EECS) Department are developing architectures and applications for group activities, including shared editing, intelligent agents, and advanced multimedia capabilities. Investigators in the Institute for Public Policy Studies (IPPS) and the Business School are exploring the social and behavioral consequences of GSS use. A major center for activity is the Cognitive Science and Machine Intelligence Laboratory (CSMIL), which serves faculty from liberal arts, business, and engineering. Current CSMIL projects involve collaborations with Andersen Consulting, MCC, Steelcase, Apple, Sun, Ameritech, and other corporate partners. Campuswide infrastructure is being established to support research and teaching.

Chapter 2 Group Support Systems Facilities and Software

Software. Michigan faculty have developed or investigated GSS software on all of the major platforms: IBM PC, Macintosh, and Unix. Recent work has focused on the latter two platforms because they are the most common on the Michigan campus. Group editors such as ShrEdit and Disted have been built in-house. Through research partnerships, a variety of other GSS software products, such as Diamond/Slate™, Aspects™, Teamfocus™, and GROVE™, have been used in studies.

Personnel. Gary and Judy Olson spearhead the GSS research effort at Michigan. Both of the Olsons are trained in experimental psychology. Tom Finholt, from the Psychology department, is interested in communication patterns and group coordination over time. Kevin Crowston is a new Ph.D. from MIT who brings his interest in organizational impact and technological coordination to the research team. Michael Cohen, from Political Science, is likewise interested in organizational impacts of GSS. Poppy McLeod, from the Organizational Behavior Department, researches interactions of group member roles and GSSs. Atul Prakash, Dan Atkins, and Ed Durfee from the EECS Department bring a wealth of technical skills to the group. Atul Prakash is interested in architectural issues related to shared work. Dan Atkins adds his knowledge of video implementation and how degradation affects satisfaction. Ed Durfee is interested in Distributed Artificial Intelligence applications to group support. Lola Killey, the technical laboratory manager, coordinates the GSS research laboratory and is responsible for hardware and software implementation.

Facilities. Campuswide high-performance networking and broadband video connections are available for GSS research. CSMIL has shared facilities to support a wide range of GSS research, including the Collaboration Technology Suite (CTS). The latter is a flexible electronic meeting room for studies of face-to-face GSSs. The overall facility is similar to a counterpart facility at Andersen Consulting in Chicago. Both contain prototype flexible furniture developed by Steelcase that allows the room to be set up to support any type of computing in a variety of physical arrangements. Michigan's CTS presently uses both Apple Macintosh and Sun workstations with GSS software running on both platforms. CSMIL also has facilities for investigating distributed synchronous work, including video conferencing in both analog and digital forms. There is also an Organizational Studies lab in the Business School consisting of networked IBM PCs. Several projects in the systems and software area are housed in the Artificial Intelligence (AI) lab in the EECS department. The AI Lab and CSMIL are linked by a high-speed network and by broadband channels, allowing studies of distributed work to occur between the two facilities.

Research. All aspects of GSS research are represented among the core faculty at Michigan. CSMIL researchers (primarily G. Olson, J. Olson, L. Killey, and P. Macleod) are focusing on synchronous collaboration among software design teams and are studying both unsupported and supported work among design teams in the field and in the laboratory. Behavioral studies focus on finding out exactly what happens to the quality of work and of interactions among members as groups use GSS tools in their work. Videotapes and logs of computer activities are routinely collected in all studies, and many methods for capturing and evaluating group process have been developed. The flexibility of the CTS is ideal for the laboratory studies of face-to-face interaction. G. Olson, J. Olson, L. Killey, D. Atkins, and A. Prakash have recently begun intensive research on GSS to support synchronous distributed work. Physically separated teams work together linked by shared computing tools and audio/video connections. This work focuses on the idea of a Collaboration Station, an integrated set of tools and communication channels that allow people to work together and have shared access to a variety of information resources. At present, small-scale studies of such groups are underway, but eventually more widespread field trials will be carried out. Other Michigan faculty are exploring architectures and systems issues for a variety of kinds of GSS software (Prakash, Durfee), including digital multimedia (Atkins). Many Ph.D. students, visiting scholars, and postdoctoral researchers are involved in the GSS research. In the fall of 1991 Kevin Crowston (Ph.D., MIT) and Tom Finholt (Ph.D., Carnegie Mellon) joined the group of active GSS researchers at Michigan.

Curriculum. A number of faculty cover GSS material in regular undergraduate and graduate courses. In addition, many special seminars for advanced students and faculty are taught.

Administrative Use. A number of groups at Michigan have used the CTS for administrative meetings. All CSMIL staff and project meetings are held in the CTS facilities. Some long-term ad hoc task forces at the University have also used it as have a small number of groups from local companies.

The Claremont Graduate School

Inception. The Claremont Graduate School Decision Laboratory was part of the design of the Academic Computing Building, which opened in 1985. The facility was based upon a similar facility (now defunct) developed by Paul Gray between 1980 and 1983, when he was at Southern Methodist University. The basic objective in creating the Decision Laboratory was to provide a full-service research facility in which to study the effects of computer support on group decision making.

Development. Like several other universities, Claremont has a strong applied focus. Because they believe that a broad range of meetings need to be supported if GSS is to be successful in industry, they have tried to provide as wide a range of capabilities as budget allows. They support visual, quantitative, and verbal decision making. They also attempt to keep pace with new technologies, such as scanners, optical storage, and multimedia, as these have become available.

Software. The principal software used at Claremont is GroupSystems™ from Ventana Corporation. Other software includes an early version of SAMM from the University of Minnesota and VisionQuest from Group Technologies, as well as both homegrown and commercial software packages used in group mode. Claremont recognized that even the best of the existing packages supported only a limited number of the activities that could take place in a meeting. In keeping with the philosophy of a full-service support environment, "Claremont Group Support Environment" (usually referred to as the CGS Environment) was developed. In this customized WINDOWS™ environment, any piece of group software can be put into a window and used in conjunction with standard software, the mainframe, and even personal software brought by a group member. That is, participants can do private work using their own or publicly available data. They can also share their work with others, send personal messages to any other participant, and scan forward or backward on meeting activities.

Personnel. Paul Gray and Lorne Olfman, carrying the Indiana "GSS genes," are the faculty members currently active in the Decision Laboratory. The laboratory is run by Jim Berkovec, an adjunct professor, with the assistance of two or three M.S. student research assistants.

Facilities. The Decision Laboratory facility consists of four separate rooms: the main laboratory, a second laboratory, a "practicum room," and an observation area. Equipment has been obtained from several manufacturers. The main laboratory contains eight workstations plus a facilitator's workstation arranged in a U-shaped design. Initially, the workstations were PC/AT's, however, they have been upgraded to PS/2 Model 70's on a token ring. Each workstation is built into a 5-foot-wide table so that two persons can work together. The screens are recessed into the tables and the keyboards are on slideout trays so that people can see one another and talk without distraction from the technology. The raised floor has multiple outlets and is surfaced with carpet squares. The floor design makes it possible to change room configuration rapidly if desired. Lighting is fluorescent, and its intensity can be varied. The room has an executive look and feel to facilitate research of senior managers and professionals in a natural environment. The second laboratory is adjacent to the first and separated from it by a divider. The divider, of the type used in hotel ballrooms, can be opened to create a large facility if so desired. The two laboratories are connected with video equipment so that it is possible to experiment with videoconferencing. The second laboratory has housed a variety of equipment, including Hewlett-Packard touchscreens and AT&T UNIX PCs. The Practicum room serves as a place where student projects are undertaken, including projects in support of the Decision Laboratory. The observation area is a small room that has one-way glass observation windows looking out at both laboratory rooms. The observation room is used as a control room and for data collection.

Research. The principal research in the Decision Laboratory is in support of Ph.D. dissertation research. For example, Hung Park completed a thesis on cross-cultural business negotiations involving U.S. and Korean firms. Susan Suchoki is working with land use planners. Jim Rhodes experimented with issue-based GSS. Munir Mundviwalla designed the CGS Environment and is now running experiments using this environment. Carl Clavadetscher is studying labor-management negotiation between teacher unions and school districts. Lorne Olfman recently used the facility to train a large number of administrators and administrative support people in the use of WINDOWS™ 3.0 and, at the same time, took data on the learning process.

Curriculum. The facility is used in support of courses in both the Programs in Information Science (such as Decision Support Systems and Expert Systems) and information systems courses in the Executive Management Program. In these courses, the room is used, in addition to specific group activities, to demonstrate software, to give hands-on experience with software, and for presentations of student projects. The facilities have also been used for a course entitled Decision Support Systems Laboratory, which is offered occasionally in the summer, and which involves students developing GSS software.

Administrative Use. Although not designated for administrative use, the facility is occasionally used by faculty groups to work on problems for which the laboratory is appropriate.

University of Hohenheim

Inception. The Information Systems Department at the Institute for Business Administration, University of Hohenheim, Stuttgart, Germany, was established in fall 1987. Initial research on computer support for groups started in 1988. The goal of this GSS research is to improve group work through the use of information and communication technology.

Development. A major focus was on the design and establishment of the Hohenheim GSS Room (or the Computer Aided Team (CATeam) room), a computerized meeting laboratory, and its conference table. This activity is currently ongoing. Furthermore, groupware products have been installed and tested for their practicality in this GSS environment and for teamwork in general. Two specific projects with special focus in the area of GSS have been started. They concern computerized teamwork and the use of coordination technology for business processes in multinational organizations. Furthermore, members of the department became actively engaged in working groups focused on group knowledge development and distributed meetings sponsored by the European Community in which European researchers cooperate to approach computer support for groupwork from a multidisciplinary perspective.

Software. Off-the-shelf groupware and homegrown customized groupware are available in the GSS environment. An easy-to-use, customized WINDOWS™ environment running H-P New Wave™ is available. The leading groupware software available in the GSS environment includes GroupSystems™ from Ventana Corporation, Lotus Notes™, Coordinator™ from Action Technologies, and Close-Up Lan™, and Comments™ from Indiana University. In addition, two German examples of groupware, "Management Priorities," a tool for team alternative evaluation, and "Mosel," a tool to support teams using morphology, are installed. In addition to applying existing groupware, the University of Hohenheim builds and tests its own prototypes. Two prototypes, one developed under WINDOWS™, the other in a Smalltalk version for OS/2, are intended to support group discussions in meetings. Future development in this area will focus on running Smalltalk in WINDOWS™ (Object Works). In cooperation with the working group of the European Community, they are engaged in developing and testing a hypercard application on a Macintosh platform for the support of group knowledge development.

Personnel. The GSS researchers of the IS Department are Helmut Krcmar, Henrik Lewe, Hans Koehler, Petra Elgass, Volker Barent, Bettina Schwarzer, and Gerhard Schwabe. Personnel of the Departments of Psychology, Communication Science, Industrial Management and Industrial Ergonomics, and International Management of the University of Hohenheim contribute to GSS research within joint research programs.

Facilities. The principle philosophy at Hohenheim is to provide GSS tools in an environment that supports the entire meeting and teamwork process. That process includes meeting phases as well as individual work phases, often performed in offices at remote locations, and the transitions between these phases. The complete GSS environment, with networked offices, and the Hohenheim GSS Room, as the computerized meeting laboratory, is designed to facilitate research on all phases of teamwork. The GSS Room provides an elaborate meeting facility and an observation facility designed to facilitate the complete and unbiased capture of the meeting processes through one-way mirrors. The meeting room will accommodate workspaces with networked computers for a maximum of 12 participants, however the room is large enough to hold additional participants. Rear projection systems are used to present public information on large screens. The meeting room is designed to be flexible and can support both computer supported teamwork and conventional meetings. The meeting participant(s) are able to decide whether and how to use the technology.

Research. Three foci for research are followed at Hohenheim. The first area, "understanding teams," is concerned with all types of tasks, work group combinations, and other variables that influence the functional and social aspects of teamwork. In the second area, "developing tools and concepts for support," the building and augmentation of computer-based tools is paramount. The third area, "evaluating tools and concepts," involves the analysis of where and when computer support for group work would be advantageous, useful, and acceptable. Within this research context, the following research questions guide activities:

1. How can work in teams be supported, coordinated, and improved by the use of GSS technology? How can these changes, especially productivity gains, be measured and evaluated?
2. Which changes in (classic) meetings are possible through GSS use? Which changes in (classic) meetings are necessary for GSS use? Which changes in (classic) meetings result from GSS use?
3. How do certain tools work and are they acceptable to the users?
4. To what extent can results of empirical studies performed in the United States be applied to Europe, especially Germany? Do studies need to be replicated due to cultural differences?

As mentioned before, two sponsored research projects relate to the GSS research activities. They are concerned with an "investigation into the effects of using coordination technologies and coordination mechanisms on the efficiency of selected management processes in multinational corporations" and on the "development and evaluation of tools for computer-supported teamwork." Research on distributed teamwork supported by video-conferencing technology is included in these projects. Experiences gained in a completed study on the use of ISDN picture telephones by German software developers can contribute to these two projects. Helmut Krcmar and Henrik Lewe are involved in the two research working groups on Cooperation-Technology (Co-Tech) supported by the European Community: Information Technology Support for Group Knowledge Development and Distributed Meetings.

Curriculum. The IS department is involved in teaching business administration and economics students. As part of several of these courses, GSS technology is demonstrated in classes and used in case analyses.

Administrative Use. The Hohenheim GSS Room is currently designed and equipped for use primarily as a research facility, therefore non-research-oriented use of the facilities by university or community organizations has not occurred. However, long-term plans call for relocating the facilities to rooms that will be more conducive to use by groups in a nonresearch context.

CONCLUSION

We have discussed these nine GSS research institutions to provide you with a taste of the variety of research that is taking place in the field. The descriptions we have provided have demonstrated that GSS research is vibrant and growing and that the future for this line of inquiry is promising. We think that, in the future, much more effort is needed to bring in researchers from diverse perspectives such as Computer Supported Cooperative Work (CSCW), GSS, computer conferencing, telecommunications, and computer science and engineering, both to broaden the perspectives from which research is conducted and to expand on the number of applications to which GSS technologies may be applied. We feel that several of the institutions discussed in this chapter have begun to progress down this path, and we are certain that many more will follow.

We have not attempted to present an exhaustive list of GSS research institutions in this discussion; therefore the majority of sites where GSS research and development work are actively being conducted have been left out. However, in order to support greater communication and collaboration between researchers at various locations throughout the world, we have included a more comprehensive list of GSS research sites, including specific contact people and addresses, in the Appendix to this chapter.

APPENDIX: GSS RESEARCH FACILITIES

The following list, the data for which was compiled by Brian E. Mennecke and Bradley C. Wheeler from Indiana University, describes some of the Group Support System research facilities in the United States and other countries. A quick survey of this list reveals that approximately half of these facilities have come on-line during the last two years. This is clearly a telling sign of increasing research activity in the field of group support systems. The list also reveals the great degree of diversity in the types of software, sizes of groups supported, and levels of usage among these facilities.

This data was collected via surveys and telephone interviews during the fall of 1991. Since many of the facilites were in the process of adding software and equipment, the survey distinguished between installed GSS software, future GSS software that was scheduled to be installed in less than one year, and for "Groupware" under consideration. Hardware availability and physical arrangement varied greatly. Responding sites were asked to classify the number of workstations that their facility would support under the classifications of time, place, and group size (large group size was fixed at 16 or more). Note that the * symbol indicates that data is not yet available or was not reported.

Boise State University
Computer Information Systems/Production Management
1910 University Dr.
Boise, Idaho 83725 USA

Telephone: 208-385-3029   Fax: 208-385-3779

Department Chair: Sue Brender
Chair Email: RISBRENE@IDBSU.BITNET
GSS Contact: Rob Anson
GSS Contact Email: RISANSON@IDBSU.BITNET
Inception Date: 12/91

	Number of Stations
Same Time/Same Place:	35
Same Time/Diff Place:	
Diff Time/Same Place:	35
Diff Time/Diff Place:	125
Portable System:	

Installed GSS Software: VisonQuest
Future GSS Software:
Under Consideration: GroupSystems™

Group Meetings/Week: *
Hours of Use/Week: *

California State University, San Marcos
College of Business Adminstration
820 W. Lost Vallecitos Blvd.
San Marcos, California 92069 USA

Telephone: 619-752-4233   Fax: 619-752-4030

Department Chair: Len Jessup
Chair Email: LEN_JESSUP@CSUSM.edu
GSS Contact: Len Jessup
GSS Contact Email: LEN_JESSUP@CSUSM.edu
Inception Date: 9/90

	Number of Stations
Same Time/Same Place:	8
Same Time/Diff Place:	
Diff Time/Same Place:	
Diff Time/Diff Place:	
Portable System:	

Installed GSS Software: IBM I-Class
Future GSS Software: Comments™
Under Consideration:

Chapter 2   Group Support Systems Facilities and Software   35

Group Meetings/Week: 1
Hours of Use/Week: 2

Carleton University
School of Business
Ottawa, Ontario K1S 5B6 Canada

Telephone: 613-788-2373   Fax: 613-788-2511

Department Chair: Roland Thomas
Chair Email: ROLAND-THOMAS@CARLETON
GSS Contact: Gregory E. Kersten
GSS Contact Email: GKERSTEN@CARLETON
Inception Date: 1/87

<u>Number of Stations</u>

Same Time/Same Place:
Same Time/Diff Place:
Diff Time/Same Place:
Diff Time/Diff Place: 6
Portable System:

Installed GSS Software: NEGOPLAN-G,GDS1
Future GSS Software:
Under Consideration:

Group Meetings/Week: *
Hours of Use/Week: *

Case Western Reserve University
Management Information & Decision Sciences
10900 Euclid Avenue
Cleveland, Ohio 44106-7235 USA

Telephone: 216-368-8913   Fax: 216-368-4776

Department Chair: Michael Ginzberg
Chair Email: GINZBERG@PYRITE.som.cwru.edu
GSS Contact: Dov Teeni
GSS Contact Email: TEENID@PRYITE.som.cwru.edu
Inception Date: 4/89

<u>Number of Stations</u>

Same Time/Same Place:
Same Time/Diff Place:
Diff Time/Same Place:
Diff Time/Diff Place: 6
Portable System:

Installed GSS Software: Spider
Future GSS Software:
Under Consideration:

Group Meetings/Week: *
Hours of Use/Week: *

Cognitive Science & Machine Intelligence Lab
Business, L.S.A., & Engineering
University of Michigan
701 Tappan
Ann Arbor, Michigan 48109-1234 USA

Telephone: 313-747-4948   Fax: 313-936-3168

Department Chair: Gary M. Olson
Chair Email: GMO@ESMIL.umich.edu
GSS Contact: Judith S. Olson
GSS Contact Email: JSO@CSMIL.umich.edu
Inception Date: 4/89

	Number of Stations
Same Time/Same Place:	9
Same Time/Diff Place:	3
Diff Time/Same Place:	
Diff Time/Diff Place:	
Portable System:	

Installed GSS Software: Aspects, ShrEdit, Grove
Future GSS Software:
Under Consideration: Diamond/Slate

Group Meetings/Week: 6
Hours of Use/Week: 25

Curtin University
School of Information Systems
Purth, Western Australia 6001 Australia

Telephone: 09-351-7685   Fax: 09-351-2378

Department Chair: Pewon Graham
Chair Email: Internet
GSS Contact: Klass Des
GSS Contact Email: KLASS@BA1.CURTIN.edu.au
Inception Date: 9/89

	Number of Stations
Same Time/Same Place:	10
Same Time/Diff Place:	

Diff Time/Same Place:
Diff Time/Diff Place:
Portable System: 10

Installed GSS Software: MeetingWare
Future GSS Software:
Under Consideration:

Group Meetings/Week: *
Hours of Use/Week: *

Electronic Data Systems
Center for Advanced Research (CFAR)
2001 Commonwealth Blvd., Suite 102
Ann Arbor, Michigan 48105 USA

Telephone: 313-995-0900   Fax: 313-995-0991

Department Chair: Marcial Losada
Chair Email: MARCIAL@CMI.COM
GSS Contact: Palmer Morrel-Samuels
GSS Contact Email: PALMER@CMI.COM
Inception Date: 11/87

	Number of Stations
Same Time/Same Place:	8
Same Time/Diff Place:	
Diff Time/Same Place:	
Diff Time/Diff Place:	
Portable System:	

Installed GSS Software: Aspects, Group Analyzer, Meeting Tools
Future GSS Software:
Under Consideration:

Group Meetings/Week: 2
Hours of Use/Week: 16

George Mason University
Decision Science & MIS
4400 University Drive
Fairfax, Virginia 22030 USA

Telephone: 703-993-1788   Fax: 703-993-1809

Department Chair: Evan Anderson
Chair Email: AEVAN@GMUVAX
GSS Contact: Minder Chen
GSS Contact Email: MCHEN@GMUVAX
Inception Date: 1/91

	Number of Stations
Same Time/Same Place:	5
Same Time/Diff Place:	
Diff Time/Same Place:	
Diff Time/Diff Place:	
Portable System:	

Installed GSS Software: GroupSystems™, VisionQuest
Future GSS Software:
Under Consideration:

Group Meetings/Week:	2
Hours of Use/Week:	12

Indiana University
School of Business
10th Street & Fee Lane
Bloomington, Indiana 45401 USA

Telephone: 812-855-9703   Fax: 812-855-8679

Department Chair:	Jeff Hoffer
Chair Email:	HOFFER@IUBACS.bitnet
GSS Contact:	Ash Soni
GSS Contact Email:	SONI@IUBACS.bitnet
Inception Date:	11/91

	Number of Stations
Same Time/Same Place:	16
Same Time/Diff Place:	16
Diff Time/Same Place:	16
Diff Time/Diff Place:	16
Portable System:	

Installed GSS Software: Comments™, VisionQuest
Future GSS Software:
Under Consideration:

Group Meetings/Week:	5
Hours of Use/Week:	15

Indiana University Collaborative Work Lab
Institute for the Study of Developmental Disabilities
2853 East 10th Street
Bloomington, Indiana 47405 USA

Telephone: 812-855-6508   Fax: 812-855-9630

Department Chair: Vicki Pappas
Chair Email: CWLAB@IUBUS.bitnet
GSS Contact: Vicki Pappas
GSS Contact Email: CWLAB@IUBUS.bitnet
Inception Date: 7/84

	Number of Stations
Same Time/Same Place:	10
Same Time/Diff Place:	
Diff Time/Same Place:	10
Diff Time/Diff Place:	
Portable System:	3

Installed GSS Software: Comments™, GroupSystems™, OptionFinder
Future GSS Software: VisionQuest
Under Consideration: SAGE

Group Meetings/Week: 6
Hours of Use/Week: 16

Instituto Tecnologico de Monterrey
Lab of Decision Support Systems
Sucursal de Correos J
Monterrey, N.L. 64849 Mexico

Telephone: 5283-582000   Fax: 5283-588931

Department Chair: Carlos Scheel
Chair Email: SCHEEL@TECMTYVM.bitnet
GSS Contact: Carlos Scheel
GSS Contact Email: SCHEEL@TECMTYVM.bitnet
Inception Date: 1/91

	Number of Stations
Same Time/Same Place:	16
Same Time/Diff Place:	100
Diff Time/Same Place:	
Diff Time/Diff Place:	250
Portable System:	

Installed GSS Software: Coordinator™, GroupSystems™
Future GSS Software:
Under Consideration:

Group Meetings/Week: 1
Hours of Use/Week: 10

London School of Economics & Political Science
Decision Analysis Unit
Houghton Street
London, NW3 1AH England

Telephone: 4471-995-7101   Fax: 4471-995-7676

Department Chair:	Lawrence D. Phillips
Chair Email:	PHILLIP1@VAX.lse.ac.uk
GSS Contact:	Lawrence D. Phillips
GSS Contact Email:	PHILLIP1@VAX.lse.ac.uk
Inception Date:	6/87

	Number of Stations
Same Time/Same Place:	1
Same Time/Diff Place:	
Diff Time/Same Place:	
Diff Time/Diff Place:	
Portable System:	1

Installed GSS Software: Hiview, Equity
Future GSS Software:
Under Consideration:

Group Meetings/Week:	6
Hours of Use/Week:	25

National University of Singapore
Department of Information Systems & Computer Science
Kent Ridge Road
Singapore, Singapore 0511 Singapore

Telephone: 65-772-2727   Fax: 65-779-4580

Department Chair:	C.K. Yuen
Chair Email:	ISCHEAD@NUS3090.bitnet
GSS Contact:	K.S. Raman
GSS Contact Email:	RAMANKS@NUSVM.BITNET
Inception Date:	7/88

	Number of Stations
Same Time/Same Place:	10
Same Time/Diff Place:	6
Diff Time/Same Place:	6
Diff Time/Diff Place:	6
Portable System:	10

Installed GSS Software: OptionFinder, SAGE, SAMM, Chinese Version of SAGE
Future GSS Software:
Under Consideration: Aspects, GroupSystems™, VisionQuest

Group Meetings/Week: 1
Hours of Use/Week: 3

New Jersey Institute of Technology
Computer Information Systems
University Heights
Newark, New Jersey 07102 USA

Telephone: 201-596-3388   Fax: 201-596-5777

Department Chair: Peter Ng
Chair Email:
GSS Contact: Roxanne Hiltz
GSS Contact Email: ROXANNE@E1ES2.NJIT.edu
Inception Date: 1/76

	Number of Stations
Same Time/Same Place:	37
Same Time/Diff Place:	30
Diff Time/Same Place:	
Diff Time/Diff Place:	200
Portable System:	

Installed GSS Software: EIES2
Future GSS Software: VisionQuest
Under Consideration: SAMM

Group Meetings/Week: 1
Hours of Use/Week: *

New York University
Information Systems
90 Trinity Place
New York, New York 10006 USA

Telephone: 212-285-6120   Fax: 212-285-6024

Department Chair: Edward A. Stohr
Chair Email: ESTOHR@STERN.nyu.edu
GSS Contact: Edward A. Stohr
GSS Contact Email: ESTOHR@STERN.nyu.edu
Inception Date: 11/91

	Number of Stations
Same Time/Same Place:	51
Same Time/Diff Place:	
Diff Time/Same Place:	
Diff Time/Diff Place:	
Portable System:	

Installed GSS Software: VisionQuest, COOP
Future GSS Software:
Under Consideration:

Group Meetings/Week: *
Hours of Use/Week: *

Queens University
School of Business
Dunning Hall, Room 131
Kingston, Ontario K7L 3N6 Canada

Telephone: 416-545-2361   Fax: 416-545-2013

Department Chair: James D. McKeen
Chair Email: MCKEENJ@QUCDN.bitnet
GSS Contact: Brent Gallupe
GSS Contact Email: GALLUPEB@QUCDN.bitnet
Inception Date: 9/86

	Number of Stations
Same Time/Same Place:	7
Same Time/Diff Place:	10
Diff Time/Same Place:	7
Diff Time/Diff Place:	10
Portable System:	

Installed GSS Software: Close-up LAN, DECAID1, GroupSystems™
Future GSS Software: Aspects, SAGE, VisionQuest
Under Consideration: OptionFinder

Group Meetings/Week: 5
Hours of Use/Week: 20

San Diego State University
Information and Decision Systems Department
College of Business
San Diego, California 92130 USA

Telephone: 619-594-5316   Fax: 619-594-1573

Department Chair: James Lackritz
Chair Email: JLACKRITZ@SCIENCES.sdsu.edu
GSS Contact: George Easton
GSS Contact Email: GEASTON@SCIENCES.sdsu.edu
Inception Date: 9/90

	Number of Stations
Same Time/Same Place:	14
Same Time/Diff Place:	28
Diff Time/Same Place:	28
Diff Time/Diff Place:	28
Portable System:	

Installed GSS Software: GroupSystems™, VisionQuest
Future GSS Software: Lotus Notes™
Under Consideration:

Group Meetings/Week: 1
Hours of Use/Week: 10

Universitat Hohenheim
Information Systems Department
P.O. Box 700562
D-7000 Stuttgart 70, Germany

Telephone: 49-711-459-3345   Fax: 49-711-459-2785

Department Chair: Helmut Krcmar
Chair Email: KRCMAR@ds.ruhll
GSS Contact: Henrik Lewe
GSS Contact Email: LEWE@rus.uni-stuggart.dbp.de
Inception Date: 1/91

	Number of Stations
Same Time/Same Place:	12
Same Time/Diff Place:	
Diff Time/Same Place:	24
Diff Time/Diff Place:	
Portable System:	

Installed GSS Software: Close-up Lan™, Comments™, Coordinator™, GroupSystems™
Future GSS Software:
Under Consideration: Lotus Notes™

Group Meetings/Week: 2
Hours of Use/Week: 24

University of Arizona—3rd Generation Room
Management Information Systems
College of Business and Public Administration
Tucson, AZ 86721 USA

Telephone: 602-621-2748 Fax: 602-621-2433

Department Chair: Jay Nunamaker
Chair Email: NUNAMAKER@MIS.ARIZONA.EDU
GSS Contact: Kendall Cliff
GSS Contact Email: CLIFF@MIS.ARIZONA.EDU
Inception Date: 1992

	Number of Stations
Same Time/Same Place:	74
Same Time/Diff Place:	74
Diff Time/Same Place:	74
Diff Time/Diff Place:	
Portable System:	

Installed GSS Software:
Future GSS Software: GroupSystems™
Under Consideration:

Group Meetings/Week: *
Hours of Use/Week: *

University of Arizona—Boardroom 2000
Management Information Systems
College of Business and Public Administration
Tucson, AZ 86721 USA

Telephone: 602-621-2748   Fax: 602-621-2433

Department Chair: Jay Nunamaker
Chair Email: NUNAMAKER@MIS.ARIZONA.EDU
GSS Contact: Kendall Cliff
GSS Contact Email: CLIFF@MIS.ARIZONA.EDU
Inception Date: 1993

	Number of Stations
Same Time/Same Place:	17
Same Time/Diff Place:	17
Diff Time/Same Place:	17
Diff Time/Diff Place:	17
Portable System:	17

Installed GSS Software:
Future GSS Software: GroupSystems™, Pen-Based Interface
Under Consideration:

Group Meetings/Week: *
Hours of Use/Week: *

University of Arizona—DIC Laboratory
Management Information Systems
College of Business and Public Administration
Tucson, AZ 86721 USA

Telephone: 602-621-2748   Fax: 602-621-2433

Department Chair: Jay Nunamaker
Chair Email: NUNAMAKER@MIS.ARIZONA.EDU
GSS Contact: Kendall Cliff
GSS Contact Email: CLIFF@MIS.ARIZONA.EDU
Inception Date: 1985

	Number of Stations
Same Time/Same Place:	21
Same Time/Diff Place:	21
Diff Time/Same Place:	21
Diff Time/Diff Place:	
Portable System:	

Installed GSS Software: GroupSystems™
Future GSS Software:
Under Consideration:

Group Meetings/Week: 5
Hours of Use/Week: 15

University of Arizona—Distributed GSS Laboratory
Management Information Systems
College of Business and Public Administration
Tucson, AZ 86721 USA

Telephone: 602-621-2748   Fax: 602-621-2433

Department Chair: Jay Nunamaker
Chair Email: NUNAMAKER@MIS.ARIZONA.EDU
GSS Contact: Kendall Cliff
GSS Contact Email: CLIFF@MIS.ARIZONA.EDU
Inception Date: 1992

	Number of Stations
Same Time/Same Place:	
Same Time/Diff Place:	20
Diff Time/Same Place:	
Diff Time/Diff Place:	20
Portable System:	

Installed GSS Software:
Future GSS Software: GroupSystems™, Group Link
Under Consideration:

Group Meetings/Week: *
Hours of Use/Week: *

University of Arizona—Enterprise Room
Management Information Systems
College of Business and Public Administration
Tucson, AZ 86721 USA

Telephone: 602-621-2748   Fax: 602-621-2433

Department Chair: Jay Nunamaker
Chair Email: NUNAMAKER@MIS.ARIZONA.EDU
GSS Contact: Kendall Cliff
GSS Contact Email: CLIFF@MIS.ARIZONA.EDU
Inception Date: 1987

	Number of Stations
Same Time/Same Place:	27
Same Time/Diff Place:	27
Diff Time/Same Place:	27
Diff Time/Diff Place:	
Portable System:	

Installed GSS Software: GroupSystems™
Future GSS Software:
Under Consideration:

Group Meetings/Week: 12
Hours of Use/Week: 40

University of Auckland
Dept of Management Science & Information Systems
Private Bag
Auckland, New Zealand

Telephone: 64-9-737-999   Fax: 64-9-366-0891

Department Chair:
Chair Email:
GSS Contact: Jim Sheffield
GSS Contact Email: J_SHEFFIELD@aukuni.ac.nz
Inception Date: 9/90

Chapter 2 Group Support Systems Facilities and Software

	Number of Stations
Same Time/Same Place:	18
Same Time/Diff Place:	
Diff Time/Same Place:	18
Diff Time/Diff Place:	
Portable System:	

Installed GSS Software: GroupSystems™
Future GSS Software:
Under Consideration: Close-Up Lan™

Group Meetings/Week: 5
Hours of Use/Week: 25

University of Calgary
Faculty of Management
2500 University Dr.
Calgary, Alta T2N1N4 Canada

Telephone: 403-220-7161   Fax: 403-282-0095

Department Chair:	Paul Licker
Chair Email:	LICKER@ACS.ucalgary.ca
GSS Contact:	Stephen Hayne
GSS Contact Email:	SCHAYNE@ACS.ucalgary.ca
Inception Date:	6/90

	Number of Stations
Same Time/Same Place:	44
Same Time/Diff Place:	108
Diff Time/Same Place:	44
Diff Time/Diff Place:	108
Portable System:	32

Installed GSS Software: Coordinator™, EIES2, GroupSystems™, Lotus Notes™, Option-Finder, VisionQuest
Future GSS Software: MUGE, GIA, GVMS, EDS, Folder, GS
Under Consideration:

Group Meetings/Week: 3
Hours of Use/Week: 32

University of California, Irvine
Graduate School of Management
Irvine, California 92717 USA

Telephone: 714-856-5246   Fax: 714-856-8091

Department Chair: Vijay Gurbaxani
Chair Email: VGURBAXA@UCI.edu
GSS Contact: Kenneth L. Kraemer
GSS Contact Email: KEN@UCIPPRO
Inception Date: 10/91

	Number of Stations
Same Time/Same Place:	10
Same Time/Diff Place:	
Diff Time/Same Place:	10
Diff Time/Diff Place:	
Portable System:	

Installed GSS Software: GroupSystems™
Future GSS Software:
Under Consideration: Lotus Notes™, VisionQuest

Group Meetings/Week: *
Hours of Use/Week: *

University of Colorado
College of Business and Administration
Campus Box 419
Boulder, Colorado 80309-0419 USA

Telephone: 303-492-3490   Fax: 303-492-5962

Department Chair:
Chair Email:
GSS Contact: Ilze Zigurs
GSS Contact Email: ZIGURS@COLORADO.BITNET
Inception Date: 1/90

	Number of Stations
Same Time/Same Place:	40
Same Time/Diff Place:	116
Diff Time/Same Place:	
Diff Time/Diff Place:	16
Portable System:	40

Installed GSS Software : OptionFinder, VisionQuest
Future GSS Software:
Under Consideration:

Group Meetings/Week: 5
Hours of Use/Week: 10

University of Denver
Management of Information Systems
2020 S. Race St
Denver, Colorado 80208 USA

Telephone: 303-871-3693   Fax: 303-871-2156

Department Chair: Don McCubbrey
Chair Email: DMCCUBBR@DUCAIR
GSS Contact: Jill Smith
GSS Contact Email: JISMITH@DUCAIR
Inception Date: 1/92

	Number of Stations
Same Time/Same Place:	15
Same Time/Diff Place:	
Diff Time/Same Place:	
Diff Time/Diff Place:	
Portable System:	

Installed GSS Software: VisionQuest
Future GSS Software:
Under Consideration: Coordinator™

Group Meetings/Week: *
Hours of Use/Week: *

University of Georgia—PC Research Laboratory
Management
Terry School of Business
Athens, Georgia 30602 USA

Telephone: 404-542-1294   Fax: 404-542-3743

Department Chair: Bob Gatewood
Chair Email: GATEWOOD@UGABUS.BITNET
GSS Contact: Bob Bostrom
GSS Contact Email: BBOSTROM@UGABUS.BITNET
Inception Date: 10/87

	Number of Stations
Same Time/Same Place:	20
Same Time/Diff Place:	65
Diff Time/Same Place:	20
Diff Time/Diff Place:	65
Portable System:	

Installed GSS Software: Aspects, Close-up LAN, GroupSystems™, OptionFinder, SAGE, VisionQuest
Future GSS Software: Comments™, Lotus Notes™
Under Consideration: Coordinator™, EIES2

Group Meetings/Week: 4
Hours of Use/Week: 14

University of Georgia—Smart Office
Management
Terry School of Business
Athens, Georgia 30602 USA

Telephone: 404-542-1294   Fax: 404-542-3743

Department Chair: Bob Gatewood
Chair Email: GATEWOOD@UGABUS.BITNET
GSS Contact: Bob Bostrom
GSS Contact Email: BBOSTROM@UGABUS.BITNET
Inception Date: 10/87

	Number of Stations
Same Time/Same Place:	32
Same Time/Diff Place:	65
Diff Time/Same Place:	32
Diff Time/Diff Place:	65
Portable System:	6

Installed GSS Software: Aspects, Close-up LAN, GroupSystems™, OptionFinder, SAGE, VisionQuest
Future GSS Software: Comments™, Lotus Notes™
Under Consideration: Coordinator™, EIES2

Group Meetings/Week: 4
Hours of Use/Week: 14

University of Hawaii
College of Business Administration
2404 Maile Way
Honolulu, Hawaii 96822 USA

Telephone: 808-956-7368   Fax: 808-956-9889

Department Chair: Jack Suyderhoud
Chair Email: SUYDER@CBAUS.cba.hawaii.edu
GSS Contact: Laku Chidambaram
GSS Contact Email: CBADLCH.UHCCVM.bitnet
Inception Date: 1/90

	Number of Stations
Same Time/Same Place:	6
Same Time/Diff Place:	4
Diff Time/Same Place:	
Diff Time/Diff Place:	
Portable System:	

Installed GSS Software: GroupSystems™
Future GSS Software: VisionQuest
Under Consideration: Close-Up Lan™, Lotus Notes™, OptionFinder

Group Meetings/Week: 6
Hours of Use/Week: 20

University of Minnesota
Information & Decision Sciences
271 19th Avenue South
Minneapolis, Minnesota 55455 USA

Telephone: 612-624-8562   Fax: 612-626-1316

Department Chair: Carl Adams
Chair Email:
GSS Contact: Gerardine DeSanctis
GSS Contact Email: DESANCTIS@UMNAXUV.Bitnet
Inception Date: 1/86

	Number of Stations
Same Time/Same Place:	38
Same Time/Diff Place:	26
Diff Time/Same Place:	
Diff Time/Diff Place:	
Portable System:	

Installed GSS Software: SAMM, Sage, GroupSystems™
Future GSS Software: Lotus Notes™
Under Consideration:

Group Meetings/Week: 10
Hours of Use/Week: 40

University of Montana
Management
Missoula, Montana 59812-1216 USA

Telephone: 406-243-4831   Fax: 406-243-2086

Department Chair:
Chair Email:
GSS Contact: Cap Smith
GSS Contact Email: BA_CAS@Selway.UMT.edu
Inception Date: 10/90

	Number of Stations
Same Time/Same Place:	24
Same Time/Diff Place:	
Diff Time/Same Place:	24
Diff Time/Diff Place:	
Portable System:	

Installed GSS Software: Comments™, Electronic Discussion System
Future GSS Software:
Under Consideration:

Group Meetings/Week: 1
Hours of Use/Week: 1

University of North Carolina at Greensboro
Information Systems & Operations Management
479 Bryan School of Business & Economics
Greensboro, North Carolina 27412-5001 USA

Telephone: 919-334-5666   Fax: 919-334-5580

Department Chair: Gerald Hershey
Chair Email: HERSHEY@UNCG.BITNET
GSS Contact: Richard Herschel
GSS Contact Email: Herschel@UNCG.Bitnet
Inception Date: 9/91

	Number of Stations
Same Time/Same Place:	25
Same Time/Diff Place:	100
Diff Time/Same Place:	100
Diff Time/Diff Place:	100
Portable System:	

Installed GSS Software: Comments™, GroupSystems™
Future GSS Software:
Under Consideration:

Group Meetings/Week: 1
Hours of Use/Week: *

University of North Texas
Business Computer Information
P.O. Box 13677
Denton, Texas 76203-3677 USA

Telephone: 817-565-3117   Fax: 817-565-4930

Department Chair:	Jack D. Becker
Chair Email:	BECKER@UNTVM1
GSS Contact:	Jack D. Becker
GSS Contact Email:	BECKER@UNTVM1
Inception Date:	1/91

	Number of Stations
Same Time/Same Place:	20
Same Time/Diff Place:	22
Diff Time/Same Place:	20
Diff Time/Diff Place:	22
Portable System:	

Installed GSS Software: VisionQuest, Comshare Commander, Knowledgeware IEW/ADW
Future GSS Software:
Under Consideration: Comments™, DECAID1, GroupSystems™, Lotus Notes™

Group Meetings/Week:	*
Hours of Use/Week:	*

University of Northern Colorado
College of Business Administration
Greeley, Colorado 80639 USA

Telephone: 303-351-2764   Fax: 303-351-2500

Department Chair:	Robert M. Lynch
Chair Email:	
GSS Contact:	Joe Alexander
GSS Contact Email:	
Inception Date:	6/91

	Number of Stations
Same Time/Same Place:	24
Same Time/Diff Place:	
Diff Time/Same Place:	
Diff Time/Diff Place:	
Portable System:	

Installed GSS Software: GroupSystems™
Future GSS Software:
Under Consideration:

Group Meetings/Week: 3
Hours of Use/Week: 10

University of Ottawa
Computer Science
150 Louis Pasteur/Priv
Ottawa, Ontario K1N6N5 Canada

Telephone: 613-564-5420   Fax: 613-564-9486

Department Chair: Luigi Logrippo
Chair Email: LUIGI@UOTTAWA.ca
GSS Contact: Stan Szpakowicz
GSS Contact Email: SZPAK@UOTTAWA.ca
Inception Date: 1/87

                                      Number of Stations
Same Time/Same Place:
Same Time/Diff Place:
Diff Time/Same Place: 6
Diff Time/Diff Place:
Portable System:

Installed GSS Software: Negoplan-G
Future GSS Software:
Under Consideration:

Group Meetings/Week: V
Hours of Use/Week: V

University of Southern California
Information Sciences Institute
4676 Admiralty Way
Marina Del Rey, California 90262 USA

Telephone: 213-822-1511   Fax: 213-823-6714

Department Chair: Jon Postel
Chair Email: POXTEL@ISI.edu
GSS Contact: Steve Casner
GSS Contact Email: CASNER@ISI.edu
Inception Date: 1986

	Number of Stations
Same Time/Same Place:	
Same Time/Diff Place:	
Diff Time/Same Place:	6
Diff Time/Diff Place:	
Portable System:	

Installed GSS Software: Diamond/Slate, Real-Time Interactive Voice/Video
Future GSS Software:
Under Consideration:

Group Meetings/Week: 3
Hours of Use/Week: 10

Western Washington University
Decision Science—College of Business
Bellingham, Washington 98255 USA

Telephone: 206-647-4817   Fax: 206-647-4844

Department Chair: Benson Earl
Chair Email: Internet
GSS Contact: Floyd Lewis
GSS Contact Email: LEWIS@Nessie.cc.wwu.edu
Inception Date: 9/83

	Number of Stations
Same Time/Same Place:	10
Same Time/Diff Place:	
Diff Time/Same Place:	
Diff Time/Diff Place:	
Portable System:	10

Installed GSS Software: Meetingware
Future GSS Software:
Under Consideration:

Group Meetings/Week: 1
Hours of Use/Week: 8

PART II

RESEARCH ISSUES IN GROUP SUPPORT SYSTEMS

CHAPTER 3

A History of Group Support Systems Empirical Research: Lessons Learned and Future Directions

Alan R. Dennis
University of Georgia, Athens

R. Brent Gallupe
Queen's University

INTRODUCTION

Empirical research into the use of Group Support Systems (GSS) has increased rapidly over the past few years. What began with rudimentary computer communications and decision support systems research in the early 1970s has now grown into a full research field within the discipline of Management Information Systems. An indication of the importance of GSS research is found in the research grants and contracts that have been awarded to conduct such studies. Government agencies and private companies such as IBM, AT&T, and NCR have contributed millions of dollars in research funds (See Chapter 2) to many public and private institutions to support GSS research.

This chapter examines the empirical research that has investigated same time/same place GSS over the last 20 years. We focus primarily on published research and major empirical studies reported in working papers (as of the summer of 1991) that evaluate the effects of using GSS meeting rooms where groups meet at the same time and place and all group members have access to a computer workstation. This excludes some valuable research that has not yet reached the prepublication stage, papers that examine exclusively asynchronous or nonproximate GSS-supported meetings (Siegel, Dubrovsky, Kiesler, & McGuire, 1986), and papers whose primary purpose was not the evaluation of GSS technology such as major GSS conceptual/theoretical/framework papers by Huber (1984; 1990), DeSanctis and Gallupe (1987), Dennis et al., (1988), and Kraemer and King (1988).

The body of empirical research into GSS has grown to a considerable size and some organizing framework is needed to group the research studies that have been conducted. A number of frameworks have been used in previous work. Dennis, Nunamaker, and Vogel (1991), employing an input-process-output framework focused on the input side, used experimental design parameters such as organizational context and group characteristics to categorize the studies. Pinsonneault and Kraemer (1989) used an input-process-output model to examine and then categorize the empirical studies mainly by output variable. Gray, Vogel, and Beauclair (1990) used a multidimensional scaling model with the dimensions identified by Pinsonneault and Kraemer to determine the relationships between GSS empirical studies. Nunamaker, Dennis, George, Valacich, & Vogel (1991) proposed a more complex theory-based interaction model of GSS effects.

Our analysis of the research literature takes a different approach. We use a historical perspective to review the GSS research conducted to date. Our review of the history of GSS research identifies four distinct phases or generations of GSS research. The first phase might be called "Roots." This was the early empirical research into computer messaging systems and individual computer support systems that was carried out in the 1970s and formed the basis for the GSS work that was to follow.

The second phase occurred during the early 1980s. This phase, which we call "Initial Explorations," focused on early efforts to examine the impacts of rudimentary GSS on group outcomes and processes. In the middle to late 1980s a series of experimental studies was conducted to compare groups supported by a GSS with traditional unsupported groups. We term this phase "Early Experiments." The fourth phase, which began in the late 1980s and continues today, concentrates on the adoption and use of GSS technology in organizational settings. This "Field Studies" phase uses field research techniques to examine the impacts on organizations when GSS technology is used. The fifth and final phase in current work is the "In-Depth Studies" phase. This phase is composed of studies that examine a particular aspect of the use of GSS technology such as the use of a particular GSS software tool, or a specific group characteristic. These studies are based on the earlier experimental work and seek to discover a deeper understanding of the impacts of these tools on face-to-face group processes.

By using a chronological approach, instead of an input-process-output theory approach, we provide the reader with a different perspective of GSS empirical research. From this historical perspective, we analyze the GSS research findings and identify areas that have been ignored or were inadequately examined. Note that we have attempted to organize studies in the order in which they were conducted (rather than published) when chronology is particularly important. In some cases, we decided to group similar studies together, rather than organize them in chronological order, which improved the clarity of the article.

RESEARCH REVIEW

Roots

The beginnings of GSS empirical research can be traced back to early work in computer messaging and decision support systems (DSS) done in the 1970s. The essence of GSS technology in face-to-face meetings is to provide computer-based communication and information exchange support for group members. Early work in using computers to support communication between group members was done using simple computer-messaging systems. The insights provided by this work formed the foundation for much of the research into computer-based information exchange in face-to-face meetings.

Chapanis and his associates (e.g., Weeks & Chapanis, 1976) were among the first to rigorously study computer messaging versus face-to-face verbal communication. An example is a study (Chapanis, 1972) in which two-person teams solved objective problems using either computer messaging, remote handwriting, audio only, or face-to-face. He found that problems took longer to solve and fewer messages were exchanged using computer messaging than using face-to-face.

Krueger (1976) compared two-, three-, and four-person groups that used face-to-face, audio only, and computer messaging. He found that participation by group members was virtually equal for computer messaging but distinctly unequal for face-to-face groups.

In two reviews of experimental work that had been conducted during the late 1960s and early 1970s on the topic of computer messaging versus face-to-face communication (E. Williams, 1977; Short, Williams, & Christie, 1976b), the authors argue that use of computer messaging strongly influences group process. Their review suggested that computer messaging seems to introduce new factors or obscure normal group processes.

The second foundation area is the early empirical work done with individual-based decision support systems. This research focused on computer support for intellectual tasks such as alternatives generation and problem solving. This early work centered mostly around doctoral dissertations completed at universities in the Boston area. Michael Scott-Morton (1970) was one of the first researchers to investigate computer support for individual decision makers. It is not widely known that, in his original work, he speculated about the impact of interactive decision systems on management teams.

Other dissertations followed (Stabell, 1974; Grudnitski, 1975; and Alter, 1975) using a variety of research techniques. Although the focus was on individual decision makers using computer support, all researchers noted that with appropriate technology and group process, individual decision support systems could be extended and enhanced to support teams of decision makers.

In summary, the roots of GSS empirical research are found in both the early computer-messaging experimental research and the original decision support system research. The computer-messaging research demonstrated that using computers as a medium of information exchange is very different than face-to-face verbal exchange. The DSS researchers noted that computer support for individual decision makers was useful but the true power of the technology lay in supporting decision-making teams. It was not until the early 1980s that researchers finally focused on decision rooms and computer support for face-to-face meetings.

Initial Explorations

The period from about 1980 to 1984 saw the emergence of a set of exploratory studies of computer-based support for group processes. Most of the studies were done in same place/same time settings, but several non-face-to-face studies that also had important impacts on future face-to-face GSS research are also considered here. These early efforts were conducted by pioneers who recognized that computer and communication technology offered the potential to improve the productivity of groups. The hardware in the early 1980s was primarily mainframe-based with communication networks connecting computers to dumb terminals. The software was written in third generation languages such as Fortran, BASIC, and Pascal. Even with this limiting technology, the early explorers set out to determine if GSS could aid face-to-face groups.

Steeb and Johnston (1981) conducted an experimental study using a specific GSS (Group Decision Aid) to compare decision performance of groups that used the GSS with those that did not. The decision task was a specialized, complex crisis scenario derived from the area of international relations. All groups were asked to reach a group consensus as to what decision to make. Results indicated that the GSS groups were more satisfied with the process and more confident in the decision they had made. The GSS groups also developed higher-quality decisions according to the experts who evaluated the decision outcomes. There appeared to be no significant differences in the group process measures between aided groups and unaided groups.

The primary purpose of a GSS research study conducted by Turoff and Hiltz (1982) was "to show that the computer may indeed be used to support group communications as an integral part of a DSS" (1982, p. 83). They conducted two experiments into the impact of computer-based support on group decision making. The first experiment was essentially an experiment into the effects of computer conferencing on group decision making that did not use an actual GSS. The second experiment, however, manipulated leadership in the group, use of a GSS and mode of group interaction (either face-to-face or computer-conference). The results indicated that use of a GSS aided the groups in reaching quality decisions more often than groups unaided by a GSS.

Chapter 3 A History of GSS Empirical Research

Floyd Lewis, in his doctoral dissertation (1982), developed a small GSS called "Facilitator" running on three Apple computers and conducted an experiment manipulating the amount of support for the group decision-making task that the groups could use. A control treatment had no support, the first experimental treatment used "Facilitator," and the second experimental treatment used a structured paper-and-pencil technique that incorporated the same features as "Facilitator." Lewis found that the use of the GSS produced decisions of higher quality, generated more alternatives per decision, and reduced domination by single group members when compared to either the control group or the paper-and-pencil group.

Kull (1982) describes a group decision-making simulation using a GSS called MINDSIGHT developed by Execucom. The five participants in the simulation were high-level executives from five different companies. They were asked to analyze a business case and then make a decision regarding a strategic problem presented in the case. The major findings from this simulation were the following: 1. The GSS must support group interaction and not inhibit it, 2. The weighting and ranking of alternative solutions is important in reaching a consensus in the decision-making process, 3. Voting support is a valuable feature of a GSS, but this support must allow for anonymous as well as public voting, 4. A GSS may not be appropriate for all types of tasks, for all complexity levels.

Gray (1983) describes the setting up of a "decision room" to support group decision making and some simulations using this room. He also discusses a group decision-making scenario in which a group of company executives must decide whether to build a new plant overseas or not. The article discusses some of the ways a GSS and "decision room" environment can assist this decision group in making their decision. Gray notes the importance of a number of factors in GSS use including the type and complexity of the group task and the level of technology sophistication.

Adelman (1984) describes the development and use of a decision support system for the design and acquisition of a new helicopter. The DSS was used in a group meeting to help the team reach a consensus decision. Results of the use of the DSS in the group setting indicated that the group discussion was more focused, that there was more support for the decision made (by all group members), and that real-time sensitivity analysis was possible in a team meeting.

Ruble (1984), for his doctoral dissertation, used a computer-based management game as the task to determine if DSS could effectively support student decision-making groups. Some groups used the DSS and some did not. Ruble found no differences between groups that used the DSS and those that did not. He speculated that either task may have been too complex for the groups to effectively use the DSS or the DSS may not have contained the proper features (such as alternative ranking) to properly support the group.

Bui and Jarke (1984) describe a system called "Cooperative Group Decision Support System." They describe the major features of the system, which include computerized support for Delphi Technique and Nominal Group Technique, a simple computer-conferencing system for group communication, and a multiple-criteria decision method called ELECTRE. In addition, they outline two examples of the use of CGDSS (faculty candidate selection and the Saw Mill Investment Problem). The major contribution of this paper is that it describes the effort necessary to develop a comprehensive GSS and the variety of decision tasks that such a system can support.

The only GSS developed by early explorers that is still widely used today (although the current version is substantially different from the initial version) is that developed at the University of Arizona. Plexsys (now called GroupSystems™) was first used in 1985 in a 16-workstation meeting room at Arizona. Applegate in her 1985 dissertation (Nunamaker, Applegate, & Konsynski, 1987) examined its use by seven strategic planning groups striving to generate ideas. These groups each met an average of three times over a three- to four-month period. The participants reported very high satisfaction with the GSS process and viewed the use of the GSS to be very important to their idea-generation process. Anonymity and the ability to work in parallel contributed to success, whereas slow network speed and the loss of a "world view" detracted.

In summary, the early explorations were remarkable for attempting to develop GSS systems and for examining the affects of using those systems. This early work is characterized by diversity of hardware and software as researchers struggled with building group support technology with rudimentary tools. The basic lessons learned, however, were (1) that GSS has the potential to improve group processes and outcomes, (2) better GSS must be developed if these systems are to be used, and (3) more rigorous research is needed before the impacts of the use of this technology is understood.

Early Experiments

The third phase of GSS empirical research is the early laboratory experiments that compared GSS groups with non-GSS groups. The intent of these studies was to explore in a more rigorous fashion the effects on group processes and outcomes of using a GSS in a controlled laboratory environment. These early experiments built on the earlier work by developing and using GSSs with similar features. They extended the initial work by using stronger research designs and more sophisticated measures to investigate the use of GSSs.

The first study in this phase was conducted by Gallupe (Gallupe, DeSanctis, & Dickson, 1988) for his dissertation at the University of Minnesota in 1985. He developed a rudimentary GSS in BASIC and then used a 2x2 experimental design that compared GSS and non-GSS groups performing simple versus complex decision tasks. He found that GSS use was particularly appropriate for complex tasks. He found that GSS groups made better-quality decisions than non-GSS groups. He also found that GSS groups were less satisfied than non-GSS groups.

The second experimental study conducted at the University of Minnesota was done by Watson (R. Watson, DeSanctis, & Poole, 1988) in 1987. He developed a GSS in the C programming language running under the UNIX operating system. This system became the Software Assisted Meeting Management System (SAMM). Watson was interested in the impact of using a GSS on consensus formation in small groups. He found that GSS groups performed an allocation task poorer on quality than did non-GSS groups and that there was no difference between the groups for amount of consensus. He also found that GSS groups were less satisfied with the process than non-GSS groups.

About the time of the Watson study, Beauclair (1987) was conducting a GSS study at Indiana University using a research GSS developed on a small local area network. Groups had to reach a decision regarding a student discipline case. Beauclair found that there were no differences between GSS groups and non-GSS groups for decision quality, time to make the decision, amount of participation by group members, and satisfaction with the group outcome.

Zigurs (Zigurs, Poole, & DeSanctis, 1988) conducted the third GSS experimental study at the University of Minnesota. This study focused on meeting process rather than meeting outcomes. Again, small size groups of three and four people were used. The amount of influence behavior experienced within the group was the major dependent variable. She found that using a GSS resulted in a more even distribution of influence in the group compared to non-GSS groups.

Ho, Raman, and Watson (1989) conducted essentially the same experiment as that by Watson et al. (1988) in Singapore. They found no differences in influence between GSS and non-GSS groups, but the GSS groups had less consensus. They attributed the differences in findings from the Watson et al. (1988) study to cultural differences, particularly in the subjects reactions to anonymity. Anonymity encouraged a more honest exchange of opinions, which is not always welcomed in Singapore, given the desire for harmony in group interaction.

Lim, Raman, and Wei (1990) used Watson's allocation task with five-member groups (half with group-elected leaders, half without) to study equality of influence and dominance. There were no differences in the equality of influence, except for the no-leader GSS groups, which had a more even distribution of influence. The dominant member in GSS groups (with and without leaders) had less influence than the dominant member in the non-GSS groups.

Tan, Wei, and Raman (1991) again used this allocation task, along with a choice task, to examine consensus and equality of influence in five-member groups. GSS groups had the highest consensus for the choice task and the lowest for the allocation task. There was no difference in the equality of influence.

Gallupe (1990) reports two studies that compared the performance of GSS groups, non-GSS groups, and the "best members" of those groups to determine if use of a GSS improved decision quality over that of the group's best member. Rank-order voting tasks using two different GSS were completed by the groups. Individual group members initially ranked a set of alternatives and then in the group process (using GSS or not using GSS) decided on a group ranking. The results were consistent in both studies. They indicated that GSS groups did not do as well as the best member of their group. More non-GSS groups did as well as or better than the best member. One explanation is that GSS use supports more equal participation by group members, making it more difficult for the best member to influence the group.

Bui and Sivasankaran (1990) studied three-member groups working on two choice tasks of differing complexity using a system similar to SAMM. For their low-complexity task, there were no differences in decision quality, and non-GSS groups were more satisfied and took less time. For their high-complexity task, the GSS groups made higher-quality decisions, but there were no differences in satisfaction or decision time.

George, Easton, Nunamaker, and Northcraft (1990) used a generate-and-choose task to compare the performance of six-member GroupSystems™ GSS groups to six-member groups without GSS support. There were no differences in decision quality, but the non-GSS groups were more likely to reach consensus in less time, whereas the GSS groups had more equal participation. They also found no significant effects due to anonymity or the presence of a randomly selected group leader, although two interaction effects were found for satisfaction and participation. Anonymous GSS groups with leaders and nonanonymous groups without leaders were most satisfied, whereas non-GSS groups with leaders and GSS groups without leaders had the most even distribution of participation.

Winniford (1991) studied the use of the GroupSystems™ GSS by five- and ten-member groups for a choice task. There were no differences in decision quality or member satisfaction, but large GSS groups chose to do more votes than the non-GSS groups.

The results of these early experiments can be summed up in one word: mixed. Some experiments showed improved decision quality, whereas others showed no effect or worse decision quality for groups using a GSS compared to those who did not. Some studies showed increased satisfaction with process and outcomes, whereas others found a decrease. What is clear is that use of a GSS did make a difference, either positive or negative, in most cases. The inconsistency of the results stands out, and researchers began to put their efforts into determining just what factors make a difference or have no effect.

Field Studies

One of the first organized field studies of this next generation of GSS technology was that by Nunamaker, Applegate, and Konsynski (1988). After studying 40 groups using GroupSystems™, they concluded that anonymity was important and that larger groups were more satisfied with GSS use than smaller groups.

A study of ten operations management groups from five public and private organizations also found larger GroupSystems™ GSS groups to be more satisfied than smaller groups (Dennis, 1991). Groups of peers reported anonymity to be less important than did hierarchically structured groups that included members with different power and status.

Subsequent case studies of GroupSystems™ use for strategic planning (Dennis, Heminger, Nunamaker, & Vogel, 1990), in the search for competitive advantage (Dennis, Nunamaker, & Paranka, 1991), in support of negotiating groups (Herniter, 1991), and in the system development process (Daniels, 1991; Hayes, 1991) have also found larger groups to be satisfied, and to perceive GSS use to be effective and efficient. A study of eight strategic management groups attributed these differences to the ability of members to work in parallel and anonymity, which led to increased equality of participation and improved communication across the organizational hierarchy (Tyran, Dennis, Nunamaker, & Vogel, 1991).

A subsequent study of the strategic-planning processes of 17 organizations (Dennis, Tyran, Vogel, & Nunamaker, 1990), later expanded to 30 organizations (Dennis, 1991), found GSS use to enhance six capabilities linked to more successful strategic management outcomes: (1) enhancing idea generation; (2) identifying key problem areas; (3) enhancing innovation; (4) communicating line managers' concerns to top management; (5) fostering organizational learning; and (6) integrating diverse functions and operations. However, the capability for top managers to communicate their views down was perceived to be hindered. These effects were attributed to parallelism, anonymity, and the group facilitator.

Carmel (1991) studied 11 Joint Application Design groups performing requirements determination for information systems (six GSS, five non-GSS). The GroupSystems™ GSS groups were more efficient and more satisfied, and group members participated more equally. The non-GSS were more structured and were better able to resolve conflict.

Jarvenpaa, Rao, and Huber (1988) conducted a field experiment in which the same three groups used three different forms of GSS technology. Groups were given unstructured problems and asked to use an electronic blackboard, workstations, or discussion (no technology). The researchers found that the technology had no effect on participation or satisfaction with the process.

McCartt and Rohrbaugh (1989) studied 14 GSS groups using the Decision Conferencing single workstation GSS. The most successful meetings were those in which the participants felt decisions had been made and action plans developed, full use had been made of the GSS technology, and there had been full, extended discussions of the issues.

GroupSystems™ was adopted by IBM in 1987, resulting in a series of research studies over several years. The first of these studied GSS use by 441 participants from 29 groups (Nunamaker, Vogel, Heminger, Martz, Grohowski, & McGoff, 1989). The participants reported GSS use to be very effective and satisfying. An analysis of actual to budgeted project plans found a 55 percent reduction in person-hours due to GSS use. Calendar time (start date to end date) was reduced by 92 percent.

Martz, Vogel, and Nunamaker (in press) found that the groups who used the GSS technology at IBM changed over time. In general, the height (number of managerial levels) and width (number of departments) of the group increased, so that later groups were more heterogeneous and less cohesive, indicating, perhaps, a growing willingness to apply the technology to more challenging problems. Interestingly, perceived task performance was found to be correlated to the size of the task: the larger the task, the greater the perceived performance.

Vogel, Nunamaker, Martz, Grohowski, and McGoff (1990) examine a study undertaken by IBM. Participants again reported high satisfaction and perceived GSS use to improve meeting efficiency and effectiveness. A study by Grohowski, McGoff, Vogel, Martz, and Nunamaker (1990) attributed this success to increasing the number of meeting participants and their participation, reducing the number of meetings, and increasing task focus during the meetings.

One area that has received recent attention is the use of GSS technology to support project teams that meet repeatedly for a series of short meetings on specific projects. DeSanctis, Poole, Lewis, and Desharnais (1991) investigated the use of the SAMM GSS by 10 project teams at the IRS. The teams used SAMM over a seven-month period for an average of six meetings. In general, the teams reported GSS use to be satisfying but expressed a desire for more training.

Dennis (1991) studied six project teams in a hospital setting over a seven-week period. All teams were given the same task—develop a project to improve customer satisfaction. Three were randomly assigned to use GSS and three to use "traditional" meeting techniques. Team member participation was consistently more even in the GSS teams than the non-GSS teams. The GSS teams reported lower initial satisfaction, effectiveness, and cohesiveness, but by the end of the study, there were no differences in satisfaction and GSS teams reported higher effectiveness and cohesiveness. The GSS team projects were rated higher for their effects on the satisfaction of two customer groups, lower on one customer group, and more difficult to implement. Although the teams found the ability to work in parallel to be important, anonymity was not seen to be important.

In summary, studies of GSS use in the field have generally found positive reactions. Participants have been satisfied and have perceived the technology to improve their effectiveness and/or efficiency. These findings are strikingly different from the findings from the early experiments, suggesting, perhaps, that GSS use in these field studies was different from GSS use in the early experiments. Several plausible differences are immediately apparent: many field studies involved large groups of managers and professionals performing complex tasks over several days using GSS that included an active process facilitator. In contrast, most early experiments involved smaller groups of students performing less complex tasks over an hour or two without an active process facilitator.

In-Depth Studies

These apparently mixed findings among the early experiments and between the experiments as a group and the field studies, led researchers to wonder what aspects of the GSS technology or the situation in which it was used influenced certain meeting processes and outcomes. This is the focus of the fifth phase of GSS empirical research that is currently under way. The research in this phase is identifiable by its in-depth focus on one (or more) specific aspect(s) of a GSS technology and or/its users. The early experiments and initial field studies were broad in scope with the intent to determine what effects GSS use might have on group process and outcomes. Phase-five research is more "drill-down" research that explores, in a narrower technology, task, and group domain, a specific use of GSS. This research aims to find not just what effects GSS use has but why and under what circumstances those effects occur. Most of these studies have been conducted using the GroupSystems™ GSS or the SAMM GSS.

Parallelism

A series of three studies at Queen's University (Gallupe, Bastianutti, & Cooper, 1991) have examined the notion that the ability for group members to work in parallel may reduce production blocking and thus may account for the increased productivity of GSS idea-generating groups. Four-member GroupSystems™ GSS groups were compared to four-member verbal idea-generating groups in all studies. The first study found that GSS groups generated a larger number of unique, high-quality ideas, and were more satisfied than traditional groups.

A second study (Gallupe, Cooper, & Bastianutti, 1990) implemented a delay into the GSS technology to simulate the blocking that occurs in traditional verbally interacting groups. This study found that the delay groups did no better than verbal groups, which implied a major blocking effect.

The third study (Gallupe & Cooper, 1991) varied the GSS treatment by imposing a strict idea-generation process on all groups. For all groups, only one idea could be generated at one time in a "first-in" procedure. That is, if an individual was first to start to express an idea, all other group members had to wait until the idea was completed before they could be next to express their idea(s). This process was felt to be most like traditional brainstorming. The results of this study showed that GSS groups generating ideas this way were less productive than traditional brainstorming groups again indicating that production blocking was indeed the major factor in GSS productivity.

A similar study at Arizona (Dennis, 1991) found nine-member GSS groups with the ability to work in parallel to generate four times more ideas than GSS groups working under similar blocking conditions. The GSS groups that worked in parallel were also more satisfied.

Anonymity

Anonymity has been one of the most-studied GSS components. Jessup, Connolly, and Galegher (1990) studied anonymous and nonanonymous four-member GSS groups performing an idea-generation task. There were no differences in overall performance or the number of supportive comments, but anonymous groups were more critical and probing, were more likely to embellish ideas proposed by others, and made more comments overall.

Jessup and Tansik (1991) then studied four-member idea generation groups with an anonymity and proximity manipulation. There were no differences due to anonymity in performance or satisfaction, but members of anonymous groups perceived the GSS meeting to have been most effective.

Connolly, Jessup, and Valacich (1990) studied four-member idea generating groups, this time with an anonymity and meeting tone manipulation. They placed a confederate into each group to provide positive or negative comments for ideas that were generated. They found that positive, nonanonymous groups were most satisfied but generated fewer high-quality ideas. Anonymous, negative groups were least satisfied but generated the most high-quality ideas.

Valacich, Dennis, and Nunamaker (1992c) studied three- and nine-member idea-generating groups. There were no differences in performance or satisfaction due to anonymity, but anonymous groups were more critical. Nine-member groups generated more ideas than three-member groups and three-member nonanonymous were more satisfied.

Group Size

Dennis, Valacich, and Nunamaker (1990) found eighteen-member groups to generate more ideas than nine-member groups, who generated more ideas than three-member groups. Satisfaction followed the same pattern as performance. In a subsequent study, Valacich (1989) found eight-member groups to generate more ideas than four-member groups but no satisfaction differences. Four-member groups perceived themselves to have been more effective than eight-member groups.

Another study was the joint Queen's-Arizona Group Size study (Gallupe, Dennis, Cooper, Valacich, & Nunamaker, 1991) comparing two-, four-, six-, and twelve-member GSS and non-GSS groups. The larger GSS groups generated more ideas and were more satisfied, but reverse was true for the smaller groups.

Fellers (1989) also studied the use of the GroupSystems™ GSS by five- and ten- member groups for an idea-generation task. The GSS groups generated more ideas and were more satisfied than the non-GSS groups, particularly the larger groups.

Another line of research related to this group size research is comparing groups to the same number of individuals working separately without communicating. Previous non-GSS research has consistently found individuals working separately to generate more ideas than groups, but three GSS studies have found the reverse: groups outperform individuals (Dennis, 1991; Dennis & Valacich, 1991; Valacich, Dennis, & Connolly, in press). Members of groups have also been found to be more satisfied than individuals working separately.

Process Structuring

DeSanctis, D'Oronfrio, Sambamurthy, and Poole (1989) conducted a study that investigated the use of decision heuristics and GSS. The task was the "Foundation Task," a task that required resolution of differing values and preferences. The decision heuristics that were varied were comprehensiveness and restrictiveness.

The SAMM GSS was used to implement the computer-based heuristics. The researchers found that restrictiveness did not affect group consensus but that comprehensiveness in the form of a general decision heuristic coupled with a computer delivery of specific heuristics (GSS) dramatically improved group consensus.

Sambamurthy and DeSanctis (1989) compared groups using two other versions of SAMM for stakeholder analysis. One version provided communication among members plus simple voting and ranking techniques. The second provided the same communication techniques plus tools supporting a sophisticated stakeholder analysis technique. In groups without strong pretest agreement about stakeholders, use of the more sophisticated GSS improved poststudy agreement, but, not unexpectedly, there were few differences for groups with high initial agreement. Groups using the more sophisticated technique also had greater confidence in their recommendations and perceived themselves to have made higher-quality decisions.

Easton, Vogel, and Nunamaker (1989) compared four-member groups with no support to four-member groups following a structured manual stakeholder analysis technique to four-members groups using a single-workstation GSS providing the same structured technique. Both structured groups generated more alternatives, made higher-quality decisions, and had more equal participation, but took more time than the unstructured groups. The GSS-supported groups were more satisfied with the process and the outcomes.

Dickson, Lee, Robinson, and Heath (1989) studied the effects of facilitation on three-, four-, and five-member groups using the SAMM GSS performing an allocation task. Groups without an active process facilitator or a passive chauffeur who solely assisted with the use of the GSS displayed less consensus than those with either a facilitator or chauffeur.

Anson (1990) also examined the effects of process facilitation. He compared six- and seven-member groups in four treatments: (1) no support, (2) an active process facilitator, (3) GroupSystems™ GSS, and (4) an active process facilitator combined with GroupSystems™. The groups in the no support treatment had lower task performance, cohesiveness, and process perceptions, whereas groups in the facilitator/GroupSystems™ treatment had the highest cohesiveness and process perceptions.

In a further study, Anson and Heminger (1990) compared GroupSystems™ groups with and without an active process facilitator. The use of GroupSystems™ with the facilitator resulted in more positive perceptions of the process and task outcomes.

Easton, George, Nunamaker, and Pendergast (1990) examined the effects of process structure in four- and five-member GSS groups performing a generate-and-choose task. This process structure divided the group communication into many separate and distinct conversations in an attempt to reduce the tendency of group discussion to focus on one topic. Groups with this structure generated more ideas, but made lower-quality decisions. There were no differences in satisfaction, participation, or consensus.

Dennis (1991) also examined this form of process structure with nine-member GSS groups. Although the groups with this process structure generated more ideas, the differences were not statistically significant.

Venkatesh and Wynne (1991) examined the use of a different form of process structuring rules by four- and five-member groups performing a generate and choose task. The treatments were no process structuring, simple process structuring (advocating the need to identify and formulate problems before attempting solutions), and complex process structuring (simple process structuring plus a specific methodology for problem structuring). There was no difference in decision time. The no-structure groups generated more alternative solutions, whereas the complex structure groups made the best overall decisions. Groups with the simple structure perceived that better communication had occurred and perceived themselves to have the greatest gain in problem understanding.

George, Dennis, and Nunamaker (1991) examined the use (or lack of use) of an overall meeting agenda by six-member GSS groups performing a generate-and-choose task. There were no differences with or without an agenda in terms of the number of alternatives, decision quality, consensus, or satisfaction.

Sengupta and Te'eni (1991) studied the effects of cognitive feedback on three-member groups performing a choice task using a specialized electronic-voting GSS. Feedback was found to improve decision quality.

Dennis (1991) examined the use of structure to decompose the task into several components by eight-member idea-generating groups. Groups that used this task structure generated more ideas than those without it. There were no differences in satisfaction.

Group Development and Studies Over Time

Dennis, Easton, Easton, George, and Nunamaker (1990) compared four-, five- and six-member groups that differed in group history using GSS for a generate-and-choose task. Established groups that had a history of working together exhibited distinct personalities compared to ad hoc randomly built groups with no group history. Members of established groups were more likely to express uninhibited comments, to question the group process, and to make directly critical comments, and the groups themselves had a less even distribution of participation. Although there were no differences in the total amount of communication, there was greater variance among the established groups.

The issue of GSS use over time, and whether user attitudes changed after they gained greater experience with the technology was considered by Zigurs, DeSanctis, and Billingsley (1989). They studied the effects of SAMM GSS use by four- and five-member groups over a series of eight meetings, and found attitudes toward the GSS became more positive as time progressed.

Chidambaram, Bostrom, and Wynne (1991) examined the effects of time and experience. They studied GroupSystems™ GSS use on group cohesiveness and the ability to manage conflict on four meetings of five-member GSS and non-GSS groups working on four generate-and-choose tasks. They found the GSS groups to have lower cohesiveness and conflict-management ability initially but this pattern reversed itself by the end of the fourth meeting.

Finally, one of the recurring questions faced by GSS researchers is the issue of typing. Will managers type? Dennis, Briggs, and Nunamaker (1991) conducted a field experiment comparing eight-member groups of senior executives who used either a keyboard or a pen-based handwriting recognition interface for an idea-generation task. Groups using the keyboard generated more ideas and were more satisfied.

WHAT WE KNOW AND WHAT WE DON'T

Summary of Findings

This body of research paints a rather cloudy picture. In most field research, GSS use appeared to improve meeting outcomes such as performance, efficiency, and satisfaction. In laboratory research GSS use has improved performance (Dennis, 1991; Fellers, 1989; Gallupe et al., 1988; Gallupe et al., 1991; Gallupe et al., in press) or had mixed effects (Bui and Sivasankaram, 1990; George et al., 1990; R. Watson et al., 1988; Winniford, 1991). Effects on member satisfaction in the laboratory have been positive (Dennis, 1991; Fellers, 1989; Gallupe et al., 1991; Gallupe et al., in press), negative (Gallupe et al., 1988; Watson et al., 1988) or mixed (Beauclair, 1987; George et al., 1990; Winniford, 1990). Influence has been more equally distributed among group members (R. Watson et al., 1988) or has seen no effect from GSS use (Ho et al., 1989; Lim et al., 1990; Tan et al., 1991). GSS use has decreased consensus (Ho et al., 1989; George et al., 1990) or had mixed effects (Tan et al., 1991; R. Watson et al., 1988).

We conclude that the effects of GSS appear to depend on a variety of factors, some of which include aspects of the technology itself, as well as those of the group and the task. The key question, of course, is what are these aspects and how do they impact meeting processes and outcomes? The fifth and current phase of GSS research is beginning to shed some light on this. Many of these studies have examined aspects of the situation in which the GSS was used, and/or specific aspects related to the technology itself.

There are many important aspects of the situation in which GSS technology is used. We consider three that previous research suggests as being very important: group size, task complexity, and task type. Eight studies have specifically examined the effects of group size (Dennis, 1991; Dennis, Valacich, & Nunamaker, 1990; Dennis & Valacich, 1991; Fellers, 1989; Gallupe et al., in press; Nunamaker et al., 1988; Valacich, 1989; Valacich, Dennis & Connolly, in press). All six that examined performance found performance to increase with group size. Of the seven that examined group member satisfaction, five found satisfaction to increase with size, and two found no differences. The message is clear: larger groups benefit more from GSS use than do smaller groups.

Another important aspect is task complexity. Two studies suggest that GSS may be more appropriate for more complex tasks, rather than simple tasks (Gallupe et al., 1988; Bui and Sivasankaran, 1990). Comparing the generally positive results from the many field studies (which have typically studied complex tasks) to the often mixed results of the laboratory research (which have typically studied less complex tasks) provides additional support for the better fit between complex tasks and GSS use.

GSS technology may also be more beneficial to certain types of tasks. For example, we are convinced that GSS technology can dramatically improve group performance and member satisfaction for generation tasks, where the group's objective is to draft a project plan, or produce a set of ideas, alternatives, opinions, information, and so forth (e.g., see Dennis, 1991; Fellers, 1989; Gallupe et al., 1991; Gallupe et al., in press). We are less convinced that GSS technology can help groups facing a choice task, where the objective is to choose an alternative(s) from a pre-specified set. For these types of tasks, GSS technology may help, but the evidence is not as clear as that for generation tasks.

Four aspects related GSS technology itself and the way they can change group interaction have also received much attention: anonymity, parallelism, structure, and facilitation. The role of anonymity has been studied both in the laboratory and in the field in at least 12 studies (Connolly et al., 1990; Dennis, 1991; Dennis, Tyran, Nunamaker, & Vogel, 1990; Ho et al., 1989; Jessup et al., 1990; Jessup & Tansik, 1991; Nunamaker et al., 1987; Nunamaker et al., 1988; Tyran et al., 1991; Valacich, Dennis, & Connolly, in press). Six of these found anonymity to have important performance effects, while five found anonymity to have few effects.

It seems likely that the importance of anonymity depends on the nature of the group and the task, particularly how secure group members feel in contributing their honest opinions. One study by Dennis (1991), for example, found groups of peers to perceive anonymity to be less important than groups with a hierarchical structure whose members had different power and status. Thus peer groups in general (but not in all cases, of course) may feel more comfortable openly sharing ideas and opinions, and therefore have less use for anonymity.

A second aspect of GSS technology that has received attention is the ability to work in parallel. The four studies of parallelism and its affect on production blocking have been consistent (Dennis, 1991; Gallupe et al., 1990; Gallupe et al., 1991; Gallupe & Cooper, 1991). All suggest that the ability to work in parallel is a significant benefit that accounts for much of the success of GSS technology.

The third GSS aspect that has received substantial research attention is the ability to structure group interaction. The results from seven studies of structure are somewhat mixed (Dennis, 1991; A. C. Easton et al., 1989; G. Easton et al., 1990; George et al., 1991; Sambamurthy & DeSanctis, 1989; Venkatesh & Wynne, 1991). Five found performance to increase with structure, one found no effect, and one found performance to decrease. Perhaps more importantly, intermediate measures of quality (e.g., the number of ideas in a generate-and-choose task) in two studies went the opposite direction from the final measures of quality (e.g., decision quality). The use of structure appears to be case specific; structure that "fits" the task can improve performance, but inappropriate structure can also impair performance.

Many GSS technology "packages" include a meeting facilitator. A facilitator can assist the group in understanding, using, and adopting the technology, as well as providing process guidance to improve group dynamics. Three studies suggest that the use of an active process facilitator improves meeting outcomes (Anson, 1990; Anson & Heminger, 1990; Dickson et al., 1989).

One final aspect is that of time and experience with GSS technology. Group performance and reactions to GSS technology may change over time, as the group gains experience with it. Three studies suggest that reactions and performance increase with repeated use (Chiambarum et al., 1991; Dennis, 1991; Zigurs et al., 1989).

Implications

The rather mixed set of findings from the studies considered here presents one overarching implication for researchers, developers, and users of GSS technology. The results of any one study will not apply to all group work, so it is also important to explicitly consider the limitations to which research findings can be generalized. We agree with Huber (1990) that even apparently subtle differences in technology (or group or task needs, for that matter) may have significant impacts on meeting outcomes.

Although effects of GSS use do differ depending upon the situation, we draw two general implications for GSS users—understanding, of course, that these implications will not apply in all situations. First, the research reviewed here suggests that groups that use GSS technology can often be more productive and satisfied than non-GSS groups. The first implication is that GSS technologies should be used when possible, especially for larger groups, when group performance and member satisfaction are important.

Second, the size of GSS groups should not be artificially constrained (Thelen, 1949), but rather should be as large as the task warrants. In short, the "optimal" GSS group size depends upon the situation (group, task, context, GSS) and in some cases may be quite large. The implication is that additional members should be added to the group as long as they have the potential to add value—new information or skills.

Many effects appear to be linked to the ability of GSS technology to provide parallel communication to reduce production blocking. The implication here for users and developers is that GSS meeting styles providing parallelism should be used where possible, although not all task activities may be amenable to electronic communication.

Anonymity also proved useful in some cases, particularly where there were power and status differences within the group. However, it appeared to have weaker effects on outcomes for groups of peers or groups that worked together on a regular basis. Although some of the potentially negative effects of anonymity were observed in some studies (deindividuation, free riding, increased criticism), they were usually minor. The implication is that anonymity should be used for groups with power and status differences. Because anonymity appears to have only a few negative effects, it may be beneficial to err on the side of using it when it is not needed, rather than not providing it when it could be helpful.

For developers of GSS technology, it is important to strive to understand what GSS aspects are useful in what situations, such as parallelism and anonymity. Clearly there are more GSS aspects that need to be considered. It will become increasingly important for developmental researchers to work closely with empirical researchers to best fit the components offered by different configurations of GSS technology to user needs. In the early years of GSS, there was little empirical research to guide developers. Developers built GSS environments, gave them to users to see what happened, and then redesigned them in an iterative cycle of design-use-redesign. Today, there is a growing base of empirical research, and although iterative development remains important, developers building on this empirical foundation can provide more successful initial environments requiring less redesign.

Future Research

The history of GSS empirical research points in a number of directions for further research. The time has now come to focus more on specific functional areas such as marketing, production, IS development, quality team processes, and so on to begin to tailor GSS tools to specific tasks. For example, focus groups are essential tools for the marketing researcher. Can a GSS tool be developed to support the special needs of marketing focus groups? Substantial systems-building research is needed to first develop these new GSS technologies, followed by both experimental and field research to determine what approaches work.

Another area of GSS research that has received little attention is the design of the group/user interface (for discussion, see Chapter 10). The user interface has been found to be an important factor in effective computer use in individual-based studies. Most GSS tools provide only one interface, and thus empirical studies have examined only one interface in most comparative studies (cf. George et al., 1990). We know very little about the impact of the user interface in GSS technology. For example, is there one best interface for each task, or should each group member be able to customize his/her own interface?

A third direction for further research is the incorporation of expert systems or knowledge-based systems into GSS. That is, meetings in which one "member" is an expert system that can provide specific insight into the task under discussion. Although this has been widely discussed, virtually no empirical research has been done.

There is also the question of time and user experience with GSS technology. Many studies have examined groups' first use of GSS technology. Yet several studies suggest that group performance and reactions to GSS technology change as groups gain experience with its use (Chidambarum et al., 1991; Dennis, 1991; Zigurs et al., 1989). More research is needed to better understand how performance and user reactions change from initial use as novices to subsequent uses as average and experienced users.

Finally, the real power of GSS technologies may not lie in how they improve group performance in meetings, but instead, in how they transform the process of group work. Many current GSS technologies designed for face-to-face work are now being extended to support groups working in different places in different times. In contrast to traditional tools for different place/different time work (such as E-mail and computer conferencing), these technologies bring all the power of face-to-face GSS technologies (e.g, anonymity, structure) into individual group member offices. Should these technologies prove as useful as their face-to-face counterparts, we may see a significant increase in productivity as the number of "meetings" requiring all group members to assemble in the same place at the same time gradually falls.

CHAPTER 4

Putting the "Group" Back in Group Support Systems: Some Theoretical Issues About Dynamic Processes in Groups with Technological Enhancements

Joseph E. McGrath
University of Illinois

Andrea B. Hollingshead
University of Illinois

INTRODUCTION

From the outset, the study of Group Support Systems (GSS) has been much more about support systems than about groups and much more about technical developments and applications than about identification and exploration of basic theoretical issues. Furthermore, the study of Group Support Systems, like work in most areas of social and behavioral science, has also seriously neglected matters of time (McGrath, 1990; McGrath & Kelly, 1986).

This lack of attention to groups, to theory, and to time is somewhat ironic considering that the early roots of this area of study grew directly out of theories of group dynamics. From the outset, efforts to provide groups with technological support for their task performance activities have been driven by three basic ideas that reflect concern with group theory and with time:

1. The idea that technologically enhanced support systems could improve group task performance effectiveness, helping groups overcome so-called "process losses" by altering group task performance processes.
2. The idea that computers could increase the range and depth of information that a given individual (or group), engaged in information-intensive work, could have access to, and also increase the speed and power with which that information could be acquired, processed, and presented for use.
3. The idea that groups using electronically enhanced communication systems could transcend the time and space constraints that burden groups that meet face-to-face—namely, that all of their members must be in the same place at the same time in order to meet.

In this chapter, we attempt to redress these imbalances of attention to groups, theory, and time. We will lay out a systematic, conceptual framework and use it to examine a wide variety of technological systems designed to modify the work of groups, giving special emphasis to group theoretic issues and to a complex set of temporal issues that these technologies involve. (Although we will use the term *technology* broadly in this chapter, most modern means for technological enhancements of work in groups involve electronic systems, so at times we will use the term *electronic* interchangeably with *technological*).

We begin the chapter by presenting a conceptual framework for the various forms in which technological systems can be used to try to enhance work in groups. We can classify the technological systems into four major types, on the basis of the function(s) that they serve for the group: inter-member communication, extra-group communication, information/data access, and member-task interaction. We then examine some issues, including temporal issues, that arise for groups with electronic systems that serve each of those four major functions. In the final section of the chapter, we draw upon a time-centered theory of groups to highlight some potential effects of Group Support Systems on group performance processes and outcomes—issues that need to be explored in future research.

SYSTEMS FOR TECHNOLOGICAL ENHANCEMENTS OF WORK IN GROUPS

Communication in the context of collaborative work in groups is a rather complex matter. If one uses the term communication broadly (as we do here), it can refer not only to transmitting, receiving, and storing information (the cognitive aspects of messages) of various kinds and from various sources, but also to transmission, reception, and storage of the affect and influence aspects of those same messages. Given that broad view of communication, we can think of each member of any particular group as being hooked up, in principle, to four functionally distinct (though not necessarily physically separate), interactive (i.e., two-way) communication systems, each of which may or may not involve technological enhancements. First, each member needs to be able to communicate to and from some or all of the other members of the current work group. A number of electronic systems have been developed for modifying within-group communication. These include video and audio phones, computer conferences, E-mail, and the like. We will call these Group (Internal) Communication Support Systems (GCSS). Second, each member needs to be able to send messages to and receive messages from a number of individuals and groups outside the group (e.g., colleagues, supervisors, and content experts). For the most part, electronic systems for modifying communication between the group, or its members, and key agencies outside the group, parallel the types of systems for internal group communication, although they serve a different function for the group. We will call these Group External Communication Support Systems (GXSS).

Third, each member needs to have access to a number of bodies of information or knowledge, from sources outside the group. Electronic systems for supplementing information available to the group or its members include systems for accessing information from databases and other archival information stores and for selecting, processing, and presenting that information. It also includes systems that access information about the group's (and organization's) own history. We will call these Group Information Support Systems (GISS).

Finally, each member needs to be able to receive task information and make task responses. Electronic systems for modifying the group's task performance processes and task products include all of the tools that can be used to structure the form of the task(s) facing the group and the form of the group's potential task responses (e.g., the "modules" often used in group decision support systems to structure idea generation, idea evaluation, agenda setting). We will call these Group Performance Support Systems (GPSS).

(These four categories are probably not as independent in practice as our description implies. Systems of each category can be viewed as related to, or even as special cases of, some of the other three categories). Those four categories are examined next.

GCSS: Technologies for the Group's Internal Communication

A number of forms of technological (electronic) enhancements have been employed to facilitate communications in work groups. Collectively, these have been called Group Communication Support Systems (GCSS), electronically mediated systems (EMS), and so on (Dennis, George, Jessup, Nunamaker, & Vogel, 1988; DeSanctis & Gallupe, 1987; Kraemer & King, 1988).

Electronic GCSS offer one major advantage and one major cost. The advantage is that, with various types of electronic communication, group members can "meet," so to speak, even when they are not all in the same place and/or

Chapter 4 Putting the "Group" Back in Group Support Systems

when they are not all acting within the same time period. The cost is that, with various types of electronic communication, group members can communicate with one another by means of only a reduced set of modalities. Various channels—auditory, visual, nonverbal, paraverbal, and so on—are precluded. The extent of that reduction of modalities depends on the particular GCSS used. The importance of that reduction of modalities depends on the particular task(s) and activities in which the group is engaged (Hollingshead & McGrath, in press). Six major types of GCSS, and some of their major distinguishing features, are shown in Figure 4.1, along with a seventh, non–technologically enhanced type—ordinary face-to-face communication—included as a baseline comparison.

The six types of GCSS in Figure 4.1 differ on two main axes: (1) the requirements they impose (and the opportunities they permit) regarding spatial and temporal distribution of group members; and (2) the modalities they provide (and those they preclude) for within group communication among group members. One important thing to note about space and time dispersion is that in contrast to face-to-face systems, all six types of GCSS permit (but do not require) group members to be spatially separated from each other—in different buildings, different cities, different countries, or merely in different rooms—while they are communicating. Three of the types permit (but do not require) group members to act in different time periods (i.e., asynchronously).

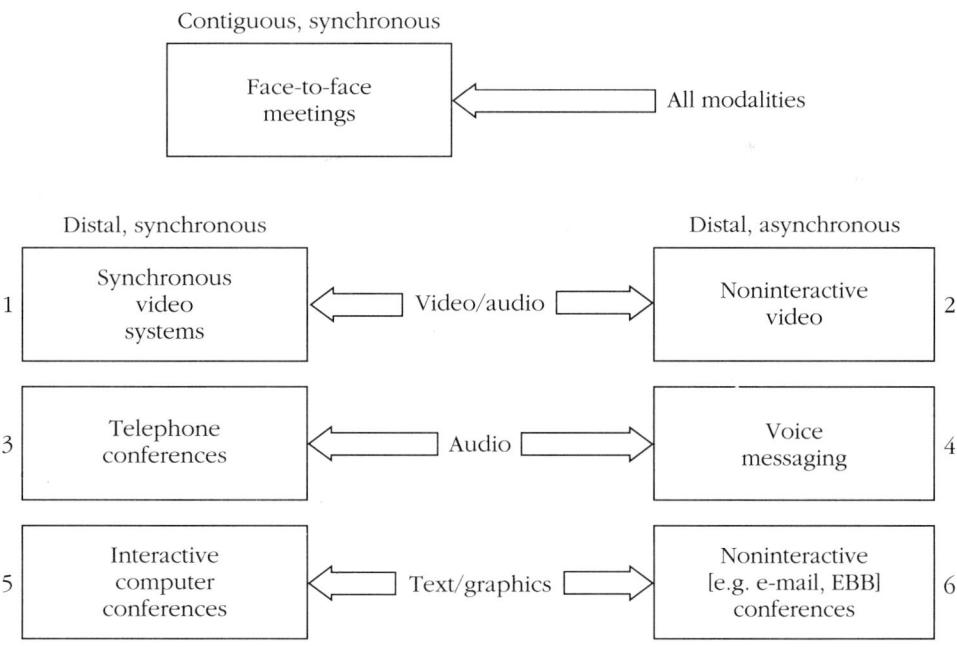

FIGURE 4.1 Six types of GCSS.

To begin with, two of the types of GCSS make use of visual and auditory modalities; they potentially can transmit written text and graphics noninteractively. Two types make use of the audio modality without any visual channel; these cannot transmit text or graphics, even noninteractively. The final two types permit transmission only of text and graphics.

1. Synchronous Video Systems. Three forms of synchronous video systems have been developed. Video walls or video windows provide continuous, interactive audio-video connection between fixed locations in each of two sites (a "commons area"); hence "automatic," low-cost continuous communication between any individuals who enter that commons area (Abel, 1990; Goodman & Abel, 1987; Kraut, Fish, Root, & Chalfonte, 1990). Videoconferences provide video-audio connections between people in two spatially dispersed locations, but at a specific time rather than continuously. Videophones link one individual with a second, specifically targeted person, in both audio and video channels.

Early in their history, such video systems were heralded, optimistically, as convenient, low-cost methods for communication among spatially dispersed coworkers, travel-free alternatives to face-to-face meetings. The reality has proven less spectacular than the promise (cf: Abel, 1990; Egido, 1990; Kraut, Fish, Root, & Chalfonte, 1990). Several factors have posed problems in their use. First, even though these systems retain both visual and auditory channels, they eliminate communication in some modalities (e.g., touch and olfactory cues) that goes with physical presence, some of which may be of value in communication, at least under some circumstances (Argyle & Kendon, 1967; Rutter & Robinson, 1981). Second, communication in the auditory and visual modalities is often seriously degraded in these systems, compared to face-to-face communication. The quality of auditory transmission in both video walls and videoconferences has proven problematic thus far; there are similar, though perhaps less serious, problems of fidelity of visual information (Abel, 1990; Abel, Corey, Bullock, Schmidt, & Coffin, 1990; Egido, 1990; Kraut et al., 1990).

There are also some serious problems in the temporal patterning of communication relating to the integration of audio and video modalities. In these systems, it is difficult to regulate the flow of inputs between the two facilities (Abel, 1990). Even though they involve considerable visual information, they apparently do not carry as much nonverbal "back-channel" information as face-to-face communication does, which can hinder smooth transitions between speakers located at separate sites. Moreover, if the sites are very distant, the time lags between transmission and feedback may differ for visual and auditory channels. Electronic transmission, though rapid, is not instantaneous in any modality, and although human interaction is not attuned to a nanosecond level, it is certainly sensitive to intervals of about 100 milliseconds or more.

Interactive exchange of written text and graphics material, missing from early systems of this type, is becoming available through recent technological developments (e.g., fax transmissions, "electronic chalk boards," and various other technologies generally referred to as "hypermedia"; see; Landow, 1990; Yankelovich, Hann, Meyrowitz, & Drucker, 1988).

2. Noninteractive (Asynchronous) Video Systems. Asynchronous groups can also use video technology in noninteractive ways (e.g., transmitting a video tape or disc from a "source" to a "target," to be viewed at a time of convenience for the target). The video material could either be recorded at the source and shipped or transmitted electronically and recorded at the destination for later presentation. For video systems, the asynchronous case imposes a strong temporal burden on communication. There are substantial time lags between composition, "transmission," and reception, and still longer ones between those stages and feedback.

3. Telephone Conferences. This type of synchronous GCSS is exemplified by the relatively familiar telephone conference—and for that matter, by the ultrafamiliar telephone call in the two-party case. There has been considerable research on such systems—much of it well summarized in E. Williams (1977). These systems eliminate not only the cues that go with physical presence (as does video, above), but also all cues in the visual modality (e.g., nonverbal behavior; information in written form). They do preserve important paraverbal aspects of speech.

Nonverbal behavior expressed through the visual modality (e.g., smiles, nods, direction of gaze) is very important as a "back-channel" for feedback in interacting groups. Its loss often creates serious problems for the group in managing the flow of speakers, pauses, interruptions, and so on—in other words, the temporal patterning of the group's communication. Furthermore, there are substantial transmission time lags for telephone conferences involving distant sites, far above the 100-microsecond level, and these can disrupt the smooth flow of conversation as we experience it in face-to-face groups.

4. Voice Messaging. Asynchronous GCSS parallel to telephone conferences are systems that entail a variety of types of voice-messaging features designed as technological enhancements of telephone answering systems (Rice & Shook, 1990). These share many of the advantages and disadvantages of telephone conferences but are not interactive.

One of the strengths of voice messaging is its presentation of paraverbal cues that can aid the expression of emotion and the interpretation of subtle meanings. The loss of such nonverbal cues represents a serious disadvantage for communication in computer conferences, types 5 and 6, discussed below.

5. Synchronous Computer Conferences. These systems permit communication among group members only via computer; hence permit interactive transmission only of written text (and graphics). This type of system imposes all of the modality restrictions imposed by the types of systems discussed above—video systems and telephone conferences—and some additional ones as well. In computer conferences, all auditory information is eliminated, and with it go the paraverbal cues of speech. These paraverbal cues serve at least two important functions in group communication: They express emotion, and they transmit subtle meanings. There have been some attempts to replace the expressive function of some of these paraverbal cues by use of special symbols and conventions in printed text (sometimes referred to as "emoticons"). These provide, at best, a very low-fidelity version of what humans do, routinely and at a high-fidelity quality, by use of paraverbal (e.g., voice inflection) and nonverbal (e.g., facial expression) cues. The vital role that paraverbal cues play in interpretation of subtle meanings in spoken speech can be partly replaced in written speech by a variety of techniques: use of longer and more complex syntax; use of jargon, argot, and other shared nonstandard language; relying on culturally shared connotative meanings; use of punctuation and format conventions; and use of redundancy. These, too, are low-fidelity, time-consuming replacements for what humans do elegantly (and eloquently) with the nonsemantic aspects of speech.

Several aspects of the temporal patterning of work differ between such computer-aided groups and face-to-face groups. First, production is slower for written (typed) text than for spoken language, even for very skilled typists. Second, reception of written text (i.e., reading) is ordinarily somewhat faster than reception of spoken text (i.e., listening), although that difference depends on type of material. Third, for communication via computer, transmission of a message is often separate from its composition and editing, costing time but potentially increasing quality; in face-to-face groups, composition, "editing," and transmission are simultaneous, saving time but at a potential cost in speech errors. Fourth, in face-to-face groups there is almost always only one speaker at a time (McGrath, 1990); in computer conferences more than one member can (and usually does) compose and send messages at the same time. Thus, computer conferences reduce "production blocking" (Diehl & Stroebe, 1987; Lamm & Trommsdorff, 1973), and perhaps reduce inhibition for low-status members (Siegal, Dubrovsky, Kiesler, & McGuire, 1986), but have at a potentially high cost in cognitive overload and disruptions in the flow of information.

6. Asynchronous Computer Conferences. Computer conferences also can be carried out asynchronously. GCSS of this type, sometimes called electronic bulletin board (EBB) and electronic mail (E-mail) systems, have proliferated enormously in recent years.

Temporal issues enter directly for these systems; members not only can be dispersed in space, they also can be "dispersed in time," so to speak. Consequently, the sequence in which messages are received and responded to is likely to differ for different participants. Furthermore, in face-to-face conversation, the temporal patterning of the actions of different members typically becomes "entrained" (Kelly, Futoran, & McGrath, 1990; McGrath & Kelly, 1986) to each other, producing a smooth and synchronized flow of conversation most of the time (e.g., smooth transitions among speakers, few long silences, and few interruptions). In asynchronous computer conferences, both the "natural order" of communications and the smooth, synchronized flow of conversation may be disrupted.

In synchronous computer conferences, the set of interactive partners is likely to be relatively small and that set is by definition a closed set. Under those conditions, people may operate on the assumption that all members receive and understand all messages more or less immediately. Hence, failure of a given member to reply in a timely fashion can be regarded as an active choice by that member. This is parallel to the assumption that we ordinarily make in face-to-face groups; but in the case of face-to-face communication we can get verification of that assumption by nonverbal and auditory channels (e.g., nonverbal feedback via smiles, gaze, head nods, and the like). In asynchronous computer conferences, however, the set of potential receivers is likely to be large, and, in any case, it is an open set. There is no automatic feedback about reception of a message, and there may be no unambiguous cues regarding acknowledgement and feedback—as there is for face-to-face communication or for synchronous computer, video, and telephone communications. Hence, there is no direct means for a sender to know that his or her message has been received by (as distinct from "delivered to") anyone, let alone by a given potential receiver. The assumption that all potential receivers have in fact read and understood a given message within a short span of time is clearly unwarranted. Hence, in the case of an asynchronous computer conference, failure of any given member to reply to a given message in a timely fashion increases ambiguity in the system.

To sum up what we have said about GCSS, these six types of GCSS differ greatly in the advantages they provide the group and in the limitations they impose on it. In general, successive restriction of modalities constrains the amount and the richness of information that can be transmitted. But, as we will discuss later in this chapter, such restriction can be a boon or a bane for the group, depending on the circumstances. Moreover, such restriction of modalities is a necessary consequence of systems that permit groups to overcome spatial and temporal dispersion. Like modality restrictions, freeing groups from these spatial and temporal constraints also brings both good news and bad news from the point of view of making work groups effective. Furthermore, GCSS are only part of the story. Three other types of group support systems perform three other functions.

GXSS: Technologies for the Group's External Communication

A second major function that technological enhancements can serve for work groups is to provide a system to support their communication with key agents external to the group. In general, the six types of support systems already described under GCSS are applicable to GXSS as well. Consequently, much of what has already been said about the six types of technological enhancements of the group's internal communication system applies, as well, to the group's external communication system.

The external communication by groups and group members has been given much less attention in the research literature than has internal group communication. Ancona & Caldwell (1988, 1990) have pioneered research showing that external relations, including external communications, are vital to effective leadership and to group success in certain kinds of knowledge-intensive work groups. But there has been little published work dealing with support systems designed to facilitate this external communication function. Research is needed on this topic.

GISS: Technologies for the Group's Information Base

In any group, each member has access to a number of bodies of information or knowledge from sources other than on-line communication within the group. At the very least, all members have, in the recent past, sent and received messages from a number of "extragroup" information sources, and still have at least some representation of those communications available (in memory or elsewhere). These "extragroup" sources include quantitative databases (e.g., sales records, production and cost data) and qualitative databases or archives (e.g., libraries, newspaper files). They also include information stores or archives that contain representations of events from the individual's or group's own histories—both formal ones (e.g, the minutes of last weeks staff meeting) and informal ones (e.g., memories of the sharp disagreement between Peggy and George at that meeting). In principle, any of these may contain information useful in the group's current performance context.

Different members of a given focal group will have direct access to different sources of potential information. No one group member has direct access to all possible information sources. But if the group can "meet" in any sense, then in principle every group member has indirect access to all of the information sources that any one member can reach. The extent to which group members fully share all information available to them, however, is always problematic, and it is a matter of considerable consequence for effective group performance. (To paraphrase: Each group member has a set of all the information available to him or her. Although the group's potential information is the union of all of the information accessible to each of the members, the actual information available to the entire group is the intersection of the information fully shared among members.)

Obtaining information from any of these sources—its initial acquisition, storage, and subsequent retrieval from storage—comes at a cost in effort and especially in time. There is an additional cost in time and effort to disseminate the information to others—that is, to communicate it within the group. Hence, information from any of these sources can be regarded as a resource that is (a) potentially scarce (that is, not everyone has all of it at the outset), (b) potentially valuable (that is, it may be useful for self or others to have it), and (c) potentially shared (that is, some information will and some will not be disseminated) within a given work group.

As noted earlier, one of the main potential advantages of the use of computers in information-intensive work has been their obvious potential for greatly increasing the range and depth of information that a given individual (or group) could have access to, and for increasing the speed and power with which that information can be acquired, processed, and presented for use.

In recent years, that speed and power has grown ever greater, as has the feasibility of providing such GISS capability to one or more members of any given group. Clearly, the problem is no longer one of insuring that group members can have access to enough extant information. Rather, the key problems in this domain now have to do with information integration and overload.

For the most part, the gaining of information from sources external to the focal group (i.e., using a GXSS or a GISS) really takes place at the individual level. Any one or more members of the group may bring information of a particular kind from a particular source into the group. But if it is to become a group resource or part of a group product, it must be shared through the group's GCSS. Given the high and rapidly increasing speed and power with which electronic media can acquire, process, and present information, it is apparent that groups with electronic GISS will continually be on the verge of disastrous information overload unless some active measures are taken to fend it off.

This poses a dilemma regarding the sharing of information. On one hand, the more group members have (and use), but do not share, information (i.e., the more each member's interactions are shaped by information available only to that member) the more group members are likely to feel that the others have "hidden agendas" and are manipulating the group, and the more group members are likely to develop mutual distrust and suspicion of one another, which certainly is not beneficial for task performance in the long run. On the other hand, the more group members share all of the information they have, the more likely it is that they will either suffer serious information overload or else ignore each other's information inputs—either of which could also hinder effective task performance.

It is important, therefore, that techniques be developed to provide efficient and effective processing, integration, and presentation of important task information. Part of the promise of electronic technology has always been its capacity to manage as well as to acquire information; we have looked to computers as the method of choice to provide means for filtering, processing, and integrating information, as well as for acquiring it. In fact, such information processing and integrating is a major function served by the fourth type of Group Support System (GPSS), to be discussed later in this chapter. But even with the best of information management systems, it is still the case that current technology for information gathering and storing is so powerful that information overload is a serious and continuing potential problem for any work group.

The problem of overload is in some respects a temporal issue. Load is always reckoned with respect to some time interval; any given level of "load" is an overload only with respect to some deadline. There are some tasks that must be done within a certain limited time period or they cannot be done at all (e.g., intercepting a missile in flight). In such circumstances, a question of overload is reducible to a matter of speed of response. But for many tasks, overload simply refers to having too many things to do at once, even though the tasks themselves do not have a critical time component. In such cases, if the operating unit can take a longer period of time to do them, then the overload problem becomes a priority and sequencing problem. Since information overload is such a potentially serious problem for groups with electronic GISS, both the temporal features and the load features of these situations ought to be given more research attention than has been the case to date.

These issues apply to the distribution and use of information in groups whether or not those groups use electronic means. But the enormous extension of speed and power of access to information that modern electronic systems provide increases the impact of all of these issues manyfold. There is a relatively recent body of excellent research on information and distribution and transmission in groups (e.g., Malone, 1986, 1988; Stasser, 1988; Weisband, 1990) that provides a solid theoretical foundation for exploring these issues. The large impact that these issues can have on effective use of GSS argues for expansion of these research efforts.

GPSS: Technologies for the Group's Performance Processes

The idea of "Group Support Systems" existed before the advent of computers, or at least before their use in such capacities. Since before midcentury, practitioners have been trying to devise ways to improve group effectiveness and specifically to help groups avoid what Steiner (1972) subsequently called "process losses." Most of the systems used in those earlier decades, however, involved what we might now call "manual" technologies; they did not involve use of electronic or other high-tech devices. Computer-based group decision support systems and decision rooms are relatively recent developments. Two facilities have pioneered those developments, one at University of Arizona (Dennis et al., 1988; Nunamaker, Vogel, & Konsynski, 1989; Vogel & Nunamaker, 1990a; Vogel, Nunamaker, George, & Dennis, 1988), the other at University of Minnesota (DeSanctis & Poole, 1989; Poole & DeSanctis, 1987, 1990; Poole, 1990). These two systems (which are described in detail elsewhere in this volume, hence are discussed only briefly here) have dominated research in this area for the past decade. They are quite distinct systems, developed along different lines, using different hardware and software, and reflecting the somewhat different purposes of their protagonists. Both attempt to provide (electronic) tools to support—and presumably to improve—group task performance.

These GPSS presume that most work groups need help in performing some or all of their task activities—for example, setting an agenda, identifying problems, generating alternatives, choosing among alternatives, negotiating consensus with one another, and so on. They provide a set of modules that the group can (sometimes, must) use to do these tasks. Each module is designed to help structure activities for a certain type of task.

These systems are intended to improve both speed and quality of group productivity. Several recent reviews (Hollingshead & McGrath, in press; McLeod, 1991) suggest that the empirical support regarding such improvement in group productivity is quite equivocal and controversial. Also, considerable evidence that use of such structuring modules in their electronic forms substantially increases the time needed to make decisions, rather than reducing it. This result is not at all surprising when you consider the consistent evidence from studies of GCSS that it takes much more time to transmit any given amount of information (or opinion) to other members of a group by typing it on a keyboard than by speaking it aloud. On the other hand, the structuring of task activities that such GPSS impose may well reduce decision time when used in a "manual" (i.e., nonelectronic) support system. Furthermore, unstructured decision making in a GCSS (that is, using an electronic GCSS but no decision support modules) is likely to take even longer than structured decision making using that same GISS and GPSS (Watson, DeSanctis, & Poole, 1988). Thus the cost or savings in task performance time may depend on effects of the GCSS with which the GPSS is coupled, as well as on the GPSS itself.

Regarding decision quality: The empirical evidence suggesting that GPSS yield increased decision quality is based on limited studies that are highly method-bound (Hollingshead & McGrath, in press). In contrast, there is considerable evidence that it is much more difficult for groups to reach consensus using electronic communication (GCSS), compared to face-to-face groups (Daly, 1990; Siegal, Dubrovsky, Kiesler, & McGuire, 1986; Weisband, 1990). Since consensus within the group is presumably a requirement for any group decision, it is difficult to see how decision quality could be increased but decision consensus precluded at the same time. Again, structuring the task may or may not improve quality of decision, but carrying out the task within an electronically mediated communication system almost certainly does not. (But, see Kraemer & King, 1988, and Kraemer & Pinsonneault, 1990, for a much more optimistic interpretation, based on review of a body of evidence that partially overlaps with the evidence examined in Hollingshead & McGrath, in press, and in McLeod, 1991).

GROUPS, TASKS, AND ELECTRONIC SUPPORT SYSTEMS

Research on the effects of electronic systems in work groups has almost totally failed to take into account the ways in which effective work in groups is contingent upon features of the group, features of the task, and features of the situation (Hollingshead & McGrath, in press). There is good reason, on both theoretical and empirical grounds (see McGrath, 1990; Hollingshead & McGrath, in press), to believe to the contrary, namely: That the effects of Group Support

Systems are not at all generic, but rather are particular to specific systems and purposes. Few effects are likely to hold across all possible systems and all uses to which they might be put. Rather, the effects obtained in any given case will almost certainly be contingent upon a host of factors, including (a) attributes of the groups and members who are using them (e.g., their task ability, experience and training, their history as a group, and their motivation to succeed); (b) type, difficulty, and other attributes of the groups' tasks; (c) features of the operating circumstances under which the task performance is taking place (e.g., temporal constraints and the possibilities and limitations provided by the particular electronic support system being examined).

The crucial question, here, is not whether or not electronic support systems improve group performance in general. Rather, the crucial question is this: What are the circumstances under which various support systems improve, hinder, or do not affect various aspects of group performance, on various kinds of tasks, for groups of various compositions and competencies?

Group and Member Characteristics

There is a vast body of research literature on effects of features of the group and its members—features traditionally referred to in group research as individual characteristics, group composition and group structure (cf: Levine & Moreland, 1990; McGrath, 1984). But for the most part it has been ignored in research dealing with Group Support Systems. It is as if researchers in this area believed that: "if you've seen one group, you've seen them all"; or: "groups are just a bunch of individuals connected by a communication system"; or even: "groups are connected networks of 'agents,' including both computer processors and individuals." We believe that none of those "as ifs" are very useful metaphors and that research that does not reckon with groups as continuing, purposive, multifunctioned, and to some degree particularized interactive social systems is unlikely to help us much in developing and applying support system to improve work in real-life groups.

Task Types

Research on Group Support Systems also needs to pay more attention to features of the task(s) that those groups are to carry out. To some degree, the modules of every GDSS explicitly or implicitly reflect the categories of a crude typology of tasks or of task processes—idea generation, proposal evaluation, alternative selection, consensus seeking, and the like. In earlier work (McGrath, 1984; Hollingshead & McGrath, in press), we presented a classification system for distinguishing different types of group tasks and relating them to one another. Some GDSS (e.g., DeSanctis & Gallupe, 1987; Zigurs, Poole, & DeSanctis, 1988b) explicitly use that task circumplex as a model from which to derive their list of modules; other systems (e.g., Nunamaker, Vogel, & Konsynski, 1989) use terms

Chapter 4 Putting the "Group" Back in Group Support Systems

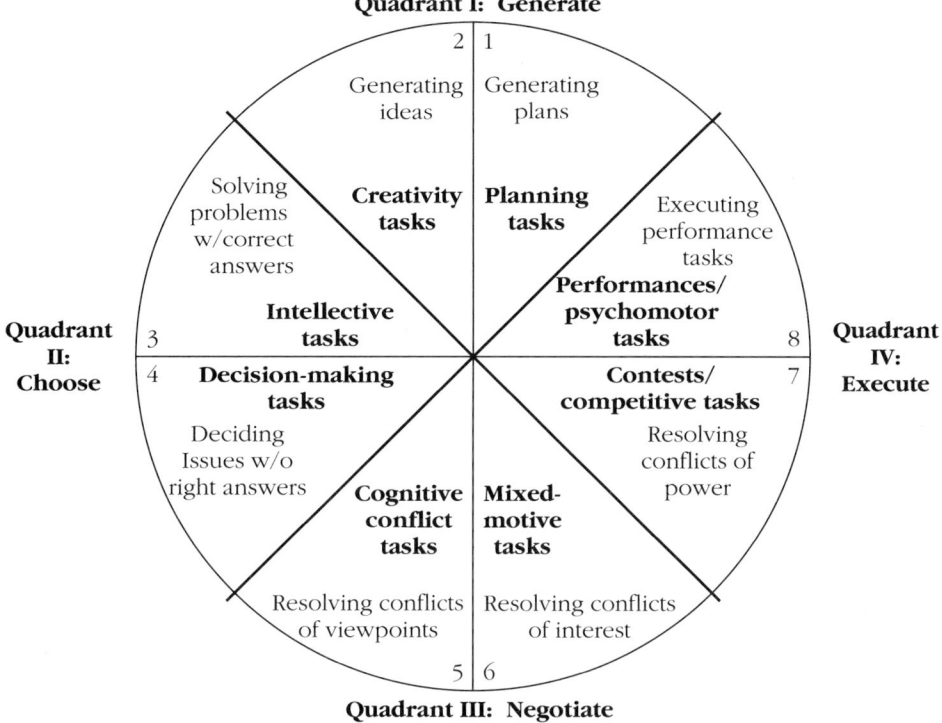

FIGURE 4.2 Task circumplex (adapted from McGrath, 1984).

and distinctions quite compatible with it. We therefore will take that circumplex schema as a useful initial guide for the present context and will draw upon it below. (See Figure 4.2).

McGrath (1984) posits four basic task performance processes, each with two major subtypes: to generate (ideas or plans); to choose (a correct answer or a preferred answer); to resolve (conflicting views or conflicting interests); and to execute (in contests against another group(s) or in competition with external standards of performance). He further posits that those four processes (or eight task types) are related to one another as the quadrants (octants) of a circumplex structure. The two dimensions defining the space of that circumplex are the degree to which the processes involve cooperation (coordination) versus competition (conflict), and the degree to which the processes involve cognitive versus behavioral activities (see Figure 4.2). Here we deal primarily with the "cognitive" hemisphere of that circumplex.

Task Types, Communication Media, and Information Richness

In recent work we have hypothesized that one axis of that circumplex space orders the task types along a dimension similar to Daft and Lengel's (1986; Trevino, Lengel, & Daft, 1987) "information richness" concept. Specifically, those authors posit (and we concur) that group tasks differ in how much they require the transmission of information that is more or less "rich" in its contents. To oversimplify: richness of information refers to how much the information contains "surplus" emotional, attitudinal, normative, and other meanings, beyond the literal cognitive denotations of the symbols used to express it. Tasks requiring groups to generate ideas (e.g., brainstorming tasks) may require only the transmission of specific ideas; evaluative and emotional connotations about message and source are not required and are often considered to be a hindrance. On the other hand, tasks requiring groups to negotiate and resolve conflicts of views or conflicts of interests may require the transmission of maximally rich information, including not only "facts" but also values, attitudes, affective messages, expectations, commitments, and so on. Tasks requiring groups to solve intellective problems (problems that have correct answers) lie in between the two extremes noted above, but nearer the "generate" category. Tasks requiring groups to reach decisions on issues for which there is not a right answer, but only an agreed-upon consensus (such as a jury verdict) lies in between the two extremes but nearer the "negotiate" category.

Daft and colleagues (Daft & Lengel, 1986; Trevino et al., 1987) maintain (and we agree) that communication media differ in the richness of the information that they can and do convey. Face-to-face communication among interpersonally involved humans is probably the richest medium; communications in standardized written form among strangers is perhaps the least rich. The electronic media in general, and computer communication in particular, are well toward the low-richness end of that continuum, compared to face-to-face communication. Hence, it is likely that those systems will yield effective task performance in groups doing tasks at or near the "generate" (low-richness) pole of the circumplex but will be very ineffective for tasks at or near the "negotiate" pole of that space. That hypothesis ought to apply to the use of electronic GCSS for tasks of various types, as well as to the use of electronic GPSS for performance modules of various types (and insofar as activities in either of those cases entail use of electronic GISS, it should hold for that category of support systems as well).

The Task/Media Fit Hypothesis

The pattern of relations reflected in the Daft-Lengel hypothesis, as we have applied it to the domain of Group Support Systems, is shown schematically in Figure 4.3. That figure presents a 4-by-4 matrix defined in terms of the four task types of the cognitive hemisphere of the circumplex (see Figure 4.2), and the four media forms discussed in relation to GCSS (see Figure 4.1). That matrix identifies patterns of differential fit between (a) the information richness requirements of the tasks in which groups might be engaged, and (b) the information richness potential of the communication media such groups might use.

The best-fitting combinations of information richness of task and media lie near the main diagonal of the matrix. Contours successively distant from that diagonal represent successively less effective fits—but for different reasons on the two different halves of the matrix.

On the one hand, task/media combinations that depart from the best-fit diagonal in the northeast direction (i.e., their media provide more richness of information than the tasks require) may be poor fits on an efficiency basis. Those groups can do their tasks effectively within the constraints of their communication medium; but their communication medium allows them to engage in information exchanges involving much more richness and surplus meaning than the tasks demand. Hence, they are always vulnerable to inefficiency brought about by the "distraction" of communications that are nonessential for effective task performance. (But this matter is viewed, later in this section, from an entirely different, group-theoretic perspective, and from that perspective such "nonessential" communications are not at all bad news).

On the other hand, task/media combinations that depart from the best-fit diagonal in the southwest direction (that is, cells with tasks that require more richness than their media provide) are vulnerable not to problems of efficiency but to problems of effectiveness and quality of performance. That is, they not only are not "distracted" by potential exchanges of too-rich information with surplus meanings; they are constrained by communication media that are not capable of transmitting information sufficiently rich to let them carry out the high-richness demands of their tasks. (But this, too, is viewed more optimistically, from a different, group-theoretic perspective, in the final part of this chapter).

Group Support Systems from a Group Theory Perspective

Some of the issues discussed thus far take on a different perspective when viewed from a group theoretic standpoint rather than from a support systems focus. The group theory formulation upon which we draw in this presentation (TIP theory; see McGrath, 1990, 1991) regards work groups as continuously and simultaneously engaged in three major functions: production, member support, and group well-being. These functions represent, respectively, contributions of the group to its embedding organization, contributions of the group to its participating members, and contributions of the group to its own continued functioning as an intact social unit.

TIP theory also regards groups as carrying out those functions by means of activities in one or another of four modes. The general form of those four modes is: I inception of a project (goal choice), II solution of technical issues (means choice), III resolution of conflict (i.e., of political issues), and IV execution of the performance requirements of the project.

Modes transcend functions. The four modes have parallel but distinguishable forms within each of the three functions. Moreover, the modes are not a fixed sequence of phases, but rather are four potential forms of activity by which each of the three functions can be pursued in relation to any given project. Groups carry out their projects via time/activity paths that consist of mode/function sequences. Although every completed project involves at least the first and fourth modes for the production function (i.e., the group gets a project and executes it), a given case may involve the second and third modes for the production function (i.e., attempts at solution of technical and conflict issues) and also may involve some or all modes of activity with respect to the member support and group well-being functions (e.g., redistribution of task roles, reallocation of status or payoff relations, socialization of new members).

Thus, TIP theory posits that natural groups may be involved in a rather complex set of activities. At any given time, any given natural group is likely to be engaged in more than one project and to be pursuing each of those projects by means of some sequence of modes of activity with respect to each of three functions. Thus, study of the work of such natural groups requires a complex set of observational tools and a complex set of expectations about meanings of behaviors that may be observed.

TIP theory insists on treating certain complexities of process as natural and as a proper focus for study, namely, the idea that groups pursue multiple functions for multiple projects by means of complex time/activity paths. Much past research on group support systems has been framed in such a way as to eliminate those very complexities, and/or treat them as "error variance." These complexities are intricately related to the issues of information richness of media and information requirement of tasks discussed above. If a group is performing only the production function for a single, simple, familiar task that has low information richness requirements, then they are likely to be able to do so by a straightforward time/activity path that involves only Modes I and IV of the production function (TIP theory's "default path"). But when there are major changes in features of the task (e.g., increased task difficulty), features of the group (e.g., new group members), or features of the situation (e.g, changes in time limits), that group is faced with a more complex situation, and the "efficient" path for those circumstances is far less simple and direct. The group may need to engage in activities related to mode II and III of the production function (i.e., technical problem solving and conflict resolution) and/or in activities related to any of the modes of the group well-being and member support functions. If so, then they will need to carry on communications that require relatively rich information exchanges—they will move downward in the matrix shown in Figure 4.3. Thus, even in a group with an apparently simple task that fits an information-poor medium at the outset, increased complexities of group, task, and situation may lead them to "migrate" southward, because their communication dimension is no longer adequate for task requirements.

Conversely, groups in early stages of their own development often may require relatively high levels of information richness in order to carry out their well-being and member support functions and to establish their task

Chapter 4 Putting the "Group" Back in Group Support Systems

Increasing potential richness required for task success ⬇	Media for Group Communication System				
	Increasing potential richness of information →			
Task type(s)	Computer systems	Audio systems	Video systems	Face-to-face communications
Generating ideas and plans	Good fit	Marginal fit Info too rich	Poor fit Info too rich	Poor fit Info too rich
Choosing correct answer: intellective tasks	Marginal fit Medium too constrained	Good fit	Good fit	Poor fit Info too rich
Choosing preferred answer: judgment tasks	Poor fit Medium too constrained	Good fit	Good fit	Marginal fit Info too rich
Negotiating conflicts of interests	Poor fit Medium too constrained	Poor fit Medium too constrained	Marginal fit Info too lean	Good fit

FIGURE 4.3 The task and media fit on information richness.

performance strategies. As those groups mature, however, they are likely to become able to carry out all of their functions, at least for routine projects, with much less rich information exchanges. As groups mature, one might say, they tend to "migrate" northward, into a region of the matrix requiring less rich information media.

Thus, the role of group support systems in the effective functioning of work groups is very complex. Furthermore, that complexity is amplified because the role of the GSS shifts over time as changes occur in circumstances and in the group itself. If we are to study these systems and learn to use them effectively in real-life contexts, we must take these complexities of group process into account.

CONCLUDING COMMENTS

The impact of Group Support Systems depends on a myriad of conditions and factors. How well a given Group Support System fulfills its intended purpose depends not only on what function the system is intended to serve (GCSS, GXSS, GISS, or GPSS), but also on features of the group and its members, the type of task the group is doing, the operating conditions under which they are working, and interactions of task with communication medium.

Furthermore, the impact of such support systems on group process and performance operates in dynamic interdependence with key features of the group, task, and situation, and therefore is contingent on the detailed, specific history of the particular group, its task, and its circumstances. Group Support Systems are implicated in each of several key functions—internal and external communications, information access and processing, and task performance. Thus, those support systems, electronic or otherwise, can aid or hinder the group in performance of processes that lie at the core of group existence. Those support systems become an integral part of the meaning of the group as a continuing, dynamic, functional social system—groups and their technologies together become dynamic socio-technical systems. It is in the spirit of exploring in depth such integrated, dynamic, socio-technical systems, we believe, that future research on group support systems should be undertaken.

CHAPTER 5

Shifting Foundations in Group Support System Research

Gerardine DeSanctis
University of Minnesota

INTRODUCTION

During the course of pursuing a research program, we occasionally find ourselves taking a moment from designing our studies, examining our subjects, interpreting our data, and so on, to reflect on the larger meaning of our pursuit. Chances are, we have traveled down our path of investigation beyond the point of no return. Nonetheless, we return to questions first asked at the time we embarked on our scientific journey: "Why is this an important research area?" "Will discoveries lead to any meaningful change in understanding or in practice?" "Are there better ways that I might conduct my research?" "What is the real goal of this line of research anyway, and am I making a meaningful contribution?" Have you ever asked yourself these questions? I know that I have, many times. I really never develop adequate answers to the questions, but the reflective process helps me to regain a perspective on what I am doing. I then leave the questions in the back of my mind and take another step forward in my research program.

Research on Group Support Systems (GSS) and related collaborative systems has been proceeding for about 10 years now, so it is time we revisited old questions, reflecting on where we have come from and where we are headed in this very dynamic research area. Indeed, much of the current volume is meant to provide us with reflections of this sort. This essay reflects on three particular questions related to the foundations of the GSS area: First, what is the goal of GSS research? Second, what are the dominant theoretical camps that underlie work in this area? Third, what is missing from current theoretical approaches and how might our theories be improved? My ruminations on these issues are no doubt influenced by my own research experiences in the area; I admit to bias at the start. But my goal is not so much to persuade the reader of my viewpoints as it is to contribute to the dialogue about the future of GSS research.

THE ROLE OF GSS IN ORGANIZATIONS

Why is the study of GSS an important research area? My own view of this issue is that GSSs are not so interesting in their own right as they are a new opportunity for studying old questions about the role of technology in organizations. Those who invest in the design, implementation, and evaluation of this new form of computing bring along certain presumptions about what the role of computing in organizations *should be*. For most of us, these presumptions are fairly optimistic; we are, alas, "technocentric" (Markus & Robey, 1988) in our belief that GSSs, like the technologies before them, have the potential to bring positive change to organizations. If change is the goal—and I believe it is—then what sort of changes are we looking for and why do we believe that GSSs might bring them about? Our approach to the study of GSSs as organizational change mechanisms depends upon our assumptions about computing technology in general and, in turn, our assumptions about the nature of organizations and the role of management in organizational success. These assumptions influence the theories that we apply to understand GSSs, our technology designs, and our research methods and interpretations (see Figure 5.1). In sum, the foundations of GSS research are rooted in specific assumptions about organizations and the role of management and technology in organizational change.

The differing assumptions that form the foundations for GSS research could be described along many dimensions, but a simple and powerful dichotomy is between *individualism* and *collectivism* as normative views of organizations. These represent polar political ideologies within western cultural life that social scientists and politicians have debated for decades, and the polemic recurs in GSS research. The tension is between the role of the individual versus the social good, the role of rationality versus emotion and values, and the role of authority versus cooperation (see Etzioni, 1988; P. Miller & O'Leary, 1989; Mitchell & Scott, 1980; Perrow, 1986). As we shall see, opinions regarding the purposes and importance of GSS research are inextricably bound up in where one's assumptions lie along these poles.

GSS as Tool: Individualism

Is the organization an assembly of individuals or an entity with rights and purposes of its own? The traditional view among economists and psychologists is

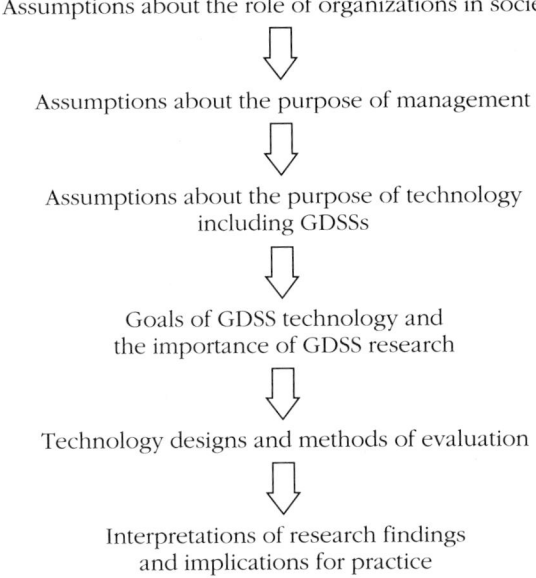

FIGURE 5.1 The foundations for GDSS research lie in our assumptions about organizations.

that the organization is an assembly of individuals. The assembly shares the same goal as that of the individual: maximization of personal gain. The goal of the organization is to maximize benefit to the individual, and so balance in the marketplace and democracy within the organization are of paramount importance. The individualistic view of organization is consistent with the classical assumption of capitalism: success of the organization brings benefit to the individual. Primary among the goals of the organization are operational efficiency and the achievement of competitive advantage.

Within the individualistic view of organizations, management is seen as a professional practice that can be applied to spur success of the enterprise so that individual workers and members of society benefit. Workers relinquish some degree of power to management to make decisions that will ultimately benefit them (Barnard, 1938). The role of technology is to aid management in its pursuit of efficiency and maximization of gain. Technology is a *tool* to be applied to enhance individual power and overcome human limitations, such as limited strength or rationality (e.g., Taylor, 1947; Waldo, 1948).

Individualistic assumptions about organizations lead researchers to view GSSs as instruments for democracy and individual gain. Theories identify the weaknesses in group, as opposed to individual, decision making (e.g., "process losses," "problems in meetings") and proceed to design technology to overcome these deficiencies (Huber, 1984a). For example, a now classical GSS design approach is to provide data, models, and communication tools to aid in information search, analysis, and reduction of equivocality (DeSanctis & Gallupe,

1987; Sprague, 1980). The "success" of the system is measured in terms of the extent to which it enables groups to make decisions more efficiently, to participate more evenly, to reason more thoroughly, to more effectively come to consensus, and to be more satisfied. These measures are typically made with the individual as the unit of analysis; individual scores are simply aggregated to yield group-level measures. Ultimately, the goal of the GSS is to bring improvements in organizational efficiency or quality of decision making, and GSS research assesses achievement of this goal.

The individualistic view places great trust in management and technology; these are instruments for organizational success that can bring efficiency and competitive gain to the enterprise. Some theories of group process, for example, have argued that greater individual participation will improve group decision quality and related outcomes (e.g., Delbecq & Van de Ven, 1971). Such a theory is derived from the individualistic ideal. As we transfer this ideal to GSS design, we hope that the technology will empower the individual to contribute more forcefully to the organization. Electronic conversational schemes that cross hierarchies or functions, large databases of facts or opinions, and voting schemes that allow each individual to provide input to a decision (Kraemer & King, 1988) are all examples of GSS functionality that are rooted in the individualistic ideal. The functions are thought to enhance participation; and enhanced participation is a desirable process because decision making and group process theories hold that participation will bring desirable outcomes (such as improved decision quality) that benefit individuals.

The individualistic perspective is at once respectful of the role of management and technology in organizations and yet ever suspicious that these mechanisms might somehow be poorly designed or be misused, thus diluting individual gain. The classic issue of whether computing brings centralization or decentralization to organizational decision making has been revisited in the study of GSS: We hope that GSSs improve participation and empower the individual, but do they? To address this question, comparative studies of the impacts of alternative GSS designs on communication and decision making processes and outcomes have been, and will remain, core to research in the area. The many studies that focus on member influence, consensus, agreement, and user satisfaction are evidence that an individualistic view underlies much of GSS research (e.g., Easton, Vogel, & Nunamaker, 1989; George, Easton, Nunamaker, & Northcraft, 1990; Watson, DeSanctis, & Poole, 1989; Zigurs, Poole, & DeSanctis, 1988).

GSS as Product: Collectivism

Opposing individualism is the view that organizations exist for the service of society as a whole, rather than for the individual. Collectivism assumes that the organization is not merely an aggregate of individuals but rather a social structure in its own right. Organizations and other institutions—including managerial authority and technologies—evolve out of the need for the culture to have meaning and order. They act as a force against social disintegration. Political theories based on the assumption of collectivism consider institutions, rather than the individual, to be the foundation of society. Thus, the nation, the fatherland, the church, or the enterprise can take priority over the individual (Etzioni, 1988), and acts of individuals can be evaluated in terms of their contribution to the social order (Parsons, 1951). Because institutions are socially constructed, their role in society varies across cultures and time periods. The collectivist assumes that management practices and technologies evolve out of the need for the particular organizational culture to have meaning and order. Organizations and managerial hierarchies are a form of collaboration that are the fabric of social orders. Individuals choose to work together and yield to authorities, customs, rules, and technologies and the like because the collaboration is essential to their social well-being (Barnard, 1938). Technologies such as GSS, therefore, are viewed as *products* of the social evolution of the organization and the larger culture of which it is a part. Because cultures vary, the *meaning* of technologies varies. Thus, any given GSS may mean different things within different organizations, or even within different groups; further, its roles and purposes may vary over time as the culture evolves. Whereas individualistic assumptions lead the researcher to be concerned with the efficiency and effectiveness brought about by the GSS, collectivist assumptions lead to an interest in the social meaning of the technology, its symbolism, how cultural practices affect technology development, and how technology, in turn, reinforces cultural norms (Feldman & March, 1981; Trevino, Lengel, & Daft, 1987).

Collectivist assumptions about organizations lead the researcher to view GSS as just one more evolutionary product to come down the pike of cultural practice. Theories don't focus on GSSs per se; rather, the cultural rules and norms that they embody are of greater interest. Because collectivist assumptions lead to few direct guidelines for technology design, they are understandably less popular among information systems researchers than individualistic assumptions. If we assume that organizations and technologies are products of culture, then the research questions of interest lie in documenting the norms or rules that the culture transfers to the GSS and the corresponding way in which GSSs influence work practice. Qualitative case study approaches based on institutional theories of organizations are more appropriate than quantitative, experimental, or field study approaches based on decision or communication theories.

ASSUMPTIONS AND THEORIES OF GSS AS ORGANIZATIONAL CHANGE MECHANISMS

The contrast between individualistic and collectivist ideologies has been witfully illustrated in the saying that economists have shown us how to make choices, whereas sociologists have shown us that we have none! Individualistic assumptions about organizations are usually associated with the fields of economics and psychology, and collectivist assumptions with sociology and anthropology. Etzioni (1988) refers to the opposing assumptions as the "I" versus "we" paradigms of organizations. The "I" paradigm treats technology as in the service of organizational efficiency and effectiveness; GSSs exist to improve individual participation and outcomes. The "we" paradigm treats technology as an institutional fabrication that embodies cultural rules and practices; GSSs exist to enforce order and commonality in group work. If there is any technological goal, it is to bring gradual improvement in the social order of the organization or community.

Individualistic assumptions lead the researcher to look for active, instantaneous change in the group or organization. A particular technology design is expected to lead to outcomes such as greater participation and improved decision making. The models of group behavior are deterministic. In contrast, collectivism assumes that technology-induced change is so embedded in cultural practice as to be hardly noticeable except over long periods of time; the models of group behavior are less deterministic, because technology is seen as only one set of forces governing the social order. Individualism leads to relatively active views of technology-induced change, whereas collectivism leads to relatively passive views (see Figure 5.2).

Which set of assumptions should drive GSS research, define our goals, theories, and methods? The issue reaches far beyond GSS to information systems research in general. For example, perhaps it is ironic that during the past decade the study of information systems to support cooperative work has occurred in

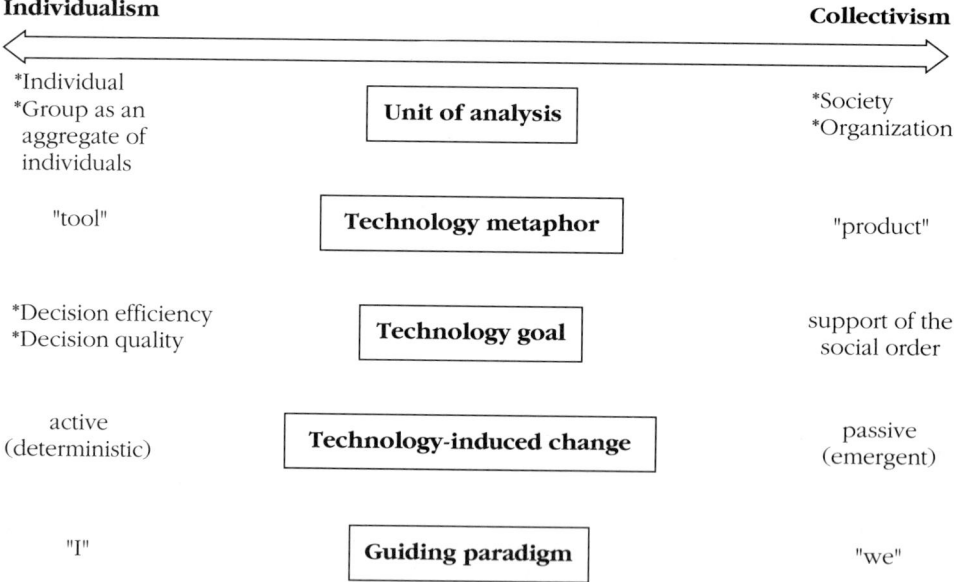

FIGURE 5.2 Opposing perspectives of technology and organizational change.

parallel with an opposing endeavor: the development of systems to gain strategic/competitive advantage for the organization (Porter & Millar, 1985). Whereas the former set of systems supposedly will help us to work together, the latter presumably will help us to beat one another in the game of economic success. We tend to think of GSS technology as advancing collectivist goals, such as "collaboration," "cooperation," and benefit to the "group." In fact, the opposite is true. GSS research has shared the same socio-political history as most information systems research: the dominance of the "I" paradigm.

In the remainder of this chapter I would like to argue the following: first, that individualistic assumptions have dominated GSS research to date; second, that there is growing interest in collectivist assumptions, and third, that neither of these is wholly adequate as a foundation for GSS research. There is something lacking in both individualistic and collectivist assumptions about technology and organizational change that hampers our theories and thus our progress in GSS research. There is a need for a shift in the foundation of GSS research such that our theories can expand beyond the polar ideologies of individualism and collectivism.

Competing Theories for GSS Research

A review of the theoretical bases of GSS research to date suggests five dominant types of theories that underlie work in the area. These are classes of theories rather than specific research models. The theories are not "competing" in the sense that one will win out or that one is superior to the other. Also, they are not entirely independent; they are overlapping in their premises and constructs. Key differences lie in their assumptions about precisely how GSSs operate as organizational change mechanisms. Individualistic assumptions are associated with the first three camps, whereas collectivist assumptions are associated with the fourth and fifth theoretical camps. Beyond this, the theories lead to slightly different foci for study and different approaches to the design and study of GSS technology.

Theories of Decision Making. A good deal of GSS research has its roots in earlier work on decision support systems (Keen & Scott-Morton, 1978; Sprague, 1980; Sprague & Watson, 1979) that, in turn, is based largely on theories of decision making put forth by Herbert Simon and his colleagues (Simon, 1960, 1976). These theories present models of organizations as collections of individual decision makers. Decision makers are viewed as desiring to maximize expected utility for personal gain, but at the same time as failing to achieve this end due to inadequacies in human judgment capacities. Decision support systems (DSSs) are designed with the goal of enhancing rationality so that individual utility can, in fact, be maximized. This is done primarily through the provision of decision models that enable the user to apply thorough and systematic (i.e., fully rational) problem solving.

Just as DSSs were designed to overcome the cognitive limitations of individuals, GSSs are designed to overcome the limits to rationality experienced by groups (Huber, 1984a; Nunamaker, Applegate, & Konsynski, 1988). Decision models, such as multiattribute utility models and risk analysis, are extended so that the preferences of a group of decision makers can be accommodated in the model. The work of Bui and Jarke (1984, 1986), L. Phillips (1986), and G. W. Dickson, DeSanctis, Poole, and Limayem (1991) illustrates GSS research that grows out of a strict decision-making view. The mathematical model is seen as the critical ingredient that the GSS provides, and the goal is to make the group capable of solving complex, information-based problems by providing models that can aggregate the judgments of group members (Hogarth, 1978; Liang, 1988).

Group Process Theories. Rational (or modified rational) decision-making views have been criticized for their failure to acknowledge that people often reject rationality in favor of conventional practice or political considerations (Cyert & March, 1963; Nutt, 1984). Group process theories argue that utility maximization is less important than the achievement of consensus or "buy in" by participating parties (Miner, 1979). Whereas decision theory approaches to GSS research have extended models of individual judgment and choice to include the aggregated judgments of groups, group process theory approaches have relied on models of small group decision making that come largely from the social psychology and organizational behavior literatures.

Underlying most group process theories is the assumption that decision making becomes more difficult as it is moved from the individual to the group setting due to the "process losses" (Steiner, 1966) associated with interpersonal interaction. Difficulties in group problem solving include: reluctance to participate, inconsistent views about the problem's components and their relationships, undue dominance by one individual in the group, premature tendency toward convergence, unproductive avoidance or escalation of conflict, and issues of leadership (Hackman & Morris, 1975). Therefore, simply providing groups with sophisticated mathematical models is not sufficient. More important is the provision of step-by-step procedures or other rules for managing group discussion that yield consensus and satisfaction by all, as well as decision quality (Noel & Wynne, 1991).

The rich literature on group decision making, including studies of group size, leadership, groupthink, risky shift, and so on, has provided a tremendous foundation for research on GSS. GSS researchers have been influenced especially by the group process models of McGrath (1984), who proposes a task circumplex for analyzing group interactions, and Hackman and Morris (1975), who propose an Input→Process→Output model of group decision making. These and related theories generally advocate improving group process through the provision of specific process interventions that promote more even participation, appreciation of multiple viewpoints, and systematic reasoning. Popular group process techniques include: brainstorming, the nominal group technique, the delphi technique, the consensus approach, devil's advocacy, dialectical inquiry, and strategic assumptions surfacing and testing (e.g., Arbel & Tong, 1982; Dalkey, 1969; Delbecq & Van de Ven, 1971; Mitroff & Mason, 1980; Osborn, 1957; Schwenk & Huff, 1986). Lamm and Trommsdorff (1973) provide a thorough review of group process techniques and the empirical literature evaluating them. GSS researchers have embedded these processes into technology and done extensive comparative studies assessing the relative value of manual versus computerized delivery of group process interventions (e.g., DeSanctis, D'Onofrio, Sambamurthy, & Poole, 1989; A. C. Easton et al., 1989; Gallupe, Bastianutti, & Cooper, 1991; Watson et al., 1988). (For comprehensive reviews of these studies see Pinsonneault & Kraemer, 1989, and George et al., 1990.)

Despite the attention given to political concerns in group process approaches, the theories are more closely aligned with individualistic than with collectivist assumptions about organizations. The group is still treated as a collection of individuals, and decision efficiency and personal satisfaction are emphasized. Theories adhere to an engineering view of organizational change, believing that failure to achieve desired change reflects a failure in the intervention provided to the group. Research hypotheses are grounded in either hard-line determinism, the belief that certain process gains should inevitably follow from introduction of technology, or more moderate contingency views, which argue that situational factors interact with technology to cause outcomes (see Gutek, 1988; Hiltz, 1988).

Communication Theories. Communication theories traditionally have focused on message exchange between two or more parties, considering information channels, message contents, and the nature of message senders and receivers (Berlo, 1977; Bormann, 1980; Schramm, 1954; Shannon & Weaver, 1949). GSS research has drawn from a variety of communication theories. A few studies have examined the individual characteristics of message senders and receivers (Hiltz & Johnson, 1990; Watson et al., 1988). Many studies have considered the number (e.g., Reder & Schwab, 1988; Zigurs et al., 1988) or characteristics (e.g., Connolly, Jessup, & Valacich, 1990; George et al., 1990) of information channels in a GSS setting. Electronic communication channels have been argued to increase deindividuation (George et al., 1990; Hiltz, Turoff, & Johnson, 1989) and to reduce media richness (Trevino et al., 1987) and social presence (Sproull & Kiesler, 1986). These theories tend to emphasize the tradeoffs associated with GSS use, and numerous studies have been conducted to compare the relative value of electronic versus face-to-face communication (e.g., Dubrovsky, 1987; Gallupe & McKeen, 1988; Hiltz, Johnson, & Turoff, 1986). In addition to considering the number and nature of channel characteristics, GSS research has also drawn on theories of discourse, such as Bales Interaction Process Analysis (Austin, Liker, & McLeod, 1990) and Sillars' Interpersonal Conflict Interaction (Poole, Holmes, & DeSanctis, 1991a), and theories of rhetorical argument (Niederman, 1990). Electronic communication is hypothesized to bring efficiency gains and more open access to intra- and interteam communication. On the other hand, there is evidence that electronic media reduce the number of socioemotional interactive sequences, inhibit interactivity, create uncertainties about the motivations and activities of others, discourage elaborated discussion, and result in weaker bonds for member support (Galegher & Kraut, 1990; Losada, Sanchez, & Noble, 1990). In assessing the tradeoffs between efficiency and effectiveness of electronic media, communication theories espouse "systems rationalism" (Rice, 1984)—the view that alternative media can bring predictable costs and benefits to the parties involved—and individualistic assumptions about organizations and technology change. But communication theories also bring a concern for the social meaning of language and action, and GSS research that attempts either to provide technology-embedded models of conversations and language (e.g., Shepherd, Mayer, & Kuchinsky, 1990) or to assess the meaning of language in the context of GSS use (e.g., DeSanctis & Poole, 1991; Poole & DeSanctis, 1990) begins to move toward the collectivist position that GSS technology is a product of the organizational context in which it is used.

Institutional Theories. The strongest collectivist position brought to GSS research has come from institutional theories that emphasize the symbolic value of information rather than its content or delivery medium (Feldman & March, 1981). Researchers within the institutional camp criticize decision, group process, and communication theorists for the "technocentric" assumption that technology contains inherent power to shape human cognition and behavior, or that technology inevitably leads to certain cost/benefit tradeoffs for organizations (Markus & Robey, 1988; Perrow, 1986). This assumption, they contend, leads to an overemphasis on hardware and software and an underemphasis on the social practices that technologies involve. According to the institutional view, technology does not determine behavior; rather, people generate social institutions, of which technology is a part (Kling, 1980).

Theoretical perspectives aligned with the institutional school include social information processing theory, which emphasizes the social construction of meaning (Salancik & Pfeffer, 1978); and symbolic interactionism, which focuses on verbal and nonverbal communication as bringing about norms, values, and other social practices (Blumer, 1969). For institutionalists, the creation, design, and use of GSSs are all part of the larger social order. The research question of interest is not "what goals does the GSS promote?" so much as "what goals is society promoting through this technology?" The GSS is but one piece in the ever evolving puzzle of social development. It follows that studies of technology and organizational change must apply dynamic models and capture historical processes as social practices evolve. Qualitative, process-oriented methods are favored over quantitative, outcome studies; and ideographic, interpretive accounts are preferred over nomothetic research designs (Barley & Tolbert, 1988).

In recent years, institutional theories and methods have come into vogue within the organization sciences, and this popularity is beginning to spread into the GSS area as well (Fulk, Schmitz, & Steinfield, 1990; Orlikowski, in press; Poole & DeSanctis, 1990). These theories tend to put a great emphasis on the social context surrounding GSSs as determinants of their eventual impacts on groups, organizations, and society at large. As GSSs move out of controlled laboratory settings into more widespread organizational use, the increasing popularity on collectivist-based theories can be expected.

Coordination Theory. Malone (1987; Malone & Crowston, 1990) has proposed coordination theory as a guiding set of principles for development and evaluation of GSSs and other forms of cooperative work systems. The approach draws from general systems theory, modern theories of organizations, and economics to provide cybernetic models of the interplay between computers, group members, goals, and activities. The interdependencies among these elements and their subcomponents can be explained, Malone argues, by drawing on principles such as feedback, information exchange, network management, and market equilibrium. Like general systems theory, coordination theory argues that the principles of coordination should apply to many domains and settings—from computers, to factories, to people. Like economic theories, coordination theory focuses on the processes of exchange that occur between two coordinating units or parties. Decision support researchers have long believed that the study of computer intelligence is a useful way to understand human intelligence (see Keen & Scott Morton, 1978; Winston, 1977). Malone extends this approach to say that studies of coordination across a wide variety of domains and settings should aid in understanding of work group coordination. Coordination theory is still in its formative stages and has not, as yet, had a substantial effect on studies of GSS use and impacts. The theory takes no explicit stand on individualistic versus collectivists views of technology, but the approach appears to favor a collectivist perspective, because the emphasis is on the entire group or system, rather than the individual:

> When we analyze the coordination...we must (at least implicitly) evaluate the actors' collective behavior in terms of how well it achieves some overall goals (which may or may not be held by the actors themselves). (Malone & Crowston, 1990, p. 359)

Missing Elements in Existing Theory

These five theoretical bases have facilitated the development of a rich literature on GSSs and related collaborative systems. Individualistic-based theories clearly have dominated the research to date, but with growing interest in institutional and coordination theories, there is a gradual shift toward collectivist views of GSS technology. Although this shift leads researchers to develop more complex and comprehensive models of groups and support systems, the range of theoretical thinking about GSSs still leaves our understanding incomplete. As GSSs are increasingly used in organizations for important group decision activities, a key question we must ask ourselves is whether our theories are sufficiently complete and useful. GSSs are no longer used by just a single group in a single location at a given time. Do our theories provide adequate understanding of intergroup relations, time lags in group communication, intercultural aspects of GSS use, and the like? Missing elements in our theories that hamper the progress of GSS research include consideration of such issues as (1) affective aspects of group decision making, (2) the moral underpinnings of group behavior and choice, (3) diversity in group membership, and (4) freedom, power, and the goals of GSS use.

Affective Aspects. Many years ago, Argyris (1971) criticized the development of computer-based information systems on the basis that they overemphasized efficiency and rationalization, inhibited openness, and reinforced the status quo. He stressed the importance of the more emotive, intuitive, and personalized approaches to the appallingly complex process of making decisions. But most GSSs have been designed on the premise that groups either act on or desire logical/empirical considerations in formulating judgments. We know that people often reject rationality and are not driven by attempts to overcome their limited rationality (Nutt, 1984; Todd & Benbasat, in press). For example, group-process theories recognize the importance of "socioemotional" communication in the successful functioning of groups. But few GSSs provide mechanisms for groups to draw on their emotions and value judgments, and even fewer theoretical models give attention to the deep role that interpersonal emotions can play in Group Support System use. There is increasing evidence in cognitive science that nonrational, emotive-based behavior can be highly functional in choice-making situations (Etzioni, 1988). Mechanisms such as quantification of affect (through numeric expression of preference) or guided language to explain reasoning (as in stakeholder analysis or problem formulation procedures) may not be sufficient to support the affective processes of group decision making.

The Moral Dimension. In addition to affect, normative factors influence how information is gathered and processed by groups and the inferences that groups draw on the options that they consider. Groups act not only to maximize individual utilities; nor are they mere actors or products within their culture. Groups consider what "should" be done in a given situation, actively searching for and evaluating guiding principles for action. They are deeply affected by "how well they are anchored within a sound community and sustained by a firm moral and emotive personal underpinning" (Etzioni, 1988). How do GSSs interact with the moral dimension of group work? For example, equal participation may not influence decision-making as much as public duty or commitment to fairness. Similarly, groups may resist GSS-embedded meeting structures choosing instead to make choices based on personal values or principles. GSS design often presumes that quick, nonvigilant decision making is counter-productive; but if groups are applying emotionally strong, generalizable principles, perhaps the quick decision is the best one. Have we given groups mechanisms for testing and applying their values and principles? Researchers may presume that resistance to GSS is due to cultural experience and unwillingness to try unfamiliar approaches to group work; but the moral imperative may overwhelm the cultural one such that groups believe they are obligated, or duty bound, to proceed in a certain fashion. Do our research methods take into account the reasons based on principles that groups may resist computer-delivered structure?

Accommodating Diversity. Organization membership, markets, and indeed societies at large, are increasingly diverse in their makeup. Although GSS researchers have considered variations in group size, leadership, and computer knowledge and experience, we have given remarkably little attention to such issues of race, gender, and cross-cultural differences in GSS design and use. (Some exceptions are Austin et al., 1990; Egbert, Jessup, & Valacich, 1991; Ho, Raman, & Watson, 1989.) Accommodating diversity in group membership means more than considering differences in typing ability or decision making experience! As GSSs are used across time, space, industry, and organizational level, issues of diversity will become paramount, and our theories need to accommodate the study of these issues. For more discussion on this issue, see the chapter in this volume by Egbert.

Freedom and Power. Perhaps the most crucial theoretical issue involves the role of the technology as instrument of individual freedom versus a form of managerial or cultural control. GSSs have been advanced for their potential to empower the individual, providing autonomy and freedom of action, and freedom from dominance (Clement, 1990). But will GSSs encourage power equalization and distributive justice, or do they act to shape group behavior, using participation as a manipulative device that advances managerial or cultural goals? (see Mitchell & Scott, 1990). Researchers have not been explicit in identifying the goals of GSS in their technology designs or in their theories. Theories that incorporate blatant consideration of issues of individualism versus collectivism, and freedom versus power, are important to our advanced understanding of the role of GSSs in organizations. As technology is increasingly applied to support group work and these systems are integrated with other computer systems in the firm, issues such as empowerment of collectivities, surveillance, discrimination, and the shaping of group reasoning become of interest. How can our theories help in our understanding of these issues?

Shifting Foundations

Much has changed since GSS research began unfolding in the early 1980s. Technology advancements are perhaps the most obvious change (e.g., local area networks, multimedia interfaces, more powerful and easier-to-use systems). But the underlying models that we use to design our systems and study their impacts have also changed. For example, researchers no longer design and evaluate one or two system features at a time; studies typically include collections, or packages, of features and evaluate their impacts. Simple input→process→output models have evolved to models that account for feedback and the environmental context in which the group works. Controlled laboratory experiments are being complimented with field studies that examine repeated use of GSSs by groups and the "success" or "failure" of using GSSs within organizations. There have also been subtle changes within the organization and social sciences at large that are affecting GSS research and will continue to affect it in important ways during the coming years: There is increasing disenchantment with rational models of decision making and with bureaucracy as the ideal organization (Perrow, 1986). There is continual questioning of the value of using computing for efficiency goals or the attainment of individual advantage (e.g., Mitchell & Scott, 1990; Rule & Attewell, 1989). There is renewed interest in case-based, interpretive research methods (e.g., Markus & Robey, 1988). And there is renewed interest in models of organizations that emphasize collectivist views and the importance of advancing the community rather than the individual (e.g., Etzioni, 1988).

Despite these trends, we still lack clear articulation of what we hope GSSs will bring to organizations and how these changes should be brought about. To date, the number of negative effects of GSS use are as numerous as positive effects (see George et al., 1990; Poole et al., 1991), and no GSS has been successful in bringing about dramatic changes in how groups operate. Moreover, groups adopt the technology in very different ways (Poole & DeSanctis, 1990), so that positive change is by no means a sure thing when GSSs are implemented. Most applications of computing have not brought substantive changes to the nature of work or organizational decision making (Rule & Attewell, 1989). Some scientists take the view that mere invention of a technology is sufficient: How society chooses to apply the technology is a matter for social scientists to observe, not determine; successful applications are to be expected in some instances and not in others. But given that GSSs target social processes, affecting how people communicate and reason with one another; and given that GSSs hold special potential for enabling new organizational forms (Huber, 1990), perhaps researchers can no longer afford to be passive observers of the technology impacts. There is ample evidence that computer systems, including GSSs, can have very different effects depending on *how* they are introduced and managed (e.g., DeSanctis et al., 1989; Markus & Robey, 1988). Why not set out an explicit, theory-based agenda on how we intend for GSSs to positively change organizations and then proceed to work with organizations to design and evaluate systems along these lines?

Such an approach argues that the shift away from decision theories and toward institutional and coordination theories cannot, and should not, be value-free. Our theories must attend to the principles that the GSS encourages—values about who the technology is intended to serve, how the technology fits into the operation of the group and its larger community(ies), how participation should take place, and what the bases for social judgments should be. Instead of a full shift to a collectivist perspective, perhaps we should consider the development of GSS features and implementation procedures that simultaneously satisfy the individual (enhance his or her gain), reflect the values and rules of the community, *and* positively change the community in some constructive way.

Some social theorists have argued that there is a need for a middle ground in theories of organizational change that recognizes the mutually dependent forces of personal freedom and collective action (Barnard, 1938). Etzioni refers to this as the "I and we" paradigm. But there are few accepted theories that include both views, and even fewer that consider the role of computer technology. Perhaps in the shifting foundations of GSS research we can give greater theoretical attention to how GSSs can "support" both reason and emotion, both individual and community, both logical and affective/moral ways of deciding. In this way GSS research might contribute to the advancement of organizations that are based less on the attainment of personal advantage and organizational profit and more on the advancement of a society that is "open, moral, loving, humane, and broadly informed" (Mitchell & Scott, 1990, p. 29) and that, in the process, heightens the knowledge and character of the individual.

CONCLUSION

If it should turn out to be the case that GSSs do not bring about the positive changes that decision and group process theorists envisioned, then what shall we do about it? Decision theories would argue that we need to improve the technology, perhaps adding more sophisticated decision models or expertise that will encourage effective adoption. Group process theories would argue that we need to improve the procedures that we provide for group members to work together. Communication theories would argue that changes in the nature of the electronic or other media may be in order. Institutional theories would argue that organizations and group members will gradually shape how the technology is used over time, so changes in the technology may be unnecessary. Finally, coordination theory would argue that there is a need for a close examination of all aspects of the system, including people, computers, and the cybernetic rules governing system interdependencies. Though all of these approaches may prove fruitful, it is also likely that none of them will yield wholly satisfactory results.

Some have argued that the social sciences are in need of "radical" theories of organizations and organizational change (Daft & Lewin, 1990). This essay has argued that radical perspectives of GSS design and use are needed—perspectives that can account for some of the missing elements in existing theory. A more expansive view of the role of GSS in organizations is needed, with clear articulation of goals with regard to who is to gain from the technology use, and why, and how. The study of GSSs provides us with an occasion to advance our understanding of organizations and the role of technology in organizational change. Expansive theoretical models that clearly articulate the goals of the technology may enable us to go beyond the status quo of technology, bringing only "business as usual" and not really transforming individuals and organizations.

CHAPTER 6

Methodological and Measurement Issues in Group Support Systems Research

Ilze Zigurs
University of Colorado

INTRODUCTION

"People see what they expect to see. The problem is, they never learn what they have overlooked."

—Weick, 1984

How are discoveries made? How is our knowledge of human behavior in groups and organizations advanced? As Weick (1984) reminds us, the world is visible to us only through the methods and measures we use to observe it. In Group Support Systems (GSS) research, as in any endeavor to understand and enhance human interaction, the methods and instruments used are critical determinants of the outcomes obtained. This chapter discusses methodological and measurement issues in Group Support Systems research. Existing methods and measures are discussed, and guidelines for future GSS research are provided.

A FRAMEWORK FOR RESEARCH METHODS

In some respects, the GSS research community is revisiting the same kinds of "growing up pangs" that the information systems area in general experienced in its formative years. In the 1970s and early 1980s, information systems (IS) researchers were proposing frameworks, identifying research agendas, and attempting to bring methodological coherence to a rapidly expanding field (e.g., Bariff & Ginzberg, 1982; Ives, Hamilton, & Davis, 1980; Mason & Mitroff, 1973; Nolan & Wetherbe, 1980).

A number of authors focused on methodologies and categorized different methods for IS research (Elam, Huber, & Hurt, 1986; Scott Morton, 1984; Williams, Rice, & Rogers, 1988). Benbasat (1984) classified IS research methods into three categories: (1) studies in natural behavior settings including case studies, field studies, and field experiments; (2) studies in contrived and created settings, including person-computer experiments and judgment tasks; and (3) setting-independent studies, such as sample surveys. Galliers and Land (1987) proposed a taxonomy of IS research approaches that separated method from the object of the research. Their taxonomy argued for an emphasis on newer approaches such as subjective-argumentative and descriptive-interpretive research. Franz and Robey (1987) categorized research methods based on the purpose (discovery or testing) and the time frame (single or multiple) of the research. Other dimensions might include by degree of control or intervention, by level of analysis, or by degree of researcher involvement. Table 6.1 summarizes potential GSS research methods, by type of method used.

The majority of early GSS research was in lab experiments, but the variety of research methods utilized has increased in recent years. In Pinsonneault and Kraemer's (1989) review, which covered published work up to 1988, approximately 65 percent of the studies were lab experiments. Since then, GSS studies published in selected IS journals in 1989 and 1990 have consisted of approximately 30 percent lab experiments, 17 percent field studies, and 13 percent design and development papers. (Note: The journals searched were the 1989 and 1990 editions of *Communications of the ACM, Decision Sciences, Decision Support Systems, Information & Management, Information Systems Research, Journal of Management Information Systems, Management Science*, and *MIS Quarterly*.)

Vogel and Nunamaker (1990b) are a good example of the types of studies that have been done or could be done using more varied methodologies, including mathematical simulation, software engineering, case, survey, field study, lab experiment, and conceptual. Reviews of research and summary papers are also becoming common, as the body of research builds.

TABLE 6.1 Potential GSS Research Methods

Action Research	Field study
Application description	Hardware/facility engineering
Archival research	Lab experiment
Case study	Mathematical modeling
Conceptual/theoretical	Meta-analysis
Content analysis	Software engineering
Ethnography	Survey
Field experiment	Theorem proof

CHOOSING AN APPROPRIATE RESEARCH METHOD

Making the right choice of a research method can mean the difference between merely confirming prior assumptions and obtaining objective findings (Weick, 1984). What is the basis for choosing an appropriate research method? Benbasat (1984) discusses three ways of deciding among strategies: (1) make an overall assessment of advantages and disadvantages of methods, independently of subject area; (2) use multiple strategies; or (3) select a strategy based on the purpose of the research and the type of area being studied. General critiques of advantages and disadvantages of different methods can be found in Cook and Campbell (1979), McGrath, Martin, and Kulka (1982), and Williams et al. (1988).

The most active debate over method choices has been the quantitative versus qualitative argument. Luthans and Davis (1982) discuss the nomothetic versus idiographic debate that started in the field of psychology—the search for general laws versus individual understanding—and the accompanying implication for methods. Luthans and Davis view idiographic approaches as being much needed in organizational behavior research, and they argue that the intensive study of one or a few cases of real employees interacting in organizations is important. Nomothetic approaches make the assumption that humans are the same, that "average is beautiful" (p. 382), and that error and variability can be accounted for or averaged out in a group. Idiographic approaches, on the other hand, or what some call the interaction approach, assume that both people and situations vary and that behavior in particular situations is a function of both.

Weick (1984) argues that IS researchers "...tend to see rationality everywhere, partly because their prior beliefs assume rationality and partly because the methods they use preserve those prior beliefs" (p. 112). Weill and Olson (1989) also see IS researchers as being embedded in a rationality assumption, a functionalist paradigm, an objectivist approach, and a deterministic model. They point out that IS researchers have ignored a more subjectivist approach, the concepts of social construction of reality, and the political nature of organizations. Indeed, they conclude that "...a premature quantification strategy has been followed by many management information systems (MIS) researchers, before a sufficient understanding of the variables and underlying relationships to be quantified is attained" (p. 76).

Although the call for more use of and respect for qualitative research is not a new phenomenon in our reference disciplines, it is only relatively recently that such methods have gained greater visibility in the IS and GSS areas. Benbasat, Goldstein, and Mead (1987) argue the importance of case research in information systems and provide detailed guidelines for how to conduct such studies. Lee (1989) provides a scientific methodology for case studies that demonstrates the legitimacy of the case study technique in the context of and by the standards of the traditional and much-revered natural science model.

There is much to be gained from qualitative methods and their focus on process. As Todd and Benbasat (1987) point out, a large body of prior research in the field of decision support systems (DSS) has demonstrated the effects of DSS use on outcomes such as decision time, decision confidence, and perceived quality of decisions. However, we still have little understanding of why such outcomes occur. Todd and Benbasat argue for more process-oriented research that opens up the "black box" of decision processes and provides understanding of how systems are being used. They focus on how best to use protocol analysis, but other process methods described include information display boards, analysis of eye movements, and computer logs. The latter method has particularly great potential in GSS research.

Quantitative research, nevertheless, continues to occupy an important place in GSS research. In spite of the many threats to validity that make quantitative, experimental research difficult to do, there exist many guidelines for dealing with these issues. Cook and Campbell (1979) and D. I. Campbell and Stanley (1963) are well-known classics. In the IS area, Jarvenpaa, Dickson, and DeSanctis (1985) discuss common problems of internal validity and provide cautions and guidelines for IS researchers. Baroudi and Orlikowski (1989) provide guidelines for increasing statistical power in studies that use statistical inference testing. And DeSanctis (1989) reviews the advantages of a laboratory setting in the context of group research in IS and discusses the challenges involved.

In the end, it is the judicious combination of multiple methods that has the most potential. Although the popularity (and accompanying prestige) of certain methods waxes and wanes, a consensus is forming that a multimethodological approach provides the greatest power of understanding the complex sociotechnological issues with which GSS research deals. Dennis, Nunamaker, and Vogel (1990–91), for example, argue that an overreliance on either field or experimental work to the exclusion of the other could be misleading. Weill and Olson, among others (Benbasat & Nault, 1990; Vogel & Nunamaker, 1990b; Williams et al., 1988), recommend a wider selection of methodologies be used, including qualitative case studies, ethnographic studies, longitudinal studies, and a combination of qualitative and quantitative methods within a study. Nunamaker et al. (1990–91) also include systems development as an important form of IS research and recommend a multimethodological approach that views systems development as the hub of research that interacts with other methods to form an integrated program. This timely trend toward multiple perspectives in GSS research will assist greatly in understanding the many complex issues that remain to be studied.

METHOD ISSUES WITHIN GSS RESEARCH

As noted earlier, the GSS field is a rapidly growing research area. This section discusses important method issues in GSS research that have emerged as the body of literature grows and expands.

Role of Reference Disciplines

The interdisciplinary nature of GSS research is evident and is both a boon and a burden. Part IV of this volume is devoted to bridging GSS to other disciplines, and the chapters in that section show the rich foundations that GSS research has to build on. The links to social and communication sciences have always been strong. For example, McGrath's (1984) framework for the study of groups has been used as the foundation for extensive programs of research at both the University of Minnesota and the University of Arizona. We have also seen explicit calls for theory-based work grounded in the reference disciplines (Jessup, 1987; Rao & Jarvenpaa, 1989).

Building on reference disciplines, however, means that we also inherit their problems (Baroudi & Orlikowski, 1989). The arguments on appropriateness and rigor of various methodologies have been and continue to be argued in our reference disciplines. As method issues arise, we need to understand how those problems have been wrestled with in other areas.

The Dependent Variable

Information systems research in general has had a long tradition of an input-process-output model, with a focus on outputs as the dependent variable. Small group behavior has been studied from the same perspective, but with greater emphasis on studying inputs (such as group composition variables) and processes (using interaction analysis) in addition to outcomes. Although we see many calls for more process research in IS and GSS (Benbasat & Nault, 1990; Franz & Robey, 1987), the link between processes and outcomes is not a clear link and warrants further investigation. Hirokawa (1982), for instance, found little evidence of meaningful and consistent causal links between group input and performance.

The small group literature contains several categorizations for the study of outcomes. Shaw (1981) summarizes the studies of individual versus group problem solving into three outcome types: accuracy of group judgment, problem-solving performance, and learning effects. McGrath (1984) categorizes outcomes appropriate to each of six task types from his task circumplex, an often-cited task categorization within GSS research. Gouran (1988) reduces the large number of possible outcomes to four categories: correctness of decision, quality of decision, utility of decision, and acceptability of decision. Gouran goes on to propose a concept called "appropriateness" which takes into account the contextual features of the decision, such as the purpose of the group and the requirements of the task.

There has also been a classic division in the small group literature between task-oriented and socioemotional outcomes (Bormann, 1975; McGrath, 1984). DeSanctis and Gallupe (1987) emphasize that GSS research should be concerned with both performance and satisfaction and should seek a balance between the two. Task performance includes categories such as effectiveness, efficiency, cognitive products, structural products, or artifactual products. Satisfaction can be personal, group-related, task-related, organization-related, or system-related. Zigurs and Dickson (1990) provide detailed dependent variables within each of these categories.

Surveys of recent empirical research in GSS (Dennis, George, Jessup, Nunamaker, and Vogel, 1988; Dennis et al., 1990-91; Pinsonneault & Kraemer, 1989) reveal that the task-related dependent variables studied most often include decision quality, decision speed, thoroughness of analysis, and consensus. The satisfaction variables that have been studied most often include decision confidence, satisfaction with process, and satisfaction with decision. Other dependent variables that have received attention include equality of influence, perceived quality of solution, and satisfaction with the system. It appears that the focus has been on a relatively narrow definition of performance, and that many satisfaction outcomes have not been studied at all. A broader view of the dependent variable would bring a richer understanding to GSS research.

Development of Measurement Instruments

Beyond defining what the dependent variables should be lies the greater challenge of operationalizing those variables. A real need exists for validated measurement instruments in GSS research, and authors need to provide more information about the measures they are using to operationalize constructs. Most published studies reveal a dearth of information about measurement instruments used. For instance, G.K. Easton, George, Nunamaker, and Prendergast (1990) measure satisfaction but say very little about the instrument they used, other than to state that it contained sixteen questions. George, Easton, Nunamaker, and Northcraft (1990) are equally silent on their satisfaction measure. Chidambaram, Bostrom, and Wynne (1990-91) used two instruments—one new and the other modified—and mention pretesting and piloting but do not provide more detail. But these sample GSS articles are not at all unusual in their lack of information on instrument validation. Zmud and Boynton (1989) examined 119 scales from 27 recent IS articles; only three of the scales met the criteria of internal consistency, validity, and use of multiple higher-level items (Venkatraman & Grant, 1986). Zmud and Boynton concluded that IS survey instruments are at a very early stage of development. Straub's (1989) review of IS instrument validation is just as telling; from a sample of 117 studies, 62 percent lacked a single form of instrument validation.

Obviously, the objective of these studies is to report results and not the process of instrument development and validation. The latter process is a major effort in itself and typically results in entirely separate publications, for example, the stream of work on developing the "user information satisfaction" construct (see Zmud & Boynton, 1989). Yet, the current dearth of information in most published work does little to promote greater validity and reuse of instruments. As Straub (1989) points out, there will always be a gap between a construct and its accurate measurement, and only through validation of instruments can we get a sense of how large that gap actually is.

System usage. System usage is an example of a deceptively simple construct that needs to be looked at more carefully. Measures of system usage have been the basis for studies of idea generation (G.K. Easton et al., 1990), influence distribution (Zigurs, Poole, & DeSanctis, 1988b), and participation (George et al., 1990; Vogel, Nunamaker, Martz, Grohowski, & McGoff, 1989–90), among others. But most measures of system usage vary from study to study, and many studies take an overly simple view of what constitutes usage.

The number lines of text entered at the keyboard has been the primary measure of system usage. However, a GSS can be supporting group activity at times other than just when group members are entering input at the keyboard. Other uses of the system might include the number and duration of views at the private or public screen (Gallupe, 1986). DeSanctis, Poole, Lewis, and Desharnais (1991) is an example of a more complex measure of system usage; they included keyboarding, looking at screens, discussing information in the system, and discussing how the system should be used. This broader view of usage helps to capture the richness of the support that GSSs provide to groups.

Decision quality. Another example of the measurement challenge is decision quality. A variety of tasks have been studied in the GSS literature, and each task type has its appropriate measure of outcome quality (McGrath, 1984). Intellective tasks by their nature have a correct answer, but most organizational tasks are not that straightforward. An important issue is how to measure decision quality for a task that has no right answer. At present, there is no consensus on the meaning of quality as a dependent variable in GSS research.

The use of "expert" judges to measure outcome quality has a long tradition in the small group literature, and there are examples of such use in GSS research (Connolly, Jessup, & Valacich, 1990; Ellis, Rein, & Jarvenpaa, 1989–90; Gallupe & McKeen, 1990). In many cases, researchers measure perceived quality, which may be confounded with perceived satisfaction. Quality has also been subdivided into outcome quality and process quality (e.g., Vogel et al., 1989–90). Useful coherence could be brought to the field by a better understanding of what each of these measures means and what each is contributing.

The Problem Of Appropriate Comparisons

Early experimental studies in the GSS area developed a tradition of comparing three types of groups: computer-supported, manual, and baseline (e.g., Gallupe, DeSanctis, & Dickson, 1988; Watson, DeSanctis, & Poole, 1988). Computer-supported groups are provided with whatever implementation of the GSS concept is being tested. Manual groups are provided with a paper-and-pencil version of the structure that the GSS provides. Baseline groups are left to interact freely, typically without instructions and without any type of support. More recently, comparisons have been strictly between GSS-supported and manual groups (e.g., Chidambaram et al., 1990–91; George et al., 1990). These three- and two-way comparisons are useful when relatively simple systems are being tested—that is, systems that support only group communication, or what

DeSanctis and Gallupe (1987) define as Level 1 systems. However, as systems become more sophisticated and support forms of group interaction that would be difficult or impossible without technological support (i.e., Level 2 and 3 systems), it becomes progressively more difficult to determine what the appropriate manual comparison group should be. If a GSS provides entirely new paths to the decision process, then a manual comparison group simply does not exist.

There are important methodological implications for this observation. Classic control group testing may be inappropriate in some cases, and that particular template should not be forced onto situations where it does not belong. One approach, still relatively rare, is to compare different technologies to each other (G.K. Easton et al., 1990; Sambamurthy & DeSanctis, 1990). Another approach has been to compare groups using the same GSS, but with subtle system differences (e.g., Connolly et al., 1990). Field sites make comparison groups even more problematic. Vogel et al. (1989–90) try to deal with the comparison problem in field research by asking for a priori perceptions on timing of manual processes and then comparing those figures to actual time spent with a GSS. Greater use of qualitative methods can help in this area, by providing depth analysis of one or a limited number of GSS groups.

The Unit Of Analysis

What is the appropriate unit of analysis for GSS research? The answer seems obvious—the group. But the group qua group is only one part of the complex interaction patterns that a GSS supports. Jessup (1987) recommends that GSS researchers use individual, group, and situational levels of analysis. Dennis et al. (1990–91) recommend that researchers study not only the meeting as a unit of analysis, but also the project that lives on over a series of meetings. Vogel et al. (1989–90) feel that it is important to address issues related to the individual, the group, the project, and the organization. Most studies to date have taken a very simple view of the unit of analysis. The common practice has been to collect individual-level data, typically affective data via questionnaires, and to average the scores of all members in a group in order to obtain a group-level data point (e.g., Chidambaram et al., 1990–91; G.K. Easton et al., 1990).

The averaging of individual scores to represent a group score, however, may present problems (Gallupe, 1986). For instance, what is the meaning of "acceptance" or "adoption" of GSS technology by the group if the analysis is only of individual perceptions or usage? Are there other ways to measure meaningful group-level variables? Gallupe and McKeen (1990) attempt to deal with this problem by measuring the same variables at both an individual and group level. They measured group decision confidence and group satisfaction by aggregating individual scores and then asked the entire group to decide on a score on the same variables. The aggregated, individual scores correlated with the verbal scores at $r = 0.79$ for group decision confidence and $r = 0.81$ for group satisfaction. The relatively high correlation is encouraging, but such attempts to get group-level measures have been rare.

Data Issues Within GSS Research

GSS research presents some unique opportunities with respect to data capture. Group Support Systems are an object of study in themselves, but they also present a sophisticated tool for the capture of research data that previously was available either through very cumbersome means or not at all. Consider, for example, the early experiments in communication networks (described in Shaw, 1981 and McGrath, 1984), in which group members were seated in cubicles that were connected by slots through which messages could be passed. Seating arrangement and slot availability were used to impose the desired communication networks, such as the circle, wheel, chain, or pinwheel. How easily and much less artificially can such networks now be imposed via electronic channels of communication within a GSS.

As GSS research evolves, the data that we capture becomes more complete and complex. Ellis et al. (1989–90) is a good example of the amount of data that can be captured in a GSS environment. In their study of computer scientists using different meeting tools, Ellis et al. gathered data in the form of videotapes of sessions, handwritten and electronic notes, information on the public screen, machine logs, questionnaires, SYMLOG questionnaires (Bales & Cohen, 1979), and verbal feedback. A recent trend has been toward capture of data on-line. Vogel et al. (1989–90) report the use of a questionnaire tool in GroupSystems™ that provides support for researchers to design on-line questionnaires dynamically and get immediate subject responses. Indeed, data has become so easy to capture that data overload can be a major problem with group research in information systems (DeSanctis, 1989).

Because Group Support Systems provide us with an unprecedented opportunity to capture comprehensive details of group member interactions, they also carry the risk of intrusiveness (Williams et al., 1988). Privacy and protection of subjects are normally governed by the rules of the agency sponsoring the research, but there are considerable variations in the degree of protection provided. As systems become more common in field sites, users' concerns with privacy are likely to increase.

Recommendations and Conclusions

Table 6.2 summarizes recommendations for future GSS research, with respect to method and measurement issues. The first recommendation is to share measurement instruments. The GSS community is a cohesive enough group that communication among members of the community is active and effective. The Hawaii International Conference on System Sciences has become a premier forum for sharing GSS work. Workshops and special symposia have been held as well, in an effort to coordinate and make more efficient the complex activity of studying group support systems. There have been notable examples of sharing of instruments in the GSS community. For instance, the Green and Taber (1980) and Gouran, Brown, and Henry (1978) measures have been used in GSS experiments at Minnesota, Arizona, and the National University of Singapore. The Minnesota GDSS Research Project recently published a working paper (DeSanctis,

TABLE 6.2 Method and Measurement Recommendations for Future GSS Research

1. Share Measurement Instruments
2. Provide More Measurement Information
3. Triangulate
4. Study Longitudinally
5. Continue Lab Studies While Increasing Field Studies
6. Increase Depth of Qualitative Analyses

Poole, Limayem, & Johnson, 1990) that includes copies of experimental materials and questionnaires used in their research program. Such efforts need to continue and be expanded to build a body of validated and used instruments.

The other aspect of sharing measurement instruments is to provide more measurement information—to provide greater detail on the background and development of the instrument in the reporting of the results. Straub (1989) suggests that IS journal editors encourage researchers to include a subsection on instrument validation in their methodology sections. Indeed, Zmud and Boynton's (1989) suggestions for IS research are especially needed in future GSS research, namely:

- Give greater attention to validity of scales, including face validity, criterion-related validity, factor analytic validity, and content.
- Use existing instruments where available.
- Revalidate borrowed instruments.
- Revalidate instruments when applying them to a different level of analysis, for example, from individual to group.

Overall, more attention needs to be given to development and evolution of measures. Zmud and Boynton make a valuable contribution by cataloging available instruments, including relevant constructs from the organizational literature. GSS researchers can benefit by using and extending this work.

The third recommendation is to triangulate. A number of authors have called for the use of multiple methods in GSS research (Benbasat & Nault, 1990; Dennis et al., 1990–1991; Vogel & Nunamaker, 1990b), and we are beginning to see the emergence of triangulation efforts. Ellis et al. (1989–90) and Jarvenpaa et al. (1988) are examples of how much can be gleaned from looking at the same data from multiple perspectives. Their 1988 paper was primarily a quantitative analysis, while the 1989 paper was a qualitative analysis of the same data.

To study longitudinally is the fourth recommendation. The vast majority of GSS research has been conducted in single-meeting contexts. Very few studies have been longitudinal in nature, for compelling reasons. Collecting longitudinal data is even more time-consuming than the already heavy burden of running single-meeting groups, and this is particularly true when large numbers of groups are desired for statistical power. There are risks of changes in group membership over time, both in experimental and field groups. Longitudinal field studies also carry the very real risk of loss of commitment from the client organization. And, whether the groups are experimental or "live" groups, external events can cause perturbations in group life that affect members' commitment to and feelings about the group.

An interesting question here is how "long" is longitudinal? The few longitudinal studies that have been done studied groups that met at most eight times (Zigurs, DeSanctis, & Billingsley, 1991) and as few as four times (Chidambaram et al., 1990–91). Chidambaram and colleagues suggest that laboratory groups can be "forced" or encouraged to develop faster than naturally interacting groups. However, in addition to the important group development that takes place over time, GSS groups also need time to adapt to the technology. The question of how long that takes has not been answered yet. Field projects that study groups over longer periods (e.g., DeSanctis, Poole, Lewis, & Desharnais, 1991) will help to answer these questions.

The fifth recommendation is to continue lab studies while increasing field studies. A most interesting phenomenon that has emerged from the body of research in group support systems has been the difference between experimental findings and field experience. The early days of experimental work resulted in mixed findings. Some GSS groups were more satisfied than manual groups, whereas others reported less satisfaction. Some studies reported higher quality in GSS than in manual groups, whereas other studies reported the reverse. As Group Support Systems began to be installed and used within organizations, the picture changed almost entirely. Great enthusiasm and acceptance of GSS was reported, with participants feeling that significant time had been saved in GSS rooms. A recent comparison of laboratory with field studies (Dennis et al., 1990–91) examined 24 variables on which the studies varied, and concluded that the results were not inconsistent—they were simply not comparable, because the studies were not comparable. What we still lack, however, is field experiments that provide semi-controlled circumstances so we can tell just what is going on in these sites.

The final recommendation is to increase depth of qualitative analyses. Although qualitative analyses are gaining more respect in our field, the few qualitative analyses that have been reported are just a beginning. This is an area in which much can be learned from the small group literature. Classic reference guides for qualitative analysis (e.g., Glaser & Strauss, 1967; Miles & Huberman, 1984) should become part of the GSS methodological toolkit.

The overwhelming conclusion that emerges from the issues discussed in this chapter is that there is no dearth of research to be done in the study of Group Support Systems. The methods by which we study GSS, the constructs we choose to examine, the measures by which we operationalize those constructs, and the instruments through which we obtain data—all these areas need more development. Through more explicit specification of means of measurement in the published papers, the GSS research community will move toward a more valid and comprehensible body of research on the real effects of Group Support Systems.

PART III

ISSUES IN THE DESIGN, DEVELOPMENT, USE, AND MANAGEMENT OF GROUP SUPPORT SYSTEMS

PART III

ISSUES IN THE DESIGN, DEVELOPMENT, USE, AND MANAGEMENT OF GROUP SUPPORT SYSTEMS

CHAPTER 7

Group Support Systems Research: Experience from the Lab and Field

J. F. Nunamaker Jr.
University of Arizona

Alan R. Dennis
University of Georgia

Joseph S. Valacich
Indiana University

Douglas R. Vogel
University of Arizona

Joey F. George
University of Arizona

INTRODUCTION

This chapter provides a summary of the major conclusions we have drawn about the effects of Group Support Systems (GSS) use, based on our laboratory and field research. Our research is motivated by both theoretical and practical issues. From a theoretical perspective, a GSS may significantly affect group and organizational processes, structures, and outcomes in ways that we have not yet envisioned. Thus, it is important to test and extend existing theories or to develop new ones. From a practical perspective, organizations need to understand the potential ramifications of these technologies, so that informed decisions about their deployment and use can be made. System developers need to understand how various contingencies impact group and organizational structuring and functioning so that more effective systems can be developed.

Our research program includes two types of research defined by Ackoff and his colleagues (1962):

1. Developmental, which attempts to create improved work methods
2. Empirical, which attempts to evaluate and understand the improved work methods.

The program has evolved through three primary phases. The initial phase which began in the late 1970s focused primarily on the development of tools and techniques to support groups of system analysts and users in the construction of information systems. The second phase began in 1984 with the construction of a special-purpose meeting room and software to support the same time/same place meetings of these design groups. The third (and current) phase began in 1987. This phase is characterized by a dramatic expansion in the research program in which the special-purpose GSS has evolved to a general-purpose group support environment (this research program, and its facilities, procedures, and software have evolved to be referred to as GroupSystems™. See Dennis et al. (1988) for a more detailed discussion on the history of the Arizona GSS research program.

In this chapter, we first discuss the theoretical foundations of our research program. These foundations provide the basis for understanding the design, implementation, and subsequent evaluation of both the GSS software and facilities. In this section, we argue that GSS design is one of four contingencies (task structure, task support, process structure, process support), along with the group, task, and context, that affects the group process and performance within these environments. Next, we discuss the key elements in the design of a GSS—the meeting room, the meeting facilitation, and the meeting software toolkit. In the third section, we focus on four of the many contingencies of GSS use in practice. We examine one example of each type of contingency, using the findings from our empirical research from both the laboratory and the field to illustrate our arguments. We end with a short discussion of general issues we have drawn from this work.

THEORETICAL FOUNDATIONS

Research on Process Gains and Losses

Prior research and theory provide a rich starting point for GSS research. However, because information technology has the ability to profoundly affect the nature of group work (Huber, 1990), it becomes dangerous to generalize the outcomes or conclusions from research with non-GSS groups to the GSS environment. For example, such commonly accepted conclusions as "larger groups are less satisfied than smaller groups," or "groups generate fewer ideas than the same number of individuals working separately" (i.e., nominal groups—see Diehl & Stroebe, 1987) have been shown not to hold with GSS groups (see Valacich, Dennis, & Connolly, in press). A better approach is to examine underlying theory that explains why these events occur and to consider how GSS use and various situational characteristics may affect the theory to produce different outcomes.

Figure 7.1 presents a high-level view of the research model that has guided our work and has evolved with our research program. We contend that the effects of GSS use are contingent on a myriad of group, task, context, and technology factors that differ from situation to situation (Dennis et al., 1988). Group characteristics that can affect processes and outcomes include (but are not limited to) group size, group proximity, group composition (peers or hierachical), group cohesiveness, and so on. Task characteristics include the activities required to accomplish the task (e.g., idea generation, decision choice), task complexity, and so on. Context characteristics include organizational culture, time pressure, evaluative tone (e.g., critical or supportive), reward structure (e.g., none versus individual versus group), and so on. Meeting outcomes (e.g., efficiency, effectiveness, satisfaction) depend upon the interaction within the meeting process of these group, task, and context factors with the GSS components the group uses (e.g., anonymity). Thus, it is inappropriate to say that GSS use "improves group task performance" or "reduces member satisfaction"; all statements must be qualified by the situation—the group, task, context, and GSS to which they apply.

To understand these interactions, we need to examine group process at a lower level of detail. Certain aspects of the meeting process improve outcomes

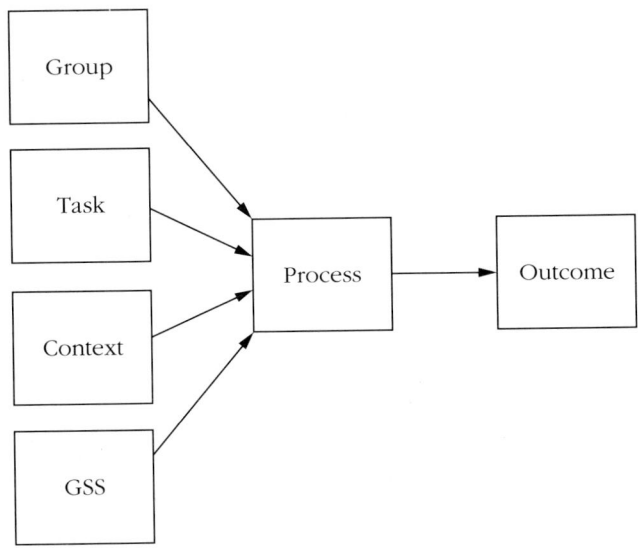

FIGURE 7.1 Research model.

(process gains), whereas others impair outcomes (process losses) relative to the efforts of the same individuals working by themselves or those of groups that do not experience them (Hill, 1982; Steiner, 1972). Meeting outcomes are contingent upon the balance of these process gains and losses (Connolly, Jessup, & Valacich, 1990). Situational characteristics (i.e., group, task, and context) establish an initial balance, which the group may alter by using a GSS. There are many different process gains and losses. Tables 7.1 and 7.2 list several important process gains and losses, but these lists are by no means exhaustive. Each of these gains and losses varies in strength (or may not exist at all) depending upon the situation.

Mechanisms for Process Gains and Losses

There are at least four theoretical mechanisms by which the GSS can affect this balance of gains and losses: (1) process support, (2) process structure, (3) task structure, and (4) task support (Figure 7.2). Process support refers to the communication infrastructure (media, channels, and devices, electronic or otherwise) that facilitates communication among members (DeSanctis & Gallupe, 1987), such as an electronic communication channel or blackboard. Process structure refers to process techniques or rules that direct the pattern, timing, or content of this communication (DeSanctis & Gallupe, 1987), such as an agenda or process methodology such as Nominal Group Technique (NGT). Task support refers to the information and computation infrastructure for task-related activities (Dennis et al., 1988), such as external databases and pop-up calculators. Task structure refers to techniques, rules, or models for analyzing task-related information to gain new insight (DeSanctis & Gallupe, 1987), such as those within computer models or Decision Support Systems (DSS).

TABLE 7.1 Important Sources of Group Process Gains

Common Process Gains	Sources of Group Gains
More Information	A group has more information than any one member.
Synergy	Each member uses information in a way that is different from the way every other member does because each member has different information or skills.
More Objective Evaluation	Groups are better at catching errors in proposed ideas than are the individuals who proposed them.
Stimulation	Working as part of a group may stimulate and encourage individuals to perform better.
Learning	Members may learn from and imitate more skilled members to improve performance.

For more information see Hackman & Kaplan, 1974; Hill, 1982; Lamm & Trommsdorff, 1973; Nunamaker, Dennis, George, Valacich, & Vogel, 1991a; Osborn, 1957; Shaw, 1981.

TABLE 7.2 Important Sources of Group Process Losses

Common Process Losses	Sources of Group Process Losses
Air Time	The group must partition available speaking time among members.
Production Blocking	Only one person can communicate at a time. This may result in forgetting ideas, not sharing ideas, or not thinking of new ideas (because of listening to the comments of others.)
Failure to Remember	Members lack focus on communication, missing, or forgetting the contributions of others.
Conformance Pressure	Members are reluctant to criticize the comments of others due to politeness or fear of reprisals.
Evaluation Apprehension	Fear of negative evaluation causes members to withold ideas and comments.
Free Riding	Members rely on others to accomplish goals, due to cognitive loafing, the need to compete for air time, or because they perceive their input to be unneeded.
Cognitive Inertia	Discussion moves along one train of thought without deviating, because group members refrain from contributing comments that are not directly related to the current discussion.
Socializing	Nontask discussion reduces task performance, although some socializing is necessary for effective functioning.
Domination	Some group member(s) exercise undue influence or monopolize the group's time in an unproductive manner.
Information Overload	Information is presented faster than it can be processed.
Coordination Problems	Difficulty integrating members' contributions because the group does not have an appropriate strategy, which can lead to dysfunctional cycling or incomplete discussions resulting in premature decisions.
Incomplete use of Information	Incomplete access to and use of information necessary for the successful task completion.
Incomplete Task Analysis	Incomplete analysis and understanding of task resulting in superficial discussions.

See Albanese & Van Fleet, 1985; Diehl & Stroebe. 1987; Hackman & Kaplan, 1974; Hirokawa & Pace, 1983; Jablin & Seibold, 1978; Lamm & Trommsdorff, 1973; J. G. Miller, 1960; Nunamaker et al., 1991a; Shaw, 1981.

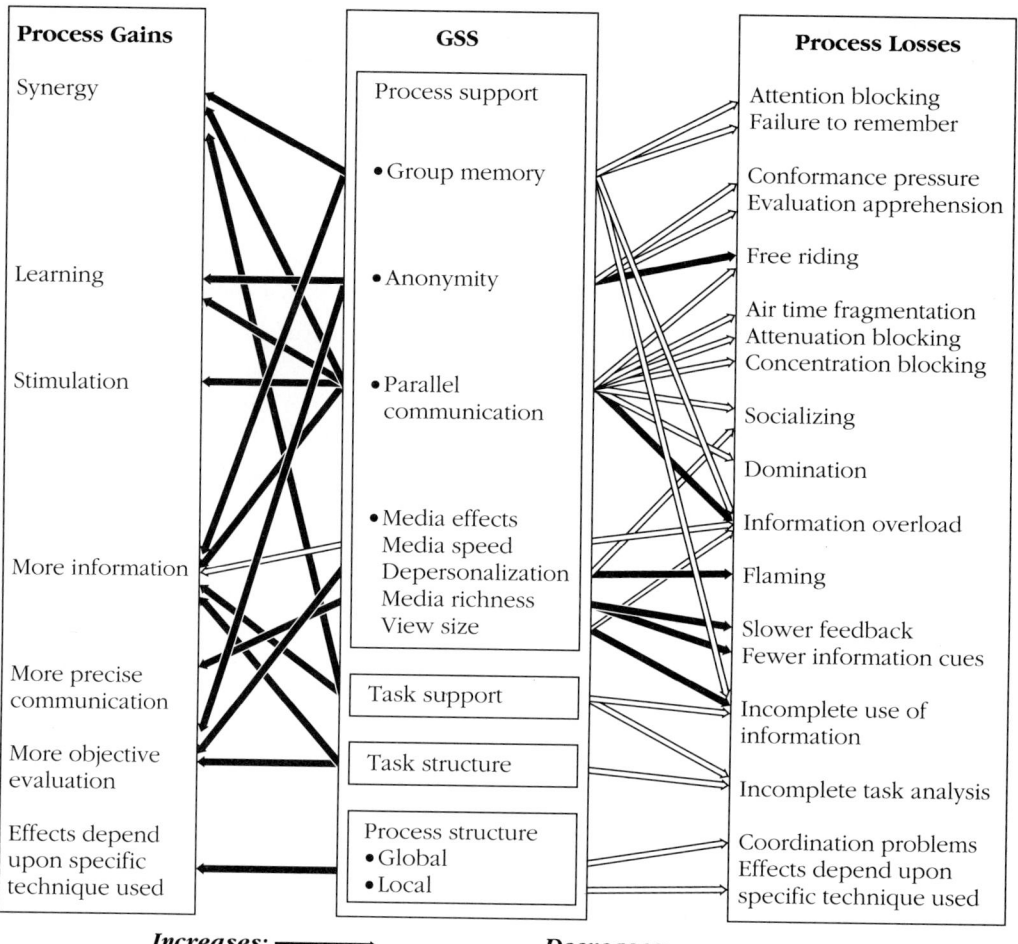

FIGURE 7.2 Potential GSS effects.

For example, suppose a group was charged with generating a plan to encourage more European tourists to visit the United States. Providing each group member with a computer workstation that enabled him or her to exchange typed comments with other group members would be process support. Having members take turns contributing ideas (i.e., round-robin), or having each member agree not to criticize the ideas of others would be process structure. Task support could include information on when, where, and how many European tourists visited last year, or about tourist programs run by other governments. Task structure could include a framework encouraging the group to consider each U.S. region (e.g., New England, California) or different types of tourists (e.g., tour clients, businesspeople), or an economic model of potential effects. We feel that a GSS can affect meeting processes through these four fundamental mechanisms. These mechanisms are not unique to GSS. The GSS is simply a convenient means by which to deliver process support, process structure, task support, and task structure. But in many cases, the GSS can provide a unique combination that it is virtually impossible to provide otherwise. In the discussion below, we hypothesize potential effects for each mechanism. These effects are those suggested most strongly by prior research, and again, this list is necessarily incomplete. As noted below, each mechanism can have many separate effects on process gains and losses, some positive, some negative. The combined effects are contingent on the strength of the preexisting gains and losses and the strength of the GSS effect on them (e.g., if the GSS reduces a weak process loss, we would anticipate few effects on outcomes). For simplicity, this discussion treats each mechanism separately; interactions are discussed later. This discussion assumes that the group actually uses the mechanisms described; any mechanism that is provided by the GSS but is not used, obviously has few effects. In our discussion of these four mechanisms, the one that has been central to our research, process support, will be emphasized.

Task Structure. Task structure assists the group to better understand and analyze task information and is one of the mechanisms by which DSS improve the performance of individual decision makers. Task structure may improve group performance by reducing losses due to incomplete task analysis or increasing process gains due to synergy, encouraging more information to be shared, promoting more objective evaluation, or catching errors (by highlighting information). Methods of providing task structure include problem modeling, multicriteria decision making, and so on. Although task structure is often numeric in nature, it is not necessarily so. (e.g., stakeholder analysis, Mason & Mitroff, 1981).

Task Support. Task support may reduce process losses due to incomplete use of information and incomplete task analysis, and may promote synergy and the use of more information by providing information and computation to the group (without providing additional structure). For example, groups may benefit from electronic access to information from previous meetings. Although members could make notes of potentially useful information prior to the meeting, a more effective approach may be to provide access to the complete sources during the meeting itself. Computation support could include calculators or spreadsheets.

Task support is also important at an organizational level. Simon argues that technological support for organizational memory is an essential part of organizational functioning (Simon, 1976). A GSS can assist in building this organizational memory by recording inputs, outputs, and results in one repository for easy access for subsequent meetings. Although the importance of such an organizational memory has been recognized in system development (e.g., CASE tools), it has not yet been widely applied to other organizational activities.

Process Structure. Process structure has long been used by non-GSS groups to reduce process losses, although many researchers have reported that groups often don't follow the process-structuring rules properly (Hackman & Kaplan, 1974; Jablin & Seibold, 1978). Process structure may be global to the meeting, such as developing and following a strategy/agenda to perform the task, thereby reducing process losses due to coordination problems. The GSS can also provide process structure internal to a specific activity (local process structure) by determining who will talk next (e.g., talk queues) or by automating a formal methodology such as NGT. Different forms of local process structure will affect different process gains and losses. For example, the first phase of NGT requires individuals to work separately to reduce production blocking, free riding, and cognitive inertia, while subsequent phases (idea sharing and voting) use other techniques to affect other process gains and losses. Process structure has been found to improve, impair, and have no effect on group performance (cf. Hackman & Kaplan, 1974; Hirokawa & Pace, 1983; Shaw, 1981). Its effects depend upon its fit with the situation, and thus little can be said in general.

Process Support. The GSS can provide process support in at least three ways, either separately or jointly: (1) parallel communication, (2) group memory, and (3) anonymity. With parallel communication, each member has a workstation that is connected to all other workstations, thus providing an electronic channel that enables everyone to communicate simultaneously and in parallel (Dennis et al., 1988). No one need wait for someone else to finish speaking. Process losses from air time, attenuation blocking, and concentration blocking should be significantly reduced. Free riding may be reduced as members no longer need to compete for air time. Domination may be reduced, as it becomes difficult for one member to preclude others from contributing. Electronic communication may also dampen dysfunctional socializing (E. Williams, 1977). Parallel communication increases information overload (as every member can contribute simultaneously). Process gains may be enhanced due to synergy and the use of more information. Increased interaction may also stimulate individuals and promote learning.

The GSS can provide a group memory by recording all electronic comments, which is typically done by many, but not all GSS (e.g., Siegel et al., 1986). Participants can decouple themselves from the group to pause, think, type comments, and then rejoin the "discussion" without missing anything. This should reduce failure to remember, attention blocking, and incomplete use of information and may promote synergy and more information. A group memory that enables members to queue and filter information may reduce information overload. A group memory is also useful should some members miss all or part of a meeting, or if the group is subjected to interruptions that require temporary suspension of the meeting (Mintzberg, Raisinghani, & Theoret, 1976). The GSS may also provide other forms of group memory that do not capture all comments. An electronic blackboard (Stefik et al., 1987), for example, may reduce failure to remember (by presenting a summary of key information) and dysfunctional socializing (by increasing task focus).

The electronic channel may provide some degree of anonymity. Anonymity may reduce the pressure to conform and evaluation apprehension but may also

increase free riding because it is more difficult to determine when someone is free riding (Albanese & VanFleet, 1985). However, when the group meets at the same place and time, the lack of process anonymity (i.e., members can see who is and is not contributing) as opposed to content anonymity (i.e., members cannot easily attribute specific comments to individuals) may reduce free riding (Valacich, Dennis, & Nunamaker, 1992). Anonymity may encourage members to challenge others, thereby increasing process gains by catching errors and a more objective evaluation. Anonymity may also provide a low-threat environment in which less skilled members can contribute and learn.

The use of electronic media may also introduce media effects that reflect inherent differences between verbal and electronic communication. These include media speed, media richness, depersonalization/deindividuation, and view size. Media speed refers to the fact that typing comments to send electronically is slower than speaking (which can reduce the amount of information available to the group and introduce losses), whereas reading is generally faster than listening (gains) (E. Williams, 1977). Electronic media are not as rich as face-to-face verbal communication, because they provide fewer cues and slower feedback (losses), but typically promote more careful and precisely worded communication (gains) (Daft & Lengel, 1986). Depersonalization is the separation of people from comments, which may promote deindividuation, the loss of self- and group-awareness (E. Williams, 1977). This may reduce socializing and encourage more objective evaluation and more error catching (due to less negative reaction to criticism and increased group ownership of outcomes) (gains). But reduced socializing and more uninhibited comments (e.g., "flaming") may reduce group cohesiveness and satisfaction (losses). Workstations typically provide a small screen view for members (e.g., 24-line screen), which can encourage information chunking and reduce information overload (gains). But this can also cause members to lose a global view of the task (Nunamaker, Applegate, & Konsynski, 1987, 1988), increasing losses due to incomplete use of information. Thus, there is much to be learned about how various media influence group processes and performance.

GROUP SUPPORT SYSTEM DESIGN

The initial focus of our research has been on supporting large groups that meet at the same place and time, although more recent work has studied small project teams and distributed groups meeting at the same time in different places (see Nunamaker, Dennis, George, Valacich, & Vogel, 1991a). This focus arose from our early work with a variety of organizations in which project teams of 10–20 members were typically assigned to address key issues.

What are the needs of large groups meeting at the same place and time? Research has shown that larger groups have a greater need for process structure (Shaw, 1981), particularly if members do not share the same information (Hackman & Kaplan, 1974). Large non-GSS meetings are usually less effective and less satisfying than small group meetings (Shaw, 1981), due to sharp increases in process losses as size increases (Albanese & VanFleet, 1985; Steiner, 1972). We concluded that, in general, high levels of global process structure and process support were appropriate.

Task structure and task support also depend on task characteristics. Because the groups with which we worked often faced strategic issues, we developed several tools providing task structure and support for strategic planning (e.g., stakeholder analysis), as well as general-purpose tools capable of supporting a variety of task structure and support needs. Because strategic tasks are often associated with political and highly competitive groups (Mintzberg et al., 1976), process-support components such as anonymity became important.

The general design for many GSS builds on three basic concepts: (1) a GSS meeting room; (2) meeting facilitation; and (3) a software toolkit. Although many different meeting room designs have been used, the minimum configuration provides a separate networked, hard disk–based, color graphics microcomputer workstation to each participant, with another one or two workstations serving as the meeting leader/facilitator's console. A large-screen video display is provided as an electronic blackboard, with other audio-visual support also available (e.g., white boards and overhead projectors) (Dennis et al., 1988).

Meeting Leader/Facilitator

The meeting leader/facilitator is the person who chairs the meeting. This person may be the group leader, another group member or, more commonly, a separate, neutral, individual who is not a group member. The meeting leader/facilitator serves four functions. First, this person provides technical support by initiating and terminating specific software tools and guiding the group through the technical aspects necessary to work on the task. This reduces the amount of training required of group members by removing one level of system complexity. Second, the meeting leader/facilitator chairs the meeting, maintains the agenda, and assesses the need for agenda changes. The meeting leader/facilitator may (or may not) take an active role in the meeting to improve group interaction (e.g., by providing process structure in coordinating verbal discussion). Third, the meeting leader/facilitator assists in agenda planning, by working with the group and/or group leader to highlight the principal meeting objectives and develop an agenda to accomplish them. Finally, in ongoing organizational settings where meeting leaders/facilitators are not group members, they provide organizational continuity by setting standards for use, developing training materials, maintaining the system, and acting as a champion/sponsor, which is key to successful technology transfer (Maidique, 1980).

Software Toolkit

Many GSS provide a software toolkit, similar to a DSS model base, that is a collection of generic tools for various group activities (such as idea generation and voting) rather than being one indivisible system to support the entire task (e.g., strategic planning). The key advantage provided by a toolkit is flexibility. Each tool provides a different approach to support a particular activity; thus the GSS can provide various combinations and styles of process structure, process support, task structure, and task support during any one meeting. Groups use many approaches and often do not proceed in a straightforward manner (Poole, 1983). The tools can easily be mixed and matched and combined with non-GSS activities in whatever order the group believes is most effective. This philosophy also enables new tools to be easily added to the toolkit and existing tools to be customized to specific needs.

Although flexibility is important, it is also important to restrict the number and type of functions available to participants (Silver, 1990). Restrictiveness provides a more powerful intervention so that groups are more likely to use the GSS as intended by its designers (which has been one of the problems with noncomputerized techniques) (Hackman & Kaplan, 1974; Jablin & Seibold, 1978). Restrictiveness promotes the use of more effective techniques and prevents less effective ones, fosters learning, promotes consistency, and provides coordination to ensure that all group members are using the same tool at the same time. However, it can also constrain creativity and exploration, limit the applicability of a system, promote user dissatisfaction, and be seen as manipulative, resulting in nonuse of the system. The GSS we have developed, GroupSystems™, balances these issues by being both highly flexible and highly restrictive. The system is flexible in that a wide variety of tools are available, but each tool is locally restrictive so that users can perform only certain functions. The selection of which tools will be used for a specific meeting is done during a premeeting planning meeting. During the meeting itself, the system is restrictive, so that members use only those tools determined to be the most appropriate during preplanning. Although agendas sometimes change, it is the group leader or the group as a whole who makes changes, not individual members. The purpose of many GSS tools is to provide process structure, process support, task structure, and task support for group interaction. Although there are many possible combinations of the process support functions (i.e., parallel communication, group memory, anonymity), GSS typically provide three distinct styles of process support that blend these functions with different amounts of electronic and verbal interaction: a chauffeured style, a supported style, and an interactive style. These three styles can be combined with each other and with non-GSS verbal discussion at different stages of any one meeting. We first describe these three styles and then consider the process gains and losses that each affects.

With a chauffeured style, only one person uses the GSS, either a group member or the meeting leader/facilitator. A workstation is connected to a public display screen, providing an electronic version of the traditional blackboard. The group verbally discusses the issues, with the electronic blackboard used as a group memory to record and structure information. A supported style is similar to a chauffeured style, but differs in that each member has a computer workstation that provides a parallel, anonymous electronic communication channel with a group memory. The meeting proceeds using a mixture of verbal and electronic interaction. The electronic blackboard is still used to present and structure information, but with each member able to add items. With an interactive style, the parallel, anonymous electronic communication channel with a group memory is used for almost all group communication. Virtually no one speaks. Although an electronic blackboard may be provided, the group memory is typically too large to fit on a screen; thus it is maintained so that all members can access it electronically at their workstations.

The interactive style is the strongest intervention (but not necessarily the "best") because it provides parallel communication, group memory, and anonymity to reduce process losses due to air time, attenuation blocking, concentration blocking, attention blocking, failure to remember, socializing, domination, interruptions, evaluation apprehension, and conformance pressure. Information overload may increase, and free riding may be reduced or increased. Process gains may be increased due to more information, synergy, catching errors, stimulation, and learning. Media effects increase and decrease process gains and losses as noted previously.

The weakest intervention is the chauffeured style (but not necessarily the "worst"), for which the GSS does not provide a new communication channel, but rather addresses failure to remember by providing focus through a common group memory displayed on the electronic blackboard. An increased task focus promoted by this style may also reduce socializing. Few other process gains or losses are affected.

Between these two styles is the supported style. When verbal interaction is used, the effects are similar to a chauffeured style; when electronic interaction is used, the effects are similar to an interactive style. Nevertheless, there are several important differences. First, although anonymity is possible with electronic communication, its effects on evaluation apprehension and conformance pressure are substantially reduced with the supported style because nonanonymous verbal communication occurs. Second, attention blocking (and possibly failure to remember and information overload) will be increased beyond that of a traditional meeting (or an interactive style) because members must simultaneously monitor and use both verbal and electronic communication channels. Third, process losses due to media speed, media richness, and depersonalization will likely be less than with the interactive style, because members can switch media as needed (e.g., if media richness proves to be a problem when using the electronic channel, members can switch to verbal interaction).

GROUP SUPPORT SYSTEMS IN PRACTICE

In this section, we discuss our empirical research, which has included both laboratory and field research, because we believe that both are important in understanding the effect of GSS and in identifying the GSS features needed for various tasks, groups, and organizations (Dennis, Nunamaker, & Vogel, 1990–1991). In general, our research has shown the use of GSS to improve meeting effectiveness (e.g., decision quality), but not in all cases. Laboratory experiments with small groups comparing GSS groups to non-GSS groups have found those using GSS to be more effective (A. C. Easton, Vogel, & Nunamaker, 1989) or have found no differences in effectiveness (George et al., 1989). Participants in field studies (Dennis, Heminger, Nunamaker, & Vogel, 1990a, Dennis, Tyran, Vogel, & Nunamaker, 1990; Dennis, Nunamaker & Paranka, 1991; Grohowski et al., 1990; Nunamaker, Applegate, & Konsyuski, 1987; Nunamaker, Vogel, Heminger, et al., 1989; Valacich, Dennis, & Nunamaker, 1991; Vogel, et al., 1989–1990) with larger groups have reported that GSS use produced more effective outcomes as compared to previous non-GSS meetings.

Effects on efficiency, the time required to complete the task, have also been mixed. Laboratory experiments with small groups have found GSS groups to take longer than non-GSS groups to reach consensus (A. C. Easton et al., 1989; George et al., 1989). However, participants in field studies (see Nunamaker, Dennis, George, et al., 1991; Nunamaker, Dennis, Valacich, & Vogel, 1991 for reviews) with large groups have reported that GSS use resulted in significant time savings. For example, after a three-day session strategic planning session with 31 managers from all parts of the firm, Frank Meyers, Senior Vice-President of Burr-Brown (Dennis, Heminger, Nunamaker, & Vogel, 1990), noted that "The process allowed us to do in three days what would have taken months to do."

Effects on satisfaction have been somewhat more consistent. One laboratory experiment with small groups found higher satisfaction with GSS support than with no support (A. C. Easton et al., 1989), whereas another found no differences between supported and nonsupported groups (George et al., 1989). Participants in field and case studies with larger groups have consistently reported GSS meetings to be more satisfying than non-GSS meetings (see Nunamaker, Dennis, George, et al., 1991a; Nunamaker, Dennis, Valacich, & Vogel, 1991).

The sections below consider how task structure, task support, process structure, and process support have influenced meeting outcomes.

Task Structure

A laboratory experiment found that small groups using the highly task-structured Stakeholder Identification and Assumption Surfacing tool (SIAS) had better quality outcomes than non-GSS groups (Easton et al., 1989). There was no difference between SIAS-supported groups and nonsupported groups using a manual process providing the same task structure, which suggests that the major contribution of the GSS was task structure. Participants in field studies have also reported that task structure was an important part of the value added by the GSS (Dennis, Tyran, Vogel, & Nunamaker, 1990). For example, task structure was central to knowledge acquisition within IBM during the construction of an expert system.

We conclude that enabling groups to apply a specific task structure can be a significant contribution of GSS, but, like the application of DSS technology, is highly task dependent. In general, more complex tasks can benefit more from task structure than less complex tasks. One conclusion from our experience is that the best approach to providing task support and structure is to provide general tools that can accommodate a variety of task-specific features. In contrast, tools that provide one specific form of task structure (such as SIAS), have received far less use than their more general counterparts.

Task Support

Although task support is not a regular part of most laboratory studies, one experiment examining task support noted that subjects first reviewed comments made earlier in the meeting and then moved to examine supporting information (Vogel, 1988). The examination of this supporting information tended to move from the most "objective" information (e.g., demographics) to progressively more "messy" or subjective information (e.g., opinions).

Task support has been a common component of meetings within IBM (Nunamaker, Vogel, Heminger, et al., 1989). Task support tools have enabled participants to review information brought into the meeting, as well as information generated previously in the meeting. "It is also an advantage to be able to bring data from outside the session. In one session, we brought in data from two other meetings and this moved the meeting right along." (IBM staff member) (Nunamaker, Vogel, Heminger, et al., 1989a). In contrast, only a few groups that we have studied have included task support (e.g., the county government). In another case, Burr Brown used task support for a multiday strategic planning session, in which divisional plans, product forecasts, and competitive strategies of rivals were provided (Dennis, Heminger, Nunamaker, & Vogel, 1990).

We conclude that task support can play an important role but depends upon the needs of the task and group. Task support may be more important to ongoing series of meetings (rather than single meetings) or more complex tasks, but the evidence is by no means conclusive.

Process Structure

A laboratory experiment studying small groups found no difference in decision quality or member satisfaction between a globally structured process and an unstructured process (George et al., 1989). However, the value of global structure for larger groups has been demonstrated in numerous field studies. Presession planning has been cited by participants as important contributions of the GSS (Dennis, Heminger, Nunamaker, & Vogel, 1990; Nunamaker et al., 1987, 1988; Nunamaker, Vogel, Heminger, et al., 1989; Nunamaker, Vogel, & Konsynski, 1989). By initially developing objectives and then building and maintaining an agenda to accomplish them, leaders felt that meetings were more successful, whereas members valued the improved clarity of their roles (i.e., information provision versus decision making). We conclude that global process structure is useful for large groups facing complex tasks, but may not have much effect on small groups or groups performing well-defined tasks.

The effects of local process structure internal to one activity were examined in a laboratory experiment comparing small groups using the Electronic Brainstorming (EBS) tool to those using the Electronic Discussion System (EDS) (G.K. Easton et al., 1990). Both tools used interactive meeting processes (no verbal communication), but EBS structured the meeting process by dividing participants' comments into several discussions, in an attempt to reduce cognitive inertia. In contrast, EDS placed all comments into one discussion. Consistent with the hypothesis that this addition process structure reduces cognitive inertia, groups using EBS generated more alternatives. However, they also produced lower-quality decisions. Groups studied in the field have had mixed opinions of EBS's approach to reducing cognitive inertia: some have perceived it to be helpful, whereas others disliked the structure (Dennis, Heminger, Nunamaker, & Vogel, 1990; Nunamaker et al., 1987).

The value of local process structure was also demonstrated in a meeting of a 17-member strategic planning committee of an extremely diverse industry association. In a two-day non-GSS meeting held the previous year, this committee had developed a mission statement that was rejected by the association's board as being too narrow for all members of the association. As part of the GSS strategic planning cycle, the committee developed a mission statement in less than two hours that was subsequently accepted by the board. The process structure imposed by the GSS ensured that every member of the planning committee participated in the development of the statement. Thus all potential objections to the mission statement were voiced and addressed in committee before the statement was submitted to the board.

We conclude that high levels of process structure that are internal to specific activities may be important in some cases but are contingent on specific tasks, groups, and organizations, which underscores the need for prior meeting planning and global process structure. The approach taken by EBS to reducing cognitive inertia appears to be successful for alternative and idea generation, but the reduced feedback, focus, and media richness impair the ability to debate issues in arriving at a decision. Thus it is useful for exploration activities but not for subsequent activities such as idea organization and consensus building.

Although some GSS have been designed without meeting leader/facilitators, we have found that a meeting leader/facilitator can play an important role in improving meeting processes and outcomes (Dennis, Heminger, Nunamaker, & Vogel, 1990, Dennis, Nunamaker, & Paranka, 1991; Dennis, Tyran, Vogel, & Nunamaker, 1990; Nunamaker et al., 1987, 1988; Nunamaker, Vogel, & Konsyuski, 1989). The issue is the same as that of process structure, process support, and so on—matching the meeting leader/facilitator's role to the group and task. The meeting leader/facilitator can be active or passive in providing technical, group dynamics, planning, and organizational support. Different groups performing different tasks will have different needs. But we anticipate that the need for planning support will continue to grow as more GSS with different capabilities become available and as more contingencies for effective use of GSS are identified.

Process Support

There are many contingencies to be considered in fitting the type of process support (chauffeured, supported, or interactive) to specific situations. The issue is one of balancing the need for reductions in some process losses against increases in others. For example, in some cases, process losses from evaluation apprehension may be such that an anonymous interactive process is required, whereas in other cases the task may require a very rich media, thus process losses from using an interactive process (with its lower media richness) would increase substantially making it inappropriate. In this section, we discuss three general contingencies: group size, task information, and anonymity. This discussion has at least three limitations: (1) there are many contingencies beyond these three that need to be studied; (2) our conclusions are only tentative, because research in this area is at an early stage; and (3) although the contingencies are discussed separately, they are highly interrelated.

Group Size. In general without GSS, process losses increase rapidly with group size (Steiner, 1972). Previous non-GSS research has concluded that in general, regardless of the task, context, or group, the "optimal" group size is quite small, typically three to five members (Shaw, 1981), because process losses quickly overtake any process gains from increased group size. Our GSS research draws a different conclusion: the "optimal" group size depends upon the situation (group, task, context, or GSS), and in some cases may be quite large.

In theory, each of the three GSS styles (chauffeured, supported, and interactive) can reduce or increase process losses in varying degrees. A chauffeured style reduces a few process losses. Thus, compared to traditional non-GSS meetings, process losses do not increase quite as fast with group size (see Figure 7.3). A supported style introduces more fixed process losses initially (e.g., media speed), but reduces the rate at which losses increase with group size. An interactive style addresses most losses (and thus they should increase very slowly with size) but introduces more losses initially. Thus, we hypothesize that interactive styles will be preferred for larger groups and supported or chauffeured styles for smaller groups.

There is some empirical evidence to support these hypotheses. One measure of process losses is participation, because it is directly affected by air time, production blocking, free riding, and so on. A laboratory experiment with small groups found that participation was the same between groups using a chauffeured style and nonsupported groups (A. C. Easton et al., 1989), suggesting few differences between the two styles. Another experiment found participation to be more equal in groups using an interactive style than in nonsupported groups, suggesting differences between the two (George et al., 1989). Experiments studying interactive styles have found per-person participation levels to remain constant regardless of the size of the group (Dennis, Valacich, & Nunamaker, 1990; Valacich, 1989; Valacich, Dennis, & Nunamaker, 1992), suggesting that process losses may remain relatively constant as size increases. Other experiments have found outcome measures such as effectiveness and member

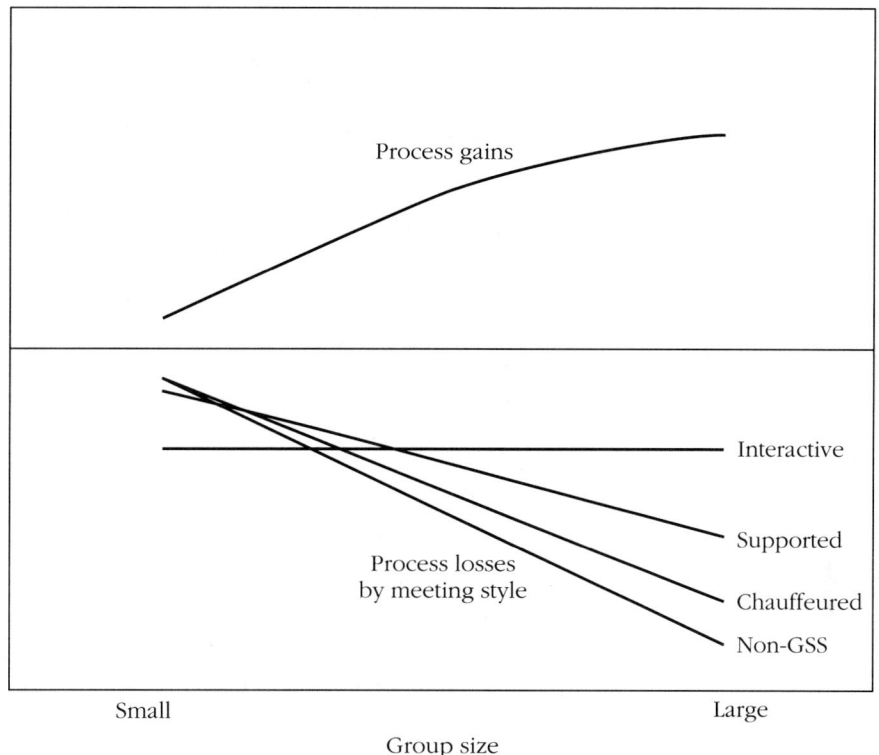

FIGURE 7.3 Process gains and losses.

satisfaction to increase with size for interactive styles (Dennis, Valacich, & Nunamaker 1990; Dennis, Valacich, & Nunamaker, 1991b; Valacich, Dennis, & Connolly, 1992). Another laboratory experiment built, tested, and confirmed a model of group performance that proposed process losses from interactive styles to be relatively constant across group size (Valacich & Dennis, 1992). Our field studies also provide some support for these hypotheses. Participants in studies with larger groups (i.e., 12–20 group members) have reported that interactive styles were more effective than supported styles (Nunamaker et al., 1989).

Task Information. The type of activities that must be performed to accomplish the task (e.g., idea generation) (Shaw, 1981) has a significant effect on the balance of gains and losses. One primary goal of most group activities is the exchange of information among members (DeSanctis & Gallupe, 1987), and thus the form of this information will have significant effects. Zack and McKenney (1989) contrast three general states of information (cf. Daft & Lengel, 1986). Ambiguity exists when there is both a lack of information and a lack of a framework for interpreting that information. Uncertainty exists when a framework exists but there is a lack of information. Equivocality exists when there are multiple (and possibly conflicting) interpretations for the information or the framework.

Equivocality requires negotiation among group members to converge to consensus on one interpretation, and media providing higher information richness are preferred (Connolly et al., 1990). In contrast, ambiguity and uncertainty require someone in the group (or the group as a whole) to provide, locate, or create the needed information or framework components. Thus the degree of media richness is unimportant; the ability of the group to rapidly gather information and framework components becomes paramount, especially if members of the group have different information, perceptions, and viewpoints.

Exploration and idea generation are more often problems of ambiguity or uncertainty than of equivocality. There are divergent activities, because members work individually to report information, propose elements of the framework, and respond to the comments of others. Prioritizing is also a divergent activity, because members work individually. In contrast, synthesizing and organizing ideas, building consensus on a framework, or interpreting the meaning of vote to achieve consensus are primarily problems of equivocality, because the group focuses on the same issues at the same time to resolve different viewpoints to converge on one interpretation.

Therefore, for divergent activities that are problems of uncertainty (such as idea generation), we hypothesize that an interactive style is more appropriate, because its parallelism and anonymity facilitate rapid development of ideas. For convergent tasks that are problems of equivocality (such as synthesis and consensus building), process losses from reduced media richness in the interactive style increase dramatically. In this case, the relatively horizontal line for the interactive style in Figure 7.3 would move beyond the lines for supported and/or chauffeured styles for most group sizes, making them more appropriate.

Our laboratory and field research provide weak support for this hypothesis. A laboratory experiment of idea generation (a task of uncertainty), found groups using an interactive style to generate more ideas and be more satisfied than verbally interacting groups (Gallupe et al., 1990). A similar study using GroupSystems™ at Indiana University had similar findings (Fellers, 1989). Experiments using purely interactive styles for generate-and-choose-tasks (tasks which begin with ambiguity but evolve into equivocality) have found no performance or satisfaction differences compared to verbally interacting groups (George et al., 1989; Winniford, 1989). The GSS groups in one of these studies also required longer to reach consensus (George et al., 1989). Groups in our field studies have typically used interactive styles to generate ideas, options, and analysis framework components but used supported or chauffeured style to resolve equivocality.

Anonymity. Anonymity is possible in interactive styles and in the electronic component of supported styles, but not with the verbal component of supported and chauffeured styles. Anonymity can affect GSS use by reducing or eliminating evaluation apprehension and conformance pressure, as well as social cues. The reduction of evaluation apprehension and conformance pressure may encourage a more open, honest, and free-wheeling discussion of key issues. However, the reduction of social cues can lead individuals to behave in ways that are outside of the realms of socially prescribed behavior. Some evidence of the deindividuation associated with the reduction of social cues has been found in some forms of computer-mediated communication, the most extreme form of which is "flaming" (cf. Siegel et al., 1986).

Changes in evaluation apprehension, conformance pressure, and social cues brought about through anonymous communication should have some effect on the meeting process, which should in turn affect the meeting's outcomes. The relaxation of social cues in anonymous GSS groups has been found in varying degrees in five laboratory experiments. Groups using anonymous GSS have been found to generate more critical comments than groups using GSS where the author of each comment was identified (Connolly et al., 1990; Jessup, Connolly, & Galegher, 1990; Valacich, Dennis, & Nunamaker, 1992). Jessup and Tansik (1991) also found that anonymous, nonproximate groups generated the most critical comments. However, only one of five experiments found anonymous groups to have increased performance compared to nonanonymous groups (Connolly et al., 1990); there were no performance differences in the other studies (George et al., 1989; Jessup et al., 1990; Jessup & Tansik, 1991; Valacich, Dennis, & Nunamaker, 1992).

Participants in field studies have usually reported that anonymity was important, particularly in cases where there were power and status differences in the group (e.g., more than two management levels present) (see Nunamaker, Dennis, George, et al., 1991). We infer that student groups in the laboratory have lower evaluation apprehension and conformance pressure, and thus although anonymity may reduce these process losses, there are fewer noticeable effects on outcomes. In situations in which evaluation apprehension and conformance pressure are high, anonymity appears to have a more significant effect on meeting outcomes.

- "People don't hesitate to voice what may be 'oddball' comments." S.L. Eichenfeld, CEO, Greyhound Financial Corporation
- "People are more willing to involve themselves in the system...because you don't have the nervousness involved in speaking to a group." manager, Hughes Aircraft
- "The anonymous and objective ranking allowed opinion to be expressed with no political ramifications." executive assistant, natural resources company

Laboratory studies of the depersonalizing and deindividuating effects of anonymity have shown anonymous groups to be more critical than nonanonymous groups (Connolly et al., 1990; Valacich, Dennis, & Nunamaker, 1992). However, evidence from the field suggests that although anonymity may temporarily increase criticalness or "flaming," the fire usually doesn't spread very far. There are some positive effects from depersonalization as well, such as the fact that it encourages more objective evaluation (Connolly et al., 1990; Nunamaker et al., 1987). Comments™ are more likely to be evaluated on their merits rather than on the power or status of their contributors. Participants have also reported that depersonalization affected the way criticism was received; criticism was seen as directed at the idea, not its contributor:

- "I wasn't as uncomfortable when I saw someone being critical of someone else's idea, because I thought 'nobody's being embarrassed here at all.' " manager, Hughes Aircraft
- "I noticed that if someone criticized an idea of mine, I didn't get emotional about it. I guess when you are face-to-face and everyone hears the boss say 'You are wrong' it's a slap to you, not necessarily the idea.... no one knows whose idea it is, so why be insulted? No one is picking on me. I think I'll just see why they don't agree with me." manager, Hughes Aircraft

Anonymity, however, is not always appreciated or warranted. One can easily envision situations in which the participants would be reluctant to suggest ideas without being recognized as the author. The tradeoff appears to be whether the ability to freely express one's opinions is more important than the desire for recognition. Anonymity may be less important for student groups performing tasks in the laboratory where evaluation apprehension and conformance pressure are low, but may be important for work groups in organizations where evaluation apprehension and conformance pressure are high—for example groups with large status and power differences among members or where there is a strong political overtone to the task.

Other Process Losses. Although much has been written about the refusal of managers, particularly senior managers, to type information into computers, we have not found this to be an issue. In the tens of thousands of person-hours that this system has been used, there have only been three instances in which participants were unable or unwilling to type for themselves. Information overload, however, has been an issue. Groups often generate a large volume of information during the idea-generation stages of a meeting. This is typically not a problem until the group attempts to synthesize the various pieces of information. The volume of information, combined with the use of a supported meeting process (as this stage requires equivocality reduction) using both verbal and electronic channels, can produce significant information overload: "It caused a real overload. But too much information is better than too little, like in a traditional group. So I'd say it was better." (manager, Hughes Aircraft). Although we have attempted to address this issue in several ways (e.g., adding keywords to ideas as they are generated to simplify synthesis), it remains a concern.

CONCLUSION

Our GSS research program has included both developmental and empirical research. Our developmental research has produced more than two dozen software tools currently in use at more than seventy GSS facilities worldwide. Our empirical research has studied GSS use in the laboratory and in the field by more than thirty-thousand individuals from more than two hundred organizations. In this paper, we have discussed several key aspects in the theoretical foundation of GSS, have illustrated how these aspects are reflected in the facility and software designs, and have highlighted the contingent nature of GSS effects. Nonetheless, much more research is needed to develop new group work methods embodied in facilities and software and to empirically test the many contingencies involved in their use.

While still recognizing the need for future research, we are convinced that the use of GSS technology can significantly improve group processes and outcomes in many cases—but effects are contingent on the situation. For example, we would expect fewer benefits from GSS use for small cohesive groups in supportive contexts, because they face fewer process losses. Based on the theoretical foundation of process gains and losses and our observations of GSS use in the field and the laboratory, we believe that GSS use may provide benefits because of the following:

- Parallel communication promotes broader input into the meeting process and reduces the chance that a few people dominate the meeting.
- Anonymity mitigates evaluation apprehension and conformance pressure, so that issues are discussed more candidly.
- Group memory enables members to pause and reflect on information and opinions of others during the meeting and serves as a permanent record of what occurred.
- Process structure helps focus the group on key issues and discourages irrelevant digressions and unproductive behaviors.
- Task support and structure provide information and approaches to analyze it.

The study of GSS is still in its infancy. It is reminiscent of the early days of the automotive industry when a motor was put into a carriage giving the world a "horseless carriage." We are now in the "horseless carriage" phase of GSS, having installed computers into existing manual processes. We need to learn how best to support groups and group meeting processes, and to build on these experiences in order to create systems that take better advantage of the abilities of technology and of groups. We may discover that many current GSS components (e.g., a facilitator) are the buggy whips of this horseless carriage phase. We are only beginning to discover what functions are robust and valuable, from which will emerge the next generation of GSS. Nonetheless, based upon our research and experiences to date, we are convinced that this technology is fundamentally changing the nature of group work.

CHAPTER 8

Group Facilitation and Group Support Systems

Robert P. Bostrom
University of Georgia

Robert Anson
Boise State University

Vikki K. Clawson
Walden University

INTRODUCTION

Numerous studies have documented widespread dissatisfaction with the process and outcomes of group meetings (e.g., Mosvick & Nelson, 1987). In an effort to improve meetings, Group Support Systems (GSS) have been developed and have become commercially available in the last three years. The field research evidence on the effectiveness of these commercial systems has been very positive. For example, IBM has documented, through a cumulative comparison of person-hours expended, a 56 percent savings attributable to GSS use (Grohowski et al., 1990). However, it is unlikely that a GSS, in and of itself, is sufficient to turn meetings into satisfying, productive events. McGoff and Ambrose (1991), describing IBM's application of GSS to over 900 group sessions, note that,

> although the technology has matured to the point where it is very easy to use by almost anyone, our experience continues to confirm that the quality of the group session is predominantly dependent on the facilitator. (p. 807)

The implication is clear: The success of a GSS supported meeting is not a given, but depends on how the GSS is applied! There is still much to be learned about how to best apply a GSS. A significant question is how to effectively plan, coordinate, and direct—to "facilitate"—the work of group members who are using a GSS. The technology itself provides some facilitation, such as the activity structuring provided through a particular software tool. Nevertheless, GSS must be used appropriately to take advantage of these capabilities. In addition, the GSS does not address other areas of group functioning, such as meeting design or managing verbal communications. These and other facilitation activities must come from people. An integration of good computer tools with effective human facilitation can lead to a more effective meeting than either by itself.

Facilitation is viewed as a set of functions or activities carried out before, during, and after a meeting to help the group achieve its own outcomes. The essential characteristic of facilitation is to help make an outcome easier to achieve. Facilitative functions may be accomplished by group members or leaders or by an external facilitation specialist. Although one person usually has the formal responsibility of being the primary facilitator for a particular meeting, facilitation must be shared by all attendees. (Throughout this chapter, we use the term facilitator to designate this primary facilitator.) All other participants and the GSS are viewed as secondary facilitators.

One cannot understand or manage GSS sessions without focusing on facilitation. One of our basic assumptions is that the facilitator shapes and guides the meeting process and the use of the GSS, rather than the GSS driving the process. The GSS is basically a set of tools that is used by the facilitator and the group to accomplish meeting outcomes. Facilitation, on the other hand, is a dynamic process that involves managing relationships between people, tasks, and technology, as well as structuring tasks and contributing to the effective accomplishment of the meeting's outcomes. The purpose of this chapter is to provide a solid foundation for those interested in understanding and studying facilitation in a GSS environment. This foundation is provided by accomplishing the following:

- By providing a framework for researching and understanding facilitation in GSS environments
- By summarizing relevant facilitation research in both GSS and non-GSS settings
- By addressing relevant issues that have been raised in this area (e.g., need for facilitator, training, etc.)
- By suggesting directions for future research in this area

The chapter begins with the development of a conceptual model of a meeting including the role of facilitation and GSS within it. This is followed by a summary of prior research in the area. Next, a general meeting facilitation framework is presented. Finally, future research directions are outlined through a discussion of key GSS facilitation issues.

MEETING MODEL

What Is a Meeting?

We view a meeting as a goal- or outcome-directed interaction between two or more people (teams, groups) that can take place in any of four environments (same time/same place, same time/different place, different time/same place, and different time/different place). Each of these environments creates different conditions that affect GSS design and usage and facilitative interventions. Most GSS facilitation research and discussion has focused on face-to-face environments (same time/same place).

Our model of a meeting, presented in Figure 8.1, is outcome-focused. It depicts a meeting as a sociotechnical systems change process. In other words,

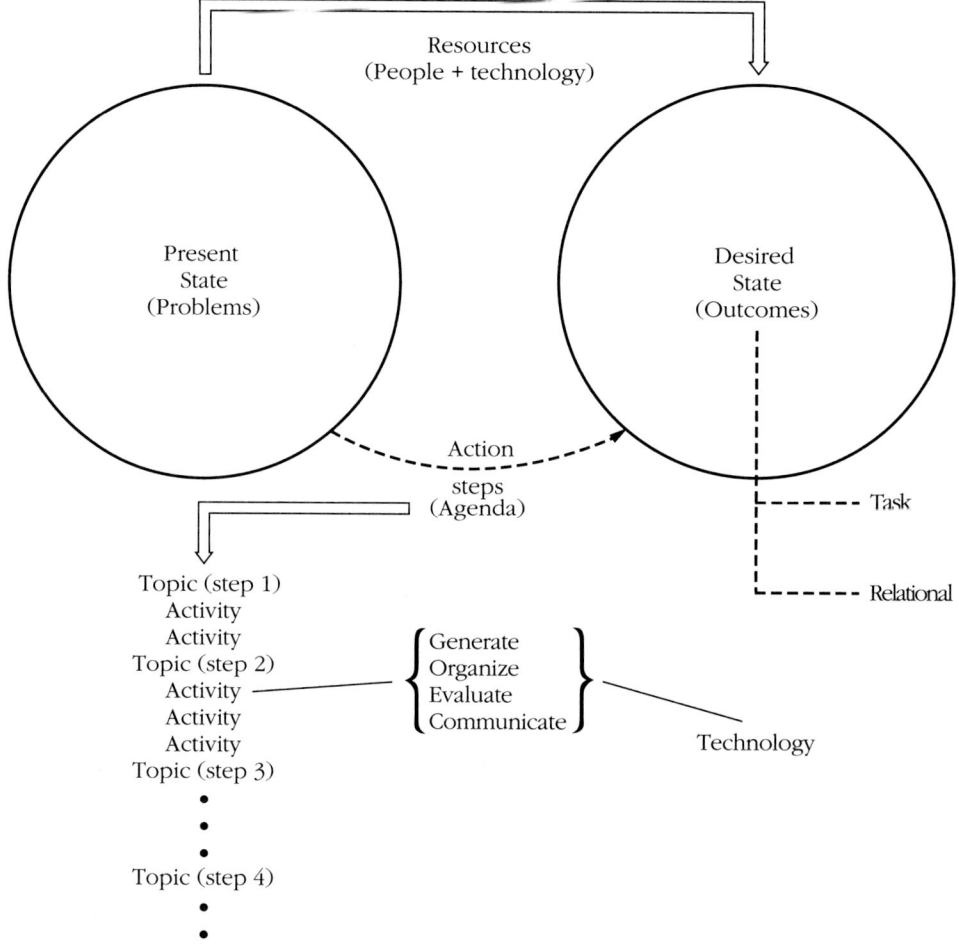

FIGURE 8.1 Goal/outcome-directed meeting.

a meeting is an interaction that utilizes a set of resources (people, technology) to transform the group's present problem state into its desired future state (accomplishing specific meeting outcomes) through a series of action steps (agenda).

Action steps can be described in terms of a core set of generic activities. That is, an agenda or agenda topic can be broken down into a number of basic information-processing activities used to accomplish that agenda or topic (see Figure 8.1). For example, to accomplish a particular topic, a group might *generate* information; *organize* the information into alternatives; *evaluate and select* alternatives; and discuss (*communicate*) their actions. These generic activities can be used to describe an agenda for any meeting task. GSS tools and other meeting technology can also be classified in terms of the activities they support, for example, generate. Thus, the facilitator can use this classification framework to help select appropriate GSS tools and other meeting techniques to be used in the meeting. (Bostrom & Anson, 1988, 1991)

Our meeting model (Figure 8.1) also depicts two general types of meeting outcomes that a facilitator helps a group accomplish: task and relational. From a task outcome perspective, a meeting brings together a set of resources (primarily people) to accomplish a task. The task provides the "content" or "what people will be interacting about" in the meeting. There are many tasks that can be accomplished in a meeting: creating a strategic plan, solving a problem, making a decision, sharing information, resolving a dispute, negotiating a contract, and so on. This fact has led some authors to develop task- (McGrath, 1984) and meeting-type taxonomies (Mosvick & Nelson, 1987).

Thus, a set of specific task outcomes is developed for a meeting. Individuals, often with very different perspectives or frames of reference about the task, are then invited to the meeting to accomplish these outcomes. From a task perspective, the meeting is used to integrate these various individual perspectives into a group frame or perspective that best represents the groups' shared understanding of the task situation and the meeting outcomes.

From a relational outcome perspective, a meeting is a relationship between people. This relationship can be broken into four subrelationships, based primarily on how participants feel about or react to certain aspects of the meeting. The first of these aspects concerns the content of interactions (*the task*). Each participant has various ways of reacting to actual products, that is, the plans, decisions, and so on, being created. The second aspect concerns the feelings that group members have toward each other (*interpersonal*); these feelings are often reflected in the amount of rapport, openness, trust, and cohesiveness in the group. The third aspect concerns the interactions going on (*process*), for example, how participants react to the agenda, activites, and GSS. The last aspect concerns how participants react to themselves and their contributors (*self*). How a person reacts to himself or herself can affect that person's self-esteem or self-efficacy and can produce certain feelings.

Each of these subrelationships (task, interpersonal, process, and self) provides a source of emotions in a meeting, and, in return, the feelings created in a meeting will influence the development and quality of these relationships. The maintenance of positive relationship in areas 1 and 2 is usually referred to as a maintenance outcome in organizational behavioral literature. We will use the term *relational* to denote outcomes in all four areas. Affect or emotions are temporary phenomena that are brought into meetings, where they are created, reinforced, or altered, and this in turn leads to more permanent or longer-term effects/relationships. Relationships are characterized by a variety of constructs such as cohesiveness, satisfaction, rapport, commitment, acceptance, comfort, and self-esteem. These relationships are obviously interrelated, (e.g., an atmosphere of interpersonal respect is conducive to positive self-esteem). Relationships also affect the achievement of task outcomes (e.g., positive self-esteem is conducive to members contributing ideas and getting involved in discussions).

The relational outcome of a meeting is to create and maintain positive emotions that will lead to constructive relationships that promote working together effectively. Thus, in an effective meeting, negative affect is not avoided but instead refocused in a positive direction. In fact, many facilitators comment that no affect (i.e., no energy) is their biggest problem.

Practicing facilitators in both GSS (e.g., L. D. Phillips & Phillips, 1990; Bostrom, et al., 1991) and non-GSS environments (e.g., Kayser, 1990; Doyle and Straus, 1976) emphasize the importance of positive affect and relationships. However, little GSS research has focused on relational outcomes especially at the affect or emotional level. O'Reilly (1991) makes a similar comment about the organizational behavior field in general. Given the importance of relational outcomes, more GSS research is needed in this area.

In most meetings, there is some combination of both task and relational outcomes to achieve. Even in cases in which task outcomes are strongly emphasized, good relationships need to be developed and maintained in order for the group to work effectively (Chidambaram et al., 1990–91; Johansen et al., 1990–1991). In other cases, the group development outcome is paramount, regardless of whether or not task outcomes are present.

Facilitation Activities by Meeting Stage

Meetings rarely die—they just keep rolling along in a cycle of premeeting, meeting, and postmeeting activities (Oppenheim, 1987). The actual meeting is but one phase of a three-phase cycle of activities that constitute a meeting (see Figure 8.2). One cycle of activity frequently sets the scene for the next cycle. What happens in the meeting phase is strongly influenced by premeeting activities, which in turn is affected by postmeeting activities of the previous meeting. These phases provide a useful means of categorizing important facilitation-related activities (Bostrom, 1989; Mosvick & Nelson, 1987; Wagner & Nagasunderam, 1988). Each phase is reviewed below.

It is important to design or plan the meeting before it convenes. The facilitator works with the group leader and/or members to develop a meeting design. An effective design focuses first on formulating the problems and outcomes to be addressed and developing an appropriate meeting agenda of the topic and activities to be undertaken (Bostrom, 1989). Next, the facilitator will select the appropriate technology (techniques, GSS tools, etc.) to carry out each activity (Bostrom & Anson, 1991). Once the outcomes and agenda are established, meeting participants can be selected and informed about any meeting preparation. Participants' roles (facilitator, decision makers, etc.) and meeting ground rules (e.g., no attack rule) need to be established. Although critical to the success of the meeting, this premeeting stage is often neglected or underemphasized in practice (e.g., Mosvick & Nelson, 1987). In fact, one of the biggest benefits of the introduction of GSS is that it forces people to pay careful attention to meeting design (Watson et al., 1991).

Both task and relational outcomes must be accomplished during the meeting. A meeting is usually divided into the three phases shown in Figure 8.2: open (setup), during (agenda), close (wrap-up) (Bostrom, 1989). During setup, the facilitator must clarify and get agreement on outcomes, make clear roles and rules, and establish a positive group affect. During the meeting, the primary responsibility of the facilitator is to help the group adapt and execute the agenda to accomplish the task outcomes (e.g., develop an action plan). The facilitator must also ensure that positive affect and constructive relationships are developed and maintained. Poor relations, that is, negative affect, can impede task-related work both during and after the meeting. Good relations, that is, pos-

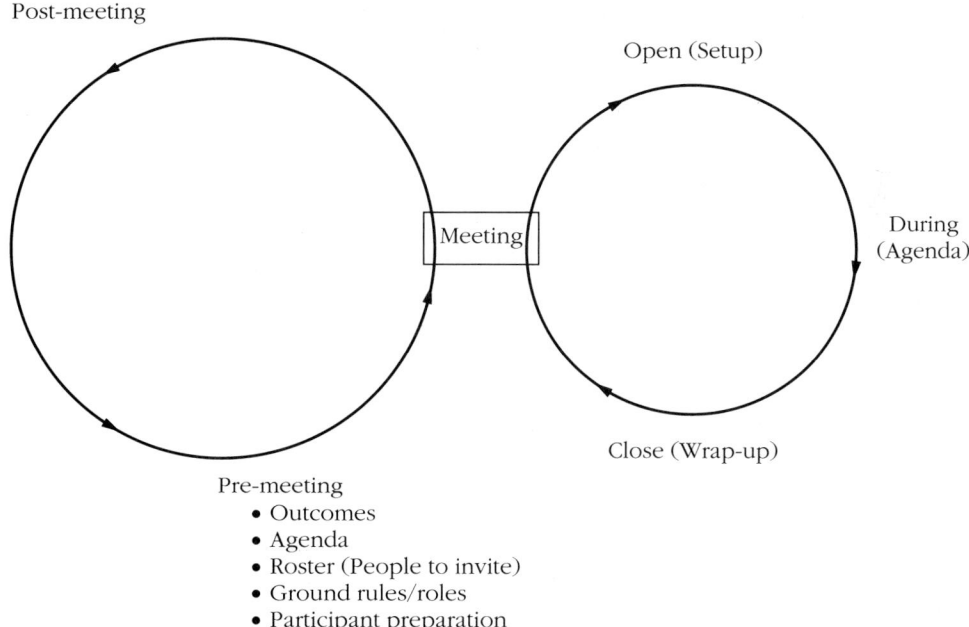

FIGURE 8.2 Meeting cycle model.

itive affect, can create a resourceful, synergistic atmosphere to accomplish the task, and to maintain group cohesion and high energy level after the meeting. During closing, facilitators usually summarize the meeting, detailing each point that requires future action (who will do what and by when, remind people of agreements, etc.).

After the meeting, the immediate dissemination of results reinforces the agreements made and maintains momentum into implementation (Mosvick & Nelson, 1987). Monitoring implementation is generally left to those responsible. The role of the facilitator, especially if he or she is not a member of the group, is minimal in this postmeeting stage. The facilitator may, however, be asked to evaluate the meeting and to suggest changes for future meetings.

REVIEW OF PRIOR RESEARCH LITERATURE

This section overviews research relevant to facilitation in GSS environments. It focuses on research from business (organizational behavior, etc.) and information systems disciplines. A recent review of psychology, social psychology, and communication literatures revealed a general scarcity of research addressing ways that group performance can be enhanced through facilitation (Hirokawa & Gouran, 1989). Our review leads to the same conclusion, especially concerning research on facilitation in GSS environments. Because organizations continue to rely extensively on groups and meetings to carry out important tasks, this lack of theoretically sound and empirically valid prescriptions for facilitating meetings is disconcerting.

In general, past research has had two major focuses. The first is descriptive, documenting problems occurring in meetings. The second focus is developing and testing structured procedures for overcoming these problems and improving meeting outcomes. The facilitation and GSS research areas are part of this latter focus.

Meeting Research

After a review of the many surveys and experimental research reports on meetings, two glaring conclusions can be made. First, meetings consume a great deal of time and effort in organizations. The prevalence of meetings makes the second conclusion all the more alarming. Most meetings are perceived to be extremely unproductive in terms of efficiently utilizing the participants' time and effectively achieving the meeting objectives.

This literature identifies a variety of problems that lead to unproductive meetings. The major problem areas are listed below (Hirokawa, 1987; Hirokawa & Pace, 1983; Monge, 1989; Mosvick & Nelson, 1987; Oppenheim, 1987; Tobia & Becker, 1990; Weinberg, 1981):

- *Poor meeting design*: The meeting lacks goals and an agenda; it is disorganized; participants are inadequately prepared for the meeting; the people

selected to participate are not appropriate choices, given the topic and agenda of the meeting; and so on.
- *Poor focus*: Participants wander off the subject; discuss irrelevant or redundant information; and so on.
- *Lack of closure*: The meeting is too lengthy; it is inconclusive; it lacks published results; and so on.
- *Poor process*: Participants do not rigorously examine or challenge opinions and assumptions; there is only a superficial discussion of the alternatives; influential members inhibit the group; and so on.

These problems occur frequently because effective guidelines or procedures are not used. The major reasons effective procedures are not used appear to be insufficient training, inexperience (Tobia & Becker, 1990), and resistance to change (Poole, 1991).

Group Dynamics/Process Interventions Research

A variety of group dynamics interventions using procedural structures to counter the meeting problems discussed above have been investigated. For example, brainstorming (Osborn, 1957) and nominal group technique (Van de Ven & Delbecq, 1974) are two popular and effective procedural structures; the Consensus Approach (J. Hall & Watson, 1970) includes fairly general guidelines and has been found to be effective; the developmental discussion technique (N. Maier & Maier, 1957; Maier & Hoffman, 1960; Miner, 1979; White et al., 1980) is an effective approach that has been studied extensively in experimental research.

Table 8.1 displays supporting research for four general intervention characteristics that appear to have the broadest positive impact on both task performance and relationships. These characteristics include structured procedures, encouraging effective task and relational behaviors, and training.

Reviewing these studies highlights several key points. First, applying structured procedures produces better results than normal group interaction. Second, more-structured interventions are generally found to be superior to less-structured or naturally occurring group interaction (Miner, 1979; Van de Ven & Delbecq, 1974; White et al., 1980). These are consistent findings throughout the structured intervention literature.

Third, broader interventions, which support both effective task and relational processes, tend to be superior to more narrowly focused interventions. Hackman & Kaplan (1974) assessed the effectiveness of a narrowly focused intervention and an interpersonal intervention (requiring discussion of task procedures before working; discussing the group's interpersonal processes during work breaks). In both cases, the intervention produced its intended effect but also produced negative spillover effects. For example, the task intervention led to improved task performance but also more interpersonal conflict and process

TABLE 8.1 Key Findings from Group Process Interventions Studies

Interventions That Broadly Improve Group Processes and Outcomes

1. Applying Structured Procedures
- providing instructions to group members (J. Hall & Watson, 1970)
- extending problem formulation (Volkema, 1983)
- extending idea generation (Ball & Jones, 1977)
- separating idea generation from evaluation (Van de Ven & Delbecq, 1974)
- delaying solution adoption (Hoffman, 1979)

2. Encouraging Effective Task Behaviors
- discussing task procedures (Hackman & Kaplan, 1974)
- applying explicit criteria (Hirokawa & Pace, 1983)
- using factual information (Hirokawa & Pace)
- maintaining focus on task goals (Dalkey & Halmer, 1963)

3. Encouraging Effective Relational Behaviors
- encouraging broad participation and influence (Hoffman & Maier, 1959)
- managing conflict constructively (Putman, 1986)
- emphasizing consensus acceptance over majority votes (J. Hall & Watson, 1970)
- applying active listening techniques (Bostrom, 1989)
- discussing interpersonal processes (Hackman & Kaplan, 1974)

4. Training
- training goup members and/or leaders (J. Hall & Williams, 1970)
- training external facilitators (Anson, 1990; Bostrom, 1989; Hirokawa & Gouran, 1989; N. Maier & Maier, 1957; Miner, 1979; White et al., 1980).

problems; the interpersonal intervention led to improved satisfaction with the group but poorer decisions.

Most of the studies have intervened with a structured procedure administered by an external facilitator. An intervention that is essentially scripted or fixed by a procedure is a highly restrictive and comprehensive type of facilitation. There has been far less attention paid to flexibly applied facilitation. Here facilitators are trained in a range of procedures and support techniques that they adaptively and flexibly apply during the meeting (Hirokawa & Gouran, 1989). It was found that more highly trained facilitators are more effective than facilitators with less training (Hoffman & Maier, 1959; Maier & Maier, 1957). It has also been found that meetings are more effective when group members and/or leaders are provided some facilitation training (J. Hall & Williams, 1970).

GSS Research

Group Support System (GSS) technology has been advanced as a means of making procedural structures available to the group and facilitating their use. There is ample perceptual and observational research evidence that GSS can positively alter group interaction processes (e.g., Zigurs et al., 1988). However, there is a mix of findings concerning the ultimate effects of GSS use on task and relational outcomes (See Chapter 2).

Differences between experimental and field study findings suggest that facilitation, among other factors, may be a critical factor in GSS effectiveness. This dichotomy has been discussed by various GSS researchers (e.g., Bostrom & Anson, 1988; Dennis et al., 1988; Dennis, Nunamaker, & Vogel, 1991). Dennis, Nunamaker and Vogel (1991) surveyed the majority of lab and field studies thus far reported. They concluded that, "the use of a facilitator can affect meeting outcomes at least as much as any other component in the (GSS) environment" (p. 124).

This conclusion is reinforced by field experience. McGoff and Ambrose (1991) and Grohowski et al. (1990) provide summary analyses of IBM experiences with applying computer support in over nine-hundred group sessions. They emphasize the critical role of a facilitator for ensuring the success of GSS supported meetings, especially their premeeting design role. Similar conclusions were reached in a recent survey of users of a keypad-based GSS (R. Watson et al., 1991).

The mixed findings among experimental studies may be due in part to differences among how groups were "facilitated" by the experimenters. Reports usually do not elaborate on how procedures are applied, so this possibility is difficult to assess. However, there have been only three studies that directly examined the effectiveness of facilitators in experimentally controlled conditions.

The first study, which compared the consensus and satisfaction of groups, provided the groups either with no facilitation (user-driven approach), technical facilitation only (chauffeured approach), or process facilitation (facilitation approach) (G. Dickson et al., 1989). It is important to note that the process facilitation treatment involved a facilitator who rigidly imposed a structured approach on the group rather than flexibly working with the group. This study found that facilitated groups had lower consensus and satisfaction than groups provided only with technical, chauffeured support. It appeared that many groups resisted the task structure unilaterally imposed by the facilitator, which negated some of its impact. On the other hand, both chauffeured and facilitated groups had more satisfaction and consensus than did user-driven groups. The authors suggested that satisfaction was related to relieving the users of concern with technical operation of the overall system.

The second study took a flexible approach to process facilitation by training a number of facilitators (Anson, 1990). The study compared groups provided with GSS or no GSS support, and process facilitator or no process facilitator support. Anson found that flexible process facilitation, whether supplied in the presence or absence of computer support, significantly improved perceptions of interpersonal relationships and group processes. Combined facilitator and computer support was most effective on average, although its effects were not significantly improved over either support applied separately.

The third study took an approach to facilitation similar to that of the second study (Anson & Heminger, 1991). The study examined groups of graduate students engaged in developing a case analysis class report. All of the groups were provided computer support for their initial analysis effort, but half of the groups were additionally supported by a process facilitator. Process facilitation consisted of flexible intervention into the group interactions, both during the meeting and the premeeting planning. The authors found that flexible process facilitation, supplied in the presence of computer support, produced significant improvements in member perceptions of group processes and task outcomes.

Summary of Research

Researchers have identified a variety of structured procedures and guidelines that can help overcome meeting problems. External process facilitation and GSS are two means of applying effective procedures outside of relying on the members themselves to do so. There is evidence that GSS can positively impact group processes, resulting in improved task and relational outcomes. There is also evidence to support the effectiveness of flexibly applied, external facilitation. Initial evidence indicates that flexibly applied process facilitation by external facilitators can supplement and/or enhance GSS effectiveness.

A MEETING FACILITATION FRAMEWORK

Overview

The purpose of this section is to present a framework for understanding and investigating facilitation in GSS environments. The framework is visually represented in Figure 8.3 and described below.

A given *source* of facilitation (external facilitator, leader, member, GSS) provides *structures* (e.g., agenda, procedures, GSS tools) and/or *support* (e.g., the facilitator administers a procedure, or deals with a disruptive participant) to a group in order to positively influence how the group accomplishes its *outcomes*. Structures provide an overall frame (represented by a rectangle around the targets in Figure 8.3) or context to activate individuals or groups to behave in a particular way. On the other hand, support activities are used primarily to maintain and promote these structures, encourage effective task and relational behaviors, and deal with disruptive influences in the meeting.

As illustrated in Figure 8.3, a facilitator, by his or her actions, attempts to influence three general targets: meeting *process*, *relationships*, and *task* outcomes. Structures are applied primarily through the development of the meeting process (e.g., agenda). These structures will influence the explo-

Chapter 8 Group Facilitation and Group Support Systems

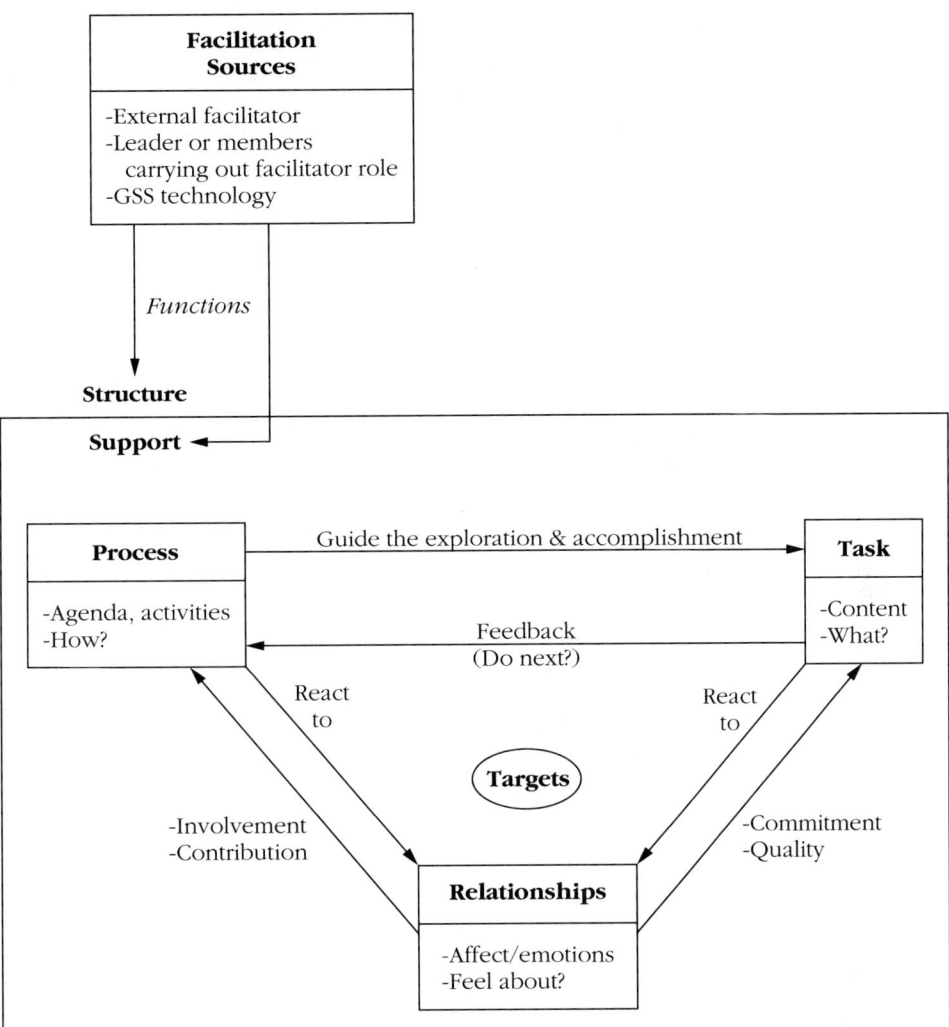

FIGURE 8.3 Facilitation framework.

ration and accomplishment of task outcomes (content: the what?) and relational outcomes (affect/emotions: feel about?). In return, the individual's and/or the group's affect-relationships will influence an individual's involvement in and contribution to the process, the quality of his or her contribution, and his or her commitment to and acceptance of the task outcomes (decision, plan, etc.).

It is interesting to note that the framework in Figure 8.3 can be applied to either the individual, subgroup, or entire group. In other words, the facilitation action can be focused on the individual and/or the group. For example, an individual engages in a particular activity (process) in order to focus on or explore a specific dimension of the task. This cognitive activity results in an individual making a contribution that leads to the development of a group cognitive frame. Thus, both individual and group frames of reference of the task are interacting in the meeting.

The participant experiences certain emotions while participating in the activity, and these feelings may change as a result of this participation. Although it is difficult to measure, the emotional life of a group is a useful concept (George, 1990; L.D. Phillips & M.C. Phillips, 1990). Emotions expressed by the group run the full range of feelings experienced by individuals. Thus, individual and group affect are also influencing the meeting process and task and relational outcomes. The facilitator intervenes into this dynamic interplay between the process, affect, and task, both with the individual and group.

In summary, facilitation, or more specifically facilitative acts or behaviors, can be described in terms of three general dimensions as illustrated in Figure 8.3:

1. Sources are the initiators of facilitative acts, including people (group members or leader, an external facilitator) or technology (GSS).
2. Targets are what the facilitative acts are trying to influence, including how the group does its work (process), the content of work (task) and/or how the group works together (relationships).
3. Functions are groupings of facilitative acts or behaviors. We have chosen two very general functions, structure and support, to categorize facilitative acts.

For example, an external facilitator (source) may need to influence how the group creatively interacts (process target) by applying a brainstorming technique (structure). The facilitator would manage (support) the brainstorming structure by acting as the recorder and by carefully summarizing each contribution. Issues concerning each of these dimensions are treated in the following sections.

Facilitation Targets

Structure and support activities may be directed at process, task, or relationships. In a meeting that emphasizes task outcomes, members are brought together primarily for their task content expertise and judgment. Their efforts to contribute to and influence the substance or content of discussions could be described as "content facilitation." Likewise, an external or third-party individual, who has specific task expertise, could be brought in as a content facilitator. However, most people use the term (process) facilitation to denote interventions to the group process or relationships. Process facilitation only indirectly influences the content of the discussion by managing the procedural and relational context of the interactions. A simple example involves a group member who facilitates the process by suggesting that ideas be contributed in a round-robin fashion, instead of facilitating the content by suggesting that the group consider a given alternative. Although computers could be used as content facilitators (e.g., expert systems), most GSS focus on improving the process. Thus, in this chapter we focus on facilitative behavior that is targeted at group process and relationships.

Facilitation Sources

There are three general types of facilitation sources: (1) external facilitators, (2) group members or leaders, and (3) GSS. All three sources may be present and involved in facilitating during a meeting, although one or another source may dominate during an activity.

The first source is the group members or leaders. In most meetings, the members and leader are the sole sources of facilitation. Because most members or leaders are invited to a meeting based on their content expertise, a triple responsibility is placed on these individuals. They must be concerned with the task-related discussions, group processes, and group relationships. This triple responsibility and a lack of facilitation skills is the major reason why traditional meetings are so often found to be inefficient and ineffective (Mosvick & Nelson, 1987).

Second, an external facilitator (EF) may be the primary source of facilitation. The EF is a facilitator specialist, invited to the meeting to apply process and relational skills. The EF is currently the dominant mode used to facilitate commercial GSS sessions. An EF is usually trained in designing and running meetings, and in GSS settings, he or she would be trained in the technology. Often the EF role within a GSS environment is split into two (which may be filled by two separate individuals). The *technical facilitator* or *technographer* is primarily responsible for operating the technology, whereas the *process facilitator* directly interacts with the group.

Finally, the GSS provides a source of facilitation through its software tools, processing routines, user interface features, and information displays. The extent to which the technology may exert a facilitative influence depends on both the extent and manner in which it is used.

There are important advantages for involving neutral external facilitators or technology for facilitation sources. Leaders or members can use the process, knowingly or unknowingly, to manipulate content (Burton, 1987). Their responsibility for process facilitation may cause important information and dissenting opinions to be lost (Gouran & Hirokawa, 1983), reduce the acceptance of meeting outcomes (Hoffman, 1982; Maier, 1963), or simply result in lack of attention to process and relational concerns.

Although it is possible for meeting participants to learn how to facilitate meetings fairly, it is not people's natural tendency (Maier & Hoffman, 1960). The primary issue is keeping process and content separate. Thus, when leaders or members do choose to both facilitate and participate, they need to keep the two roles separate. They need to signal in some way (e.g., sitting down in an empty chair) that they are stepping out of the facilitator role and into the role of group participant and vice versa. GSS environments actually facilitate this role delineation because one usually becomes a participant when one enters information into the system. In fact, GSS environments provide many advantages of EF and may allow members or leaders to facilitate their own meetings more successfully.

Facilitation Functions

The notion of functions is drawn from the group dynamics and leadership literature. Based on the pioneering work of Benne and Sheats (1948), a number of specific facilitative functions have been suggested that describe what needs to take place in a group in terms of leader and/or member behavior (Quinn, 1988). Some examples of functions include organizing, initiating structure, summarizing, clarifying, harmonizing, and energizing.

In our model, we have summarized these functions into two very general functional categories, structure and support. This is appropriate given the tutorial or overview nature of our model. Specific research studies may want to define more precise facilitative functions/role profiles (for example, see Chilberg, 1989).

Structure

Facilitators provide structures to establish a frame or context to activate individuals/group into a particular way of behaving. In a meeting context, structures primarily include the following:

1. Meeting outcomes.
2. Role specialization: participants are assigned specific roles (for example, devil's advocate, facilitator, decision-maker, and so on), for an activity, phase, or entire meeting.
3. Rules to follow during an activity, phase, or entire meeting.
4. Procedures to accomplish an entire meeting, a specific meeting phase, or a specific activity.
5. Techniques/technology to carry out procedures.

A facilitator works with the group leader (and participants) to establish meeting outcomes. The facilitator then designs the meeting by picking relevant roles, rules, procedures, and techniques to accomplish desired outcomes.

As noted above, roles, rules, and procedures can have different application scopes. Some have a narrow scope and apply only to single activity, whereas others have broad scope and apply to the entire meeting. Most rules are role- and/or activity-specific, such as the rules defining the devil's advocate's role or a brainstorming activity (VanGundy, 1988). However, some rules may be designed to operate throughout the meeting process. For example, a "respect rule," (i.e., respect individual differences) enforced by the facilitator and/or members at all times, may be established to promote good relationships and encourage people to contribute.

A facilitator has many different resources to utilize in developing a structural design for a meeting. Different sets of structures have been defined for meeting, agenda, and activity levels (e.g., Bostrom, 1989; Chilberg, 1989; Poole, 1991; VanGundy, 1988). For example, VanGundy (1988) summarizes an extensive array of procedures to carry out specific activities such as generating (e.g., brainwriting, excursion) and evaluating (e.g., sticky dots) information. These structures are best viewed as structural templates that are often customized for specific group and task situations and adapted or modified during the actual meeting.

Similarly, a facilitator may use a GSS to provide structure for organizing group and/or individual thought processes and actions. A GSS tool in most situations automates a particular procedure to carry out a specific activity, for example, the brainwriting procedure is used to generate information. However, given the nature of computer technology, certain structural components that provide additional structuring capabilities are "embedded" in the technology. Examples of these added components found in GSS implementations are simultaneous idea exchange and input, anonymity, electronic recording and display and enhanced information processing capabilities (Bostrom & Anson, 1988). By its design, a GSS tool establishes a particular structure to which a facilitator may add supplemental structure, for example, rules of brainstorming (no evaluation of items generated, etc.). It is this combined collection of structures to which a group responds when using GSS technology.

Although structures usually focus on the process and task dimensions in our model, they can directly or indirectly support the relationship dimension. For example, many activity procedures (including those in GSS) serve directly relationship outcomes by providing opportunities for involvement and reducing dysfunctional behaviors. In some cases, rules are used to develop desired relational behaviors (e.g., no personal attacks, respect individual differences).

Support

Facilitator support activities are used primarily to enact structures, encourage effective behavior, and deal with disruptive influences. Gouran and Hirokawa (1986) provide a useful taxonomy for understanding support activities and the relationships between structures and support. They view any behavior or interaction as having three potential influences on meeting outcomes. First, it may have *promotive influence* by facilitating the accomplishment of meeting outcomes. This type of influence is often referred to as "process gains" (Steiner, 1972; see Nunamaker, Dennis, George, Valacich, & Vogel, 1991, for discussion of group and GSS process gains). Second, it may have a *disruptive* influence by inhibiting progressive movement, thus, incurring "process losses" (Nunamaker, Dennis, George, Valacich, & Vogel, 1991). Third, a behavior may act as a *counteractive influence* if it neutralizes or negates the disruptive interaction and restores progressive movement toward meeting outcomes. Facilitation support activities or behaviors are usually promotive, encouraging effective task and relational behaviors (see Table 1 for examples); or counteractive (e.g., challenging relevancy of information when someone wanders off the topic).

Effective structures are both promotive and preventive (minimizing disruptive influences, and thus avoiding the need for counteractive influence). For example, a GSS can promote equal participation and reduce or prevent people from dominating communication. However, structures may not be used as intended or may need to be modified to accomplish meeting outcomes. Thus, some of the primary functions of support activities are to maintain, reinforce, promote, and adapt the structures being used.

All support activities in meetings are carried out through communication acts using verbal, nonverbal, and GSS channels. Thus, the heart of good facilitation support is effective communication skills. Several authors have outlined some of the major skills required to effectively facilitate in GSS environments (Bostrom et al., 1991; McGoff et al., 1989; L.D. Phillips & M.C. Phillips, 1990). For example, frame-clarification skills that clarify, verify, and help make meaning of an individual's or group's frame of reference or language are important skills. More research is needed on how support skills can be enhanced by, or designed into, a GSS.

FUTURE RESEARCH ISSUES

Introduction

In this section, future research directions are outlined through a discussion of key GSS facilitation issues that include the following:

- The necessity of a facilitator in GSS environments
- Facilitating in different GSS environments
- Developing facilitation skills

Our outcome is to highlight critical research questions and issues relevant to facilitation in GSS environments. Recent research agendas for the general area of facilitation are available (Broome & Keever, 1989; Hirokawa & Gouran, 1989). Our agenda complements these. As pointed out in the review of research, little research has been carried out in the facilitation arena. Therefore, the research agenda is large and challenging. Before discussing the research issues, we introduce adaptive structuration theory as a general theoretical framework to study facilitation in GSS environments.

A Theoretical Perspective of Facilitation

Adaptive structuration theory (AST; see Chapter 15 for discussion) has been applied in GSS research by Poole and DeSanctis (1987, 1990), DeSanctis and

Poole (1991), Anson (1990), and Gopal (1991). AST, like other sociotechnical theories, conceives technology use as a social practice that emerges over time. AST suggests that meeting outcomes are not a direct result of structures introduced through technology or facilitation. Rather, these outcomes reflect the manner in which groups appropriate and modify these structures. From an AST perspective, the role of facilitation is to select and present beneficial structures to groups in a manner that encourages their faithful appropriation.

A key construct within AST is appropriation. Appropriation is the process by which participants invoke or enact available structures (e.g., GSS, agenda, etc.) and thereby give meaning to them (DeSanctis & Poole, 1991). AST posits that the success of an appropriation is determined by three dimensions: the *faithfulness* (in respect to structure's design principles) of the appropriation, the group's *attitudes* towards the structures, and the group's *level of consensus* (i.e., agreement on how structures should be used). As we discussed earlier, a facilitator affects all three of these modes through support activities: faithfulness through promotion and maintenance of structure; attitudes through activities that develop positive affect; and consensus through monitoring the group's reactions and making appropriate adjustments.

Because of the newness of GSS technology, an external facilitator is often used to ensure proper selection of GSS structures and to provide support to ensure successful appropriation (McGoff et al., 1989). When an external facilitator is not present, a few group members take over this role (DeSanctis & Poole, 1991). Once a group has learned the GSS technology (design principles and how to use) an external facilitator may not be needed. On the other hand, any facilitator who lacks the knowledge of and comfort with a GSS will have a difficult time selecting appropriate structures and guiding the appropriation process (Anson, 1990). Understanding structures, especially those provided by GSS, and the appropriation process is critical to facilitating GSS meetings.

AST provides a general framework for investigations. More specific theories or frameworks can be used as supplements in detailed investigations. For example, the substitutes for leadership theories (e.g., Howell et al., 1986; S. Kerr & Jermier, 1978) provide concepts that may be useful in exploring and describing potential interactive effects between GSS and human facilitation sources.

Is a Facilitator Necessary in GSS Environments?

Many people who promote GSS as a substitute for a human facilitator answer "no" to the question of "is a facilitator necessary?" They argue that business cannot afford the expense of an external facilitator and that a "good" GSS should be capable of providing the group with the facilitation needed. It should be obvious from our discussion that we believe the answer to this question would be a resounding "yes!" Given the current state of GSS technology, a human facilitator is definitely required. A GSS can provide some facilitation support, but it cannot be a total substitute for a facilitator.

Consequently, the important question is not, "is a facilitator necessary?" The important question is, "how can different sources of facilitation (people, GSS) be combined to effectively design and support meetings?" Research in this area has been limited and exploratory. Very little is known about how different sources might interact when used together. Although we know that a GSS can support faciliting such things as in-meeting participation and dominance control, we are not sure how to build more facilitative functions into a GSS. Most GSS provide support only in the meeting, and do not address, for example, the critical premeeting phase. How can we design GSS to facilitate the entire meeting cycle and system? The integration of other technologies into GSS, such as expert systems (e.g., acting as facilitation advisers) and database (e.g., capture group/meeting history), will be important in answering this question. However, a great deal more needs to be learned about the process of facilitation and facilitator interventions before expert system advisers could be effectively designed.

A second question is related to the tradeoffs between using external facilitator, group members, or GSS as the facilitator. In the long run, organizations cannot rely on a pool of external facilitators to run all their meetings. As more facilitation functions are integrated into GSS, the need for an external facilitator is expected to decrease. A GSS with greater facilitative capabilities may allow the group members to facilitate their own meetings and still provide substantial content involvement. However, the issue of training group members to effectively use the GSS must be addressed and studied for the goal of self-facilitation to be realized. With increased GSS sophistication, the facilitator specialist role may evolve into one of providing consultation to groups on how to effectively design and run GSS supported meetings.

Much conceptual and empirical work remains to develop and test the effects of various structural and support characteristics of combined human-computer facilitation. Appropriation analysis (DeSanctis & Poole, 1991) could explore the effects of different combinations of facilitation and GSS interventions. The development of a set of structural dimensions that could be used to define different classes of facilitation and/or GSS interventions would greatly expedite these research efforts. The collection of structures provided in a GSS environment could then be described and differentiated using these structural dimensions. Poole (1991) and Anson (1990) document some initial efforts to develop these dimensions. Other rich areas for future research include how GSS and/or facilitation training, GSS experience, different GSS designs, and other contingencies can influence patterns of appropriation in groups.

Facilitating in Different GSS Environments

Typically, group interaction takes place in a face-to-face environment, with the group working together at the same time and place. However, GSS and other collaborative technologies have expanded the types of environments in which meetings can take place to include the same time/different place, different time/same place and different time/different place. There appear to be three key parameters that would influence facilitation in these different environments: the availability and richness of communication channels, the immediacy of feedback, and the means of coordination.

All GSS facilitation research has been carried out in same time/same place settings. Thus, it is necessary to gather various forms of research data (cases, surveys, experiments) on facilitation in these other environments along the lines suggested in the previous section. Our facilitation framework (Figure 8.3) is applicable to these other environments, although the mechanisms to provide structure and support would vary. Same time/same place environments provide a variety of rich communication channels (verbal, nonverbal, GSS), immediate real-time feedback, and multiple means to coordinate activities. In different time or place environments, especially different time, the facilitator would have to rely more on the GSS to provide special mechanisms to enrich communication, gather and assess feedback, and monitor and coordinate activities (e.g., agenda). What mechanisms (tools, features, etc.) are needed for someone to be able to effectively facilitate in these different environments?

The core of any collaborative system is the shared group space. In current different time/different place systems (electronic mail, video- or teleconferencing, bulletin boards), this is primarily a communication/discussion space. This communication space lacks the process-structuring, outcome-directed space found in most GSS different time/different place environments. These GSS lack the communication space of non-GSS tools. A communication space is needed to support GSS facilitation. Ways to integrate these technologies to support facilitation need to be explored either by providing linkages between GSS and non-GSS tools and/or integrating non-GSS tools into a GSS. Research studies carried out using different time/different place tools may provide a source of good ideas and data, especially those that focus on people who facilitate activities in these environments (e.g., S. R. Hiltz et al., 1991a, 1991b; J. C. Smith and Vanecek, 1990).

The availability of different meeting environments creates more meeting design alternatives because the facilitator can combine different environments to accomplish a meeting outcome(s) and agenda that unfolds over time. For example, a useful combination is different time/different place followed by same time/same place. One of the authors recently participated in a meeting to develop changes to an undergraduate curriculum. The suggested changes were generated and an initial evaluation of changes was done first in different time/different place mode. This was followed by a GSS-supported face-to-face meeting to decide on which changes to actually implement. How do we effectively combine different environments to accomplish a meeting's outcomes?

Research exploring the effects of different combinations of environments is needed. In addition, some researchers have argued that different GSS environments should be used depending on the group development stage, for example, face-to-face environments should be used in early stages of group development when interpersonal relationships are being formed (Johansen et al., 1991; Kutsko and Smith, 1991). These types of contingency hypotheses need to be investigated including their reverse formulations, for example, how can a facilitator overcome obstacles in environments that are not face-to-face environments to effectively develop group relationships.

Developing Facilitation Skills

In this chapter, we have argued for the importance of facilitation skills in GSS environments. Given their importance, the critical research questions become the following:

1. What are the key or core facilitation behaviors and skills within a GSS environment? How do these differ from traditional environments?
2. How do we develop and/or select people with these skills?
3. Are some individuals or "personalities" predisposed to developing facilitative behaviors? Is there a facilitative personality profile?
4. How can GSS technology and/or facilitators be used to teach facilitation skills to individuals? Groups? Organizations?

One would expect to have a solid body of literature to draw on in pursuing questions 1–3 yet this is not the case (see Clawson, 1991, for research summary). Empirically based answers to all three questions are needed in both GSS and non-GSS environments. Evidence does indicate that the facilitator's training and experience with technology is important in the GSS environment (Anson, 1990; McGoff et al., 1989). How do we help current or future facilitators integrate GSS technology into their toolkits?

In agreement with Hirokawa and Gouran (1989), we do not anticipate research ever to lead to specific detailed prescriptions for facilitating groups. However, general strategies, skills, and concepts can be developed, taught to facilitators, and applied in a flexible manner in various meeting contexts. We generally have a good understanding of issues that make meetings unsuccessful (e.g., poor design) and successful (e.g., good design). Facilitation strategies and skills can be developed to effectively address each of these areas. For example, one of the most common meeting design problems is the lack of clear outcomes. An effective strategy a facilitator might employ is helping groups formulate explicit outcomes. Thus, outcome development skills become essential to effective facilitation.

Based on the above assumptions, we have developed a training program for facilitators in both GSS and non-GSS environments. Our research (Anson, 1990; Bostrom et al., 1991), along with the earlier research on facilitator training (see Table 1), has demonstrated that people can be trained in these skills. However, our training program is only a second-generation prototype. More detailed responses to questions 1 and 2 above are needed to provide good training guidelines. We need to know what a complete skill set is; what good training methods are; how training should be sequenced; etc. The question also arises about who to train (facilitator specialists, team leaders and/or members, all of these)? If group members or leaders are to be trained to act as the facilitators, what techniques do they need to know in order to effectively handle their triple responsibilities for meeting process, content, and relationships.

Although none of the GSS facilitation studies found significant overall differences between individual facilitators, some specific differences were discovered (G. Dickson et al., 1989; Anson, 1990). Organizational behavior research has also identified personality differences in successful individuals in facilitation-related roles (Hamilton, 1988). Thus, researching the issue of a "facilitator personality" might help guide the development of facilitator selection guidelines.

Evidence already exists to suggest that the introduction of GSS into an organization can help develop good meeting facilitation skills. For example, R.T. Watson et al. (1991) found that GSS forces people to design better meetings. Question 4 above invites exploration of this important issue. Can GSS be a catalyst for learning facilitation skills? Can a GSS be used as a training simulator in teaching people facilitation skills? It is also important not to overlook the teaching role of the facilitator. For example, having a facilitator explicitly mark out what and how skills are being applied could accelerate the learning curve of members. Thus, similar research questions can be generated for the facilitator role and the combined human-computer facilitation roles.

Many research strategies can be utilized to generate answers to the questions raised above. Developing profiles of excellent facilitators through modeling will be particularly important early on. The research generated in this area will provide guidelines for training programs; selection criteria for hiring and placing facilitators; and useful information for GSS designers on how to design more facilitation functions into their software.

Future Research Summary

Space does not permit an exhaustive discussion of all the specific research possibilities. Rather, our outcome has been to identify an appropriate focus and general directions for future research. We believe that the introduction of GSS will create a renewed interest in the neglected area of facilitation. GSS environments provide an ideal research setting for researchers from different disciplines to study facilitation. Thus, we would strongly encourage multidisciplinary research efforts. In addition, we would suggest that researchers follow the guidelines recommended by Hirokawa and Gouran (1989). They have suggested that an appropriate approach to facilitation research and training is to focus on general skills, strategies, and concepts that can provide guidance in generating specific behaviors that can be applied across a number of contexts. This implies that facilitators should use their own judgment in applying their skills, rather than imposing facilitation techniques and procedural structures in a lockstep, prescribed fashion. Although this research approach is necessary to fully assess facilitation, it does complicate the assessment of cause and effect. Utilizing some of the research approaches outlined in this section (e.g., appropriation analyses) might help deal with this issue. The use of qualitative research methodologies will also be required.

CONCLUSION

The promise of technology will always rest within people, not machines (Pasmore, 1988). Computer technology to this point has been designed as a personal invention to enhance personal performance. However, as GSS technology and collaborative group work are assimilated into the business mainstream, we cannot underestimate the importance of supporting this transition with solid skill and conceptual training in both technology and facilitation. Preparing organizations and groups for both the GSS explosion and for working collaboratively will be critical. This chapter has outlined a number of issues that need to be explored to make this human-computer facilitation successful.

CHAPTER

9

Flexspace: Making Room for Collaborative Work

Richard B. Polley
Lewis and Clark College

Philip J. Stone
Harvard University

INTRODUCTION

Consider the setting in which you are reading this book. Chances are that you are sitting at a desk in a private office. Such spaces support solitary activities like reading, writing, and working at computer terminals. If you are like most American office-dwellers, the door to your office is open. This is your concession to collaborative work. You have indicated a willingness to be "interrupted" by co-workers and visitors. Now ask yourself how many people your office can comfortably accommodate. What kind of collaborative work does your office facilitate? Unless you are very near the top of your organizational hierarchy, it is unlikely that your office can accommodate more than four people or that it includes table-top work space for more than two.

Conventional office design is "sociofugal," driving us away from central meeting spaces into private offices. "Sociopital" alternatives—such as the ubiquitous open offices that have evolved from office landscaping first proposed by the German Quickborner team—tend to bring out the agoraphobic in most of us, forcing us together at the expense of privacy and control. An office with a lockable door is both a refuge and a symbol of power. Territory ensures us both access to resources and a place in which we have an advantage over "intruders."

TIME AND SPACE

Working lives tend to be defined by boundaries of time and space. For the majority of us, "work" takes place somewhere between 8:00 A.M. and 5:00 P.M. Monday through Friday in a private office. However, the concept of "flextime" has been with us for several years (Glueck, 1979; Ralston, et al., 1985). It has been demonstrated that allowing employees to define their own work hours — within reasonable bounds — increases both satisfaction and productivity.

Stone and Luchetti (1985) proposed an office design that could be characterized as "flexspace." Their "activity setting" (see insert, pp. 172–177)* was designed to ease the office worker into a more collaborative use of space. They proposed incrementally adjustable walls so that "home bases" (private offices) could be gradually reduced in size as workers began to use private space less often and shared space more often. Expensive resources could be kept in shared space to maximize their use. Tables would be modular and thus could be configured for the specific group size. If you were currently sitting in this "office of the future" you would probably be reading this in a comfortable library chair rather than at your desk. Stone and Luchetti proposed solving the problem of accessibility by having each person carry an infrared communication device, with receptors in the ceiling keeping each person in constant touch with a communications center. The proposal was that the office shown here would gradually be phased in. Space would be charged back to occupants at a gradually increasing rate so that the full cost of office space would eventually appear as an item in the budget line that could be traded off for other resources, including access to equipment, assistants, and use of shared spaces.

GSS FACILITIES: A CRITIQUE

Social science knowledge, especially group dynamics, should contribute to an appropriate design of computer-based facilities for collaborative work that reflects a dialectic between theory and practice. Consider, for example, three rooms at universities that were especially constructed to facilitate collaborative work: these pioneering endeavors and the experience people have in using them offer useful lessons for implementing future collaborative environments.

The first room, shown in Figure 9.1A (Dennis et al., 1988), has the advantage of putting participants in face-to-face proximity, although the distances are somewhat far for comfortable interpersonal communication (E. Hall, 1966). The sides of the "horseshoe" are flat, and people are seated in a U-shaped configuration, making communication with people more than one seat away and sitting on the same side of the table difficult. Communication between two people sitting next to one another will be private rather than public because the interpersonal distance is too close for other than fairly intimate conversation

---

*Illustrations by Robert Luchetti, Michael Tingley, and William Cromar; copyright by Robert Luchetti Associates, January 1992.

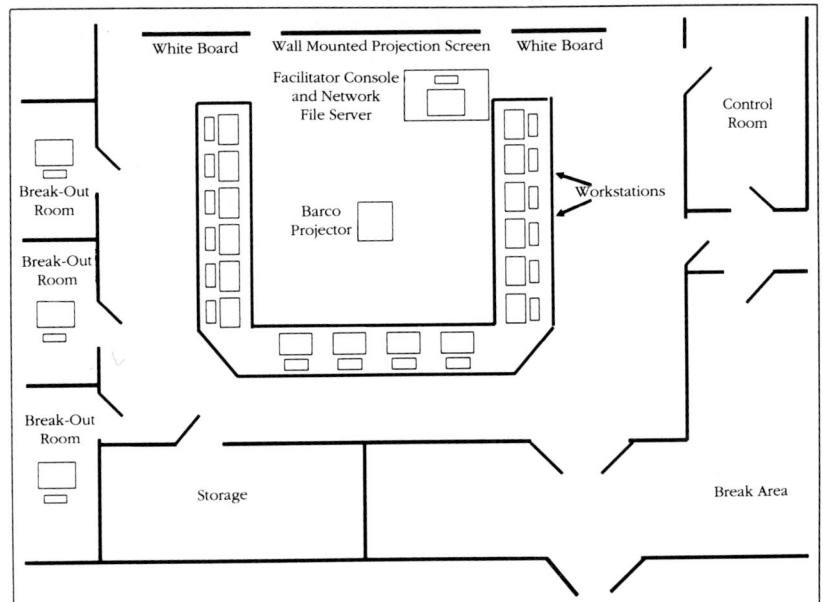

FIGURE 9.1A PlexCenter.

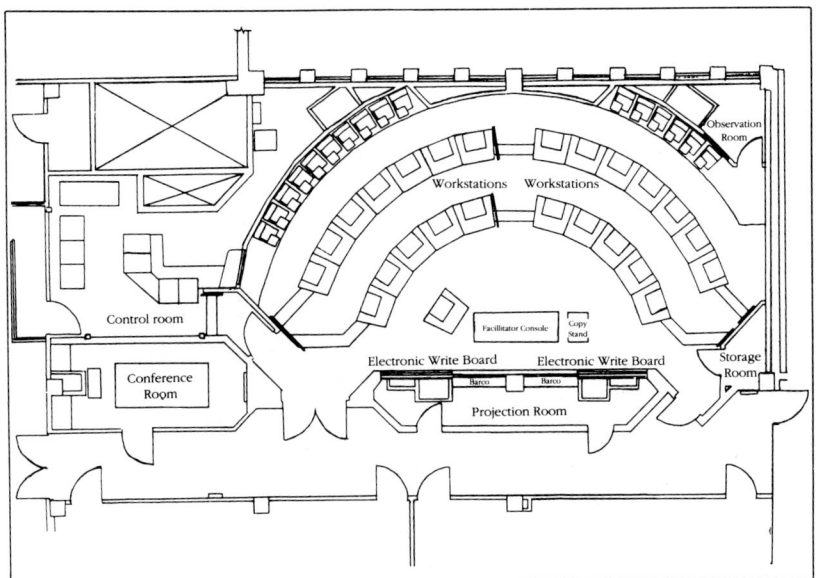

FIGURE 9.1B Decision room for larger groups. (Figure 9.1 is reprinted by special permission from the *MIS Quarterly,* Volume 12, Number 4, December 1988. Copyright © 1988 by the Society for Information Management and the Management Information Systems Research Center at the University of Minnesota.)

"On the left you will see that..."

"I'd better call Mike and Rebecca. There's no way I can get this done by myself..."

"...Hmm. I never expected to find this—I didn't even know they'd done it..."

"I'm not sure that we can accept these terms. What will Joe say if we..."

"Let's make a separate file out of it and dump it in the empty folder at the upper left..."

"Was that really the most recent quote? Jane is checking it now..."

"Great! This fax makes it much clearer…"

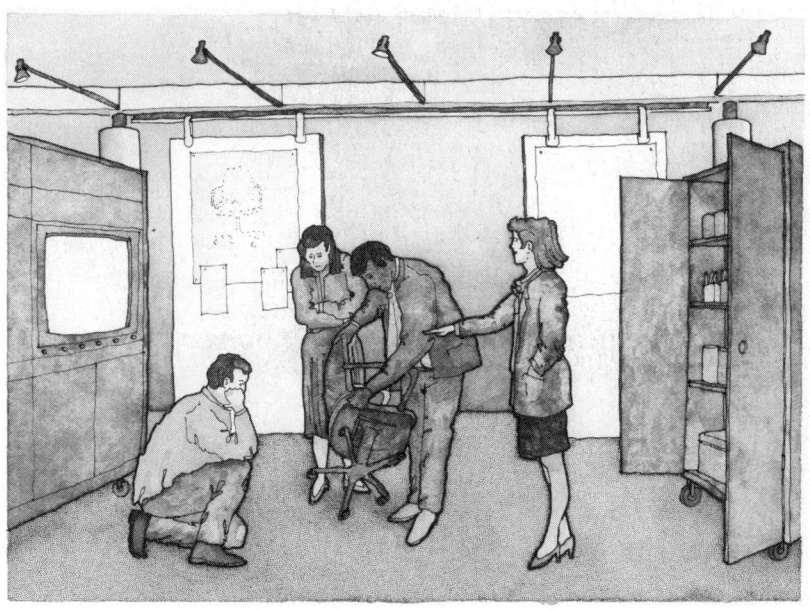

"If we could just simplify the lift and then…"

"If we can get this back to them today, we've got a chance…"

"There was this one case that showed how you could…"

"I'm not sure that we can..."

"...I'm glad we have gotten this resolved..."

(E. Hall, 1966). The open end of the U has a control unit and a projection screen contributing to a hierarchical structure guided by a facilitator (Sommer, 1969), even when the group is intended to be democratically self-run. Finally, the computer monitors are somewhat intrusive, making it difficult for those who "face" one another across the table to engage in face-to-face communication.

The second design (Figure 9.1B) shows a larger room (Dennis et al., 1988) in which the rows of stations are curved, thus allowing members to see one another. The long distances between people from one end of a bank of stations to the other and the difference in elevation between the front and back banks require loud conversations that encourage speech-making (E. Hall, 1966). In legislative congresses, speakers generally step to the front to deliver important addresses, but this facility ties the speaker to a seat by making computer support stationary. In an attempt to facilitate verbal communication, these problems may actually have been exacerbated; microphones have been installed at the work stations.

These two facilities share a lack of flexibility. The tables are arranged in a fixed configuration and comfortably accommodate groups of only one size. Many of the difficulties discussed above are solved by the facilities proposed by Cornell and Luchetti (1989). Their "ELMER" (Electronic Meeting Room) provides independent, movable units that can be networked in varying numbers and configurations (Figure 9.2). A laboratory with these units would have a wide variety of configurations ranging from one full group to a variety of concurrent task groups.

Our third example is a recently built human-computer interaction laboratory that was designed to incorporate twelve ELMER-like units. Its planners and builders encountered major problems in design and implementation that underscore the difficulties in translating theory into practice. The facility included one large meeting room and one smaller meeting room, in addition to two individual "breakout rooms". The large room could be used for groups of up to 24, because the units were designed to allow two people to share one computer. Small groups could be held concurrently in the two rooms and individuals could work in the small breakout rooms. This was a nice idea, but the units turned out to be too wide to fit through the internal doors and can be moved between the two meeting rooms only by wheeling them outside and back in through the rear entrance. Moreover, the units are slightly too small for two people and each comes with a fixed shelf installed across the front at ankle-barking level. Because the monitor is placed on a fixed shelf below table level, it is at a correct angle only if the user is of the proper height. Finally, the unit was designed in such a way that the cord for the mouse runs out the front of the unit, which reverses the mouse orientation so that the user has to move the mouse in the opposite direction of the desired cursor movement.

Lighting can be a difficult problem in computer-based environments, whether for individual workstations or collaborative work settings. In the case of the interaction laboratory, a constant glare was found on both the glass top and the monitor screen because the glass tops do not employ any nonglare coating and the ceiling light fixtures are standard flourescents. To correct the

FIGURE 9.2 Six carts in a circular arrangement with triangular infill tops; monitors in various postions.

glare problem the designer created, all units are now located around the edge of the large room, so that they are not directly underneath the light fixtures, thus neutralizing the advantage of having movable units. Because this did not completely solve the problem, the designer added plywood hoods, thus eliminating the advantage of clean work surfaces.

SOME MISTAKEN PREMISES OF COLLABORATIVE WORK

In order to design outstanding environments for the support of collaborative activities, it is necessary to look beyond issues of logistics, good design, and ergonomics and also consider some assumptions about group work that are likely to be mistaken. These mistaken assumptions not only stem from many managers' "Theory X" hierarchical thinking but also from the traditional ways social scientists have regarded groups. McGrath (1991, p. 149) points out:

> [M]ost group theories purport to be about groups in general and, by implication, about naturally occurring groups. But the groups we meet in those theories, like the groups used in most studies, differ markedly from the kinds of groups we meet in everyday affairs. The groups that inhabit our theories and experiments are of a relatively constant membership. Their activity entails going about some experimenter or supervisor-assigned, singular, simple, well-practiced task—and nothing

else. Those groups never have to decide which tasks to do or to do next. They never have to make do without essential materials, personnel, or other resources, they never have to reckon with disputes, with "freeloaders," and so on—unless, of course, those are the specific issues of concern for the theorist-experimenter.

McGrath argues that, to the contrary, most groups "we meet in everyday living ...have variable membership from one occasion to another...are embedded within larger social aggregates" and are engaged in "complex sequences of interdependent tasks that compose a larger 'project'," with "often more than one such project going on at the same time."

Another common mistaken assumption that social scientists make is that all the important group dynamics occur when the full group meets. McGrath (1991, p. 152) argues instead:

> Much of the work of natural groups gets done by individuals or subgroups, acting when the "main" group is not in session: One member of a research team has an insight that solves a key problem for the whole team, two group members go into town in early morning to pick up supplies needed for the group's work that day, and so on. Thus, even the observation of "all" group meetings and the recording of "all" group actions and communication still cannot capture the totality of the flow of work in that group, much less the totality of group life beyond direct task performance.

Group Support Systems therefore should not only address activities when the group meets as a whole, but also the coordination and communication needs when the group breaks out into several task activities. If a GSS is to support the collaborative process of the group, then not only must it coordinate what Johansen (1988) described as "same place, same time" activities of the group as a whole, but also the delegated activities that take place in different places and different times. A productive group is not just one that meets effectively as a whole, but one that also functions in a smooth, organic way, even when its members are not all together.

The physical facilities for supporting groups should provide adequate resources and flexibility to support these diverse group processes. A meeting room may be equipped with all the latest technologies, but if it is only targeted to serve larger or smaller groups in various work arrangements, then it is decidedly less than optimal. Even if a room has been thoroughly thought out to accommodate various size groups and work configurations but there are no nearby places for breakout activities and socializing, then the collaborative process as a whole is not adequately addressed.

Instead of designing decision-making rooms that resemble updated "war rooms" of a Dr. Strangelove tradition, we should focus on creating collaborative environments that not only facilitate task work, but also support a group's well-being and address the needs of its participants. Building group loyalty, commitment, and a sense of inclusion can be just as important as getting the work done, especially in groups that need to bring out the best from their participants (Hirschhorn, 1991).

What is needed for this is a change of mindset regarding the support of collaboration somewhat analogous to the mindset change from Theory X to Theory Y (McGregor, 1960) or to Theory Z (Ouchi, 1981), or Likert's (1961) more gradual transition from System I to System IV. A Theory X of collaboration is the top-down management of groups in which groups do tasks as they are told. A Theory Y of collaboration is more like the groups McGrath (1991) described, with groups taking more initiative and responsibility for their own development and evolution. As with the slow drift toward Theory Y, we are likely to experience some false starts in which the new assumptions are given lip service by skeptical leaders and managers—the period of what R. Miles (1975) referred to as the human relations approach, that warm and fuzzy detour on the road from authoritarianism to a human resources approach that recognizes the value of attending to employees' suggestions. To facilitate this mindset transition, it is helpful to specify the assumptions of the old mindset and then consciously strive to change them. We propose eleven well-entrenched assumptions that should be addressed.

1. Groups are Most Always Formed Through an Orderly Planning Process. Some groups are a fixed part of the organization chart, starting with the board of directors, but other groups form in response to contingencies that arise or are bottom-up initiatives to take advantage of new opportunities. A newly formed team should be able to obtain suitable settings for its activities with minimal negotiation and hassle. Organizations should be outfitted to respond to such unplanned space requirements, making it easy for people to collaborate spontaneously.

2. Work Teams Maintain a Constant Size. After a team forms, members may be added or leave to join other projects. Consultants may be brought in. Teams should have access to work places appropriate to the number of participants and the task at hand. For each team activity, a setting should be chosen that is neither too crowded nor too large for the number of people participating. Some groups will move their meeting place according to the number of people expected. Others should be able to adjust their current meeting space boundaries to accommodate their current size.

3. Each Work Team Does Primarily One Thing. Most work teams experience project life cycles. Various activity settings and levels of computer support are needed for a group's diverse tasks. Although brainstorming sessions, for example, may be facilitated through Group Support Systems, the availability of a technology should never drive the decision of whether or not to use it. Computer support in group meeting rooms should be sufficiently unobtrusive so as to allow the team members to ignore it at times when face-to-face interaction is preferable.

As groups go through their life cycle, they commonly go through repeated cycles of differentiating into several breakout or task groups and then integrating back together again into a group as a whole. Both the physical environment and the computer support system should facilitate this microlevel recurrent division of labor and its reintegration. These transitions of differentiation and integration should be effortless and not disrupt the group process—transitions that Stefik and Brown (1989) call "seamless."

The intensity of a group's activities also often fluctuates greatly over the group's life cycle, creating constantly changing support needs regarding both the physical environment and computer support. At some times, the group as a whole will be fairly dormant, with a few members working on a task. Project deadlines create a last minute flurry of activity, a charrette in which all resources are taxed to a maximum.

4. Work Teams Last Indefinitely. Some teams last as long as the organization, but Peters and Waterman (1982) firmly advise that project teams should have goals that they can attain within less than six months. Organizations need to take care that unnecessary groups do not become entrenched fixtures of an organization's bureaucracy. Although a group may need to generate member commitment during its life cycle, it also needs to be loosely coupled enough so that members can easily move on to other activities. Instead of thinking of the organization as having what Durkheim (tr. 1984) would call an "organic solidarity" with groups fixed in relation to one another like organs of the body, it is more helpful to think of the organization as being highly "recombinatory."

5. Each Group Has One Leader. Flexspace should allow a group to choose whatever leadership arrangements are appropriate to its current task and life cycle stage. Some groups at some point will have multiple task leaders, each with his or her own area of expertise. Other groups will divide their leadership between a task and a social leader, with the social leader looking out more for the welfare of the group and the needs of the participants. Still other groups will not designate leaders but will strive to share leadership among equal members. Some groups will have a leader at the head of a class, addressing the group as an audience, whereas others will informally include the leader among them. Negotiating groups may line up on two sides, with a leader on each side, but will convert to a more mixed arrangement that brings together partners of each side once basic negotiations are settled.

Computer-based technology for collaborative activities may contain what Pool (1990) would call a "soft determinism" for still additional leadership roles. Some technologies provide for a scribe role to record the discussion process. This person is likely to take a leadership role in shaping the record of the discussion to provide a clearer picture of the agenda than a transcript of the discussion would show. Although others may monitor the recording process as projected on the screen and suggest occasional changes, clearly this person has a position of power, having what amounts to a "last word" unless challenged. Some tensions indeed may mount between this person and the other leaders in the group as the record unfolds, especially those parts of the record that set the future agenda for the group, including who will do what when.

Other new leadership roles that may be softly determined by computer-based technologies are the coordinator role (especially important for groups meeting at different times and in different places) and the integrator role taken by the person who brings together the different suggestions that may have been recorded into a summary statement. The importance of the coordinator role was recognized over a decade ago by Hiltz and Turoff (1978). They found that networked communications were more successful if someone took this role, rather than leaving it up to haphazard management. The importance of having an integrator becomes evident in meetings in which all participants have computer keyboards and all their brainstorming gets captured by a computer. Without a good integrator, reports generated by collaborative activities end up being bulleted lists with little coherent organization.

These additional roles give further reason to expect groups to have multiple leaders, with the leadership functions changing over the life of the group.

6. Groups Meet at a Regular Time and Place. Elaborate and rigid facilities work well if meetings can be scheduled well in advance. Often, however, important work is a result of impromptu, even accidental meetings. Group members should be equipped to consult resources such as their databases wherever they happen to meet. Portable equipment and easily reservable settings allow users to establish impromptu meetings that facilitate these serendipitous interactions. If team members travel frequently, these meetings are likely to occur at airports and hotels.

Instead of having the technology support group work tied to one place, it is better to have a group's files easily accessible on laptop computers that members can take with them to wherever they meet. These computers should be programmed to automatically update their hard disk bases whenever they are linked by phone to the organization's electronic network. In this way, group members work with current information wherever they happen to be.

7. Those Who Work in Offices Participate in Only One Group. Those who work in offices often participate concurrently in several project teams and adhoc groups. Davis and Lawrence's (1977) *Matrix* proposed an innovative organizational structure for coordinating among teams with overlapping membership, but at the time there was little technology available to support the communication explosion generated by their proposal. Consequently, they cautioned organizations to adopt the new structure only as a last resort, when classic management theory failed to provide adequate flexibility.

Computer networks operating in a WINDOWS™ environment provide the necessary technological support for matrix organizations. When each participant at a team meeting has a computer terminal, each terminal's display can include a window through which a participant receives and responds to messages from groups elsewhere in the organization. Whenever a message comes in, the participant usually can find an opportunity to type in a brief response within a few minutes without disrupting the group discussion. This capability makes it possible for a member of multiple teams to be "present" in more than one meeting at once. Often, a member with particular expertise will be called to a meeting only to answer one or two questions. By using computer access, this member's time is not wasted in sitting through a lengthy meeting and waiting for the questions to arise.

8. A Group Draws Upon Nearby Participants. Organizations that assume group activities draw on nearby participants naturally assign group meeting places to one department or another. Each group space becomes part of a department's turf and is used by others only with special permission. Organizations that make good use of cross-function teams should make group spaces available to the entire organization so that they serve the organization as a whole.

As organizations seek to participate in a global economy, many project teams span organizations. Rosabeth Kanters's (1989) *When Giants Learn to Dance* emphasizes the importance of "pooling, allying, and linking across organizations" in order to achieve synergies of "value multiplied." Organizations then have to consider, of course, what information they will share with outsiders.

Erving Goffman's (1959) dramaturgical analysis differentiates between the "frontstage," where public performances take place, and the "backstage," where the team prepares in private for these encounters. Effectively designed activity settings acknowledge this distinction. Backstage areas should provide ready access to all necessary information and technology, but access may need to be restricted to insiders. A separate frontstage area can then give outsiders access to appropriate levels of information and technology without unnecessary delays for security processing or putting an organization's security at risk.

9. Teams Should Be Insulated From Surrounding Activities So They Can Do Their Work. Groups need privacy in order to do their work, but too much isolation can let a group engage in *groupthink*. As Irving Janis (1972) demonstrated well with case studies, groupthink occasionally can have disastrous consequences. One challenge for a modern organization is to provide each group with the privacy it needs to do its work well and yet keep the group's activities within an organizational context.

Instead of assuming that there is one optimal solution regarding privacy, groups should be empowered to vary their privacy according to their current needs. By providing what Sundstrom and Altman (1989) call *boundary control* over their work setting, groups can create total privacy to concentrate on tasks but at other times open their boundaries to feedback and suggestions from others.

10. Team Members Share Information Equally. This premise may hold true when openness prevails among the members of an organization as well as with outside consultants and contractors. Quite often, however, information relevant to a group's activities may not be shared among all group members. A consulting company, for example, that has several clients in the same business sector may be contractually bound to keep information about its client from any of its employees who consult for one of the client's competitors. Dual careers may create additional reasons not to share information. For example, a member may have a spouse who works for a competitor or a government regulatory agency.

Organizations have to balance the risks of information getting out against the losses of missed opportunities. Instead of designing offices that put the organization always on the side of security, an office setting should provide controls to vary security arrangements according to the situation at hand.

11. Office Tensions Mainly Stem From Internal Group Dynamics. Managers have learned to focus on internal group dynamics as a source of tensions. This is likely a consequence of experiences in family and other primary groups, as well as sensitivity training courses on how to manage interpersonal tensions. However, because groups within organizations compete for resources, it is often the tensions between groups that can cause organizations the most trouble. Teams have a natural tendency to compete with one another, especially if there is a fixed pie of resources to be shared. In the process, overall goals of the organization are likely to become secondary.

One way to reduce these problems is to have overlapping memberships so that participants can inform their colleagues how issues are perceived by others. This purposeful overlapping, however, increases problems of coordination among group members, making it more necessary for team members to work asynchronously.

Designers of group support software should also give consideration to how their software can help one group keep other groups informed of what they are doing without interfering with the group process of either. One benefit of such software should be a significant reduction in the amount of time that groups spend speculating about—and perhaps building on false assumptions about—what others are saying or doing.

FLEXSPACE DESIGNS FOR COLLABORATIVE WORK

Given the years of experience and billions of dollars invested in outfitting offices in which individual position corresponds to place, it should be some time before comparable experience is gained about group work to result in ready-made resources for collaborative environments. This outfitting should eventually involve a complimentary implementation of computer-based resources for networking and collaboration together with a diverse range of suitable activity settings. These computer-based supports should include procedures for an almost effortless booking of appropriate settings as they are needed.

No collaborative environment is likely to succeed, however, if inadequate attention is given to providing each participant with an adequate "home base," a place that each employee can call his or her own and outfit as he or she desires. Collaboration must be complemented by reasonable opportunities for reflection and privacy. Although some thinking can be done in shared, library-like environments, other activities need one's own work area, where work can be spread out as desired. People tend to be remarkably territorial, and increased demands for shared activities with others create a greater need for a home base to which one can retreat. Home bases also are a sign of having an identity within the organization, of belonging and being included.

Several companies that outfit offices have been examining how their traditional line of meeting tables or private work stations can be supplemented with appropriate group support resources, such as the ELMER units described above. Partly because collaborative work has only recently been emphasized, these new lines of exploration have only begun in the last few years.

Although a major Korean office furniture manufacturer has aggressively entered the American market, few ideas regarding collaborative work environments are likely to come from Asia. Japanese office workers usually sit at desks in open areas that are subject to far too much noise and confusion for most Westerners. Whereas Westerners often seek to be at the office periphery near a window, Japanese office workers like to be near the center where the action is. Being assigned a desk at the periphery near a window in Japan does not connote high status, but suggests that the person has little to contribute to the organization and may as well stay out of the way and enjoy the view.

Instead, models for designing collaborative environments come from those who collaborate best and who think about how collaboration takes place. Already, many Americans are veterans when it comes to working in teams. Although their horizon may be limited by their range of experience, we find that many have no trouble in identifying what does *not* work for them. Such experiences combined with suitable programs of theory and research should provide the most promising path for developing outstanding collaborative environments.

A VANGUARD CASE: OFF-SITE TRAINING CENTERS

One sign that organizations are becoming increasingly aware of the importance of having environments that support collaboration is the increasing use of conference and training centers. The concept of using specialized centers for conferencing and training, rather than using in-house facilities or regular hotels, is fairly new. The International Association of Conference Centers (IACC), which certifies centers, was founded in 1981. Yet a considerable amount of experience has been gained in recent years that could further our understanding of how environments can support or hinder collaboration.

Conference and training centers have several origins. Most are residential commercial centers, open to any organization. Others have been developed by organizations—including Xerox, Motorola, AT&T, and Arthur Anderson—for their in-house training. A few have been built by educational institutions, such as the Center for Creative Leadership in North Carolina and the Harvard Business School's Advanced Management Program.

These centers strive to serve diverse forms of collaboration by providing what IACC calls a *total meeting environment*. This translates into providing a full range of activity settings needed to facilitate different aspects of collaborating. The IACC conference standards, for example, include the following:

- Meeting rooms of appropriate size and arrangement, with suitable presentation resources
- Guest rooms that are larger than average in order to provide adequate, well-lighted work or study space, in addition to a place to sleep
- Sufficient breakout rooms to support task teams or training exercises
- Continuous availability of refreshments so groups can schedule breaks at their own convenience
- Private dining that supports confidential discussions during meals
- Copying and communication services, including fax, transcribing, and so on

In addition, many centers feature libraries, reading rooms, rooms with computers, and small offices, not to mention a wide variety of recreational facilities that support both team and individual activities as well as paths to stroll and talk. Some also feature outdoor "low-risk" and "high-rope" exercises designed to stimulate problem solving, personal challenge, openness, and team building.

Because of wide differences in what kinds of collaboration are sought, as well as differences in educational philosophies, these environments for collaboration will vary considerably. This is especially true in regards to the number of people who are expected to work together or be trained as a group. Most centers are designed to handle groups of twenty to fifty, but a program like Harvard Business School's Advanced Management Program regularly processes classes of a hundred with great success, drawing on a carefully thought out environment for this purpose. Some facilities are geared to the traditional lecture theater, augmented with the latest display technologies. Other facilities are designed to facilitate case discussions, using a semicircular seating arrangement—with access corridors for the discussion leader—so that participants and leaders can see one another and interact easily. Still other training programs have their participants doing exercises in small teams, with the groups as a whole meeting only a small fraction of the time.

Clearly there are lessons to be learned from the veteran users of these centers about how different kinds of collaboration are best supported. One straightforward way to achieve this would be to survey both leaders and participants about how their training environments frustrated or facilitated them. Business travelers who were surveyed for suggestions in planning hotels were often found to be extraordinarily sophisticated in how they selected hotels and even developed various innovative strategies to make hotel rooms more bearable. Similarly, many professional trainers representing various educational backgrounds, professional meeting planners, and professional conference coordinators—as well as managers who participate in various programs at different centers—should be able to supply valuable insights regarding the relevance of various conference resources to their particular needs. The survey questions would be a modification of those in Appendix A, targeted for various types of off-site training and conferencing.

By surveying users of various state-of-the-art conferencing sites, an overview could be obtained about what resources best support each type of collaborative process. Because a surprisingly large proportion of off-site training now involves learning computer-related procedures, such surveys should also shed considerable light on the ways that computers can be successfully incorporated.

Innovations in off-site collaborative environments, because they would be used so intensively, should have a trickle-down impact on the resources provided for on-site collaboration. Managers will become more sophisticated in collaborating, making more demands for suitable resources at their workplaces. Most important, these innovative centers should make apparent the unsuitability of traditional assumptions for today's collaborative activities.

IMPLICATIONS OF FLEXSPACE FOR FUTURE RESEARCH ON GROUPS

McGrath (1991) acknowledges that it is much harder to do research on a group if it is all over the place and repeatedly breaking out into various subgroups. Scientists like to have their subject matter under the microscope where they can watch it carefully. Yet it is unfair to ask a group to not take advantage of the immediacy of spontaneous thought and instead wait to develop an idea until it can assemble in the decision room under the watchful eye of the researcher. By then, the immediacy of the idea will have evaporated.

It should be noted, however, that GSS procedures create an electronic trail of information that may be a useful tool in itself for studying group process. Researchers can examine trails of information to compare those groups that are more successful in one way or another with those that are less successful. In addition, the electronic mail features of GSS software may be employed to request group members to fill out research instruments describing recent group events when they get back to their home bases. Instead then of having to corral groups within the artificial constraints of the observation room, groups can be followed through their natural sequences of activities.

To track the transition from a Theory X to a Theory Y orientation of collaborative work, it will be necessary to begin collecting data on the current state of the organization. We propose either a questionnaire or structured interview made up of questions raised by the eleven mistaken premises of group work (see Appendix A). If these data were collected over time—along with the electronic communication record, any available measures of interpersonal and group behavior, and outcome measures—we could begin to assess the progress being made toward optimizing computer-supported collaborative work.

CONCLUDING COMMENTS

Options for supporting group work will continue to expand, increasing pressures for an organization to decide what is consistent with its objectives and organizational culture. Some years ago, a research group at Xerox took the rather radical step of outfitting their meeting room with bean bag chairs. Today, networked laptop computers that are radio-linked to databases and electronic networks could be casually spread around the room on these chairs while colored electronic displays of the group's thinking illuminate the walls. Adequate support for collaborative work, however, is not handled by creating a few formal or informal high-tech showcase settings, but by creating a coherent "groupware" program (Johansen, 1988).

Unless care is taken to reconsider "premises about premises" in light of organizational objectives, organizations will continue to create environments for long-term, fixed-sized single-purpose groups with designated leaders that are formed by orderly planning processes for organizational hierarchies in which each person and each group has a place. Such environments will encourage groups to draw upon nearby participants and insulate them from other activities. Taking a static view of collaborative work, in which groups meet at regular times and places, these organizations will not empower groups to adjust to their changing life cycle needs regarding differentiation and integration or boundary management.

Many organizations instead should choose coherent groupware—combining an inventory of appropriate physical environments and several levels of electronic networking—to support serendipitous encounters, different types of group meetings, breakouts into task forces, informal rump sessions, evolving social and task leadership, privacy management, and concurrent membership in multiple groups. This support will not only enable companies to be more responsive to increasingly complex environments of constantly changing contingencies but also empower workers to participate more effectively and help organizations attract a more participative, committed work force.

APPENDIX A:
QUESTIONS FOR A STRUCTURED INTERVIEW ON FLEXSPACE

A. The Team

1. Whose decision was it to establish this team?
2. Who determined membership in this team?
3. How did you decide where to hold team meetings?
4. How many members are there in your team?
5. Has the team maintained a constant size and constant membership over its life? If not, how much has membership varied?

6. Has your team continuously engaged in the same sort of work over the life of the team? If not, describe the life cycle of the team.
7. How long has your team been in existence? How much longer do you expect this team to exist in its present form?
8. Has there been a single leader of the team? If not, has leadership been shared or rotated?
9. Is the team leadership integrated into the team or clearly differentiated from other members?
10. Are you aware of any significant interpersonal tensions within your team? If so, how much of an impact do you feel these are having on the effectiveness of the team?

B. On-Site Facilities and Computer Support

1. Did you encounter any difficulties in finding a place to meet?
2. Does your team have a regular meeting time and place? If not, have you experienced any difficulty in reserving appropriate space for your meetings? If so, is appropriate space available in your organization?
3. Are your present meeting spaces adequate to your needs? If not, what sort of spaces would you like to have available? Are such spaces currently available anywhere in your organization?
4. If team size has varied, have you been able to schedule appropriate space for the size of each meeting?
5. Has sufficient computer support been accessible to the team when it has needed it?
6. Has computer support ever intruded into and interfered with face-to-face interaction in the team?
7. If the team has gone through cycles of differentiation into smaller teams and reintegration, have sufficient *breakout* spaces been available to accommodate the various subgroups?
8. Are there aspects of your current computer support that create or necessitate particular leadership roles, such as coordinator or recorder? If so, what sorts of roles are present?
9. Do you regularly meet in a facility that has been committed to the exclusive use of your team or of your department?
10. Are the home offices of all team members in close proximity? If not, how have you decided on where to meet?
11. How have your team's space needs varied over the life cycle of your team's activities?

Chapter 9 Flexspace: Making Room for Collaborative Work

C. Coordination with Other Teams and External Members

1. Are you currently a member of other teams in the organization? If so, has your membership in one team created any problems in receiving updates and communications from the other teams of which you are a member?
2. Does your team include members from outside the organization? If so, are there any security problems involved in getting these members access to your meeting facilities?
3. How insulated from surrounding activities does your team need to be? Is it necessary to completely close the team off from outside distractions?
4. If you were to meet in a setting in which other members of the organization could drop in and out, would spontaneous participation from these members be useful?
5. Can the information with which your team is dealing be comfortably shared with all members of the team? Can it be shared with people outside the team? If not, what are the risks involved in breaches of security? Has the need to restrict access to information in any way inhibited the development of ideas and solutions?
6. Are you aware of any conflicts between your team and other teams within the organization? If so, how much of an impact do you feel these are having on the effectiveness of your team?
7. Are there aspects of your team's work that should be shared with other teams in the organization? Do you currently have mechanisms for sharing this information?

D. Off-Site Facilities and Computer Support

1. Do team members have access to computer support and data when working outside the organization? If not, is it because it has never been requested or because there are problems such as data security or budgetary constraints?
2. Does your team ever use off-site meeting facilities? If not, do you think it would be helpful to do so? If so, what aspects of the team's work are most likely to be done off-site? What off-site facilities are most needed?
3. What sort of off-site facilities might be useful to the team? Why would it be more appropriate to seek these facilities off-site rather than have them provided on-site?

CHAPTER 10

The User Interface in Group Support Systems*

Paul Gray
The Claremont Graduate School

Munir Mandviwalla
The Claremont Graduate School

Lorne Olfman
The Claremont Graduate School

John Satzinger
University of Georgia

INTRODUCTION

To the user, the system is the interface (Moran, 1981). For decision support systems, human-computer interactions can be analyzed in terms of Bennett's (1983) three questions:

1. What does the user see at the terminal?
2. What must the user know about what he or she sees at the terminal?
3. What can the user do with the system to accomplish the purpose of using the system?

---

* Portions of this chapter in somwhat different form appeared in Gray (1988), Gray and Olfman (1989), and Mandviwalla et al. (1991).

Chapter 10 The User Interface in Group Support Systems

These three questions, originally formulated for individual DSS design, apply equally well to Group Support System design. In considering GSS design, several additional factors have to be considered:

1. The design of the "public screen(s)."
2. The interaction between the public screen and the individual screen.
3. The design of the individual's workstation in the group environment.
4. The interaction among the participants.
5. Cognitive style differences among participants.
6. Cultural differences among participants.
7. The content of the specific meeting to be supported.
8. The type of information used by the group (text, numeric, database, or visual) in its deliberations.

These additional considerations increase the dimensionality of the interface problem. In terms of what the user of a GSS sees, the focus is on both the private and public screens. What the user must know includes individual and cultural style differences. What the user does with the system includes interactions with other participants and possibly a chauffeur and/or facilitator.

In this chapter, we explore the issues involved in interface design. We limit the discussion to GSSs in which all the participants are in the same room at the same time, that is, a system in which the group is involved in a conference whose purpose is either cooperative work or decision making. (For a discussion of other GSS arrangements, see DeSanctis and Gallupe, 1987; Johansen, 1988; or Johansen, 1991.) Our examples include interfaces developed between 1983 and 1991 at the University of Arizona, The Claremont Graduate School, and at XEROX Palo Alto Research Center (XEROX PARC). The University of Arizona and XEROX PARC interfaces are described in Gray and Olfman (1989). The Arizona GSS is described in more detail in Chapters 2 and 7. The Claremont Graduate School interface, called the CGS Environment, is described as an example at the end of this chapter.

THE INTERFACE IN A GROUP SUPPORT SYSTEM

In a GSS used to support conferencing, the basic structure is that of a set of individual DSS terminals interconnected by communications (Huber, 1984a; Bui & Jarke, 1986; Gray, 1987). What distinguishes a *same time/same place* GSS from an office automation system built around a local area network is that the participants are not only in the same room but also work together simultaneously on the same problem or decision. In so doing, the GSS requires software that supports the group as a whole and hardware/software combinations that can cope with periods of high demand when the group is performing a joint function such as information entry, voting, or ranking alternatives.

ISSUES IN DESIGN

Issue 1: The Design of the "Public Screen(s)"

The public screen is typically a display at the front of the room that is seen by everyone in the conference. Its purpose is to provide a common focus around which the discussion flows. In most current systems, only one person controls what is shown. Design decisions that have to be made involve technical, organizational, and cost issues. The distinctions are not clear-cut because the technology affects what can be done organizationally, organizational imperatives can drive technical decisions, and budget limitations may be decision factors. The following is a brief discussion of the design considerations for the public screen.

One Screen or Multiple Screens. Public screens involve projection of some display device. Each screen is limited to the lesser of the underlying resolution of the display device and the projection device. For example, CGA graphics from a PC are limited to 80 characters per line and 25 lines. Projection devices on the market are related to the resolutions available in CGA, EGA, and VGA formats, with each step in increasing resolution coming at escalating cost.

In many situations, the small amount of information available on the PC screen is just not sufficient. This is particularly true for many situations in which windowing is desired to compare several alternatives simultaneously. Therefore, Arizona (in its large facility) and Claremont use multiple public screens, each of which may be windowed, and XEROX uses a full-wall, rear-projection system that is bitmapped. Experience in multiscreen video indicates that people can absorb information from several sources simultaneously. Multiple screens can be used in various ways. For example, the screens may project long lists that require more than 25 lines, or one screen may have reference information on it (e.g., historical performance graphs, the meeting agenda), while another has currently changing information (e.g., charts belonging to the presentation being made). One screen may show the base case in a spreadsheet while the other shows the "what if" case.

During multinational discussions in which the same information has to be displayed in several languages, multiple screens become imperative because otherwise the information in each language has to occupy a small window on the single screen.

Resolution. Usually the intent is simply to project the same display on the public screen as on an individual workstation screen, such as the chauffeur's. In this case, the resolution decision is simple. The problem becomes more complicated if the private screens are high resolution. For example, if the workstations are 19-inch screens that provide pixel resolution so that two 8 ½-by 11-inch typewritten sheets can be displayed in "what you see is what you get" mode, it becomes extremely expensive to project information with the same resolution. Such resolution is available on the very large public screen at XEROX PARC (Stefik, 1987).

High resolution is needed in systems that support complex visual decisions such as those involved in creating packaging or engineering designs. Consider a group discussing a packaging design for a new product to be produced in Country A for sale in Country B. By using the graphics capabilities on the public screen, people from both cultures can see how the package will appear and can alert one another about culturally sensitive issues such as symbols or colors (see Issue 6 below).

Although higher resolution can increase the amount of information displayed on a single screen of given size, there are limits to the smallest lettering that the eye can discern. The desire and need for an ever-increasing amount of information displayed will push GSSs toward multiple high-resolution public screens.

Color versus Monochrome. Both systems at Arizona and one at Claremont use color projection. XEROX uses monochrome. Cost and resolution considerations both enter into this choice. Color is more expensive for a given resolution. The choice, however, is almost predefined. Public screens should match the private screens of individual workstations.

Speed of Response. The public screen (and private screens) should paint as quickly as possible. Thus, the underlying computer driver should have quick response. In a world in which they have the latest personal computers on their desks, executives will not put up with waiting for the screen to paint. If the GSS is tied to a mainframe, high-speed communications must be provided. 1200 or 2400 baud does not do; 9600 baud or better is recommended.

Location of Screen. The public screen is an integral part of the physical facility design (see Chapter 9 by Polley and Stone). In this section, we discuss the interface considerations in screen location.

The public screens must be visible to everyone. The usual arrangement has been to put the screens in the front of the room. In the large Arizona system and at XEROX PARC, people sit in a row and face the large screen, which is rear projected. In the small Arizona system and at Claremont, people are in a U-shaped arrangement where they can see one another and can also see the screen. However, in the U-shape, people who are close to the screen are at an angle, and people who face the screen are furthest away. If a curved screen is used to increase the sharpness of the display for people who view head-on, then the screen starts blurring for people who view it at large angles.

The U-shape allows everyone to talk directly to everyone else on a line of sight but makes public display design more difficult. Putting the public screen perpendicular to the discussion (as was done in the original setup at the Minnesota facility (DeSanctis & Gallupe, 1987)) forces people to choose between face-to-face discussion and the public screen. Putting people in rows makes it easier for them to read the public display but reduces eye contact and results in verbal discussion flowing principally between individuals sitting close to one another and between individuals and the chairperson.

The choice of seating arrangement is also affected by the culture in which the meeting takes place. For example, the U-shaped arrangement would not be appropriate for a negotiation in Japan because there people want to be physically opposite one another.

Controlling Public Screen Content. Whoever controls the public screen controls the flow of the discussion. Thus, the person who decides what is shown has power in the meeting. One approach is to give control to the conference chair or to the chair through the chauffeur. A second approach, used in the Minnesota GSS software (DeSanctis & Gallupe, 1987) is to allow any individual to control the content of the public screen. A third is to have some form of Roberts Rules of Order in which the person currently speaking can display his or her work on the public screen. A fourth is reflected in the Arizona software (see Chapter 7). The control problem becomes more complex with multiple public screens and/or multiple languages.

Cost. The larger the screen, the easier it is to view. Larger screen areas can also support increased resolution in the underlying drivers. However, increased resolution usually implies increased cost of the projection equipment. Furthermore, because large display systems have small markets, there are diseconomies of scale as screen size increases.

Issue 2: The Interaction Between the Public Screen and the Individual Screen

Relation of Private Screen to Public Screen. What is shown on the public screen should also be available on the private screens, particularly when a presentation is being given. For example, suppose someone is giving a briefing by projecting a series of charts using presentation graphics software. People should be able to look at that chart on their private screens as well as on the public screen. Furthermore, they should be able to leaf through the presentation both forward and backward. In a sophisticated system such as Colab at XEROX PARC, the public screen is available on demand in a window on the private screen.

It should be possible to move the contents of the private screen to the public screen. Thus, if an individual has an idea (e.g., a favorable "what if" case) he or she should be able to have his or her private screen displayed for everyone to see. The rules of the meeting will determine whether participants can do this at will or if they must go through the chauffeur or the chairperson.

Editing Capability. At the next level of sophistication, individuals should be able to edit or annotate the copy of the public screen on their private screens. Such editing capability can facilitate cooperative work. For example, if a contract is being negotiated, an individual may want to edit the text currently displayed and send it to the public screen. By windowing the public screen or by using multiple public screens, the alternative proposal and the original can be placed side by side and can be seen by everyone.

Language Choice. For multicultural GSS, group members should be able to work in their own language on their private screen irrespective of what language is being shown on the main public screen. For presentations, they should be able to leaf through the charts in the language of their choice. Where near-simultaneous translation is provided (see Issue 6), they should be able to view what is on the public screen on their own workstation in their own language.

Issue 3: The Design of the Individual Workstation in the Group Environment

Group Environment. The individual sits at a workstation that provides him/her with work space, data entry device(s), and a private screen. Because a GSS involves interpersonal interactions, the physical environment provided to group members individually and collectively is an inherent part of the human interface. The design of the work station requires attention to ergonomics. The work space should be comfortable in seating (knowledge workers spend a lot of their time sitting!), lighting, and ambiance. The last implies an executive "look and feel" for the facility. Ample space should be available to lay out documents, notepads, and other personal items.

Input Devices. A variety of input devices can be used including: (1)keyboard, (2) bit pad, (3) mouse, and (4) touch screen. A fundamental decision has to be made whether a particular piece of software will be keyboard-based (e.g., Minnesota) or nearly keyboardless. The conventional wisdom is to try to make real systems for executives as nearly keyboardless as possible. Although the younger generation was brought up on computers and is, on the whole, keyboard skilled, middle-aged managers often are not or have a "typing-is-for-secretaries" attitude. At Claremont, the keyboard is in a slide-out drawer under the table that allows it to be stored when not in use and increases the work space available to the participants. In multilingual situations, the required keyboard mappings increase the complexity of using typewriter input.

The mouse, the bit pad, and the touch screen are all alternatives to the keyboard. The touch screen requires the least skill and learning time. However, the resolution (smallest size that can be pointed to) is not as good as that for a mouse and some people become quite tired of pointing at the screen. The bit pad allows people to write and draw, although the resolution is often quite poor. Furthermore, many people's handwriting is difficult to read. The introduction of a number of pen-based computers in 1991 may presage improvement in this technology. The mouse requires some training, but more and more people have mouse skills.

Finally, voice input is on the horizon. Unfortunately, voice input has been on the horizon for over thirty years and has not yet been realized commercially in computing on a large scale except for voice mail. The exact time of its arrival is therefore problematic. Whether voice input can be used in face-to-face GSS still needs to be determined because of the problem of distinguishing voices when several members of the group are talking simultaneously. The computers used for private work would have to identify the voice(s) of their users. Furthermore, it is not clear that private work can be done verbally because the user's voice interferes with the meeting and loses some of the benefits of anonymity. Experience with sorting voices in audio- and videoconferencing should help with voice input.

The Private Screen. People should be able look at one another while talking in a meeting. This goal is achieved by recessing the private screen in front of the participant so it is not a barrier to the line of sight. Selecting the size of the private screen involves a design tradeoff. To make screens less obtrusive, small screens are preferred. However, to increase the amount of information seen, larger screens are required. Bitmapped screens increase the amount of information that can be shown. However, reading small type can be a problem for middle-aged executives.

Color versus Monochrome. The choice of color versus monochrome affects the private screens as well as the public screen. Color, even though it costs more for a given resolution, adds a dimension to the information displayed. However, many software designers do not understand how to use color effectively. The continuing improvements in color resolution should make this issue disappear. When they choose color combinations software designers should be particularly cognizant of the color-blind male because the probability of having one or more color-blind participants becomes significant for large groups.

Number of Persons per Screen. The Arizona and Claremont systems (Gray & Olfman, 1989) are set up so that two or more people can work comfortably at one workstation, whereas at the XEROX PARC system, (Stefik, 1987), in general, there is one person per screen. Having multiple people per screen allows small subgroups of participants to discuss responses and reinforce one another. Such reinforcement often generates increased interaction during a meeting. A single-user arrangement provides greater privacy but may result in individuals losing themselves in the screen rather than participating with the group.

Interaction of the Individual with the System. Because to the user the system is the interface, the designer must pay particular attention to how individuals interact with the system. The user should view the system as easy to use, efficient, easy to learn, and easy to relearn after some time away from it. (Users may have large time intervals between successive uses and forgetting does take place.) Most executives do not respond favorably to interfaces that require complex keystrokes, many steps, or use unfamiliar or hard-to-remember terminology. A computer system is viewed as inefficient if it takes as much time as a non-electronic competitor (such as pen and paper). Such a system will not be used. Participants in electronically supported meetings range from computer naive to computer expert. For the naive participant, the interface should be sufficiently simple that the user can participate in all supported aspects of the meeting. A user who cannot participate is likely to become hostile toward the system and not participate fully in the meeting.

Chapter 10 The User Interface in Group Support Systems

Considerable strides have been made in recent years in creating interfaces that feel comfortable to users. Furthermore, many organizations have chosen such software packages as their standard interface; hence, users are accustomed to good interfaces. To keep this feeling of comfort, the GSS should provide interfaces that are similar to what users see when working alone.

Customization to individual user needs is possible and can take several forms. One way to customize is to set up the information available to the user so that it is relevant to the meeting. For example, with a small amount of advance planning, every meeting participant can be given access to the agenda, the presentations, and the background documents relevant to the current meeting on their private screen. Although the information is customized to the usage required for the meeting, the look and functionality can be the same from meeting to meeting. Customization of look and feel can be carried one step further. Namely, if the person who will sit at a particular terminal is known, the information can be presented in a form that matches that person's cognitive style (see Issue 5).

Another form of customization is possible when users are allowed to do private work using their own software and data as well as group work. Such customization can be done if the electronic environment on the private screen allows the user to manage the work space on the screen by using a windowing environment. This entails providing tools that help users manage their group and personal work, bring in and take out files, and bring in and set up their own software.

Issue 4: Interaction Among Participants

In this section we examine two forms of communications beyond the verbal that are possible because of GSS and computer mediation: shared screens and electronic mail.

Shared screens. Screen-sharing software is becoming widely available as an aid to cooperative work. Such software allows two or more people to see the same information on their individual screens. At the simplest level, for example, using the voting capabilities of the software at Arizona, every participant sees the same screen and can interact with the screen but not directly with people sitting at other screens. At the other extreme, the Colab system by Xerox (Stefik, 1987) carries screen sharing to the level of WYSIWIS (What You See Is What I See).

Shared screens are not a complex issue if the mode of the GSS is synchronized and top-down. That is, if each person sees the same screen format and if the meeting leader decides what work will be performed and when it will be performed. However, screen sharing is an important issue when private work is performed (as in the Claremont and XEROX systems) and it is possible for individuals to become "out of sync" with the group. There are interface design tradeoffs here. Working on the same item provides common focus, whereas being able to work on different items enhances flexibility. If people can get out of sync, the designer needs to provide tools that allow individuals to get back "in sync" with the group. One approach, taken by the CGS Environment (see below) is to provide a "Groupbox," similar to an E-mail mailbox, that serves as a cache for all information about group interactions. A participant can catch up to the group by accessing the Groupbox. The philosophical viewpoint is that everyone in the group has the opportunity to participate whenever they choose to. An alternative approach is to insist that individuals participate on the group's time schedule. In this case, a time limit is attached to certain transactions such as votes. For example, if a response is not received within 5 minutes, an automatic abstention is entered. Mixes of the two approaches can be used.

Communication among Participants. A GSS makes it possible for participants to use electronic mail to send messages to one another. Electronic mail can be used to form alliances ("I agree with Jane. Let's back her"), indicate response to the current speaker (a "mood meter" is included in the systems at MCC and at Minnesota), and send other information either to everyone or to specific individuals.

Sending messages electronically, however, like passing paper notes, can be obtrusive. The sound of the keyboard clicking in a meeting while someone is talking can be considered rude. With keyboard interaction, the identities of the sender and receiver become known. In the above example, participants would realize who is behind the newfound support for Jane. An alternative is to provide discreetness by extending the mood meter approach to create many predefined messages that can be sent using only mouse input, or mouse input plus a few keystrokes.

Issue 5: Cognitive Style

The designer should not assume that all users of a GSS have the same cognitive style or that they come from the same cultural and language background. Cognitive style refers to the way an individual understands information most effectively. Cognitive style differences imply that a "one size fits all" approach to interface design should be avoided. For example, some people prefer columns of figures, whereas others prefer bar graphs. Although a GSS is designed for group use, the technology permits the information display to be custom tailored to individuals. A thoughtful designer will create interfaces that allow the user to select the form of presentation. Many commercial software packages allow users to set "profiles" according to their wishes. Thus, a participant may create a chart as a bar graph and have it displayed as a line chart on the public screen and as a table by someone else on their private screen. (Note, however, that some of this advantage is lost if private screens are shared.)

Issue 6: Cultural Differences

It is important for designers to remember that cultural differences have to be accommodated in design of the interface. Issues include presenting information in different languages, translating from one language to another, and recognizing that colors and icons have different meanings in different cultures (Gray, Olfman, & Park, 1988).

Group process is a set of behaviors. GSS provide tools that help organize and formalize these behaviors. To establish rapport in a cross-cultural setting, individuals from each culture must understand their counterparts' underlying beliefs and assumptions. The difficulty of achieving rapport is best underscored by the difficulty of understanding jokes and humor from radically different cultures. What is funny in one culture is not necessarily funny in another. Similarly, it is important to understand how groups achieve outcomes. Each group in each culture has a set of rules and norms of behavior it follows in trying to reach closure. The computer lays an extra layer of behavior on top. People from different cultures can perceive the same graphics or images in different ways. Little is known about the implications of this phenomenon for GSS. One helpful way of gaining insight about this problem would be, for example, for a group of Americans to observe the process of making a decision in a Korean "decision room," and vice versa. Even if the participants do not speak the language, simply observing what users see, what they must know, and what they can do prior to undertaking a joint session should help improve the process.

Translation in a GSS meeting involves both voice and text. To gain an understanding of the translation process, we first consider voice translation.

Two types of voice-to-voice language translation systems are usually provided: simultaneous and sequential. Simultaneous translation provides "real-time" translation from one language to another. In a voice-to-voice simultaneous translation, the listener hears the words of the speaker in his or her own language just after the words are spoken. The speaker continues without interruption and is generally only minimally aware of the translator's presence. Simultaneous translation is not word by word but depends on phrases and sentences to achieve the necessary context. As a result, even if the speaker is bilingual, he or she cannot tell whether the translation is accurate. In sequential voice-to-voice translation, a spoken sentence (more likely a paragraph) is retold in another language after it has been completed. The speaker hears the translation and waits until it is finished before continuing.

Because small, low-priced machines to support high-speed, high-accuracy translation between any pair of languages will most likely not be available for a long time, in the short term, computer-generated information (text, spreadsheets, graphs) will have to be handled by skilled facilitators who translate the material and type it in. On-line dictionaries, transliteration tools, and idiom translators will provide computer assistance to facilitators. Depending on the decision-making context and the methods available, translation can greatly slow the group process.

Issue 7. Content Specific to the Meeting

The GSS and its interface are inexorably intertwined with the content of the meeting. If only a single GSS package is used to support all meetings at a particular facility, then the major requirement is that the interface be reasonably consistent within that package. However, except perhaps for facilities that are rented out to solve a specific class of problems, a wide variety of topics are discussed at meetings. To support them, different computer packages are used. The interface designer is faced with several problems:

1. Providing *consistency* across the range of packages and across the range of meetings.
2. *Integrating* the pieces of a meeting into a whole.
3. Providing *memory* from one meeting to the next.
4. Providing *meeting administration*.

Consistency. Although research results, described later in this chapter, indicate that complete consistency is not necessarily desirable (or, for that matter achievable), participants in supported meetings do need to be able to deal with the variety of computer packages that they see. One approach is design all packages so that they mimic a commonly used interface such as WINDOWS™.

Integration. Most meetings cover more than one subject, even if they are on one topic. Usually an agenda specifies the sequence of items to be considered. Often the agenda items overlap or use common information, such as the capital budget or the project schedule. Provision has to be made in the interface so that participants can integrate this common information.

Meeting Memory. Most meetings do not occur in isolation. Many are heartbeat, occurring at regular intervals. Others convene periodically as needs arise. For ongoing meetings, meeting memory is particularly useful. An advantage of GSS is that it is possible to provide meeting history on line. The interface should provide access to minutes, documents, attendees, presentations, and other electronically stored material from previous meetings. (See Chapter 11 by Hoffer and Valacich for further discussion.)

Meeting Administration. Another aspect of the intersection between interface and meeting content is meeting administration. It is useful to use the interface to present information about the meeting such as the agenda, the name and location of the attendees, minutes of previous meetings, and so on. Strategies for displaying this information include using multiple public screens for permanent display or using hypertext buttons or pull-down menus to provide the information on demand.

Issue 8. Information Input and Output

Participants in a meeting interact with a variety of forms of information, including textual, numeric, database, and visual. The interface gives them access to this information and must be capable of providing input and output in each of these forms.

Textual. The simplest and most widely used form of information is text. In group situations documents, such as reports, proposals, or contracts, are often the basis for the discussion. GSS software provides text entry, editing, and retrieval capability. For example, group participants using brainstorming software can enter text, edit their own text, and request that the system retrieve text created by others. The facilitator can edit the output of the group. The Minnesota SAMM system provides both a group scratch pad and a private scratch pad; the group scratch pad can be viewed on the public screen, but the private scratch pad can be seen only by its originator.

A designer must decide what level of word-processing capability to provide. It is axiomatic that the more sophisticated the word processor, the fewer the participants who are able to use its full capabilities. Conversely, providing a minimal word-processing capability creates frustration and gives participants the impression that the system is unsophisticated and untrustworthy.

A particularly useful feature for an interface is the ability to put two documents or two versions of the same document next to one another on the screen so that participants can do comparisons and, if they like, edit one or both of them.

A feature at the next level of sophistication for document editing is group editing capability. Using an editor with this feature, a member of the group can make changes (blue line) and can identify himself or herself as the proposer of the change, if he or she so desires.

A feature at yet a higher level of sophistication is hypertext. For example, if a group is discussing a particular document, hypertext can be used to bring up definitions of terms, backup information, or even whole documents. This is done by pointing to a particular item and either clicking on it with a mouse or touching it with a finger on a touch screen. These sensitive areas are called *buttons*. The button approach in hypertext is used much more extensively in Executive Information Systems (EIS) than in GSS.

Numeric. Many group business discussions center around numeric information such as balance sheets, income statements, or spreadsheets. A spreadsheet, for example, may be used to present information to a group, to allow inquiry, that is, *drill down,* about the numeric information, or, in more sophisticated systems, allow GSS participants to ask *what-if* questions.

Drill down is a form of hypertext. It refers to the ability to point at a particular number and bring up supporting information. For example, if a user is concerned that total sales are low, he or she can use a mouse to click on the sales number to bring up a new table that shows the distribution of sales by territory or division or salesperson so that the source of the discrepancy can be understood. Drill down information need not be numeric. It could be a text note explaining the number, for example, "Don't worry. The check is in the mail".

Because the participants in a meeting have different levels of computer expertise, numeric information should be arranged so that the most important information is visible on a single screen. If several levels of detail are being presented (e.g., total sales and sales by region), the information must be organized so that successive levels of detail are presented one screen at a time. This requirement can be onerous because the amount of information on a standard screen is limited to 2000 characters (80 characters/line, 25 lines). For example, a typical spreadsheet, such as Excel, shows only 10 columns and 20 rows on a single screen unless columns or rows are compressed.

As discussed in the section headed *Cognitive Style,* some people prefer columns of figures, whereas others understand numeric information better in graphical form. It is often wise to present the same information two ways, as numbers and as a graph. An additional level of sophistication in a group setting is to allow individuals to select the graphic form they want to see on their own screen.

Database. Whether the group has access to a database customized for its needs or uses the organizational database, the interface designer needs to consider how the GSS provides access to that database. Query languages, such as SQL, require some training to be used effectively. If a skilled chauffeur is used by the group, then a complex query system is acceptable. However, for untrained users, simple database query schemes need to be provided.

Visual. Much of the work to date on GSS has focused on verbal and numeric decision making. The typical tasks for which GSS have been used (e.g., idea generation, alternative selection and voting, group writing, and financial "what ifs") all deal with words or numbers. Yet many decisions inherently involve two or three dimensions. For example, decisions on

- package and product design
- land use
- corporate logos
- organization charts
- office layout
- land use organization charts

all involve visualization and usually require one or more group meetings.

Drawing programs, CAD programs, and Geographic Information Systems (GIS) are available at relatively reasonable cost. These programs provide the capability both for creating the visuals about which decisions are to be made and for modifying them. Object oriented programs promise to make interactions with these programs widely accessible.

The public screen in a GSS provides everyone a view of the visual alternative being considered. Copies can also appear on the individual private screen. For simple tasks, such as approval of a logo, individuals can be given the use of drawing, CAD or GIS programs to do visual "what ifs." However, the ability of executives to use such programs is generally much less than their ability to interact with text. Therefore, a technical assistant familiar with the particular program being used is called for.

Object Orientation. Advances in graphics, particularly object orientation, offer great promise. An example is THINX, a package produced by Bell Atlantic Corporation that operates under Microsoft WINDOWS™. The package integrates drawing, object, text, database, and spreadsheet capabilities. Because the WINDOWS™ metaphor is becoming widely used, individuals are developing the skills needed to use packages such as THINX to create their own graphical "what ifs."

The THINX screen not only shows the drawing, but also the tools available. These include the following:

- A palette of standard objects (e.g., chairs and tables in an office layout)
- The conventional drawing palette
- The results of the underlying calculations done on a database.

The user can add, delete, and move standard objects, can change their size, thickness, and color, and can change their price or other attributes. The objects are linked to an underlying database and spreadsheet so that as objects are added or deleted, inventories of items, total costs, and other computed values are changed. Thus, to make changes in the design, the user only needs to manipulate what he or she sees on the screen, and the interface takes care of the changes in data. We believe that this is the direction that GSS interfaces must head.

EXAMPLE: THE CGS ENVIRONMENT (CGSE)

The Claremont GSS Support Environment (or CGS Environment for short) illustrates the application of many of the principles presented here. It supports group and individual work, a high and low level of synchronization in meetings, and such common meeting functions as communications and information sharing. The conceptual design of the system consists of a "meta-environment" that allows users to move seamlessly from activity to activity, performing either group or individual work. Thus, they can use the best available software for each activity. The meta-environment concept is based on the assumption that each meeting is planned and a custom system is constructed for each meeting or set of meetings. The initial implementation of the CGS Environment was as a WINDOWS™ 3.0 (Microsoft Corporation) application constructed with the Bridge Toolkit (Softbridge, Inc.). The system takes advantage of standard WINDOWS™ features such as mouse, pull-down menus, high resolution VGA graphics, direct manipulation interface, overlapping windows, and icons.

Background

Existing GSS software packages support business teams when the task at hand starts with problem definition and when the issues to be supported are verbal. They do not provide support for all group activities during a meeting. For example, the group's work may benefit from traditional single user software such as presentation programs and spreadsheets. Furthermore, little support is provided for individual work by meeting participants. It is difficult to exit any of these systems to undertake other activities not supported by them and then return. One approach is to expand a highly capable package, such as

GroupSystems, so that it contains the functionality needed for all types of group activities. Another is to create a "meta-environment" that allows users to move seamlessly from activity to activity, using the best available software for each activity. The CGS environment adopts the second approach.

The design emphasizes ease of learning, ease of relearning, minimum keystrokes, and ease of use. Furthermore, many meetings are high-pressure situations of limited time duration. Participants want to deal with the content of the meeting, not with the particulars of the system. *Customization* is used to make the system more transparent to the user. The interface refers directly to the content of the current meeting. The user has access to background data and tools relevant to the meeting and can consult them privately. Participants can work in or out of synchronization with the rest of the group. Furthermore, participants can bring their own software and data to the meeting and work with it.

The User Environment

If the meeting is customized to include every feature in the CGS Environment, users will see the following:

1. A windowing environment that allows the user to see several applications on the screen at once
2. A menuing interface, customized to the meeting, that allows the user to select the functions wanted
3. Access to the following functions:
   data about the meeting
   connection to the mainframe
   electronic mail
   the user's own data files
   applications for individual work
   the data files and group work
   tools to manage group and individual applications
     available on the network
4. The minutes of the meeting as they are being recorded and as a printed record for later use
5. On-line help in using the interface

The main menu of the CGS Environment (shown at the top of Figure 10.1) provides the following headings:

Meeting	Information about the current meeting and its participants
Information	Access to "information packages" associated with the current meeting
Group	Tools to support group interaction such as communications
Personal	Individual management of their group and individual work

Tools   Tools available for this meeting
Help   Access to on-line help.

The user can select any of the menu items to begin work. Because this menu has the same functionality as WINDOWS, it is familiar even to many first-time users. The menu has been customized, however, to provide the user with access to the tools he or she needs for the meeting. Figure 10.1 shows the details of the major menu items provided in the first implementation. Figure 10.1 is a representative sample of what can be done; it is neither limiting nor exhaustive.

Meeting. The Meeting menu contains commands related to the meeting itself. The functions performed by the individual commands are the following:

1. Current meeting (date, time, objective, scheduled participants, and a seating map of the current attendees)
2. Agenda
3. Previous meetings (minutes, participants, and information items about previous meetings of this group)
4. Future meetings
5. Minutes (If a group member is taking minutes, they are accessible at any time to all participants.)
6. Action items
7. Groups (select, edit, and create different groups in the system)
8. Meetings (Select, edit, and create different meetings) (Figure 10.2)

Groups and meetings are administrative tools. Because teams need several or regular meetings on a topic, the meeting data is kept in a database. The database stores information about past meetings and about meetings in preparation. The database thus allows customization information to be kept as part of each meeting. A meeting is always associated with a group. The *Groups* command is used to change to a different group and see the meetings for that group.

Information. A particular meeting agenda may deal with several topics. Each agenda item may require different application support and background information. To reduce the cognitive load of the user by freeing him or her from having to know how to retrieve files created in different applications and to provide the advantages of electronic storage (e.g., ease of editing and what-if capability), the *information package* was created. A typical information package will contain several items (computer files) packaged together by context. For example, the *Proposals* command in the Information menu (Figure 10.1) displays a spreadsheet and text describing the proposal and its merits (Figure 10.3).

The Information menu contains the different information packages put together by the meeting planner (Figure 10.1). Thus, each meeting will display a different set of submenu items in the Information menu. The labels of the information packages are used as the names for each of the submenu items. When

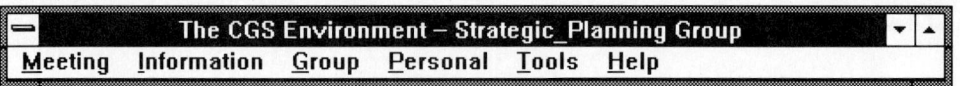

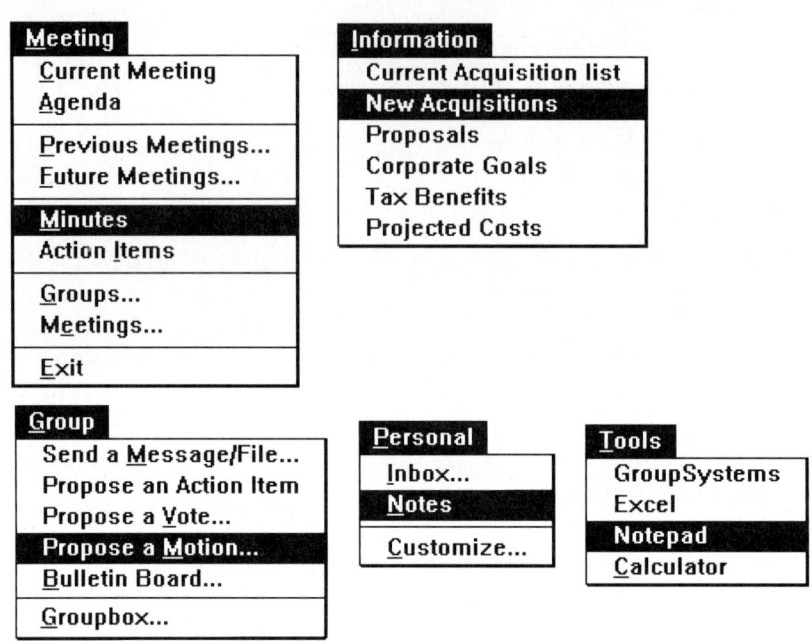

FIGURE 10.1 Main menu and submenu commands for a typical meeting.

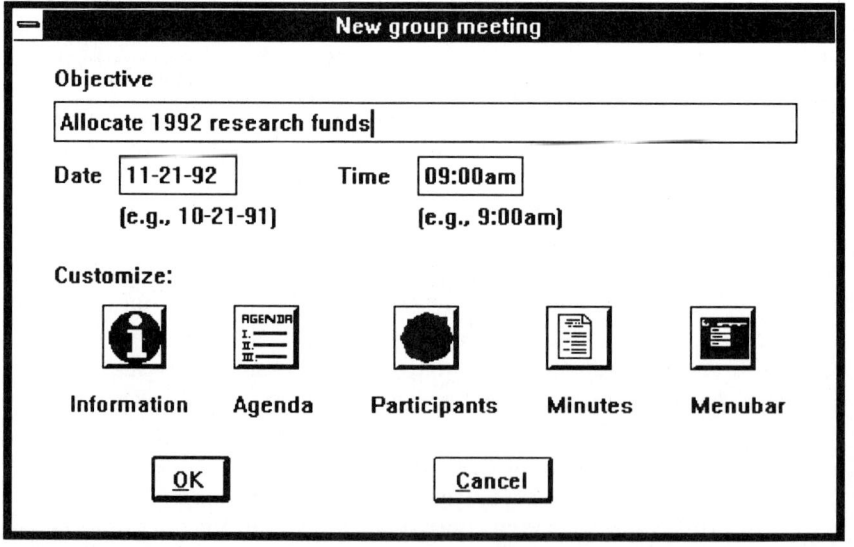

FIGURE 10.2 Preparing for a meeting.

Chapter 10 The User Interface in Group Support Systems

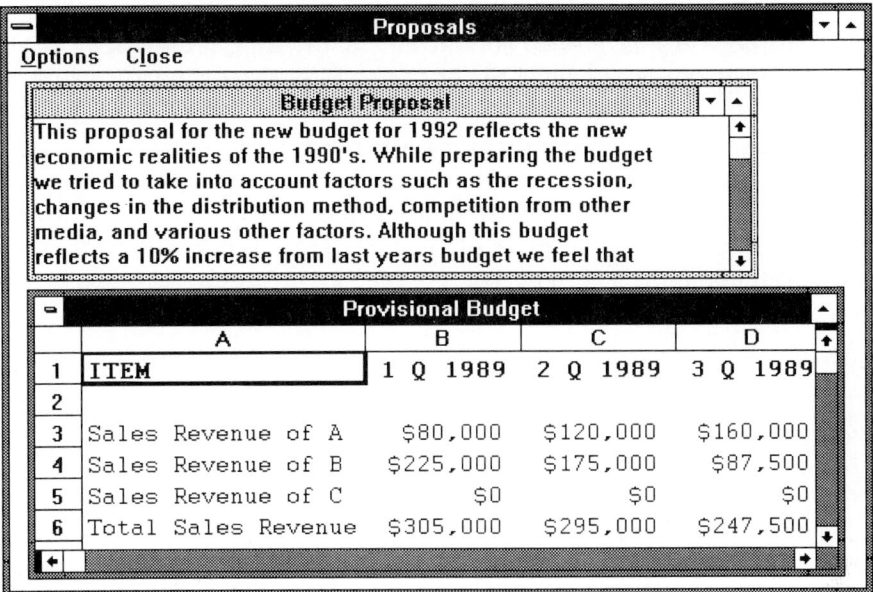

FIGURE 10.3 Example of an information package.

the participant selects an information package, typically one or more files are displayed on the screen. Depending on the choices made by the meeting planner, the file(s) may be displayed in the following:

- A simple dialog box
- An independent window
- The application program (such as a spreadsheet) in which they were created

Participants can be passive or active. They can view the information, or if they have the computer skills, they can manipulate it. If there is an underlying application, that underlying application program is accessible for what-if analysis or other work.

Group Interaction. At the group level the system provides tools to support interaction among participants during the meeting (Figure 10.1). The tools are the following:

1. *Messages and file sending.* One-line messages are sent to other meeting participants or broadcast to the group. If required, one or more files are enclosed with the message. This tool is designed to serve as a convenient substitute for passing notes and disks back and forth.
2. *Voting.* This command enables participants to propose votes. To set up a vote a participant selects the command, types in the vote, chooses from the vote-type options, and sends out the vote. Once the vote is sent out, it appears in the Groupbox (see below) of all the participants. A participant

can either respond to a vote or ignore it. Votes can have time limits. When all the votes have been submitted (or the time limit reached), the system informs the vote originator of the results. The originator can, if he or she so chooses, forward the results to all the participants' Groupboxes.

3. *Bulletin board.* The bulletin board serves as an anonymous suggestion box or mood meter.
4. *Groupbox.* Groupbox is a public mailbox that will hold all the transactions (e.g., proposed motions) of the meeting. Each participant has a unique Groupbox for each meeting.

Personal

The Personal menu commands help the individual manage group interaction and group and individual work (Figure 10.1). The main tool is the *inbox*. The distinction between the Groupbox and the Inbox is the same as the distinction between an office mailbox in which mail is received and an inbox on a desktop. The Personal menu is designed to help the individual manage his or her interactions and work, whereas the Group menu is designed to support the actual interaction. The *Customize* command in the Personal menu is used to set various options and is not discussed

Tools. The Tools menu accesses the different application programs that the meeting planner decided to make available (Figure 10.2). When a participant selects an application from this menu it is loaded for use. Both group and traditional single-user applications can be made available.

Summary and Conclusions

The CGS Environment expands GSS capabilities beyond those provided by existing GSS packages. It is based on the assumption that in a GSS environment, participants should be able to undertake a variety of tasks, including individual work. To create a full-service environment that permits retrieving, sharing, and generating information among group participants, the CGS Environment extends conventional GSS software in several dimensions. The CGS Environment allows the users to do the following:

1. Work with several applications simultaneously in a windowing environment, not just a single GSS package
2. Access and use their own applications and files as well as applications resident on the mainframe and the server
3. Work in or out of synchronization with the rest of the group
4. Obtain access to "information packages" specific to the current meeting

The specific information and tools available in a meeting are customized to that meeting. In effect, each meeting becomes its own virtual world. This approach solves the classical "please give me one more feature" problem faced by software designers. That is, no matter how rich a particular package, almost every user group imposes an additional requirement to meet its needs, and that requirement differs from group to group and even over time for the same group.

With the availability of the CGS environment, it becomes possible to explore the potentialities and implications of private work in a GSS environment. Although talked about for 10 years, private work capabilities have only rarely been implemented in same place/same time GSS. In fact, some early systems provided spreadsheet analysis, such as Mindsight at Execucom (Wagner, 1982) or the Decision room at Southern Methodist University (Gray, 1983). Observation of people doing private work with spreadsheets showed that independent work during meetings was possible and aided meeting outcomes.

Previous research on GSS has centered on studying groups using particular software packages. These packages have specific views of how meetings are conducted and constrain users to that format. In a sense, they are closed systems. The CGS environment promises a more open system that permits users much greater freedom in planning and running meetings.

NEEDED RESEARCH

Although each GSS that is developed attempts to create a simple, consistent, easy-to-use interface for the software modules included, little systematic research has been done on GSS software interfaces. The assumption has been that an interface that appears to work well for an individual will work well with a group of users.

One study (Satzinger, 1991) examined the issue of interface consistency in a suite of applications that are used together. This research applies directly to GSS because most GSS software packages provide a number of different applications for multiple users working on a single task. These packages typically attempt to maintain as close to perfect interface consistency as possible across applications. The study considered the question of whether such perfect consistency is possible or even appropriate.

Two alternative approaches for developing a GSS are to continually expand a software package so that it contains all required functionality or to create a meta-environment that allows the best of available software packages to be included. In the meta-environment approach, the GSS includes software modules and applications from a variety of developers and hence does not necessarily have consistent interfaces. The effects of consistent versus inconsistent interfaces across these applications becomes increasingly important as managers and professionals work with more and more applications for both private and group work.

Three types of interface consistency can be defined (Grudin, 1989):

- Internal consistency: consistency of interface attributes within the application, such as object names, screen layout, and selection technique.

- Analogical consistency: correspondence of objects, attributes, or relationships in the application to the world outside the computer application.
- External consistency: features of one interface correspond to features of another interface known to the user.

Unfortunately, it appears impossible to obtain all three types of consistency simultaneously. Even a GSS designed from scratch to include all required functionality in one "consistent" package will fall short of this goal.

Satzinger (1991) studied the effects of interface consistency across applications (external consistency) while controlling for analogical and internal consistency. The research model proposed that the effect of interface consistency on ease of learning and use would depend upon the degree of integration of the applications, the degree of simultaneous use of the applications, and the training environment provided. As discussed in Issue 7, GSS applications are moderately integrated, multiple applications are used in a given meeting, and training on the use of the GSS must be conducted quickly. The training emphasis is placed on the group task rather than the functionality of individual applications.

Studying the effects of interface design choices for a specific GSS in a controlled laboratory experiment requires manipulating attributes of the interface. That is, several alternate versions of a complete GSS must be developed for use by groups in experimental sessions. Such development is expensive and time consuming and may not be generalizable to other GSSs. Furthermore, using an existing GSS introduces the possibility of confounding the results because some subjects are familiar with the interface.

To conduct a series of experiments that manipulate attributes of the interface, single-user training prototypes of two GSS modules were developed. The interface of each module could be changed easily without affecting the degree of integration or degree of simultaneous use of the two modules. Various versions of the pair of modules, differing only in degree of consistency of the interface across applications, were used in training sessions. Differences in user learning and satisfaction with the GSS were measured. This approach also has the advantage that it avoids confounding the results by providing an interface that is unfamiliar to the subjects.

The two modules are called NUCLEUS and PIPELINE. NUCLEUS is used to create and maintain records of people, the work groups formed, and the information they generate. PIPELINE supports communication among people and work groups defined in NUCLEUS. The experiment manipulated the "look and feel" of the interface by providing consistent versus inconsistent menu hierarchies (command language syntax) and screen layouts (object display syntax). Consistent menu hierarchies facilitated performance as expected. However, contrary to expectations, inconsistent screen layouts across applications also increased performance. When multiple applications were used in a work session, learning and use were facilitated if each application had a distinctive visual appearance. A distinctive appearance helped users form a separate and more accurate conceptual model of each application.

A follow-up experiment, underway at the time this chapter was written, uses NUCLEUS and PIPELINE to examine the benefit of consistency in the use of names for objects and commands across applications (semantic design). Studies of interface consistency are also reported in Kellogg (1987) and Nielsen (1989).

CONCLUSIONS

The three interfaces used in this chapter range in complexity from the character-based menus of the GroupSystems software developed at the University of Arizona to the sophistication of WYSIWIS of Colab at XEROX PARC. It is worth thinking about these interfaces in terms of Bennett's (1983) paradigm: "What does the user see? What must the user know? What can the user do?" The Arizona system is the simplest to use. This simplicity is obtained at the expense of user flexibility. The user must know how to type and has to know (or learn) the rules by which the system works. In the CGS Environment, a user sees the WINDOWS environment and must be able to master elementary aspects of WINDOWS. In the mouse-driven WYSIWIS system at XEROX PARC, with its emphasis on cooperative work and information sharing, the user has the most information displayed and has the greatest freedom of action. This experimental system is designed for use by computer professionals. Because of its sophistication, even if the system is made available to executives and other knowledge workers, it is likely that it will require some time to learn all the possibilities of what can be done.

In thinking about these interfaces and how they are being used, it is clear that the combination of GSS hardware and software provides a powerful capability for human parallel processing. During conventional meetings, in which Roberts Rules of Order are followed and everyone speaks in turn, ideas are presented sequentially, and the conversation jumps around from topic to topic. In GSS arrangements, the participants can all "speak" at the same time; therefore more efficient creation and recording of ideas take place. The piggybacking of ideas is not lost because, as people work, they can see the input from others on the same topic and hence can add their responses to the discussion.

The interface is a critical success factor for decision support systems that is as important as the availability of appropriate software tools and proper training. The design of the interface for Group Support Systems is more complex than that for the individual work station. It involves consideration not only of the private screen, but also of the public screen(s), the relation of the public screens to the private screens, the physical environment of the facility (e.g., lighting), the response time of the network, the interaction among the participants, the differing cognitive styles of participants, and cultural differences. In short, the interface has to be designed using the systems approach.

CHAPTER

11

Group Memory in Group Support Systems: A Foundation for Design

Jeffrey A. Hoffer
Indiana University

Joseph S. Valacich
Indiana University

INTRODUCTION

Researchers frequently view organizations as information-processing systems, and memory is a central concept in this perspective on organizations (Galbraith, 1977). *Memory* is the facility to retain, recall, and manipulate history. Memory includes a repository of information as well as mechanisms to capture and to search for information in the repository. *Organizational memory* is a sharing of interpretations among the individuals in an organization. Besides history, memory may also include perceptions of today and expectations of the future.

Organizational theorists view *organizational memory* as composed of standard operating procedures, role descriptions, and cause maps, among other concepts (Walsh & Ungson, 1991). Of interest are the structure and content of memory; the processes for acquiring, accessing, and maintaining memory structure and content; and the consequences of memory on organization behavior. Some view organizational memory as ambiguous or artificial (Argyris & Schon, 1978). At a minimum, organizational memory is the collection or constellation of the memories (shared or isolated) of its organizational members, fraught with potential inconsistencies of interpretation.

Work groups present a special situation for organizational memory since the responsibilities of the group focus attention on sharing specific information.

This would suggest a group memory concept. Groups hold a series of meetings and engage in other interactions over time. In support of group memory, groups need the following:

1. Access to a wide range of information internal and external to the organization as well as internal and external to group process
2. The ability to dynamically and easily capture, store, and integrate information generated by group interactions and about group process
3. Support for use of both quantitative and qualitative decision models and aids (Valacich, Vogel, & Nunamaker, 1989)

In addition, information resulting from group deliberations and interactions (whether in meetings or from other activities), as well as information external to the group, typically forms the foundation for future group meetings and interactions.

One distinguishing feature of organizational, especially group, information processing is *data sharing.* Information held in public repositories (such as meeting transcripts, bulletin boards, corporate databases, and commercial data banks) is readily shared. Information held in personal repositories (such as personal files, E-mail folders, and local information systems) is likely to be inconsistent and must be explicitly transmitted or opened to be shared (Huber, 1984a). Information processing at the organizational and group levels typically involves several managers who try to converge on a similar interpretation. Organizational information processing must cope with diversity not typical of the information processing and memory of a single individual. Organizational information processing must bridge disagreement, ambiguity, and diversity in interpretations (equivocality) distinct from the information activities of isolated individuals (Daft & Lengel, 1986). Organizational memory, in whatever form, is a major source and repository of data in these interactions.

In modern organizations, various formal, shared repositories for organizational and group memory exist. These include knowledge bases, databases, word processing files, E-mail folders, office automation files, computer conferences, and other electronic and nonelectronic information storage systems. In particular, corporate databases have achieved special prominence because information is deemed a valuable and persistent organizational resource (McFadden & Hoffer, 1991).

A *database* is the shared understanding about an organization found in computerized records. A database is a group memory that is shared and is used at least for formal information processing. In addition, database technologies are now used as a base for Group Support Systems (e.g., Heminger & Valacich, 1991; Mandviwalla, Gray, Olfmund, & Satzinger, 1991). A corporate database is a repository of data about business transactions, market forecasts, product descriptions, physical and human resources, and a host of other components of group memory. Computerized repositories, like databases, are the source of many, if not most, printed reports on business performance, past organizational behavior, and results of decisions.

This chapter merges concepts of organizational memory and database management to lead to principles that can guide both organizational and database researchers in the design of computerized support for group memory. Viewing group memory in light of database technologies is necessary and insightful for two reasons. First, the development and use of advanced information technologies (like GSS built on a database platform) can cause us to reexamine various organizational theories, including those about organizational memory (Huber, 1990). Huber specifically proposes the more frequent development and use of computerized databases as components of organizational and group memories. He suggests that research is needed to understand what incentives are necessary for those organizational members whose actions produce new information, to share information, and to maintain the quality of information.

Second, the organization memory and database management fields have evolved separately, yet each addresses aspects of a single phenomenon—shared information. Thus, database researchers could learn much about the role of database technologies and the organizational imperatives for managing data by studying organizational memory. Organizational researchers could learn about the storage of and access to communal information (memory) from a dominant technology for business information processing.

This paper will accomplish these goals by discussing how a GSS, supported by a database foundation, can be designed to support group memory. The paper begins with an overview of theories and research on organizational learning and organizational memory. We then discuss the general requirements for a group memory, including group decision making and other activities that draw on a group memory. This is followed by an elaboration on specific requirements for managing group memory and a discussion of how these match with the capabilities of current database technologies. The paper concludes with a suggested high-level design for a group memory structure as part of a Group Support System.

OVERVIEW OF ORGANIZATIONAL LEARNING AND MEMORY

Organizational theorists often viewed organizational memory within the context of organizational learning. An organization learns if, through its processing of information, the range of its potential behaviors is changed (Huber, 1991). Organizational learning is based on four related constructs:

1. Knowledge acquisition—obtaining knowledge
2. Information distribution—sharing information that leads to new information or understanding
3. Information interpretation—information is given one or more commonly understood meanings
4. Organizational memory—means by which knowledge is stored for future use (Huber, 1991)

Chapter 11 Group Memory in Group Support Systems

These constructs are summarized in Figure 11.1 (adapted from Huber, 1991). In this scheme, organizational memory is subdivided into two subprocesses: (a) storing and retrieving information and (b) computer-based organizational memory. Obviously, these are not totally separable processes.

The storing and retrieving mechanisms for organizational memories are often inadequate. Cognitive deficiencies of human memory, personnel turnover, information overload, lack of knowledge of the existence or location of data, and other such factors are often suggested as limiting the effectiveness of organizational memories. When organizational members, due to such limitations or specialization of duties, "do not know what they know" (Huber, 1991), organizational and individual learning is retarded. Thus, for any organization and its members, learning is a primary goal to more effectively process information, and organizational memory is the primary tool for such learning. Further, computerized memories are offered as an aid for group activities and information processing. To lay a foundation for our discussion of organizational and group memory, we first outline the elements of organizational learning that set expectations for organizational memory.

Constructs and Processes	Descendants
Knowledge Acquisition	Congenital Learning
	Experimental Learning
	Experiments
	Self-Appraisals
	Serendipity
	Learning Curves
	Vicarious Learning
	Grafting
	Searching and Noticing
	Scanning
	Focused Search
	Performance Monitoring
Information Distribution	
Information Interpretation	Cognitive Maps and Framing
	Media Richness
	Information Overload
	Unlearning
Organizational Memory	Storing and Retrieving
	Computer-Based Organizational Memory

FIGURE 11.1 Organizational learning constructs and processes and descendants (adapted from Huber, 1991).

ORGANIZATIONAL LEARNING

Organizations learn by encoding inferences from history (memory) into routines that guide behavior (Levitt & March, 1988). Behavior is an evoked, repeatable response and is an adaptation of stored routines, much as the muscles of an athlete learn certain moves without the overt direction of the brain. Behavior is purposeful and is viewed as picking an appropriate action by matching the current situation (pattern) with past situations (patterns), rather than consciously choosing among alternatives. Actions are extensions of history more than the result of anticipating the future.

Organizational learning deals with either cognitive changes or behavioral changes by the organization (Fiol & Lyles, 1985). Cognitive change results in new shared understandings and conceptual schemes by organization members; behavioral changes are a change in the range of potential behaviors of organizational members (Huber, 1991). The literature on organizational learning has been summarized as reflecting two basic perspectives: the systems-structural perspective and the interpretive perspective (Daft & Huber, 1987).

The *systems-structural perspective* emphasizes the acquisition and distribution of information as a resource that is necessary for learning. The systems-structural perspective focuses on the process of learning. Message routing (the distribution of messages) and message summarizing (compression of ideas without loss of meaning) are important processes. The *interpretive perspective* focuses on a deeper reason for information exchange. In the interpretive perspective, information has utility because it can reduce uncertainty and equivocality and can therefore change one's understanding about the external world (Daft & Macintosh, 1981). Uncertainty can be simply defined as the absence of information. This is distinct from equivocality, which can be defined as the existence of multiple and conflicting interpretations about a situation. Uncertainty and equivocality are reduced, in part, by collecting and organizing information into shared repositories.

Many factors influence the ability of repositories to aid in the information gathering, equivocality reduction, and subsequent understanding within a GSS. Factors such as the capacity of the communication channels available (media richness), the flexibility of the representation schemes, and the ease of sharing information among group members all influence information gathering and understanding. Further, these concepts—channel capacity (see Chapters 4 and 12 for a discussion of this topic), ease of use (see Chapter 10), and sharing—influence the utility of a GSS to support the development and use of an organizational memory.

Organizational learning, thus, can be viewed as the acquisition and sharing of assumptions and cognitive maps among organizational (group) members (Shrivastava, 1983). Learning can occur when individuals compare their own assumptions and maps to what actually occurs. This comparison may result in two types of learning, single- and double-loop learning (Argyris & Schon, 1978). In single-loop learning, misconceptions are corrected (facts changed) within a fixed infrastructure. In database terms, the content of the database changes, but the structures or data relationships remain. In double-loop learning, organization norms, strategies, assumptions, and structures are fundamentally changed. For a database, this would appear as new or redefined relationships as well as changes to the data content. Double-loop learning requires a more flexible repository that supports dynamic changes to both the structure and content of the repository.

The constraints of using a computerized repository, such as a database, as a foundation for memory cause learning to be systematic and restricted. A more flexible option for an organizational learning repository might be a knowledge base (Srivastava, 1983). However, even the most dynamic object-oriented structures (for example see Carlson & Ram, 1990) require knowledge to be stored, accessed, and defined using specific constructs. Thus, actual implementations of organizational memory in even the most dynamic data management models may prove to be problematic and incomplete. (Readers wishing to learn more about organizational learning are referred to *Organization Science,* Volume 2, number 1 [1991].)

Organizational Memory

"Organizational memory refers to stored information from an organization's history that can be brought to bear on present decisions" (Walsh & Ungson, 1991, p. 61). The content of an organization's memory can limit its perspective and alternatives or, especially when shared and integrated, can expand the visible options. Thus, an organizational memory can be used to both develop and answer questions. However, the ways in which memory is structured and stored will affect its accessibility and usefulness. For example, technologies that act as organizational memory aids need to handle ad hoc and unanticipated queries and to store many types of information. These technologies also must be adaptable to a variety of purposes to best encourage memory use and evolution.

The existence of memory at the organizational level is not embraced by all organizational researchers. For example, Argyris and Schon (1978) argue that organizational memory is only a metaphor; in contrast, Sandelands and Stablein (1987) raise the possibility that organizations are mental entities capable of thought. It is unclear whether or not information processing ideas, derived from work on biological organisms, can be extended to social and organizational phenomena (Walsh & Ungson, 1991).

Walsh and Ungson (1991) identify three critical elements to an understanding of (and, hence, support for) organizational (and group) memory: the retention structure of memory, what they call locus of organizational memory; the processes by which the contents of organizational memory are manipulated (acquired, stored, and retrieved); and the ways in which the use of organizational memory affects group processes, organizational outcomes, and performance.

Retention and Memory Processing. The central component of organizational memory is information about critical decisions made and problems solved. Typically, the information can include issues that triggered an event, how a situation was handled, and the consequences of an organizational response. This information is usually distributed across six different storage facilities: humans, culture, transformations, structures, ecology, and external archives (see Table 11.1—adapted from Walsh & Ungson, 1991). Thus, a comprehensive electronic repository for organizational memory needs to draw from each of these facilities and needs to store a diverse set of information. However, not everything can be recorded in the organizational memory; a good deal of experience is unrecorded simply because the costs are too great (Levitt & March, 1988).

Role of Organizational Memory. Organizational memory serves three roles (Walsh & Ungson, 1991): informational (knowledge), control (reduces transaction costs by focusing on relevant options), and political (dependence and influence on actions of others). Thus, memory acts to frame a new situation. When decisions are made within such a framework, they are likely to be more effective and to meet with less resistance than those considered without reference to organizational memory.

Such frames appear as individual- and organizational-level schemata and heuristics (user views in database terminology), which act as filters and reference points to retrieve, process, and interpret data. These may block, obscure, simplify, or misrepresent event history. They are formed from a subset of experiences to facilitate (simplify) information processing. Douglas (1986) suggested

TABLE 11.1 Retention Facilities (adapted from Walsh & Ungson, 1991)

Storage Facility	Type of Information	Storage Requirements
Human	experiences, recollections, assumptions, values, beliefs, and formal records	use flexible data management technology for diverse knowledge
Culture	language, symbols, stories, frameworks, personal networks	retain and transmit to avoid unintentional alteration
Transformations	process knowledge, standard operation procedures, agendas	use rules and past transformations to guide current processes
Structures	organization structures that follow and copy job descriptions, patterns, titles, and role labels	inherit properties of general object
Ecology	physical layout of workplace	compress differences in space and time
External Archives	former employees, observers, news media, competitors, regulatory bodies	access and merge with internal data sources

that all members of a group may retrieve similar information from organizational memory (a kind of groupthink variation for organizational memory). However, the support of multiple and even conflicting (dialectic) memories could encourage learning by forcing a deeper investigation and a questioning of assumptions.

Thus, a single shared database may not be the ideal. This suggests a profound departure from classical data management thinking that a common conceptual, if not physical, data repository is desirable in an organization. Although multiple operating pictures can cause confusion and wasted reconciliation time, the ability to keep multiple perspectives on what has happened causes a closer examination of the organization.

A shared group memory structure can include checks for inconsistencies among the multiple views of the same information. Organizational memory is distributed, large, and complex. The distributed and multiple views support greater coverage and comprehensiveness. Thus, a support system (a computerized organizational memory management system) should be helpful to both group and organizational functioning.

GROUP DECISION MAKING AND THE ROLE OF GROUP MEMORY

Group work typically involves many task phases and therefore requires different types of process support. Herbert Simon (1960) characterized the basic decision-making process as consisting of three major phases: intelligence, design, and choice. During intelligence activities groups develop and share information and search the environment for conditions calling for decisions. During design activities groups develop and refine alternatives for possible courses of action. Choice involves selecting an alternative or course of action from those available. Simon's model suggests a flow of activities from intelligence to design to choice, with the option that at any phase there may be a return to a previous phase. Although this view of group decision making suggests a simplistic and a somewhat rational approach, our experience suggests that these three phases are generic activities—groups may perform one, two, or all activities, and in any order depending upon the task being performed. Nonetheless, it is likely that retention structures for the group process and outcome are required.

Within these generic group decision making activities—intelligence, design, and choice—there are several possible informational needs in which on-line, computerized memories can be used to enhance the group process. Further, in complex problem environments, it is unlikely that any decision can be made in a single interaction (meeting) with a relatively small and fixed group (Huber, 1990; Mintzberg et al., 1976; Witte, 1972). The completion of the process may necessitate multiple steps (meetings) lasting months or years, potentially involving new and different organizational members. Thus, there are numerous motivations for the development of dynamic and accessible group memories to support ongoing group processes. Several of these motivations are discussed below.

Common Organizational Information

Information such as organizational mission, goals, objectives, and basic policies is common and relevant to a wide variety of groups within an organization. As such, this information should be readily available to be accessed and potentially integrated into the context of group deliberations where appropriate. Not to do so means that the organization runs the risk of seeing groups proceed toward consensus on a path that might well violate existing organizational policies or goals.

Relevant External Information

As organizational environments become increasingly complex and interrelated, information external to the group and organization that might impact group decisions should also be made available. Much information is readily available and virtually free of charge (for example, federal, state, and local economic information). Additional information is available through private services at varying prices dependent, in part, on the subject matter and specificity of the information. The key is to be aware of available sources and have effective processes to monitor, access, and integrate relevant external information when appropriate.

A second type of external information that should be accessible in the context of group work is information about prior, similar problem contexts. Once accessed, this history can be used to evaluate the current situation so more effective strategies can be developed. Furthermore, the requirements for these external linkages may be different from group to group and from member to member within a single group.

Education of New Group Members

An important function of a group and organizational memory will be to bring new group members "up to speed" about information gleaned from prior group sessions. Groups tend, by nature, to have changing memberships due to including new or temporary members with specific interests when needed, conflicting time commitments, lack of interest, absenteeism, or turnover. Excessive amounts of time that new members spend learning about their group and their tasks is time that could otherwise be spent in moving forward on current group issues.

Session Continuity Support

In addition to bringing new members up to speed, an important function of group memory will be to provide continuity between current and prior events. For example, the outcomes of one interaction or meeting could serve to establish the agenda for the following meeting. Thus, the time required to review prior meeting material could be minimized without jeopardizing the group's ability to stay focused in moving forward towards resolution of a complex problem. Within a GSS, meeting and process continuity could thus consist of static support for browsing through previous meeting minutes and also dynamic support for provision of keyword searching and work flow management.

Response to Change

Current organizational environments are more competitive, complex, and turbulent. Thus, effective organizational performance requires faster responses to a more changing environment. An automated repository can contain the results of crisis scenarios and "game playing" in anticipation of future events. These group and organizational memories can thus be used to assist in responding to changing environments by allowing fast access to preprogrammed responses.

Group Coordination and Work Flow Management

A critical element in determining the success of a group activity is the amount of coordination, or team work, the group possesses. As groups get larger and more distributed or as members join the group to fill a short-term need, coordination becomes more critical. Many activities are sequenced such that activity A must be preformed before activity B (for example, a contract cannot be filed until it is signed). Further, many activities may require the use of a specific, scarce resource for completion. Thus, the effective tracking, monitoring, and coordinating of individuals and resources is critical to effective group processing and performance.

For more than a nontrivial problem, this coordination will be very difficult without the aid of computer-based systems and memories to aid in the scheduling and sequencing of events. The results of such improved coordination should lead to more effective time management of both human and capital resources, coordination of group activities both within and across sessions, and improved meeting processes and group interactions.

Support for Distributed Groups

Due to the downsizing of organizations, it is unlikely that any one organization will have all the expertise needed to solve all problems (Huber, 1990). It is more likely that organizations will solicit expertise as needed. Also, as decision and communication technologies such as GSSs become more pervasive, there is a greater likelihood that groups (or remote experts) distributed by both time or space could be effectively supported in a multifaceted goal-oriented meeting. (We say "multifaceted goal-oriented meeting" because we recognize that computer conferencing and electronic mail now effectively support groups for more communication-intensive activities.) Thus, technologies such as advanced database management systems that can support such distributed processing will be needed (see McFadden & Hoffer, 1990 for a discussion of the complexities associated with distributed processing from a technology perspective).

Creation of a Group and Organizational Memory

A broader objective of GSS technologies, beyond the support of discrete group processes, lies in capturing and recording information that supports the creation of an organizational memory. As such, information from multiple group sessions can be integrated with additional external and internal organizational information to provide a foundation of information from which an organization can continue to benefit. Information can be more conveniently shared between various projects, thus minimizing tendencies to "reinvent the wheel." High-level information can serve as a guideline for the development of more specific support data.

SUPPORT FOR THE DESIGN OF GROUP MEMORY

In the previous section we presented several general ways in which computerized memory can be used to support groups. In this section we build on those ideas by suggesting general design principles for supporting group memory within a GSS. This is done by extending the description of group memory above into specific group memory management capabilities. We do this within the context of database management, the primary approach for supporting data sharing in organizations. Within the construct of database management, we include such technologies and methodologies as database management systems, data dictionaries, data modeling, query and natural languages, knowledge bases and expert systems, and public data banks.

The Relationship of Database Management to Group Memory Management

The purpose of database management technologies is to encourage data sharing as well as minimal and consistent data storage, and to provide easy and flexible access to data. Although database technologies can support individuals, they typically support work groups or larger segments of an organization. Database systems provide needed capabilities, as well as exhibit certain limitations, for the support of group memory. These capabilities and limitations will be reviewed in the next two sections, respectively.

Database System Capabilities for Group Memory Management. Twelve capabilities of modern database systems, as viewed from a group memory perspective, are listed in Table 11.2. Current database technologies (primarily those based on the relational data model), to some degree, provide all of these requirements.

Group memory demands support from a wide variety of *retrieval* tools for scanning, focused search, and performance monitoring (Huber, 1991), which are information acquisition steps in organizational processes. Also important is the ability to retrieve information based upon associations (for example, all responses to a particular idea or all the comments related to the second-best decision solution). Further, because group memory is potentially so vast, group

TABLE 11.2 Group Memory Management Capabilities

Capability	Description
Data retrieval	browsing, selection, extraction, sorting, grouping, and comparing data from memory
Keyword indexing	finding data within context, such as by data, time associations, or source
Concurrency management	coordinating memory updating so each group member sees the most current data and their actions to update are independent of input sequences
Security restrictiveness	maintaining private or restricted access memories as required; allowing group members to change only those memory contents for which they are authorized
Anonymity	protecting, as needed, the source of group memory contents
Ease of joining/access	allowing access to memory and participation in group processes by any authorized group member at any time or from any access point
Unequivocality and fairness	providing a single, shared source of knowledge, equally accessible to all group members, and in which each contribution is treated equally
Continuity and consistency	permitting the seamless transfer of data generated in one group activity to another, without having to recall this history from outside the group memory
Validation and integrity	imposing rules or structures that identify errors and that add meaning; applying group screening through which false claims can be handled
Knowing what we know	finding where information is stored, what the information means, and how to gain access to it
No explicit routing	broadcasting knowledge (or making accessible this knowledge) to all with the right to see, without having to explicitly send this knowledge to anyone (and potentially not sending it to someone with a need to know)
Multiple interelated views	allowing each group member to locally arrange a subset of group memory of interest to them into a structure that is easy and meaningful for their purposes; grafting the memories of new group members into the group memory
Extensibility	extending/evolving data and procedures for handling data as more knowledge is collected; this is done with parsimony and often with nonlinear growth

memory must be *indexed* to facilitate filtering, organization, and finding desired information. This might be done by placing keywords on units of information or by building a network of folders for logically grouping information (Snyder & Lynch, 1990). Smart indexing (Huber, 1991) is also essential to reduce the burden in capturing group memory. Smart indexing would relieve group members from having to anticipate every way by which group memory contents might be retrieved.

Since group members may be *concurrently accessing* group memory, controls are needed to insure that one group member cannot lock out others by claiming exclusive use of parts of the memory. Further, group memory management must guarantee that group members are aware when changes have been made to group memory and that changes made by different group members do not interfere with each other (Greif & Sarin, 1987).

Often there needs to be *restricted access* to information in group memory. For example, access and changes to details of specific decisions, crises, or surprises should be restricted to those group members with the authority for such actions. El Sawy, Gomes, and Gonzalez (1986) propose a 2 by 2 grid for categorizing public and restricted institutional (group) memory (see Figure 11.2 adapted from El Sawy et al.). Semantic group memory is more factual and objective, usually having only one interpretation. Episodic group memory is more narrative and difficult to classify, and often it has multiple interpretations. *Anonymity* provides a form of security in that the source of information in memory is protected (although a GSS may still tag information with its source). Anonymity appears to facilitate the collection of a richer group memory by encouraging new contributions and challenging debatable views independent of the contributor's influence (Connolly, Jessup, & Valacich, 1990).

It should be relatively easy for organizational members *to join and participate in* group processes and to be socialized into groups, in contrast with face-to-face interactions. Some have speculated that people will join more electronically supported groups than face-to-face ones (Finholt & Sproull, 1990). Consequently, database support for group memory must provide the socialization to the group: to easily see history, to determine where the group is in its process, to identify who is in the group, to recall participant expectations, and so forth.

The support of group memory should diffuse power, thus increasing a sense of justice and *fairness* to organizational processes and decisions. Privileged access (access granted on the basis of factors other than formal authority or expertise) to group memory should not be supported, so competitive advantage within the group cannot occur. A computerized database reduces individual effects and equivocality, unless multiple views are explicitly supported. Such fairness and unequivocality should lead to less resistance in the implementation of decision choices than to those formed within less communicative environments (Walsh & Ungson, 1991).

Group memory transcends all group tasks, and the information captured in one group activity is often needed for another activity. Thus, support for group memory must provide for the *continuous* passing of *consistent* information

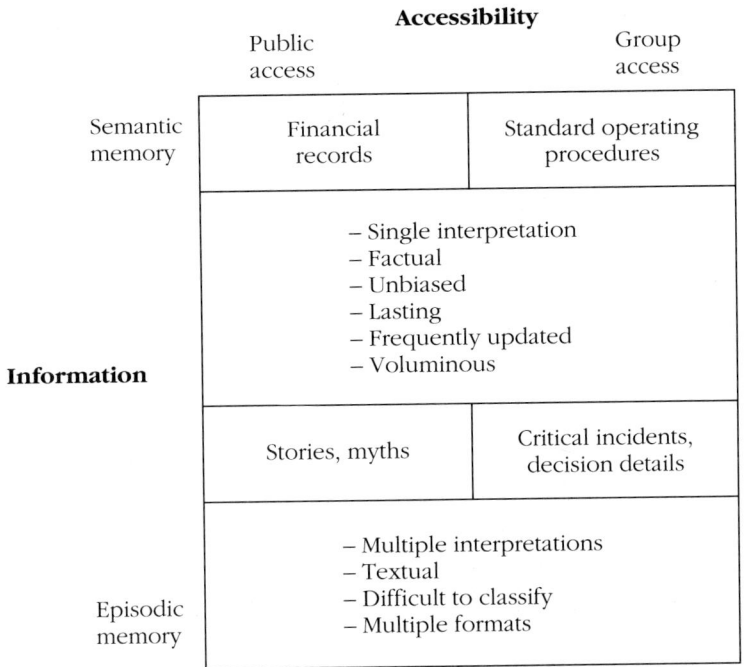

FIGURE 11.2 Group memory security and restrictiveness.

between group members and activities, even when the group interactions are asynchronous. An inaccurate shared group memory can lead to widespread confusion, poor decisions, lack of confidence, and wasted efforts in resolving errors. The restrictiveness of database structures impose business rules which *validate* and provide *integrity* to group memory. Such rules also give added meaning and consistency to shared data.

Possibly the most fundamental group memory capability is *knowing what the group knows,* or managing metadata. Except for systems that routinely index and store "hard" information, organizations (and groups) tend to have only weak capabilities for finding where a certain item of information is known to the organization (Huber, 1991). Simply providing an index to group memory sources could go a long way toward facilitating group interactions.

Group members with potentially synergistic information often do not know who else could benefit from that information, so they do not *route* information to the proper destinations (Huber, 1991). A shared group memory, as a central, but passive, repository, implicitly routes all knowledge to all with the rights to see.

Multiple views of group activities need to be "grafted" together as new members are added to the group. Also, each group member should not be burdened by having to sift through unwanted data. Members need to see just that portion of group memory required in the structure most convenient for their tasks. The ANSI 3-schema architecture and associated concept of data independence (McFadden & Hoffer, 1990) allows each group member to view and interpret data within their own schemata or cognitive map/frames.

It is inevitable that group memory will grow as group learning takes place. Group memory must be able to be *extended* without disrupting current contents (unless current knowledge is refuted by the new information). Also, new procedures to manipulate information must be able to be written by simply referring to existing group memory, without having to create new data repositories when existing ones suffice. Procedural knowledge should be included as easily as factual information.

DATABASE SYSTEM LIMITATIONS FOR GROUP MEMORY MANAGEMENT

Four limitations of current computer data management technologies restrict their usefulness for supporting group memory. First, current databases are media of *low richness* (Daft & Huber, 1987). For example, a computerized group memory can induce group members to see phenomena as distant and remote, stable, abstract, unequivocal, and to concentrate on hard measurements and rational expectations. Knowledge bases can add richness to group memory by including judgments and alternatives. Feelings, emotions, values, and processes need to be added to further improve the richness of computerized group memory repositories. Object-oriented and multimedia technologies, now just emerging for data management (e.g., Carlson & Ram, 1990), will also improve the richness of databases by allowing images, pictures, voice, and procedures to be handled consistently with numerical and textual information.

Second, automatic retrieval of information from preprogrammed data access procedures may cause a situation to be handled as a *routine decision* when a nonroutine response is called for (Walsh & Ungson, 1991). Alternately, the restrictiveness of a database may limit retrieval capabilities, and, hence, cause nonroutine responses when routine responses would have been appropriate, if only the group could have seen the relevant data.

Third, current shared database technologies are based on a fundamental *principle of consensus* on data definitions, ownership, and content. Conflicts over such a philosophy can reduce the benefits of a database, or, even more seriously, invalidate the group memory. When just a few group members ignore the database and operate from individual memories, the database may become useless. Until conflicting views can be tolerated by computerized databases, database technologies will be reduced in value as platforms for group memory.

Finally, group memory is potentially very large, lacks a clear structure, and must often be captured passively. Storage of data must happen as part of group activities, without group members having to explicitly classify data within a complex database structure. Because of the potential size, technology must filter messages coming into group memory to determine not only where to store reflects our preoccupation with decisions and answers, rather than with interpretations and questions. Drucker (1974) illustrates the problem:

> The key...is that the Westerner and the Japanese mean something different when they talk of "making a decision." In the West, all the emphasis is on the *answer* to the question. Indeed, our books on decision making try to develop systematic approaches to giving an answer. To the Japanese, however, the important element in decision making is *defining the question.* The important and crucial steps are to decide whether there is a need for a decision and what the decision is about. And it is in that step that the Japanese aim at attaining consensus. Indeed, it is this step that, to the Japanese, is the essence of the decision. The answer to the question (what the West considers *the* decision) follows from its definition. During the process that precedes the decision, no mention is made of what the answer might be...Thus the whole process is focused on finding out what the decision is really about, not what the decision should be. Its result is a meeting of the minds that there is (or is not) a need for a change in behavior. (pp. 466–467)

Our hunch is that GSS research has been inconclusive because the bulk of it focuses on answers rather than questions, outcomes rather than inputs, and structure rather than process. When we discuss sensemaking in this chapter, we argue as if sensemaking precedes decision making in a linear sense when, in fact, both processes operate simultaneously. Just as sensemaking shapes events into decisions, decision making clarifies what is happening. We isolate sensemaking here because sensemaking processes are different from decision making processes, and because we feel that the nature and processes of sensemaking are underdeveloped in GSS research compared to decision making.

The case for more attention to sensemaking will be developed in the following way. First, we discuss the nature of sensemaking and introduce the distinction between uncertainty and equivocality to differentiate sensemaking processes from judgment and choice processes of decision making. Second, having described sensemaking, we then discuss five ways in which individuals engage in sensemaking. These five processes, paraphrased from Weick (1985), are often truncated by computer aids, which explains why the enthusiasm for these aids are often muted (Kraemer & King, 1988, p. 140; Johansen, 1988, p. 128). We then explore the advantages and disadvantages of computer aids for sensemaking in the context of unaided and aided meetings. The potential advantages and disadvantages represent hypotheses to be tested, challenges for GSS design, and grounds for skepticism about GSS claims. We conclude the chapter with a brief review of implications for research, development, and practice.

SENSEMAKING IN EQUIVOCAL CONTEXTS

This essay is grounded in the imagery of sensemaking, rather than the imagery of problem definition (e.g., Smith, 1989) favored by GSS researchers, in order to highlight a set of issues whose neglect provides a plausible explanation for why existing support systems have met largely with mixed results. Sensemaking is about meanings rather than problems, and that is a difference that makes a difference. Sensemaking involves efforts to construct moderately consensual definitions that cohere long enough for people to be able to infer some idea of what they have, what they want, why they can't get it, and why it may not be worth getting in the first place. Sensemaking is about negotiation and construction of a mutually shared agreement of what causal linkages and outcome preferences constitute a confusing event. To simply call these activities of negotiation and construction "problem identification" is to miss the important point that to label a small portion of the stream of experiences as "a problem" is only one of many options. The stream could also be labeled a predicament, an enigma, a dilemma, or an opportunity. Each of these labels has a different implication for action. If it is a problem, then solve it; but if it is a predicament then accept it; if it is an enigma then ignore it; if it is a dilemma then define it away; and if it is an opportunity then exploit it. To call something a problem is the outcome of sensemaking. Furthermore, the problem often starts when something is labeled a problem. A problem is not some preexisting condition that is recognized, identified, or formulated. Instead, it is something that is constructed, something that is reified, something that need not be solved (e.g., simply getting something labeled as a problem may be sufficient to affirm one's power to manage meaning and that affirmation may be all that the task requires).

The genesis of sensemaking is a lack of fit between what we expect and what we encounter. To see this, we need to change the traditional preoccupation of decision studies with the user's question, "which course of action should we choose?" and look instead at an earlier point in time where users are unsure whether there is even a decision to be made. The question in this earlier period of confusion is, "what is going on here, and should I even be asking this question just now?" This difference can be seen by contrasting uncertainty and ignorance with equivocality and confusion.

Ignorance occurs when there is uncertainty and too little information. As information increases, ignorance decreases (Galbraith, 1973, p. 4). Uncertainty can be resolved through objective analysis because it consists of clear questions for which answers exist (Daft & Lengel, 1986, pp. 556–557). For example, a computer facility's management team is told to plan for data storage demands in a year. At first, team members are uncertain about which new storage devices to buy. Yet this task is clearly framed (assess current capacity, project application growth, identify capacity of potential new devices) and analytical methods can be applied to generate answers. Reducing ignorance is a fairly straightforward task.

Confusion occurs when equivocality and multiple, conflicting interpretations exist about an organizational event (Daft & Macintosh, 1981, p. 211). Confusion "leads to the exchange of existing views among managers to define problems and resolve conflicts through the enactment of a shared interpretation that can direct future activities" (Daft & Lengel, 1986, p. 557). For example, the computer facility's management team is given the responsibility, as part of its charter, to "plan for the future." How shall they do this? How far in the future: six months or three years? What is the scope of this planning: particular departments or all divisions? Should the team focus on existing technology (such as IMS) or emerging technology (such as object-oriented database systems)? Are these even the right questions to be asking? Nobody knows the answers to these questions, so the team must create a shared sense of order by defining and organizing the potential issues in order to meet this charter responsibility. Reducing confusion through sensemaking, when compared to reducing uncertainty through decision making, is often a convoluted, messy process.

One way to distinguish between ignorance and confusion is in terms of two dimensions used by Thompson and Tuden (1959) to describe decision-making strategies. These two dimensions are (1) extent of agreement on cause-effect links and (2) extent of agreement on preferences for outcomes. Their argument is that agreement on both dimensions favors decision making by computation strategies, disagreement on both dimensions favors inspiration strategies, agreement only on cause-effects favors compromise strategies whereas agreement only on preferences favors judgment strategies. Our argument is that Thompson and Tuden's framework, influential as it has been, captures a relatively late stage in group action and leaves a great deal unspecified. We would argue that it omits the most crucial stage in the process. To see this, think again about the contrast between ignorance and confusion.

When people are *ignorant* about causal linkages and preferences in a decision context and experience uncertainty, they know how much agreement exists among them on causation and preferences, but they do not know which decision option is the best. The question of which is the best option is, however, an explicit question, and they adopt one of four strategies to answer it. People experience uncertainty because they do not yet have an answer to the question of options, but they do know that some kind of answer is possible. And they

	Outcome preferences	
	Agreement	Disagreement
Causal linkages — Agreement	computation	compromise
Causal linkages — Disagreement	judgment	inspiration

FIGURE 12.1. Decision making strategies (from Thompson & Tuden, 1959, p.198).

know that as more information is obtained, they will have a better sense of what that answer might be.

When people are *confused* about causal relationships and preferences, their lack of understanding is much more basic. "Participants are not certain about what questions to ask, and if questions are posed, the situation is ill-defined to the point where a clear answer will not be forthcoming" (Daft & Lengel, 1986, pp. 556–557). The question of equivocality is not so much "is this the best option?" but rather "is there sufficient determinacy for us even to declare this to be an occasion that needs a decision?" A question like this reflects the existence of "multiple and conflicting interpretations," which is the hallmark of equivocality. Confusion exists because a shared interpretation of causation and preferences has *not* yet emerged.

When people are confused, they cannot determine whether agreement about preferences is high or low, because they have not yet agreed on an event about which questions of preference and causation can even be asked. The activity of bracketing and framing an event as a decision, with some amount of agreement concerning its causal structure and some amount of agreement on preferences for its outcomes, is a process of sensemaking. Sensemaking reduces equivocality and confusion. Once the event has been framed, then activity *within* that frame transforms the "givens" of a causal structure and a preference structure into a decision; this is a process of decision making that reduces uncertainty and ignorance.

When people are confused, they do at least five things to reduce equivocality: act, triangulate, affiliate, deliberate, or contextualize. These sensemaking processes produce at least two outcomes. First, potential cause-effect links begin to emerge, as do preferences for some effects over other effects. Second, as potential linkages and preferences begin to emerge, interpretations of their nature and strength begin to be compared and people discover that they agree or disagree on these interpretations.

The combination of causal linkages + preferences + interpretations + agreements *together* forms the relatively patterned uncertainty that people have come to designate as a judgment or choice situation. This patterned uncertainty then makes it possible for people to address Thompson and Tuden's question: Which decision strategy should we use? The question of strategy is a traditional question of decision making. However, from the perspective of sensemaking, the patterned uncertainty that enables people to worry about strategy is the *output* of sensemaking and equivocality reduction. The input to sensemaking is a diffuse sense of unease that perhaps something needs to be done, although no one can say for sure. The question—what decision making strategy should we adopt?—literally makes sense only *after* the decision context has itself been shaped and given definition by processes of sensemaking.

This process of prior shaping and sensemaking is often missed in GSS studies because it usually occurs before data collection ever begins. The agents of this prior sensemaking are people like experimenters who craft decision scenarios that will be handed to subjects, leaders who create meeting agendas that list decisions to be made, and schedulers who decide that the time is right for the group to meet in a decision room. Once these people have framed the decision, then the decision makers themselves are in effect presented with a *fait accompli.* This often means that the decision makers confront a problem that makes more sense to someone else than it does to them. Thus, when the participants start to make decisions, the options and issues they face have not been informed and shaped by their own efforts at sensemaking, the information available is not necessarily as rich as it could have been had their own sensemaking efforts generated it, and the decision itself is not framed in a way that makes the best use of whatever competencies they feel they bring to the task. In light of these shortcomings, all of which can be traced to short-circuiting the sensemaking process, it is not surprising that decision quality suffers and that enthusiasm for a decision's implementation is muted.

ACTIVITIES OF SENSEMAKING

Although sensemaking is a complex, ongoing process involving simultaneous induction and deduction and simultaneous thought and action, the following discussion is structured as if it were not. For the sake of exposition, we have adopted a convention used earlier (Weick, 1985) in which sensemaking is described as the construction of meaning using five different activities. These five categories are analytical rather than empirical; they were chosen to highlight different features of the sensemaking model. Sensemaking as a retrospective process is most visible in the activity of *action,* sensemaking as a consensual process is most visible in the activity of *triangulation,* sensemaking as an interactive process is most visible in the activity of *affiliation,* sensemaking as a cognitive process involving inference is most visible in the activity of *deliberation,* and sensemaking as a historical process is most visible in the process of *contextualization.*

Each of these activities makes a different contribution to the construction of meaning. Although it might seem as if affiliation is some kind of "master category," given the centrality of interaction in sensemaking, affiliation that is passive rather than active, homogeneous rather than diverse, impulsive rather than thoughtful, and contemporary rather than historical, should generate interpretations that collapse as soon as other groups or individuals are encountered (see Janis, 1982, on groupthink).

We assume that people who are confused by equivocal events gain more understanding of these events as they use more sensemaking activities. Interaction helps alleviate confusion, but more so when action is taken and multiple sources of data are compared and the results are pondered and the confusing event is placed in a context. It is the contemporary nature of these five activities that seems most threatened when confused people are expected to define and resolve their confusion in front of computer screens. The magnitude of this task is artificially reduced when the task is described as one of problem identification rather than sensemaking. It is our intention to convey an appreciation of this larger, messier process of sensemaking, so that designers are made more comfortable when they constrain and excise some of its features.

SENSEMAKING IN MEETINGS

An important part of our challenge to GSS researchers is the elusive concept of a well-run meeting. Many descriptions of well-run meetings exist (e.g., Hackman, 1990; Larson & LaFasto, 1989; Schwartzman, 1989). The traits of a well-run meeting in one context may be those of a poorly run meeting in another context (Steiner, 1972). Nevertheless, in the following discussion we will assume two idealized types of meetings: a "well-run" meeting and a "poorly-run" meeting. For our purposes, a well-run meeting is characterized by an appropriate number of participants who have a moderately diverse set of experiences, skills, knowledge, and influence (Hackman, 1987, pp. 324–327). In addition, participants have sufficient decision-making authority as well as productive conflict, competent leaders, commitment toward a common goal, and interpersonal skills (Hackman, 1987). These elements interact to create, among participants, a shared interpretation of which causal linkages and outcome preferences plausibly constitute the equivocal event. Participants need not agree on the specific strengths of the linkages or the specific form of the preferences, but they ought to agree on which linkages and preferences need to be discussed and which do not. In addition, well-run meetings ought to foster the kind of teamwork that will enable the interpretation to be implemented.

A poorly-run meeting is characterized by the opposite characteristics: homogeneous participants who are incompetent, uncooperative, insensitive, overly dominated, poorly led, and who disagree about the common goal.

Individuals who try to make sense of an equivocal event by means of a poorly-run meeting typically either fail to converge on a plausible shared interpretation or succeed in converging on an implausible shared interpretation. A critical challenge that GSS researchers need to answer is this: In order for GSS to work as sensemaking aids, meetings must be well-run. But if meetings are well-run, then participants do not need a GSS. Researchers who find where this statement is wrong will, we believe, have found the real value of GSS as sensemaking aids.

In the following discussion (summarized in Tables 12.1 and 12.2) we presume that most goals of GSS interventions match the qualities of well-run meetings. The potential advantages and disadvantages that GSS aids provide, as compared to unaided meetings, represent hypotheses to be tested. We have not sought to identify all of the issues but have, instead, selected just a few to illustrate the impacts of a GSS aid on sensemaking in meetings.

Action*

People learn about organizational events when they prod them to see what happens (e.g., Salancik, 1979). Through numerous iterations of trial and error, people discover things they did not know, learn which of their behaviors produce a desired effect, and often learn what the environment is and why it behaves as it does. This basically retrospective process can only occur if the person does something, such as walking around, touching, speaking, observing, hearing, and smelling, that evokes a reaction. This is akin to empirical medicine: physicians begin treatment so they can learn what they are treating from the patient's response. Diagnosis often follows treatment and is inferred from differential responses to the active intervention.

Unaided Action. Meetings provide individuals with at least two opportunities for kinds of trial-and-error activities that differ from those when they act alone. Because meetings isolate participants from the event, trial-and-error experiments are symbolic and vicarious. Furthermore, interpretations are based on indirect feedback, which is more subject to distortion.

An initial advantage of meetings over singular action is that participants can be used as remote event representatives, with their responses replacing an event's responses. Because meeting participants cannot act directly on the event, they must experiment vicariously by articulating questions and statements for the group. Saying something is an organizational action (Schwartzman, 1989, p. 40) that experts can react to based on their expectations of the probable outcomes of such experiments. For example, a financial planner proposes cutting expenditures by 25 percent. In response, the marketing and production directors bluster that such an action will have damaging effects on an upcoming new product launch. Upon hearing and seeing this reaction, the financial planner adjusts her interpretation of the budgeting proposal to incorporate the new information (that the new product may suffer, that the directors reacted strongly against the proposal). The financial planner has substituted the directors' response for that of the customer.

A second advantage is that many meetings convene to create an event that is self-contained and requires no interaction with individuals outside the meeting. In these situations, participants can act on the socially constructed event directly and make sense using a wider range of action tactics than they could when working alone. For example, labor contract negotiations are self-contained because propositions, bluffs, and arguments produce, for experts, directly observable manifestations of the relationship that is being enacted. Participants start "treating" their adversaries and by doing so, learn what their proposals and behaviors mean when they see the reaction of adversaries. Although the negotiators must answer to constituencies outside the meeting, the negotiation process itself remains independent of those processes.

---

*We offer here only brief descriptions of the five sensemaking strategies. For a more thorough discussion, see Weick (1985).

TABLE 12.1 Group Sensemaking in Meetings—Potential Positive Contributions of GSS

Strategy Treatment	Group With No Aid: Advantages*	Group Using a GSS Aid: Disadvantages*
Action	Isolation from the event creates a lack of direct feedback and over-reliance on memory and prediction Lack of evidence leads to Type I and II errors	Event simulation allows multiple representations, through vicarious, trial-and-error experimentation
Triangulation	Information overload can cause use of biased heuristics Consensus-seeking behavior can prevent use of diverse measures	Aid can manage large volumes of hard data Communication access to diverse, external information sources
Affiliation	Group dynamics can induce uneven participation Polarization can encourage premature adoption of dominant interpretation Groupthink can prevent consideration of contrary yet plausible views Conflict can prevent consensus	Aids that prevent process losses can improve discussion Aid WYSIWIS features enable negotiation from common referents
Deliberation	Discussion can interrupt thinking Audience effects can prevent creativity Inappropriate pace can disrupt reasoning	Imposed social protocols increase task enabling deeper concentration Task focus improves consideration of several approaches Personal workstation enables offline deliberation Artifacts can act as group memory
Contextualization	Physical and cognitive meeting context can trap participants into narrowly constructed mindset	"Organization as information processor" metaphor can help make sense of events

*Advantages and disadvantages are not meant to correspond directly

TABLE 12.2 Group Sensemaking in Meetings—Potential Negative Contributions of GSS

Strategy Treatment	Group With No Aid: Advantages*	Group Using a GSS Aid: Disadvantages*
Action	Participants can act as event representatives and provide feedback Participants can construct an event within the confines and context of the meeting	Simulation aids with a biased or incomplete representation can mislead confused people
Triangulation	More people means more information and measures available Different views can guard against use of homogeneous measures	Anonymity features prevent assessment of idea source pedigree Limited strategies imposed by aid limit discussion to homogeneous measures
Affiliation	Meetings encourage more participation, which surfaces more diverse views, which leads to more stable shared interpretations Participants can enact roles and relationships Participants can provide social support for group	Decreased social communication prevents role and relationship building, comparison of views, and negotiation of differences Increased diversity of views can prevent consensus Imposition of strategies prevents emergent, innovative approaches
Deliberation	Diverse views introduce new information, which induces different reasoning patterns Artifacts can serve as "group memory" and can be reviewed later when they make more sense	Parallel informtion-creation features overload participants' cognitive capabilities and force attention on the aid rather than the event "Media effects" force attention on the aid, rather than the event
Contextualization	Diverse individual histories can spark the creation of new mindsets Group's experience can become a metaphor for future sensemaking episodes	Participants may follow only a "computer logic" mindset High density of information may overwhelm figure-ground identification skills and impair memory, abstraction, and induction

*Advantages and disadvantages are not meant to correspond directly

Meetings, compared to working alone, can intensify at least two barriers to trial-and-error activities: constrained tactics and acceptance of implausible interpretations.

First, a meeting usually separates participants from the event that they want to understand and this limits the variety of tactics they can use to purely intellectual actions such as remembering and predicting. Both of these are fallible cognitive processes. For example, bank branch operations staff cannot observe directly why three separate branches regularly receive negative customer reactions. When they sit in a meeting room, they can't look around the branch, talk to clerks, stand in lines, park, or do other things that may cause the negative evaluations. Occasionally, participants who trust their imaginations can present the results of their intellectual experiments to others and narrow the cognitive gap between the meeting and the real event, perhaps even enough to make satisfactory sense of the event. But for many events, and many people, imagination is suspect.

Second, when individuals cannot evoke direct feedback from an event, two consequences are likely. First, they lose confidence in a plausible interpretation because confirming evidence is absent. Thus, they are more prone to make a Type I error. Second, they may gain more confidence in an implausible interpretation because disconfirming evidence is absent. This Type II error can lead people to stop their sensemaking search and employ an ineffective decision strategy.

Aided Action. When individuals meet in a decision support facility, they are still physically isolated from an event, but they gain one advantage over unaided group sensemaking: group event simulation.

Participants can simulate experience for group interpretation and thereby make better use of the knowledge carried by event representatives. However, to do this, GSS aids must be viewed less as aids built to improve group processes and more as aids built to represent *a* view of an organizational event. GSS aids have the potential to simulate more aspects of an event for vicarious observation than is possible in unaided meetings.

Individual decision support systems that simulate organizational events, currently developed and used by organizations, could be adapted to help people construct ideas about causal linkages, preferences, and interpretations in a group setting. For example, a computer program that simulates actual manufacturing line flows could be used by purchasers, manufacturing engineers, or personnel planners to test how different production assumptions affect line behavior. Multiple trial and error tests on the simulation could be analyzed and interpreted in a short period by meeting participants with different agendas.

A simulation aid can be a threat to sensemaking in at least two ways. First, any computer program that simulates an event imposes the programmer's interpretation on users (Crowston & Malone, 1988), which could conceal linkages, preferences, and interpretations that people need to consider. Second, a simulation aid works only for organizational events that can be modeled accurately, which is a serious limitation when the basic issue involves confusion (Smith, 1988, p. 1500). Confused people don't know which questions to ask and can't agree on which causal linkages, preferences, and interpretations need to be discussed. They are grasping for sensible anchors in a stream of nonsense. If an aid offers only anchors based on abstract assumptions using machine-compatible data, then confused people may have little idea of what to do with the abstractions. If they proceed anyway, sensemaking tends to be arbitrary and shaky. For example, resource allocation based on political processes probably cannot be modeled because the actors involved seldom divulge their true tactics. If designers speculate about these tactics, and build those speculations into the model, then the result may be more confusion instead of less.

Existing GSS aids seem to offer few action advantages over unaided meetings because they do not overcome the two main action deficiencies present in unaided meetings: event isolation and constrained experimental tactics. Individuals meeting in a room where GSS technology can operate are *still* isolated, physically and cognitively, from most organizational events. Even a good computer-based simulation of an organizational event can only decrease the cognitive distance between a meeting room and a programmer, not necessarily between the room and the event itself.

Triangulation

Triangulation is a normal practice of scientists (e.g., Jick, 1979; Huff, 1981) and, just as scientists use a variety of measures to make sense of confusing phenomena, so do members of organizations.

> Triangulation, however, can be something other than scaling, reliability, and convergent validation. It can also capture a more complete, *holistic*, and contextual portrayal of the unit(s) under study. That is, beyond the analysis of overlapping variance, the use of multiple measures may also uncover some unique variance which otherwise may have been neglected by single methods. It is here that qualitative methods, in particular, can play an especially prominent role by eliciting data and suggesting conclusions to which other methods would be blind. (Jick, 1979, p. 603)

For example, think again about the computer facility management team and their task of planning for the future. Current usage statistics, transaction volume projections, and what-if analyses are not sufficient by themselves to provide unequivocal data about an organization's future information systems needs. The conclusions from these data need to be checked against qualitatively different sources such as customer interviews, informal conversations with users and management, visits to vendors' research and development labs, analysis of questions phoned to the help desk, and the speed with which new applications get approved and developed. These measures each present their own weaknesses, but together they enable the team to converge on an interpretation of what could plausibly happen in the industry and what is possible to implement in the organization. "The key point is that the convergence involves qualitatively different measures, not simply increasingly detailed refinements, ratios, and comparisons within the same set of measures. What survives in common among the several measures is something that is sensible rather than fanciful" (Weick, 1985, p. 53).

Unaided Triangulation

When individuals triangulate in meetings, they gain at least one important advantage over triangulating alone. In meetings, the participation of experts with diverse experiences can increase the variety of measures used by the group to make sense of equivocal events (Smith, 1988, p. 1499). Simply put,

> there is more information in a group than in any of its members. Even if one member of the group (e.g., the leader) knows much more than anyone else, the limited unique knowledge of lesser-informed individuals could serve to fill in some gaps in knowledge (Maier, 1967, p. 240).

For example, some people prefer to draw conclusions from qualitative measures (e.g., conversations, observation), whereas others prefer quantitative measures (e.g., surveys, analytical models). When alone, individuals stick to their preferred methods and often miss key information. Together, these individual preferences are supplemented when participants with opposing preferences expose the limitations in these measures and the group works to overcome these limitations.

However, meetings also tend to intensify an existing threat to triangulation (information overload) and create a new one—social conformity pressures. Greater diversity of measures produces increasing volumes of information, which, at some point, overwhelm peoples' capacities for memory, attention, and analysis. To counter the overload, confused people may call on biased heuristics (Tversky & Kahneman, 1974, p. 1124), miss useful information, and increase confusion rather than reduce it.

A further problem with groups is that they often encourage consensus-seeking patterns of behavior (Janis, 1982). Consensus-seeking groups focus on a limited set of measures in the interest of agreement and ignore measures that would introduce contradictory evidence (Janis' "mindguard" concept, 1982, pp. 40–41). When individuals move into meetings, they often face conformity pressures that encourage them to give up their unique interpretation, even if it represents a better solution (Myers & Lamm, 1976, p. 603; Schlesinger, 1965, pp. 225–243). Although conformity dynamics can improve group cohesiveness and social identity (Tajfel & Turner, 1986, p. 16), they pose a continuing threat to triangulation because they limit input.

Aided Triangulation. Individuals in aided meetings benefit from at least two triangulating tactics that are not available in unaided meetings.

Eisenhardt (1989) found that executives who made successful decisions "routinely paid close attention to quantitative indicators such as daily and weekly tracking of bookings, scrap, inventory.... They preferred these operational indicators to more refined accounting data such as profit" (p. 551). GSS aids can manage large volumes of hard data for participants who are limited by their own cognitive processing capabilities. GSS aids that capture real-time data at the source and present it to participants in understandable form can make the data more accessible to groups.

Second, a GSS aid can provide communication access to diverse information sources not represented in the room (Huber, 1990, p. 55). Sometimes electronic information sources such as databases, document bases, video bases, audio bases (Johansen, 1988, p. 183), and image bases (Rorvig, 1989) can provide diverse measures of an organizational event. For example, a video-based GSS aid with tapes of customers standing in line at a bank may provide nonquantifiable information about customer line behavior that helps branch architects resolve confusion about the genesis of complaints. Unfortunately, existing GSS aids seem limited to only text-based information sources such as electronic mail or electronic conferences.

GSS aids do not guarantee triangulation, however. Anonymity may reduce social barriers to participation; however, it can also raise communication barriers to triangulation because it removes social cues from messages. In one study, the aided group "members, and particularly the leaders, found the anonymous nature of [electronic] messages irritating, as they could not always put the message in the context of the group discussion" (Jarvenpaa, Rao, & Huber, 1988, p. 658). Knowing who said what and how they said it lets people infer meanings of messages because they know the speaker is an expert (or a novice), is a potential beneficiary of the decision (or a loser), and is influential (or peripheral). Aid-induced anonymity strips these cues from communication and prevents individuals from assessing the credibility of the measure's source.

Existing GSS aids, by virtue of their technical limitations, do not yet incorporate the diverse strategies that are associated with triangulation. They are too structured and too similar to improve much on unaided sensemaking discussion (Ellis, Gibbs, & Rein, 1991, p. 51; Johansen, 1991, p. 186). For example, aids that impose the Delphi procedure only provide measures that represent quantitative estimates of event qualities (McGrath, 1984, p. 74).

Affiliation

People learn about organizational events and construct meanings when they compare what they see with what others see and then negotiate some mutually acceptable version of what exists. The highly symbolic character of most organizational life makes it necessary to construct much of the environment if any stability is to be achieved. When confusion is high, it is especially important to know what other people think and where their analyses converge and diverge with one's own.

Unaided Affiliation. A meeting represents an intentional effort to facilitate sensemaking through affiliating. When individuals interact face to face, they can compare views, negotiate shared realities, and produce a plausible shared interpretation about an organizational event more quickly, because group conversation replaces separate dyadic conversations spread across different time periods and different contexts.

Meetings can encourage fuller participation by more individuals. Individuals in dyads may be reluctant to compare their views if they perceive that a partner holds contradictory views. Conflicting views threaten the very existence of the dyad (Simmel, 1950, pp. 118–144). In meetings, reluctant individuals may be more willing to air potential conflicts because less is at stake. They may believe at least one other participant shares a similar view and may therefore feel less threatened in offering their view for comparison (Asch, 1958, p. 9; Lamm & Myers, 1978, pp. 185–186). Once this barrier to participation falls, individuals can become more active in the discussion and assume more personal responsibility (Brickner, Harkins, & Ostrum, 1986); this often makes people more secure in their differences.

With fuller participation in well-run meetings comes at least three affiliation advantages over working alone: more discussion of contrary views, easier construction of member roles and relationships, and better group cohesion through social support dynamics.

First, more active participation by more group members brings contrary interpretations to the surface, which can then make the group's interpretation more stable and implementable once it is constructed. Participants who hold back their personal views often refuse to accept the interpretation negotiated by the other participants (Maier, 1967). If the group cannot agree on which causal linkages and outcome preferences ought to be discussed then the subsequent task of selecting a decision strategy (Thompson & Tuden, 1959, pp. 198–205) will be performed ineffectively.

Second, meetings are an important sensemaking tool for organizations because they define, represent, and reproduce the social entities and relationships the organization uses to achieve its objectives (Schwartzman, 1989, p. 40). "Individuals can use meetings to read and/or see their place in particular social systems" (Schwartzman, 1989, p. 312).

Third, the prevailing view of meetings, that meetings exist to solve problems, can be reversed—problems exist to create meetings (Schwartzman, 1987, p. 288). In this latter sense, people look for some pretext to assemble meetings that then give them an opportunity to support each other, reaffirm their own unique internal system, and fine-tune relationships (McGrath, 1990, pp. 33–34).

Meetings, however, can impair sensemaking. If participation is uneven, because of processes such as social loafing (Williams, Harkins, and Latane, 1981, p. 309; Kerr, 1983, pp. 820–821), conformity pressures (Asch, 1955), audience effects (Zajonc, 1968), and distraction (Baron, 1986), then comparison, negotiation, and convergence are truncated, and the reality constructed from truncated social processes tends to be less plausible and implementable.

Uneven participation may also encourage premature adoption of a dominant interpretation. Polarization processes, in which individuals give up their initial judgment to move toward group consensus judgments (Myers & Lamm, 1976, p. 603), can lead to the problem of groupthink, where participants "show interest in facts and opinions that support their initially preferred policy and take up time in their meetings to discuss them, but they tend to ignore facts and opinions that do not support their initially preferred policy" (Janis, 1972, p. 10). For example, Special Assistant to the President Arthur Schlesinger opposed plans for the Bay of Pigs invasion of Cuba. However, because the Joint Chiefs of Staff, CIA, and Department of Defense clearly supported the plans (the dominant view), Schlesinger suppressed his views (a subordinate view), which then led the group into a groupthink situation (Schlesinger, 1965, pp. 227–242). Polarization and groupthink processes produce consensus, but only because they encourage people to ignore large amounts of data that contradict that consensus. Equivocality is willed out of existence rather than reduced to a workable level.

Although too much consensus too soon is a potential drawback of meetings, the opposite problem, too little consensus too late, is equally possible. Participants may disagree on the criteria for assessing what is sensible because of conflicts among their self-interests. Although some conflict may enable the group to frame better decisions (Gallupe, DeSanctis, & Dickson, 1988, p. 292), especially for innovative tasks (Maier, 1967), conflict must be managed (Forsyth, 1990, p. 382; Vancil & Green, 1984) or it can spiral and produce even more equivocality (Steiner, 1972, p. 118; Barnlund, 1959, p. 59; Maier, 1967). Balancing between too much and too little conflict, and consensus that occurs too soon or too late, are difficult management problems that cannot be resolved simply.

Aided Affiliation. Participants in aided meetings seem to gain two advantages of affiliation over those in unaided meetings, though the extent of these advantages is unclear.

First, a GSS aid that shapes social procedures used in a group can overcome some of the process losses that impair sensemaking. In unaided meetings, dysfunctional processes such as low participation, polarization away from innovation, and conflicting interests can prevent effective comparison, negotiation, and the free exchange of ideas. Several studies (Pinsonneault & Kraemer, 1989, p. 205) suggest that aid features can attenuate some of these dysfunctions. For example, anonymity can diminish evaluation apprehension and conformity pressure and enable participants to discuss ideas more candidly (Nunamaker, Dennis, Valacich, Vogel, & George, 1991; Gallupe, DeSanctis, & Dickson, 1988, p. 291).

Unfortunately, GSS aids that improve specific social interaction protocols block the emergence of more customized, group-specific approaches that fit the unique situation of equivocality they face (Ellis, Gibbs, & Reim, 1991, p. 51). A GSS aid seems "to impose an implicit 'agenda' on the group that acts to structure the group process" (Gallupe, DeSanctis, & Dickson, 1988, p. 290). The group may spend more effort coping with this implicit agenda than with the multiple views themselves.

Second, WYSIWIS (What You See Is What I See) features can increase the ability of participants to build a common set of linkages, preferences, and interpretations because they focus the social construction process on common referents (Ellis, Gibbs, & Rein, 1991, p. 50). How much of an advantage GSS-based WYSIWIS features offer participants over the use of manual WYSIWIS devices (such as overhead slides and whiteboards) depends on at least the specific features of the GSS aid and the complexity of the task. Jarvenpaa, Rao, and Huber (1988) found that an electronic bulletin board seemed to provide more value to a group than conventional methods in building a shared interpretation (p. 660). Workstation-based WYSIWIS features, however, seemed to provide less advantage and, in some cases, were indistinguishable from conventional methods (p. 662).

GSS aids also hold the potential to interfere with affiliation tactics that individuals use in unaided meetings. Existing GSS aids seem to decrease social support communication (DeSanctis, Poole, Lewis, & Desharnais, 1991, p. 19; Watson, DeSanctis, & Poole, 1988, p. 474; Sproull & Kiesler, 1986, p. 1509), which makes consensus building more difficult. Aids that increase participants' focus on the task often do so at the expense of social support processes that manage conflict (McGrath & Hollinghead, 1991, p. 27; DeSanctis & Gallupe, 1987, p. 592). Aids can even discourage conversation (Jarvenpaa, Rao, & Huber, 1988, p. 658), which undercuts the social foundation of sensemaking.

Existing GSS aids seem to reinstate the classic dilemma in small groups between quality of ideas and acceptance of ideas. As diversity of ideas increases, quality increases, but acceptance decreases. As diversity decreases, the opposite happens. Gallupe, DeSanctis, and Dickson (1988) observed that their aid produced "more diversity of ideas, hence more effort to reconcile competing views," which led to more disagreement about the final decision than in unaided groups (p. 291). They argue that the advantage of aided groups appears largely when problems require heavy mathematical analysis. We suggest two other explanations for the failure of participants to reach consensus about the decision. First, the design of the aid may exclude several means of sensemaking and make it difficult for groups to agree on causal links, preferences, and interpretations. Second, the aid may impose the wrong decision-making strategy (Thompson & Tuden, 1959, p. 198) for the pattern of agreement on causal links and preferences that the group has achieved.

Deliberation

Individuals learn about organizational events through slow and careful reasoning, during which they formulate and compare ideas, simulate events cognitively, reflect on feedback, and, finally, induce plausible patterns. When this reasoning process is extended over time, partially formed connections are allowed to incubate and become clarified, irrelevancies are forgotten, later events are used to reinterpret earlier ones, and all of these processes are used to edit, simplify, and make more meaningful the initial puzzling inputs. Deliberation is basically a slow process. When information comes too fast, people revert to habitual categories and stereotypes and fail to explore novel linkages, preferences, and interpretations of the equivocal event.

Unaided Deliberation. The fast pace of social interaction in meetings can make deliberation more difficult. Slow, careful reasoning is hard when members expect each other to think on their feet and come up with quick answers (Shure, Rogers, Larsen, & Tassone, 1962). Groups assigned a task tend not to discuss strategies for dealing with the task (Hackman & Morris, 1975, p. 66). When they do, however, this often leads "to more positive ratings of group atmosphere, increments in verbal interaction, greater satisfaction with leadership and flexibility in performing tasks" (Hackman & Morris, 1975, cited in Forsyth, 1990, p. 287; Kelly & McGrath, 1985, p. 405). In short, equivocal events may require periods of deliberation that last longer than a single meeting. For this reason, single meetings may impair sensemaking.

Nevertheless, unaided meetings need not preclude deep reasoning. Because more diverse views are aired in meetings, individuals hear new information that stimulates new thinking. New information may bridge gaps in individuals' reasoning (Vinokur & Burnstein, 1974, p. 313) and enable people to reason more deeply than if they had not come to the meeting. Deeper reasoning can be contagious and participants often build on each others' ideas (Steiner's additive task, 1972, pp. 32–33).

Meetings also produce artifacts (minutes, handouts, visual aids, notes, and audio or video tapes), which individuals can review later. These artifacts provide a form of organizational memory (Schwartzman, 1989, p. 40) and can stimulate ongoing deliberation after the meeting.

The central issue, however, is that the pace of social interaction in meetings can prevent individuals from reasoning deeply about equivocal events. There are at least three reasons for this: First, participants interrupt each other, and in doing so interrupt trains of thought, especially if information contradicts beliefs. Second, simply being in the presence of others can distract individuals who are deliberating because mere presence can heighten anxiety and arousal in equivocal situations (Zajonc, 1968, p. 65). Higher levels of arousal produce more perceptual narrowing and more reliance on earlier learning, both of which make it harder for people to make new connections that reduce equivocality (Easterbrook, 1959). And third, meetings generate their own pace of thought and action. If the fastest thinker dominates the meeting, then the desire to compare favorably to him or her (Festinger, 1954, p. 131), may tempt others to accelerate the pace of their thinking. To do so, they may adopt more superficial levels of reasoning, which means incomplete deliberation. On the other hand, the participants' thinking may slow down to the pace of the least skilled person in order to maintain group cohesiveness (Steiner, 1972, p. 28). Or groups may meet for as long as they have time available, regardless of task complexity (Parkinson, 1957; Varela, 1971, p. 158). Any discrepancy between pace and task demands can lead people to forget salient points and miss important connections (Kelley & Thibaut, 1968, p. 70).

Aided Deliberation. We see GSS aids as providing four advantages to deliberation in meetings:

First, meetings that are filled with interruptions and distractions can be improved by GSS aids that direct attention toward the event for longer periods (Pinsonneault & Kraemer, 1989, pp. 205–206; Gallupe, DeSanctis, & Dickson, 1988, p. 290). Because unaided groups tend to converge quickly on a problem-solving approach or solution and ignore alternatives, aids that block this temptation are an advantage.

Second, GSS aids may enable participants to consider more alternatives more thoroughly, increase the total deliberation time, and result in more stable interpretations (Pinsonneault & Kraemer, 1989, p. 210). In the absence of agreement on linkages and preferences, groups that try to make sense of equivocal contexts need more time to explore their tentative interpretations because they don't know what questions to ask or what steps to take next. Because unaided groups tend to shorten this exploration, we see the increased time induced by a GSS aid as a potentially valuable asset to sensemaking.

Third, when participants work at their own GSS workstation, they can pursue their own line of thinking and they do not have to wait for others to finish speaking or to catch up with their line of reasoning (Gallupe, DeSanctis, & Dickson, 1988, p. 292; Nunamaker, Dennis, Valacich, Vogel, & George, 1991; Watson, DeSanctis, & Poole, 1988, p. 474). However, because individuals in unaided groups can also go "offline" with a notepad, we wonder if this capability is unique to GSS aids. If a GSS offline aid makes more sensemaking tactics available than does a paper and pencil offline, then the GSS aids have a clearer advantage when deliberation is used.

Fourth, charts, graphs, text, notes, and other computer-printable artifacts that can serve as "group memory" (Gallupe, DeSanctis, & Dickson, 1988, p. 293; Nunamaker, Vogel, & Konsynski, 1989, p. 149) can sometimes be produced more easily from a computer aid than from manually generated artifacts, especially accurately scaled graphics. As with artifacts created during unaided meetings, participants can think about these at their leisure away from the meeting.

Despite the preceding advantages, existing GSS aids can also make deliberation more difficult. In unaided meetings, participants create information serially, one speaker after another. As individuals speak, other individuals follow the line of reasoning and usually filter their own emerging thoughts before contributing them (Grice, 1975, p. 45). The resulting information represents cumulative, filtered thoughts that are often relevant to causal linkages and preferences under current analysis. However, because GSS aids employ parallel information creation (Nunamaker, Dennis, Valacich, Vogel, & George, in press), information can flow toward participants from several directions at once. This has at least two effects on an individual's cognitive processing capabilities. First, the sheer volume of information that needs to be analyzed can overload an individual's processing capabilities (Miller, 1978; Jarvenpaa, Rao, & Huber, 1988, p. 657). Second, the simultaneous input of information requires that an individual engage in multitasking cognition (Jarvenpaa, Rao, & Huber, 1988, p. 658). When information overload and multitasking demands increase, arousal increases, attention becomes more selective, and people become more conscious of their agitated condition rather than the task, all of which reduces performance.

Demands for perceptual multitasking create difficulty in deliberation. GSS aids provide multiple windows and perform multitasking quickly, whereas deep reasoning often requires sustained focus on just one aspect of an event at a time. If the aid, or the person guiding the aid, switches among features quickly (text processing to drawing to database access) the thinker may be unable to develop a consistent line of reasoning. This problem of "constant context switching" means that

> users constantly have to adjust to a changing visual environment rather than focusing on the data. The user is also forced to remember things seen in one view so that he or she can use the other view effectively. This means that the user's short-term memory is occupied with the incidentals rather than with the significant issues of analysis. (Donoho, Donoho, & Gasko, 1988, p. 58)

Some GSS research suggests that such "media effects" cause participants to become confused about the task they are performing (Nunamaker, Dennis, Valacich, Vogel, & George, 1991), which, in a context already shot through with confusion, cannot be considered an aid.

Finally, the mechanics of interacting with the GSS aid can distract deliberation (Watson, DeSanctis, & Poole, 1988, p. 474). Participants who type poorly, are computer-phobic, or become overly engrossed in the aid itself (Jarvenpaa, Rao, & Huber, 1988, p. 658) may be more aware of the interface than the object of judgment.

Contextualization

People learn more about an organizational event when they relate it to other comparable events, stored as mental images, whose links are better understood. "Meanings are mental images that we create to help us interpret phenomena and develop a sense of understanding" (Kreps, 1990, pp. 25–26). Three important summarizing devices that enable people to create these mental images are labels, metaphors, and platitudes.

> Labels tell *what* things are, they classify [e.g., decentralization, leadership, excellence]; metaphors say how things are, they relate, give life [e.g., personal develop-

ment as gardening, organization as garbage can]; platitudes conventionalize, they standardize and establish *what is normal* [e.g., democracy must be built anew in each generation]. (Czarniawska-Joerges & Joerges, 1990, p. 339)

Labels, metaphors, and platitudes link the present with the past and provide compelling images *if* those images are shared. When people fail to contextualize, they use limited information and reinforce erroneous assumptions about an equivocal event rather than move to different orders of reasoning.

Unaided Contextualization. Meetings provide individuals with at least two contextualizing advantages, although both are indirect:

First, the diversity of knowledge, expertise, and mindsets embodied in a meeting's membership create opportunities to identify related contexts. Each new use of labels, metaphors, platitudes, archetypes, and stories provides individuals with new or forgotten contexts that move them into new orders of thinking. For example, a new marketing analyst may be confused about what to make of a recent downturn in her industry. Could the downturn reflect a long-term trend, a short-term correction, or a seasonal cycle? The perspective of a longtime industry expert, who can relate other historical events to the downturn (e.g., "it's like the fiasco of 1975"), could help the marketing analyst make a more informed guess about what the downturn means.

Second, the group's experience in the meeting will become part of that group's history. This experience has an indirect impact on sensemaking, because the group is building context for future sensemaking sessions. New stories and metaphors emerge *about* that history. This new lore about who felt what, what issues were discussed, and how things worked out will provide a context in the future when participants recall the episode.

Unfortunately, unaided meetings also raise at least one new barrier to contextualization. Individuals in meetings can get trapped into a narrowly constructed mindset imposed by their physical context (a room away from the event) or by their cognitive context (discussion dwells solely on intellectual processes). Both traps limit the ability to "get out" of the context and identify comparable historical events.

Aided Contextualization. We see one potential advantage to contextualization provided by GSS aids.

Use of computers, over time, can instill an "organization as information processor" mindset (Galbraith, 1973), which can be useful to some sensemaking episodes. Groups that can place an equivocal event in this context can focus on the role of information in constructing causal linkages, outcome preferences, and shared interpretations.

However, this indirect advantage may be negated by two direct disadvantages. First, participants who rely too heavily on a GSS aid may find they have no alternative but to accept the logic of the incomplete representation provided by the aid (Seely, Brown, & Duguid, 1989, p. 18; Blair, 1990; Dreyfus, 1979,

p. 288). They then try to build a shared interpretation of an inherently cryptic event without the benefit of additional meanings provided by summarizing devices. The tendency to treat the aid's view of reality may become especially pronounced in meetings where leaders or circumstances strongly encourage using the aid as a primary sensemaking tool.

Second, the high density of information provided by GSS aids may overwhelm the synthesizing abilities of confused individuals. Synthesizing tactics require a mixture of memory, abstraction, and induction to create a higher order, cohesive conception of causal links and outcome preferences. When information density becomes too high, individuals find it difficult to sustain all three simultaneously.

CONCLUSION

The purpose of this essay has been to give voice to our concern that existing GSS aids are relatively insensitive to the fact that groups spend just as much time trying to resolve confusion through operations that construct meaning as they do trying to resolve ignorance through operations that construct decisions. The preceding comparisons suggest that existing group support systems provide more decision support than sensemaking support and are therefore not exactly *group* support systems. For example, aids that increase meeting pace, decrease social interaction, prevent emergent approaches, and isolate participants from events may improve decision making, but they do so at the expense of sensemaking.

Our review suggests, however, that there are occasions when aids conceptualized within the context of decision making can assist sensemaking. Existing support systems may provide some help with the sensemaking strategies of action (they provide simulations) and deliberation (they provide more input for thought but at the risk of too much too fast); they provide a small assist to triangulation (access to more diverse data sources) and to affiliation (by inducing more equal participation through anonymity); and they provide no significant improvements in contextualizing (access to memory and metaphor are not improved, although this could be changed).

If existing aids have only modest relevance for sensemaking, and if sensemaking is basically an untidy activity that is sensitive to the style of leadership exhibited in a meeting, and if the adequacy of sensemaking is what makes for most of the difference between a well-run and poorly-run meeting, then it is not surprising that GSS aids work best in well-run meetings, because the aids are incidental to what is happening and benefit from whatever is happening. The aids become more central and more relevant as the meeting moves from sensemaking to decision making. Thus, the question that has haunted us throughout—"if group support systems aid sensemaking only when a meeting is well run, then why do people need a group support system?"—may be a question that has not yet been addressed. The support systems that are present in well-run meetings are not *group* support systems, they are *decision* support systems. And decisions are not what the well-run meeting is about. Still unanswered is the question of what effect a *sensemaking* support system has on a well-run meeting. That question is unanswered because it has yet to be asked. What have been tested instead are systems that help decision making directly and sensemaking indirectly. A well-run meeting tends to be a meeting that is strong on all five of the strategies we have reviewed, and therefore the group sensemaking process is buffered against interference from whatever decision support system is draped around this process. If a meeting is deficient in sensemaking strategies of action and deliberation, then existing decision aids can improve sensemaking. If the meeting is deficient in triangulation, affiliation, and contextualizing, then decision aids will not be of much help. The tantalizing question is, what kind of sensemaking aid might be of more help?

If GSS research is to become more sensitive to sensemaking then it will have to overcome the smaller handicap of a past history of preoccupation with decision making and the larger handicap of a Western tradition that condones this preoccupation. The way out of this blind alley seems to be the very same tactics we have discussed throughout. If existing GSS research is equivocal rather than uncertain, then intensified action, triangulation, affiliation, deliberation, and contextualizing should clarify the questions that need to be asked next. If these processes work for groups, then they should also work for the scientists who study groups. If they don't, then their failure should point the way to improved work on sensemaking. In either case, there should be a better fit between people and technology.

PART IV

BRIDGING GROUP SUPPORT SYSTEM APPLICATION AND RESEARCH TO OTHER DISCIPLINES

CHAPTER 13

A Theory of the Effects of Group Support Systems on an Organization's Nature and Decisions

George P. Huber
University of Texas

Joseph S. Valacich
Indiana University

Leonard M. Jessup
California State University, San Marcos

INTRODUCTION

What are the effects of Group Support Systems (GSS) on group processes and group outcomes? This is an important question. A decade of research provides answers, and current research will provide still more. Another question, more important for many of the same reasons, has largely gone unasked and unaddressed, probably because both researchers and practitioners were understandably preoccupied with the first question. However, because we have learned a good deal about the answers to the first question, and because GSS are increasingly making their way into organizations, it is time to address the second question: "What are the effects of GSS on the nature and outcomes of the organizations within which and for which the groups function?"

In a previous work (Huber, 1990), we set forth a general theory of the effects that computer-assisted communication and decision-aiding technologies have on organizational design, intelligence, and decision making. In developing the theory, we drew upon and integrated the work of researchers from the fields of information systems and organizational science. The theory was quite general in that it encompassed a variety of advanced information technologies (e.g., electronic mail, computer conferencing, decision support systems). We noted, however, that there is a clear need for researchers to specify more precisely the particular technology of interest when they develop hypotheses to be tested empirically. We also noted that, as more is learned about the effects of computer-assisted communication and decision-support technologies, it may be found that even subtle differences among technologies can result in important differences in their effects.

The current chapter is offered in this spirit of delineation. Its purpose is to apply the general theory of our previous work to the specific context of Group Support Systems, one particular class of computer-assisted communication and decision-aiding technologies. This effort helps pave the way for critical empirical investigation of the general theory and also highlights the practical importance of understanding the effects of specific technologies.

The conceptual theory of GSS effects presented here assumes rational organizational actors. However, we believe that the theory fits for even highly politicized or power-driven organizations. That is, we believe that people use technologies to advance their self-interest or otherwise enhance the quality of their lives. Thus, as we did for the more general theory, we make here the fundamental assumption that organizational participants will use advanced information technologies in ways that increase their effectiveness in fulfilling both individual and organizational goals.

Presented next is a description of GSS, titled, "The Nature of GSS." With several variations of GSS now in use and more on the way (see Chapter 2), it seems most appropriate to discuss, generally, the nature of the system to which the theory applies. The conceptual theory is then presented, with discussion of relevant constructs, concepts, and propositions. Finally, the chapter ends with a discussion of implications of the theory and recommendations for both researchers and practitioners.

The Nature of GSS

The evolution of GSS, from a technological and conceptual perspective, is evident in the changing definitions that have appeared across time. For example, Huber originally described Group Decision Support Systems (GDSS) as, "...a set of software, hardware, and language components and procedures that support a group of people engaged in a decision-related meeting..." (1984a, p. 195). DeSanctis and Gallupe later presented a definition that included some nontechnological "process" elements. They wrote of systems, "...which combine communication, computer, and decision technologies to support problem formulation and solution in group meetings..." (1987, p. 589). An even broader definition was later provided by Dennis and his colleagues when they describe an electronic meeting system as "an information-based environment that supports group meetings, which may be distributed geographically and temporally ... [which] ... includes, but is not limited to, distributed facilities, computer hardware and software, audio and video technology, procedures, methodologies, facilitation, and applicable group data" (1988, p. 593). This chronological sequence suggests an evolution toward a more general, encompassing view of GSS. Consequently, here we define GSS broadly as the collective of computer-assisted technologies used to aid group efforts directed at identifying and addressing problems, opportunities, and issues. By "groups," in this context, we mean both face-to-face groups supported by GSS technology during a meeting and also groups whose members are physically separated but who use GSS technology to exchange information either synchronously or asynchronously.

Toward a Conceptual Theory

As noted above, the conceptual theory presented here is adapted from our earlier conceptual "theory of the effects of advanced information technologies on organizational design, intelligence, and decision making"(Huber, 1990). This earlier theory, summarized as a set of integrated constructs and concepts, was induced from a set of theoretical propositions. Here we tailor this earlier, general theory to the context of GSS to develop a conceptual theory of the effects of Group Support Systems on an organization's nature and decisions. This latter theory is summarized in Figure 13.1 as a set of integrated constructs and concepts.

THE THEORY

Associated with each concept in Figure 13.1 are propositions. If a person accepts as valid multiple propositions, then he or she can use induction to infer the superordinate concept. If a person accepts a concept, then he or she can deduce the subordinate propositions. Propositions, being less general, are also less abstract. In this section we articulate our theory by discussing the propositions associated with the concepts of Figure 13.1. The propositions evolve from our prior work and from examinations of recent research on group processes and GSS.

Concept 1: *Availability of GSS* leads to the *use of GSS*. (We intend for "availability" to mean existence, accessibility, and suitability.) Group Support Systems have properties different from more traditional group support technologies. As a result, the *availability of GSS* (Construct A) extends the range of communication and decision-aiding options from which potential users can choose. On occasion, the whole GSS, or one of its technological features, will be chosen for use, and when chosen wisely, its use will lead to improved task performance. This positive reinforcement in turn leads to further *use of the GSS* (Construct B).

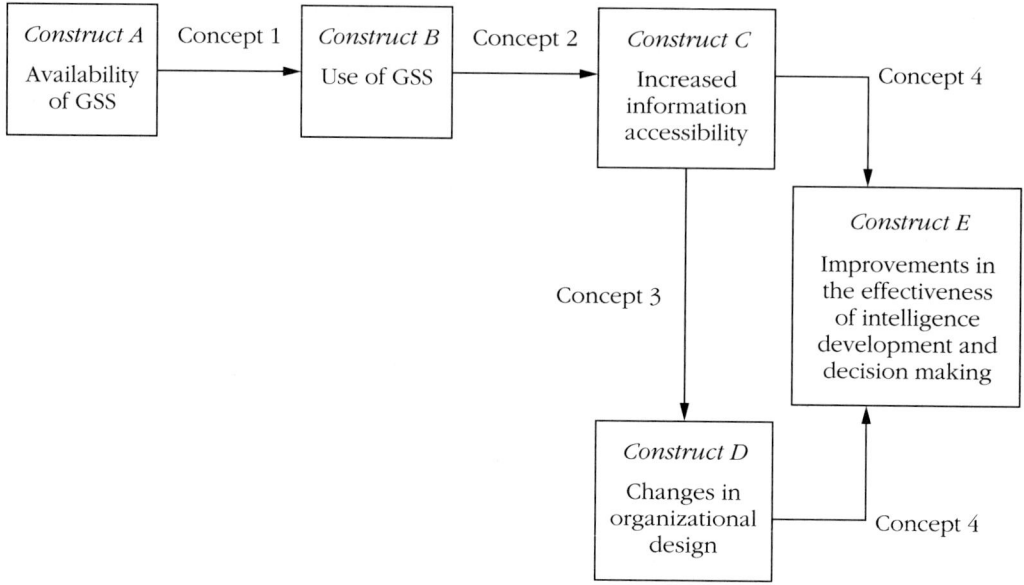

Concept 1: Availability of GSS *leads to* use of GSS
Concept 2: Use of GSS *leads to* increased information accessibility
Concept 3: Increased information accessibility *leads to* changes in organizational design
Concept 4: Increased information accessibility *and* changes in organizational design *lead to* improvements in the effectiveness of intelligence development and decision making

FIGURE 13.1 Conceptual theory of the effects of Group Support Systems on group and organizational design, intelligence, and decision making. Adapted from Huber (1990).

Because the conceptual theory of this chapter is concerned with the effects of GSS use, and because of space constraints, we do not here review additional, more theory-based arguments that support Concept 1. Fulk, Schmitz, and Steinfield (1990) discuss these arguments in detail.

Besides the rationale just noted, recent organizational experiences with GSS also support Concept 1. For example, Poole, DeSanctis, Kursch, and Jackson (1991) report the experiences of four groups in one organization using a GSS over a period of six months to one year. Although they report that system use varied—as adoption was effected by a plethora of factors—one general conclusion, which directly supports Concept 1, was that over the period of observation all groups chose to use the GSS, and in a majority of the groups, use increased (at varying rates). Another example, supporting Concept 1, is that although GSS use within IBM was initially limited to only one manufacturing site and only a limited variety of groups (Nunamaker, Vogel, Heminger, Martz, Growhoski, and McGoff, 1989), IBM later made GSS technology available to many more of its sites and has still more facilities scheduled for deployment (Growhoski et al., 1990). This broadened deployment has coincided with an increase in the number and variety of groups using the GSS, such that backlogs for facility use are common and upper management has on occasion preempted the GSS for its own use.

Research on technological diffusion makes clear that availability of useful technologies does not always lead to their use (cf., George, Valacich, & Nunamaker, forthcoming; Meyer & Goes, 1988; Rogers, 1983; Van de Ven, Angle, & Poole, 1989). A variety of factors and forces can intervene and preclude use. Thus Concept 1 will not be substantiated in every instance. For example, one of four groups in the Poole et al. (1991) study reported above reduced its system usage over the observation period. If instances of nonuse are thoroughly investigated, so that the cause of the lack of validation is identified, this "negative" case analysis (Eisenhardt, 1989b) can lead to refined, valid propositions and theory. Indeed, one goal of Poole and his colleagues' use of adaptive structuration theory is to explain why and how some groups adopt GSS whereas others do not. Readers interested in GSS adoption issues are encouraged to refer to Chapter 15 by Poole and Jackson for a discussion. Useful insights into the process of end-user adoption of GSS developed within the organization by research and development units are provided by Applegate (1991).

Concept 2: *Use of GSS* (Construct B) leads to *increased information accessibility* (Construct C). Concept 2 flows from several propositions presented in Table 13.1. These are discussed below.

TABLE 13.1 Concept 2 and Related Propositions

Concept 2—Use of GSS Leads to Increased Information Accessibility

Organizational-Level Effects

1. GSS use leads to a larger number and variety of organization members participating in problem-solving conferences.
2. In a given situation, GSS use leads to an increased and more uniform distribution of information across organizational levels.
   2a. In a highly centralized organization, GSS use increases the accessibility of lower-level units to information about the organization's policies and overall situation.
   2b. In a highly decentralized organization, GSS use increases the accessibility of upper levels to information about situations at lower organizational levels.
3. Whereas traditional meetings have been used to support communication from the organization's sensing units to its decision units, GSS use leads to increased information accessibility for the decision units.

Effects on Organizational Memory

4. GSS use leads to increased availability of information generated during meetings.
5. GSS use leads to increased availability of information from "outside" the meeting.

In organizations without GSS, people with potentially useful contributions to make to a problem-solving conference are sometimes precluded from participating because they are remote in terms of time or distance. GSS technologies, particularly distributed networks or video conferencing, greatly enhance the feasibility of participation by those so separated. A result is that:

> **Proposition 1:** GSS use leads to a larger number and variety of organization members participating in problem-solving conferences.

A second line of reasoning also leads to Proposition 1. A number of studies indicate that GSS enable even face-to-face participants to communicate more effectively and efficiently (cf., DeSanctis, Dickson, Jackson, and Poole, 1991; Nunamaker, Dennis, Valacich, Vogel, and George, 1991; Post, 1992). Sometimes this result follows from the capability of the technology itself and other times it follows from the more efficient communication processes that seem to develop or be developed in GSS-supported groups.

Additional evidence supporting Proposition 1 appears in the growing body of GSS field research (see Chapter 3 for a general literature review; see also Chapter 7). A specific example of how a GSS can affect the number and variety of meeting participants is described by Dennis, Heminger, Nunamaker, and Vogel (1990). They report the experiences of one company in which a GSS effectively supported 22–26 group members in each of several strategic planning meetings. This was contrasted to prior nonsupported sessions in which only 8-10 members were able to participate. The communication and structuring efficiencies made possible by the GSS were credited as enabling this change, resulting in a transformed planning process that was no longer limited to only a few high-level participants. This transformed process included a wide variety of functional managers from different areas of the company and this broadened participation, in turn, resulted in more easily implementable solutions and a more efficient planning process.

Because use of a GSS allows a larger number and variety of organizational members to participate in problem-solving conferences (Proposition 1), it will in many cases enable a larger proportion of the organization's levels to be better informed about the organization's *overall* situation. This leads to our next proposition:

> **Proposition 2:** In a given situation, GSS use leads to an increased and more uniform distribution of information across organizational levels.

Corollaries to Proposition 2 are:

> **Proposition 2a:** In a highly centralized organization, GSS use increases the accessibility of lower-level units to information about the organization's policies and overall situation.

and

> **Proposition 2b:** In a highly decentralized organization, GSS use increases the accessibility of upper levels to information about situations at lower organizational levels.

An example of the outcome predicted with Proposition 2a appears in the Dennis, Heminger, Nunamaker, and Vogel (1990) field study noted above, where the CEO felt that the inclusion of more people in the GSS meeting served to increase the information available to lower- and middle-level managers—"A lot more people are on board with an understanding of what went on...People walked in with narrow perceptions of the company and walked out with a CEO's perception" (p. 117).

Of course GSS use facilitates upward communication as well, and this fact leads to Proposition 2b. A particularly interesting form of support is the special case where the GSS allows users to communicate anonymously. GSS laboratory experiments (e.g., Connolly, Jessup, & Valacich, 1990; Jessup, Connolly, & Galegher, 1990; Jessup & Tansik, 1991; Valacich, Dennis, & Nunamaker, 1992) and field observations (e.g., Dennis et al., 1990; Growhoski et al., 1990) suggest that the anonymity feature, when employed, tends to promote relatively uninhibited group interaction, for example, more open and candid generation and evaluation of ideas. In the field study of GSS use cited above, one IBM manager concluded that "the meeting could not have been conducted manually and that anonymity first allowed the meeting to be conducted and, second, to be productive"(Growhoski et al., 1990, p. 377).

Decision makers often use meetings as devices or occasions to become informed, about either general conditions or particular situations, by representatives from environmental scanning units (e.g., market research units) or internal monitoring units (e.g., production control units). It seems likely that the GSS-provided feasibility of including within meetings representatives of such sensing units (see Proposition 1) would lead to the decision makers' obtaining information that is more timely and wide ranging. Thus we conclude that:

Proposition 3: Whereas traditional meetings have been used to support communication from the organization's sensing units to its decision units, GSS use leads to increased information accessibility for the decision units.

An interesting and useful feature of GSS is that they can be used to create, organize, and disseminate an electronic record of all of the data exchanges and data displays used during the meeting. Graphical, tabular, or text displays developed during a meeting, messages exchanged electronically, minutes, documents, or conclusions compiled during a meeting, all can be indexed, recorded, and distributed much more readily than their counterparts in a meeting not supported by GSS. Thus we conclude that:

Proposition 4: GSS use leads to increased availability of information generated during meetings.

(The reader is urged to see Chapter 11 by Hoffer and Valacich on the role of GSS in the development of organizational memory.)

People in meetings often encounter an unexpected need to tap external information sources before they can complete their task (e.g., they may need new estimates of production costs given a meeting-generated revision to a planned product mix or production schedule). Research by Growhoski and his associates (1990) and by Valacich, Vogel, & Nunamaker (1989) demonstrates that, to the extent that the GSS includes technologies for retrieving such information, the information will be used. Example technologies are computer-assisted systems for accessing experts, expert systems, organizational and extraorganizational databases, or electronic records of previous meetings. We conclude, then, that this GSS feature, this capability for accessing "outside" information during a meeting, often increases the usefulness and use of an organization's technology-based organizational memory.

> **Proposition 5:** GSS use leads to increased availability of information from "outside" of the meeting.

Propositions 1 through 5 are associated with Concept 2, the idea that GSS use leads to increased information accessibility. Propositions 6 through 11 are associated with Concept 3.

Concept 3: *Increased information accessibility* (Construct C) leads to *changes in organizational design* (Construct D). Propositions for Concept 3 are presented in Table 13.2 and are discussed below.

Let us first turn to the design of the organization's decision units. Proposition 6 and its corollaries address how GSS use can influence this design. The propositions presented in support of our prior concept, Concept 2, suggest that GSS use leads to increased information accessibility. This increased information accessibility is achieved through more effective means for accessing a greater number and wider variety of participants and an enhanced ability to access experts and computer-based memories. It seems reasonable to believe that enhanced information accessibility, through whatever means, will influence the design of the formal decision unit.

> **Proposition 6:** GSS use leads to changes in the number and variety of members comprising the formal decision unit.

A person's membership in a formal decision unit is often granted and required because the person possesses some information or expertise critical to the unit's task. Propositions 3, 4, and 5 inform us that some types of information or knowledge that traditionally were brought to a decision unit in the minds or briefcases of its formal members can now, if the unit's GSS have certain features, be accessed from other sources and through other media. This possibility is greatest when the nature of the needed information is clear at the outset; the possibility is less when the nature of the information needed must be discovered during the group's deliberations. This suggests that:

> **Proposition 6a:** When a decision unit's problem is relatively well structured, when at worst the situation is uncertain rather than ambiguous or equivocal, GSS use leads to a smaller number and variety of members comprising the formal decision unit.

Chapter 13 The Effects of GSS on an Organization's Nature and Decisions

TABLE 13.2 Concept 3 and Related Propositions.

**Concept 3—Increased Information Accessibility
Leads to Changes in Organizational Design**

6. GSS use leads to change in the number and variety of members comprising the formal decision unit.
    6a. When a decision unit's problem is relatively well structured, where at worst the situation is uncertain rather then ambigious or equivocal, GSS use leads to a smaller number and variety of members comprising the formal decision unit.
    6b. When a decision unit's problem is relatively unstructured, where the task is more one of understanding the problem or interpreting the issue, GSS use leads to a greater number and variety of members comprising the formal decision unit.
7. GSS use results in less of the organization's time being absorbed by decision-related meetings.
8. GSS use changes the locus of decision making.
    8a. If the organization's upper echelon seeks the satisfaction or developement of lower-level managers, then GSS use leads to more decentralization, particularly in a highly centralized organization.
    8b. If the organization's upper echelon seeks enhancement of its control over operations, then GSS use leads to more centralization, particularly in a highly decentralized organization.
9. GSS use reduces the number of organizational levels involved in authorizing proposed organizational actions.
10. GSS use leads to fewer intermediate human nodes within the organizational information-processing network.
    10a. GSS use reduces the number of organizational levels involved in processing messages.

We hasten to note that Proposition 6a is formulated and presented in an organizational context, in which a variety of pressures exist to keep decision units as small as practicable.

The situation described in Proposition 6a contrasts with the situation where the exact nature of the required informational inputs is unclear at the outset, either because the situation is not well understood or is subject to multiple interpretations. In such a situation, it is often desirable to include a larger number or wider variety of people in the decision unit so as to ensure that relevant insights, perspectives, and expertise are not lacking. Because GSS can enhance the effectiveness of problem structuring (Poole & DeSanctis, 1990; Poole, Holmes, & DeSanctis, 1991) and can facilitate communication within large groups (Dennis, Valacich, & Nunamaker, 1990; Valacich, Dennis, and Nunamaker, 1992), it seems reasonable to believe that:

Proposition 6b: When a decision unit's problem is relatively unstructured, where the task is more one of understanding or interpreting the situation, GSS use leads to a greater number and variety of members comprising the formal decision unit.

Other motivations for increasing the size of the formal decision unit can be found in the work of Dennis et al. (1988) and Nunamaker (1991). These researchers suggest that the inclusion of more organizational members may ease the execution of a plan or decision (by including those members who are needed for success that might not otherwise be included in the process), may aid organizational learning, and may help overcome political issues related to decision buy-in, ownership, and rewards.

We earlier argued and referenced the fact that GSS use leads to more effective information sharing within meetings. This suggests that individual GSS-supported meetings would be shorter or that fewer would be required to deal with any particular issue. It follows that:

Proposition 7: GSS use results in less of the organization's time being absorbed by decision-related meetings.

The GSS field observations of Growhoski and his associates (1990) suggests that, indeed, use of GSS leads to a reduction in the number and duration of meetings.

Because the focus of this section of the conceptual theory is the effects of GSS on organizational design, we do not delve into the effects of GSS on group process and structure. We believe, however, that it would be very useful to link group-level design issues (e.g., formation and development, interaction, status, power, roles, leadership, norms, etc.) to organizational design issues, because they are very much interrelated.

Proposition 8 and its corollaries address the locus of decision making within an organizational hierarchy. They follow from Propositions 2, 2a, and 2b, which assert that GSS use leads to more uniform and generally increased information availability at all organizational levels. It follows that this increased distribution of information tends to increase the number of levels that are qualified, with regard to information, to make a decision. In other words, it enables decision making to occur across a greater range of hierarchical levels with little or no loss in quality. The hierarchical level that would actually make a particular decision would depend on the overall objectives of the organization and the inclinations and availability of the relevant decision makers at the various levels. Thus, it seems likely that:

Proposition 8: GSS use changes the locus of decision making.

Corollaries to Proposition 8 are:

Proposition 8a: If the organization's upper echelon seeks the satisfaction or development of lower-level managers, then GSS use leads to more decentralization, particularly in a highly centralized organization.

and

> **Proposition 8b:** If the organization's upper echelon seeks enhancement of its control over operations, then GSS use leads to more centralization, particularly in a highly decentralized organization.

Let us first examine Proposition 8a, pertaining to organizations in which the top echelon's dominant goal is to maximize decision quality. Consider the use of a GSS to support information exchange in a meeting in which the participants span multiple hierarchical levels and in which one or more of the participants must subsequently make a decision based on what was learned in the GSS-supported meeting. Here, the information accessibility provided by GSS (see Proposition 2) enables middle- and lower-level managers to learn from top managers about the organization's problems, policies, and priorities, and to learn from any participant about possible side effects of various choices. We believe the result will be that top management, thus assured that lower-level managers understand these matters, will more often permit and encourage more decentralized decision making.

The reasoning supporting Proposition 8b is as follows. Top management, even though it is often more aware of overarching matters that might determine the quality of a decision, might hesitate to centralize the associated decision process because it recognizes its relative ignorance of the local situation. However, use of a GSS, especially a distributed GSS, enables top management in some cases to acquire richer, more timely information about the local situation and thus to centralize the decision process with no loss of decision quality.

Empirical studies directed at the effect of GSS (or any information technology) on the hierarchical locus of decision making should assess top management's dispositions on these matters. Some sophisticated thinking about the effects of computer-supported information technology on centralization is that of George and King (1991). Propositions 8, 8a, and 8b follow from the arguments presented, but are not directly based on empirical studies and certainly require further investigation.

Proposition 9 follows from Propositions 2, 2a, and 2b and is an elaboration and extension of our earlier work.

> **Proposition 9:** GSS use reduces the number of organizational levels involved in authorizing proposed organizational actions.

More specifically, our reasoning associated with Proposition 9 is as follows. We discussed earlier (Huber, 1990) how organizations commonly involve several levels in authorizations because each level in the hierarchy has unique knowledge or decision-specific information that qualifies it to apply criteria or decision rules that other less well-informed levels cannot apply (cf. Meyer & Goes, 1988, p. 904, 905). If individual levels have or can appropriately apply information of only one type, then the greater the number of discrete information types that are required, the greater will be the number of hierarchical levels that are involved in the authorization process. Because GSS makes information sharing more effective, in some cases they enable an organizational level to obtain current information or background knowledge that was previously unavailable to it, and thus enable it to apply criteria or decision rules that it was previously not qualified to apply. By increasing the number of criteria or decision rules that each level might be able to apply, GSS reduces the number of levels required to authorize proposed actions.

Let us turn now to the density of the organization's structure. We believe GSS use leads to organizations having sparser structures.

> **Proposition 10:** GSS use leads to fewer intermediate human nodes within the organizational information-processing network.
>
> **Proposition 10a:** GSS use reduces the number of organizational levels involved in processing messages.

Propositions 10 and 10a operate at the organizational level and address the number of *intermediate* human nodes and organizational levels in the organization's information-processing network. In our earlier work, we pointed out that the human nodes of the organizational information-processing network carry out tasks ranging from straightforward relaying to elaborate interpreting, tasks that more and more can be performed by various information technologies. Thus, the use of information technologies for these tasks will tend to result in the elimination of these human nodes and sometimes the elimination of managerial levels. Do GSS, as a particular technology, serve to replace humans as intermediate nodes in the organization's information-processing network? In some cases, we think they do. In other cases, we think not.

When GSS increase the benefit-to-cost ratio of a meeting so greatly that GSS-supported meetings become the medium of information exchange in place of networks of nodes that communicated synchronously with only one other node at a time, then the reasoning and conclusion of the above paragraph apply. However, in the many situations in which communication mediated by an intermediate human node between the sensor the decision maker is efficient, timely, and satisfying, then it seems that meetings would be unnecessarily costly and would not replace organizational units as information-processing mechanisms and Propositions 10 and 10a would not apply.

Concept 3 and Propositions 6 through 10a dealt with the effects of GSS on the nature of organizations. Concept 4 and its associated propositions deal with the effects of GSS on organizational decisions.

Concept 4: *Increased information accessibility* (Construct C) *and those changes in organizational design* (Construct D) *that increase the speed and effectiveness with which information can be converted into intelligence or intelligence into decisions, lead to organizational intelligence being more accurate, comprehensive, timely, and available, and to decisions being more timely and of higher quality, that is, increased information accessibility* and the corresponding *changes in organizational design* lead to *improvements in the effectiveness of intelligence development and decision making* (Construct E).

The four propositions associated with Concept 4 follow from the earlier arguments, references, and propositions, and so we treat them more briefly in spite of their importance (see Table 13.3).

Proposition 11: The computer-assisted information acquisition and interpretation technologies that characterize GSS cause GSS use to lead to organizational intelligence that is more accurate, comprehensive, timely, and available.

Proposition 11a: GSS use leads to more rapid and more accurate identification of problems and opportunities.

Proposition 11 and 11a are based on the assumption that both internal and external information sources are accessible, accurate and comprehensive. Otherwise, garbage in, garbage out. Proposition 11 and 11a follow from the thinking surrounding Propositions 3, 4, 5, 10, and 10a.

Proposition 12: GSS use leads to higher-quality decisions.

We mean for the word "quality" in Proposition 12 to be broadly interpreted, to include, for example, timeliness. Proposition 12 follows from the facts that the quality of an organizational decision is largely a consequence of both the quality of organizational intelligence and the quality of the decision-making processes. Thus it follows from all of the previous propositions. Especially it is founded on the idea that, by facilitating the sharing of information, GSS increase the quality of the decision-making process, and that by aiding in the analysis of information within decision units, GSS use increases the quality of decision making. This idea is supported by much of the laboratory and field research reviewed by Dennis and Gallupe in Chapter 3.

Proposition 13: GSS use reduces the time required to authorize proposed organizational actions.

TABLE 13.3 Concept 4 and Related Propositions.

Concept 4—Improved Information Accessibility and the Corresponding Changes in Organizational Design Lead to Improvements in the Effectiveness of Intelligence Developement and Decision Making
11. The computer-assisted information acquisition and interpretation technologies that characterize GSS cause GSS use to lead to organzational intelligence that is more accurate, comprehensive, timely, and available.   11a. GSS use leads to more rapid and more accurate identification of problems and opportunities. 12. GSS use leads to higher-quality decisions. 13. GSS use reduces the time required to authorize proposed organizational actions. 14. GSS use reduces the time required to make decisions.

Proposition 13 follows from Proposition 10, which dealt with how GSS use leads to a reduction in the number of levels involved in authorizing an action. Because GSS use reduces the number of levels involved in authorizing an action and will thus reduce the number of times a proposal must be "handled"(where "handled"refers to activities of a logistical rather than a judgmental nature), it seems likely that GSS use will reduce the time required to authorize proposed organizational actions.

Proposition 14: GSS use reduces the time required to make decisions.

Proposition 14 follows from the earlier propositions about rapid identification of problems and opportunities, about fewer intermediate nodes in the organizational information-processing network, about fewer levels involved in authorizing proposed organizational actions, and about reductions in the organization's time being absorbed by decision-related meetings. Proposition 14 is frequently supported by anecdotal evidence from field observations. For example, a group vice-president in one GSS field study concluded that, "the [GSS-supported] process allowed us to do in three days what would have taken months to do [without the GSS]" (Dennis, Heminger, 1990, p. 116).

SUMMARY AND RECOMMENDATIONS

In an earlier work (Huber, 1990) we presented a general theory of the effects of advanced information technologies on organizational design, intelligence, and decision making. In that work, we called for the development of theories tailored to specific types of advanced decision and communication technologies. In response to that call, in this chapter we developed a more specific theory, a theory of GSS effects on the same three phenomena (organizational design, intelligence, and decision making), here noted more generally as the organization's nature and decisions.

Although we believe that this theory of GSS effects is a good start, we note that GSS vary from implementation to implementation, and we therefore repeat our previous observation that even subtle differences between advanced information technologies may have profound effects. Small differences between GSS forms seem to account for the sometimes conflicting results of early GSS research (see Chapter 3). Further, organizational tasks, contexts, and participants can vary widely from one implementation to the next (see Chapter 4). Therefore, we offer our rather general conceptual theory of GSS effects to researchers for further refinement and, ultimately, testing, so that a more accurate theory can be formulated.

The theory of GSS effects presented here, and our previous theory of the effects of advanced information technologies, fit within the domain of organizational science, because organizational science has always been concerned with the processes of communication, coordination, and control and, as is apparent from GSS research, the nature and effectiveness of these processes are changed

Chapter 13 The Effects of GSS on an Organization's Nature and Decisions

when GSS are employed. Without this organizational perspective, we are likely to limit our understanding of GSS use and effects; findings from organizational science should be used to guide GSS research.

There is also a practical importance to enhancing our understanding of the effects of GSS. As development and use of these systems increases, organizational administrators will want and need to anticipate the effects of GSS implementations on the structure and functioning of their organizations. In order to aid organizational administrators in anticipating these effects, GSS researchers must seek to understand the underlying factors that cause GSS to affect an organization's nature and decisions.

CHAPTER 14

Behavioral Decision Theory and Group Support Systems

Terry Connolly
University of Arizona

INTRODUCTION

A couple of years ago I asked a group of my graduate students to put together a bibliography of empirical studies investigating the effectiveness of spreadsheet programs—Lotus 1-2-3, Visicalc, and the like. These hugely popular programs are heavily advertised in the trade journals in terms that seem clearly to promise that their use will improve the user's effectiveness as an analyst and decision maker: "explore options," "what-if thinking," "optimize your choices," and so on. As a student of how people make decisions, I was curious about how these claims to improve decision making had been demonstrated and documented.

As it turned out, the project was a failure. My students were unable to find any substantial body of research that would demonstrate to a reasonable skeptic that a spreadsheet program bought to improve someone's decision making would earn its keep. (There may be such evidence, of course, that my students simply failed to find. I suspect not, however). They had no trouble finding lots of very broad claims, a number of supportive anecdotes, and some grateful testimonials from spreadsheet users. Very little of this, however, provided the level of proof one would ask of, say, the claim that a new fuel additive would actually improve your car's gas mileage or that some new detergent does actually wash whiter. According to what my students were able to turn up, the best-selling decision-aiding software does not seem to have irrefutable, independent demonstration of its effectiveness, let alone any rich connection to studies of how people made decisions before spreadsheets, and what might have been wrong with that process.

The concern is not limited to spreadsheet programs. Quite generally, research on how people actually make decisions and development of technology to help them do better have proceeded almost independently of one another (e.g, Tolcott and Holt, 1987). The first effort, which we shall refer to here broadly as "decision behavior research," has been concerned with understanding what people actually do when they make decisions, solve problems, arrive at judgments, and perform similar, more-or-less intelligent, purposive, conscious mental activities. The second body of work, which we shall refer to broadly as "decision aiding," has been concerned with the development of normative rules, computational support, and technology intended to be helpful with the aid of which people should make decisions more effectively, or at less cost of time and effort. GSS, the focus of this book, are, of course, the fruit of decision aiding aimed at groups. Decision behavior and decision aiding should have a great deal to say to one another, if only because of the practical dangers of trying to improve what one does not understand. So far, they have said very little. The purpose of this essay is to try to stimulate the conversation.

DECISION BEHAVIOR RESEARCH

Other chapters of this book have presented a very thorough picture of the current status of GSS efforts. In this chapter we shall sketch some of the issues that decision behavior researchers work on, sample some of their findings, and suggest some of the challenges that these findings present to the GSS designer.

Most research in decision behavior has been framed at the level of the single individual, and is thus relevant to group processes only indirectly. Two points strengthen the connection. First, the participant in a GSS may be relatively less embedded in the group than he or she would typically be in a face-to-face group (see Kiesler, Siegel, & McGuire, 1984), so that understanding of the individual acting alone may serve as a better point of departure than would the usual assumptions about individuals relatively tightly coupled to other group members. The second point is that groups may well be used as instruments to offset the imperfections of individuals working alone. For example, the issue we consider in Section 1 of this chapter, group idea generation, is of interest primarily because of the demonstrated shortcoming of individuals as idea generators. Groups are simply too costly and inconvenient to use for tasks a single individual does well. The use of a group, with or without GSS support, is thus often a reaction to concerns about the adequacy of the single decision maker. Understanding the individual decision maker thus provides a useful springboard for exploring the decision-making processes of groups and the effectiveness of systems designed to help them.

The following sections take up three issues that have been studied by decision behavior researchers and that seem to have some promise for GSS researchers and designers. The first, group idea generation, is relatively well developed, and effective GSS tools are already emerging, though linkage between the technology and the underlying cognitive processes is somewhat sketchy. The second, overconfidence and hindsight bias, has both solid basis in decision behavior and potentially high relevance to the GSS context, but I know of no serious GSS development of the issue thus far. The third area, which concerns the representation and analysis of judgment policies, has a rich background, good application history, and a well-developed computer-based technology, but has yet to reach full flower in GSS applications.

I make no claim to comprehensiveness, either of promising topics or of coverage within each. The three areas are sketched only in outline, and a few entry-level references are provided for readers who wish to dig more deeply. The intent is merely to illustrate some active areas of decision behavior research, and to suggest their possible relevance to GSS researchers.

IDEA GENERATION

To make a good decision or solve a problem well you need to come up with at least one good alternative and be able to identify it as such. How good are we at generating alternatives? Plenty of evidence suggests that we are significantly limited idea generators. For example, Gettys and Fisher (1979) asked students to come up with as many ideas as they could to solve such problems as the parking shortage on their campus, how an out-of-town visitor who had lost his wallet might survive, and other practical problems. They found that even the most ingenious respondents produced only a tiny fraction of the ideas on a master list of proposals accumulated from many students.

A slightly subtler failure of imagination was demonstrated by Fischhoff, Slovic, and Lichtenstein (1978). These researchers constructed fault trees showing the variety of reasons a car might not start—a fault in the electrical system, the fuel system, the mechanical system, and so on, each area spelled out in some detail—and asked subjects to assess the relative probability of each being the cause of a particular failure to start. They found that, when they collapsed large portions of the tree and simply labeled them as "Other causes," the probability assigned this group was substantially smaller than had been assigned to the several components that made it up. Apparently, the subjects (even professional mechanics, presumably very knowledgable about cars) failed to bring to mind the various components that had been swept into the "Other" category, and thus underestimated their contribution to failure possibilities.

The implication of these and many other studies (see Maier, 1970, and Hogarth, 1987, for useful introductions) is that we may approach problem solving and decision making with a much poorer grasp on the factors involved and alternatives available than we need. One common response has been to assign groups to generate ideas, on the very plausible assumption that group members will have a wider range of information and ideas to contribute, and may stimulate one another. Group "brainstorming," a technique invented by Alex Osborn in the mid 1950s, was designed to maximize this stimulation by forbidding criticism, urging quantity rather than quality of ideas, and encouraging modification of and piggybacking on the ideas of others (Osborn, 1957). Dozens of related group processes have since been proposed (see Van Gundy, 1981, for a survey).

Unfortunately, there is little evidence that any of these techniques actually work, in the sense of yielding more or better ideas than the same number of people working alone for the same period of time and then pooling their outputs. For group brainstorming, the best studied of these techniques, the evidence is now clear: individuals brainstorming alone and later pooling produce more ideas, of a quality at least as high, as do the same number of people brainstorming in a group (McGrath, 1984). Diehl and Stroebe (1987) suggest three possible reasons: (a) People may be shy about proposing wild ideas in front of others and thus hold back ideas (evaluation apprehension); (b) Group members see little connection between their efforts and the group output as a whole and therefore make less effort to contribute (free riding); (c) In groups, only one person can talk while the others listen (or at least wait for their chance to talk); thus participants may forget or be talked out of ideas before they get a chance to propose them (production blocking). Though there is evidence that all three processes operate, Diehl and Stroebe conclude that production blocking is the main villain.

This conclusion is consistent with our own findings with the University of Arizona GSS. One of the tools available in that GSS is an idea-generation support system called EBS (for Electronic Brainstorming). In using EBS, a participant sits at a terminal that shows the theme question at the top of the screen (e.g., "What could be done about the campus parking problem?"). He or she types in a suggestion (up to five lines) and sends off the file, which is immediately replaced by another file containing the same question and a suggestion offered by another participant. The first participant adds a comment, sends the file, receives another randomly drawn file, and so on, until the session is concluded. As the file builds, the user can scroll to and fro through the comments. Thus, whereas someone noting ideas on a wordprocessor has only his or her own earlier ideas to look back on, the EBS participant can look back on a loosely-knit chain of ideas generated by others. The hope is that this chain of ideas will provide enough stimulation to generate useful new ideas without incurring the "production blocking" costs associated with normal face-to-face interaction.

This hope has received substantial support, at least for large groups from a recent series of experiments with the EBS systems (Valacich, Dennis, & Connolly, 1991). Using a variety of problems, group sizes, incentives and input formats, we found that EBS groups larger than a dozen or so members generated more ideas than did the same number of individuals brainstorming on their own and later pooling output. Given a thirty-year history of precisely the opposite result from face-to-face group brainstorming, we are very excited about this result and are eager to further understand and extend it. For example, the simple file-passing procedure might be usefully modified to allow longer or shorter periods of thinking, to change as the session moves forward, to involve more or fewer other participants, or to subdivide and structure the problem to selectively allow different expert or unfamiliar inputs. We regard the demonstration of EBS superiority to be something of a breakthrough and are eager to exploit it.

It does seem clear that the removal of production blocking is not the whole story, as Diehl and Stroebe suggest. In an earlier study using smaller groups (Connolly, Jessup, & Valacich, 1990), we manipulated two factors: Whether or not comments were identified by the name of the member who made them (anonymity); and, using confederates, whether the tone of the responses to others' comments was supportive or hostile. Both factors had a substantial effect on idea output, with groups in which members remained anonymous and used a critical, evaluative tone being the most productive. Both also had a substantial (though precisely opposite) effect on participant satisfaction, with groups in which members identified themselves and used a supportive tone most satisfied. These results appear inconsistent with any simple account of what motivated the participants (evaluation apprehension, free riding, or other), and seem to call for a more complex theory including both motivational and cognitive elements. (Interestingly, in this experiment, self-ratings of productivity tended to follow the satisfaction measures rather than actual output, so there was a large and negative correlation between actual productivity and self-rated productivity. The implications for GSS evaluations that turn on self-report are obvious and worrying.)

Overall the connections between basic decision behavior research and GSS application are relatively well developed in the idea generation area. On the one hand is a well-established literature showing that individuals can use help in generating ideas to solve problems, but that group brainstorming is not the solution, despite its obvious promise. On the other hand we have a specific technology, EBS, that addresses production blocking, the primary obstacle to effective idea generation. With the recent experiments of Valacich et al., the two have come together and produced the first version of a superior idea generator. With more development and refinement, it may become the routine technology for the idea-generation phase of decision making and problem solving.

HINDSIGHT AND OVERCONFIDENCE

Decisions are made with a view to the future consequences of present actions, and the future is uncertain. Decision behavior researchers have thus been primarily interested in how people cope with uncertainty and particularly with how their coping corresponds to the formal models provided by probability theory. Researchers have looked at such questions as how people combine information about two uncertain events ("If it rains on Sunday and if Jim shows up for the picnic"); how they revise their opinions in the light of new information ("I fancied Black Arrow in the 3.30, but now I learn that his regular jockey is not available"); and how they deal with conditional probabilities ("How likely is it that I have this disease, given that the test came out positive?") Any of the regular decision behavior texts (e.g., Hogarth, 1987; Yates, 1990) will provide a useful overview of this work. (Von Winterfeldt and Edwards' 1986 book on decision analysis also has an especially good section on this problem.)

Perhaps the simplest of all these probability questions is this: How good are we at estimating probabilities? One probability estimate is common enough that it has attracted a distinct research literature. It examines our judgment of how likely we are to be right in making a particular assertion—that is, our level of confidence in our judgment. We feel some degree of confidence in our judgment of a defendant's guilt, of the commercial promise of a new product, of a job candidate working out well, of our being able to beat the train to the crossing, of it raining tomorrow. How well do these confidence judgments correspond to objective probabilities?

In most predictions like this, there is no obvious way to test our confidence levels (unless we foolishly assigned a probability of 1.0 or 0.0 to some event). Unlikely events do, in fact, sometimes happen, and near certainties sometimes fail to happen. In some special circumstances, however, we can collect the relevant data. Weather forecasters, for example, routinely estimate the probability that it will rain tomorrow. If we collected a sample of, say, a hundred days on which a particular forecaster had assigned a 60% chance of rain, we could then check to see if it actually did rain on about 60 days, or noticeably more or less. Similarly, professional racing tipsters offer large numbers of predictions that are easy to check afterwards. Simple experiments could ask people factual general-knowledge questions ("What's the capital of Iowa?") and ask them both for an answer and a rating of confidence in that answer. If confidence reflects accuracy, we would then expect questions answered with high confidence to be mainly right, those with low confidence mainly wrong, and other classes in between.

In fact, the only group we know of that has this property (known as "good calibration") is weather forecasters. Their estimates of rain probability are astonishingly close to the actual frequency of rain on specific days (see Murphy and Winkler, 1974). In contrast a large body of evidence using one form or another of the general-knowledge quiz procedure has regularly found subjects to be considerably over-confident: The answers to which they assign confidence levels of 10 on a 1 to 10 scale turn out to be correct only about 70% of the time, those they give a confidence rating of 5 turn out to be correct only about a quarter of the time, and so on (e.g., Fischhoff, Slovic, & Lichtenstein, 1977). Similarly, subjects asked to construct 98% confidence intervals around their estimates of factual questions (e.g., "What percentage of your classmates here prefer scotch to bourbon?" "How many eggs were produced in the United States last year?") give intervals so tight that the true value falls outside them a third of the time or more (Alpert and Raiffa, 1982). (Appropriate 98% confidence intervals would, of course, fail to contain the true value only 2% of the time).

A related phenomenon, hindsight bias, can be considered as "overconfidence of the past." The core of the effect is that, once we know how some situation turned out, we see the events leading up to that outcome as relatively inevitable and suppose that people who were in the situation at the start could have anticipated this unfolding. We thus have a difficult time making the empathetic leap to how uncertain the future must have seemed at the time. Looking back on Pearl Harbor, for example, we are amazed at how the participants did not see it all coming. Interestingly, the effect seems to work even when we are looking back on our own earlier judgments. We recall having been more sure at the time than we actually were who was going to win the election or how a scientific experiment was going to turn out (Slovic & Fischhoff, 1977).

Hindsight bias raises serious questions as to the extent to which we are able to learn from experience. In some studies with business students analyzing business cases (Connolly & Bukszar, 1990; Bukszar & Connolly, 1988) we found that students had no trouble interpreting the same set of events and decisions as leading to either a very successful, or a very unsuccessful, outcome. Students who were told the bad outcome judged that the decision made earlier had been ill-considered, too risky, and based on inadequate information. Those told the good outcome found the initial decisions sound and competent. The results were unchanged when the students saw the outcome generated randomly by the toss of a coin. Discussion among groups of students failed to eliminate the effect. It is difficult to see quite what (other than glibness in analysis) is learned when the same set of case materials can as easily be interpreted as leading to a good or a bad outcome.

Fischhoff (1982), in a careful review of research on these two phenomena, points out that simply warning people of their existence or urging them to try harder has little or no effect. Indeed, both biases have proved quite resistant to debiasing efforts. The one approach that seems to have real promise in both cases involves getting the subjects to search for and integrate disconfirming information. Slovic and Fischhoff (1977), for example, reported reduction in hindsight bias when subjects were asked to explain the occurrence of the event they believed had *not* happened. Lichtenstein and Fischhoff (1980) found that overconfidence was markedly reduced when subjects were given a brief but intensive personalized training on their own earlier responses in a similar task. In neither case, it should be noted, did the bias disappear; it was simply reduced.

Do these processes generalize to any substantial extent from the laboratory to the real world? When, for example, we examine the decision making leading to the Challenger shuttle disaster are we seeing, first, overconfidence of the launch controllers in the success of a risky mission and, second, a hindsight bias in the later investigators that made the earlier decisions seem foolhardy? The honest answer is that we simply do not know—as we noted earlier, the circumstances under which the effects could be detected are rarely found outside conscious experimentation. For the GSS designer, however, it seems prudent to examine the possibility that the effects are real and that remedial designs might be needed.

There has, as far as I know, been no serious experimentation with these effects in computer-supported groups. A full-scale program of research along these lines would be very interesting, and seems relatively straightforward. One might start with student groups generating confidence ratings of simple estimates or guesses about general-knowledge matters and move on to groups of substantive experts forming complex assessments in matters of professional significance. Across-time designs would allow exploration of hindsight effects across the same range. As a comparison baseline, a simple averaging of individual judgments (cf. von Winterfeldt & Edwards, 1986) would suggest whether groups that interact differ in any systematic way from those that simply pool individual estimates (paralleling the "real versus nominal groups" comparison used in brainstorming studies).

My own initial hypothesis would be that group interaction would generally tend to increase overconfidence (cf. Sniezek & Henry, 1989; Castore & Murnighan, 1978). In part this would flow from the information effect (see, e.g., Oskamp, 1967) in which confidence, but not accuracy, increases steadily as subjects received more information. Remedial strategies might draw on the findings concerning marshalling of contradictory evidence noted above and echoed in the earlier literature on devil's advocacy and dialectical planning (e.g., Mitroff and Emsholf, 1979). Though remediation will, clearly, be a challenge to the ingenuity of the GSS designer as well as to the skills of the experimenter, an initial line of approach might explore ways in which the group might be induced to search out and keep in play evidence supporting multiple and unfavored hypotheses. Ideas from legal adversary procedures might also be of value here.

In summary, then, overconfidence and hindsight represent a cluster of decision behavior concerns that seem hardly to have penetrated the GSS world, despite their evident potential for posing practical problems. It seems relatively straightforward for GSS researchers to probe the possibility that the effects translate into their sphere of concern. Supposing they do, there are a few leads in the decision behavior literature that might be developed into effective remedial strategies in working GSS. The potential value of a bridge in this area between the two disciplines appears to be quite good.

EXTERNALIZING JUDGMENTS AND POLICY CAPTURING

A central part of the activities we think of as requiring human judgment is a many-to-one transformation, that is, a mental process by which several items of information are boiled down to a single overall judgment. For example, a physician examines a patient's symptoms and test results and boils the information down to a diagnosis. An expert livestock assessor looks at a hog's bodily dimensions and appearance and makes an overall judgment of the animal's worth. A new-products manager examines a product's features, profitability, and test-market results and assesses its overall potential. Similarly, faculty admitting students to graduate school, weather forecasters predicting tomorrow's weather, horse bettors picking their bets, and personnel managers rating a candidate's potential: In each case one can think of the final overall judgment as in some way derived from a larger set of information inputs or cues. In each case we also tend to associate the combination process with expertise, with subtle and complex weighings and combinings of information.

Although the above examples are generally considered processes of inference, of discovering some true state about the outside world, they are quite parallel to other many-to-one judgments involving preference. I might, for example, express my overall preference for alternative vacation packages described by several features, for cars described by their price, performance, appearance, and reliability, or for restaurants described by their location, price, and type and quality of food. In these cases the combining process has no "right answer," in the sense that others looking at the same evidence should reach the same overall judgment—you probably like different vacations, cars, and restaurants than I do. But the same many-to-one process seems to be involved, and researchers have approached many of these preference processes in much the same way as they have the inference processes noted above.

Any introductory decision making text (e.g., Arkes & Hammond, 1986; Yates, 1990) will provide dozens of examples of studies of processes like these. In broad outline such studies aim to represent what the judge is doing in the form of a rule by which he or she combines the input information into the output judgment. For example, if the inputs are in convenient numerical form, like test results, the rule might be a simple weighted average or a rule involving more complex mathematical forms. (Note that the rule "represents" the judge only in the sense of producing, as well as the researcher is able, the same overall outputs as the judge does for the same set of inputs. There is no claim that the judge is, in fact, computing a weighted average or whatever the form of rule is.) The general procedure, known as "policy capturing," is to present the judge with a set of cases (patients, candidates, hogs, or whatever) and ask for judgments of each. When inputs and outputs are simple numerical scores, standard statistical techniques such as multiple linear regression are used to derive a best-fit model of the judge. Other techniques are used in less amenable circumstances.

After dozens and dozens of studies in this general framework (see, e.g., Brehmer & Joyce (1988) for reviews), some clear and surprising findings have emerged:

1. The judges in these tasks typically describe their combining processes as using quite a large number of factors or cues and in quite complex ways. For example, "Factor 1 is important only if Factors 2 and 3 are both high, otherwise, Factor 1 doesn't matter."
2. The best-fit models of the judges generally use very few factors and combine them in quite simple ways. For example, a simple weighted average of two or three factors often fits the judge (i.e., produces overall judgments that are near as possible to his) as well as any.
3. When there is some objective criterion for what the judge is trying to estimate (e.g., a later post mortem report on the disease the physician was trying to diagnose earlier), the simple model described in (2) does at least as good a job as the actual judge, and often significantly better. Further, a model based on what the judge claimed to be doing invariably works worse than the judge (a finding with some worrying implications for developers of expert systems, amongst others).

Once again, it is easy to sketch some very promising bridges from this body of work to the world of the GSS developer. Let us, for a concrete example, consider support for a group that is trying to evaluate candidates for some important post in their organization, such as the presidency of a university. A file of information has been assembled about each candidate—education, employment history, letters of reference, impressions from interviews, and so on. Somehow the group is charged with distilling this mass of information, perhaps on hundreds of candidates, into an overall rating for each, at least sufficient to select out a "short list" of half a dozen candidates. Once again we see the many-to-one process, but this time repeated between group members as they struggle not only to form a personal evaluation of each candidate but also to shape the group's ratings.

There is, clearly, huge potential in this setting for conflict between group members, on both inference (Just how strong is the candidate's record on minority hiring?) and preference issues (How much weight should be given to this factor, compared to his skills in external fund raising?). Indeed it is surprising that such groups ever reach sufficient consensus to report out a recommendation. When they do, it is often in the spirit of unsatisfactory compromise and covert politics. How might a GSS help?

One approach has been extensively developed, at least for two-person conflicts, by Hammond and his associates (e.g., Hammond, 1971). He considers, for example, a possible contract (with its many provisions) presented to the two sides in a labor-management negotiation. Each negotiator forms some assessment of how favorable it is to her side. But, lacking any very clear self-insight into exactly *why* she gives it that assessment (i.e., her weighting of the relative importance of each contract element), she is not likely to be very good at subtle shifts that might make it more attractive. Further, she is most unlikely to understand her opponent's weights and thus to see how the contract could be modified to make it more acceptable to the opponent. With both sides lacking the insight into their own and their opponent's "judgment policies," it is hard to see what they can do other than strive for maximum concessions on each contract issue. Impasse is the likely outcome.

In an old study, Flack & Summers (1971) worked with pairs of such negotiators who had just completed a long and bitter settlement of a labor dispute. They first conducted policy capturing for each individual and presented the results in primitive computer graphics both to the individual and to his opponent. The results were extraordinary: Each pair of negotiators was able almost at once to devise contracts that both parties liked, many more satisfactory than the deal they had in fact hammered out in months of painful traditional negotiation. The policy capturing, coupled with graphical feedback, allowed each party to better understand both his own and his opponent's weighting scheme, and this apparently allowed rapid development of contracts satisfactory to both sides.

As interest in formal negotiations grows in the GSS context (see, for example, Jelassi & Foroughi, 1989), the implications of this line of work should not be missed. Policy capturing at the individual level could be readily implemented as an optional GSS tool, especially since initial discussion should surface some shared understanding of what the key issues might be. Discussion could then center around the actual weights participants are found to be applying, rather than around those they think they are applying, or those others assume they are applying. It may well be revealed that parts of the debate are appropriate subjects for expertise, and if that expertise is not already in the group, it could be obtained. For example, Hammond & Adelman (1976) report on a highly emotional debate over the choice of appropriate ammunition for the Denver police force. The opposing parties were found by policy capturing to hold quite different weights for three crucial aspects on which bullets differed: stopping power, lethality, and ricochet danger. However, the objective characteristics of different types of ammunition were identified as an objective matter, and this was resolved by scientific testimony from ballistics experts. Once this subissue was resolved, it was discovered that one particular type of ammunition was acceptable to the warring parties, and consensus was rapidly reached. There is, of course, no guarantee of such a happy outcome, but the general strategy seems to have clear implications for GSS developers.

The key idea here is the concept of a "judgment policy," a set of rules that, when given the same inputs as the real judge, yields an approximation of the judge's output. Using this idea together with the now well-developed technology of "policy capturing," by which such rules may be discovered, we can describe what an expert is doing with some precision, whether it be forming an inference or expressing a preference. A body of research based on these ideas has found that judges often have poor insight into their own policies and those of others; that real policies are often simpler than their owner thinks; and that computer graphics provides an ideal interface for feeding back these discoveries to the individual involved. Each of these elements seems to fit naturally into a GSS context and provides both an account of why satisfactory agreements may be hard to come by and the outlines of a set of techniques for improving the process.

CONCLUSIONS

This chapter, to reiterate the initial statement of purpose, is not intended as a comprehensive outline of research topics bridging decision behavior and GSS. It is simply a sampler of three issues that seem to me to be worth developing. The first, idea generation, has received a good deal of attention from GSS developers, and recent work suggests that useful payoffs are now attainable. The second, overconfidence and hindsight bias, in contrast, has a substantial research literature in decision behavior, but no GSS work so far, despite the apparently clear potential. The third, policy-capturing and related techniques, falls in between, with some application beyond the decision behavior laboratory but lacking full-scale development within GSS.

The field, then, is wide open. On the one hand there is a large and growing body of research in decision behavior that explores how people actually make decisions and judgments and the factors that make these processes more or less difficult and more or less successful. On the other hand is an increasingly sophisticated body of GSS tools and procedures whose broad purpose is to improve and facilitate human decision making. The two areas have grown and flourished to date with almost no serious interaction between them; the strengths and weaknesses of each clearly reflect this isolation. Our purpose in this chapter has been to urge that they start to talk to one another, and to suggest a few examples of the issues that might come up if they do so. There is no shortage of profitable topics for the conversation.

CHAPTER 15

Communication Theory and Group Support Systems

M. Scott Poole
University of Minnesota

Michele H. Jackson
University of Minnesota

INTRODUCTION

The roots of the communication discipline go back at least as far as Plato and Aristotle, who recognized that public speaking and deliberation were essential activities of a vital society. Aristotle, Cicero, and Augustine, among other classical authors, wrote treatises on rhetoric as the art of public speaking. Throughout its history, the study of communication has focused on the process of communicating, which includes the creation of messages, their delivery, and the reactions they provoke in audiences.

The two principal models of the communication process have been shaped by the communication contexts and media they refer to. Studies of public address and mass media communication emphasize the creation and delivery of messages to large audiences and the assessment of message effects. They tend to model communication as one-way transmission with delayed or indirect feedback. In contrast, studies of communication in personal relationships, groups, and organizations adopt a more interactional framework, which emphasizes the personal exchange of messages between individuals or groups who can give each other direct and immediate feedback. They model communication as a two-way, interactive process or transaction.

The emergence of new technologies such as GSS, which combine aspects of both interpersonal interaction and mass media, presents something of a challenge to communication theory. With new technologies, the line between the various contexts begins to blur, and it is unclear that models based on mass media or face-to-face contexts are adequate (Rice, 1984). Indeed, although communication theory can contribute to the study of GSS, research on GSS and other new technologies is also stimulating new developments in communication theory.

Communication research is rich with themes relevant to the study of GSS. This essay focuses on four areas of communication research that seem particularly promising: studies of differences in communication media, group communication research, research on argumentation and reasoning, and rhetorical studies. These certainly do not exhaust the communication theories applicable to GSS research. Not covered by this essay is relevant work on the social information processing model (Fulk et al., 1990), network analysis (e.g., Contractor & Eisenberg, 1990), relational communication (e.g., Courtright et al., 1989), cognitive bases of communication (Knapp & Miller, 1984), philosophy of communication (Scott, 1967; Cherwitz & Hikins, 1986), and critical theory of communication (e.g., Finlay, 1987).

Communication Media Research

Communication occurs through many different media, including written text, face-to-face interaction, meetings, large convocations, telephones, teleconferences, computer conferences, and electronic mail. This array of possibilities provides a wide range of choices for GSS design (see the chapter by Polley and Stone for a discussion of design choices). DeSanctis and Gallupe (1987) illustrate a few of these possibilities. They distinguish GSS along two dimensions, whether they support face-to-face or dispersed groups and whether the groups meet over short or long periods. They posit different combinations of media for different types of GSS. For example, in dispersed short-term groups, they posit that computer-mediated communication over networks combined with audio-teleconferences might be used. For long-term dispersed groups, they argue that computer-supported videoconferencing is a workable model. Of course, many more media combinations are possible, and different GSS features may embody different media. A GSS that supports both public and private message exchange, for example, gives groups channels similar to both electronic mail and computer conferencing; members may pick and choose which they employ. Given the range of media possibilities, how does one determine which media to integrate into a GSS? To answer this question, several more fundamental issues must be addressed: What theoretically meaningful dimensions can be used to distinguish media? What effects do different media have on the communication process? Are some media more appropriate than others under various conditions?

At least four different dimensions have been defined to distinguish communication media and explain their effects. Short, Williams, and Christie (1976; Rice, 1984: pp. 56–65) define media in terms of their *social presence*, which refers to the degree to which media allow a communicator to establish a personal connection with others. It is operationalized by having participants in a communication exchange evaluate the medium used on semantic differential scales such as "unsociable-sociable," "cold-warm," and "impersonal-personal." A high-presence medium is rated toward the sociable, warm, and personal end of the continuum. Short et al. report rankings of five media in order of increasing social presence: business letter, telephone, multispeaker audio, television, face-to-face discussion. Rice (1984) comments that social presence differences are linked to restrictions that the media place on nonverbal cues; as we move from written to face-to-face media, communicators are able to transmit and interpret an increasing range of vocal and visual nonverbal cues. The importance of nonverbal cues in conveying emotions and subtleties of meaning may well explain differences in social presence perceptions.

Trevino, Lengel, and Daft (1990) distinguished media in terms of *information richness*. The information richness of a medium is its capacity to facilitate shared meaning among communicators. Daft and his colleagues highlighted the importance of this function by noting that equivocality—the existence of multiple and conflicting interpretations—is a central feature of organizational life. In order to act effectively, organizations must reduce equivocality and create shared frameworks of meaning. Information richness refers to the varying capacity of media to reduce equivocality and depends on a "blend" of four criteria: the degree to which a medium provides immediate feedback, the capacity of the medium to transmit multiple cues, the use of natural language versus numbers, and the personal focus of the medium. Trevino et al. (1990, p. 76) generate the following ordering of media in terms of increasing richness: bulletin, special report, memo, note, letter, electronic mail, telephone, face-to-face. Although social presence and information richness seem rather similar, it is important to note that social presence distinctions are based on interpersonal concerns, such as the warmth and personalness of communication, whereas information richness distinctions are based on information-processing considerations such as equivocality or uncertainty reduction.

A third dimension for distinguishing media is their *symbolic meaning* (Rice, 1984; Trevino et al., 1990). There are at least two levels of symbolic meaning of media. A medium can add symbolic meaning to messages it carries, as when a handwritten note, as opposed to a typed one, conveys extra personal concern. Beyond the symbolic value they add, media are symbols in themselves; using a GSS may signal to others that the group is progressive and trying to learn about itself.

A fourth dimension is the degree to which media "bind" time or space, referred to here as *bindingness*. Ong (1982) and Innis (1972), among others, have distinguished media that provide permanent public records (e.g., writing, a database in a GSS) from those that carry transient messages (e.g., speaking). Media such as writing bind time by preserving past events, decisions, and actions for future use. Ong (1982) traces profound changes in human memory and thought patterns to the shift from oral to written to print to electronic media, each of which binds time to a different degree. Media also differ in the degree to which they are capable of joining geographically separated actors and areas, binding space, and by how tight this binding is (i.e., by how fast interchanges can be managed and how tightly they can be monitored). Innis (1972) has discussed the role of spatially-binding communication media such as the telegraph and radio in political and economic change.

Given the four dimensions of social presence, information richness, symbolic meaning, and bindingness, what effects do media have and what conditions dictate when various media are appropriate? The literature on media effects is rather large, and it is beyond the scope of this essay to summarize it (for reviews, see Johansen, 1977; Poole, Shannon, & DeSanctis, in press; Rice, 1984; Williams, 1977). However, some examples are illuminating. Both social presence and information richness have been shown to influence media choice in organizations (Rice, 1984; Trevino et al., 1990). Interestingly, information richness predicts media choice accurately for high-performing managers, but not for low-performing ones; Trevino et al. suggest that sensitivity to media differences and ability to select appropriate media are important managerial skills. As might be expected, high-social-presence media are generally regarded as more appropriate for emotional or conflictive communication, whereas low-social-presence media tend to be selected for task-oriented communication. In the same vein, high-information-richness media are better for highly equivocal tasks, whereas low-richness media are better for low-equivocality tasks. However, there are enough exceptions to these rules to warn us against accepting them uncritically. Context also plays an important role in determining social presence, information richness, and symbolic meaning, and thus the most appropriate medium. For example, an e-mail message from one manager to another about a decision may be taken to be low social presence if the first manager had refused to meet the other personally, but it would be considered high social presence if it were a "hi there"-type note between managers who had never met.

Some research on GSS has employed these dimensions. Hiltz, Johnson, and Turoff (1986) posit differences between face-to-face meetings and computer conferences based on social presence differences. Poole, Holmes, and DeSanctis (in press) predicted conflict management differences between GSS-supported meetings and nonsupported meetings based on social presence differences and on differences in time-bindingness. Because there are many different types of GSS, each with its own configuration of media, it is tempting to posit that predictions can be based on combinations of media effects along different dimensions. This raises an interesting question: Where along the information richness and social presence scales do GSS lie? It seems likely that different GSS might have quite different classifications on these dimensions.

There are many unsettling findings and unanswered questions regarding communication media effects. Information richness and social presence ratings are not particularly stable; ratings for the same media differ across contexts, samples, and types of communication (Rice, 1984; Fulk & Schmitz, 1988; Zmud, Lind, & Young, 1990). The problem of shifting and uncertain classifications along the dimensions is especially troubling for media such as electronic mail and GSS, which represent complex combinations of media. Then, too, how do we predict the ultimate impact of media combinations? Are the impacts of technologies such as GSS, which combine several media types, predictable by additive combinations of the individual media effects? Or are some media effects more important than others? Much research remains to be done before we will fully understand media effects.

Communication Processes in Group Decision Making

Group decision making is one of the main foci of communication research (Cragan & Wright, 1990; Fisher, 1980). Communication research on this much-studied topic is unique in that its primary focus is interaction processes. Communication has gone as far as any field has in attempting to satisfy McGrath and Altman's (1966) argument that adequate theories of groups must be based on analysis of the entire input-process-output chain.

In effective group decision making, a set of individuals—each with his or her own goals and motivations—must somehow coordinate its disparate tendencies and activities so that unified group action emerges. How does this occur? Two communication theories can be integrated to provide a useful model for GSS research. The Socioegocentric Model of group decision making (Hewes, 1986) describes a baseline, which represents the social dynamics that occur in a set of nonunified individuals. This set of individuals is temporarily unified—turned into a group—by structuring processes enacted in group communication, as described in the Theory of Adaptive Structuration (Poole & DeSanctis, 1990; Poole, Seibold, & McPhee, 1985, 1986). The effectiveness of these structuring processes determines decision making effectiveness, and the various factors that influence structuring processes are the key determinants of decision making.

Introducing his socioegocentric model of groups, Hewes (1986, p. 279) explains: The term "socioegocentric" is derived from Piaget's early developmental studies of "egocentric speech." Piaget notes that children ranging in age from 3 to 8 years engage in speech characterized by "remarks that are not addressed to anyone...and that...evoke no reaction adapted to them on the part of anyone to whom they might chance to be addressed." In the most developmentally advanced type of egocentric speech, "collective monologue," children give the structural appearance of engaging in a dialogue (for instance, appropriate turn-taking) but without managing to sustain the meaningful connectedness usually exemplified in adult speech.

The explanation for egocentric speech is that children have two goals—playing and relating to other children—but can only devote sufficient attention to one, their own play, due to human information-processing limitations. However, because they are aware of the importance of social interaction, children give the structural appearance of dialogue to their comments.

Many groups exhibit this same disjointed character, which might be termed the "cocktail party syndrome" (Poole, 1991). As in many "conversations" at cocktail parties, people make vacuous comments only loosely related to previous statements. But these comments seem connected, because people use various means of connecting them, such as referring to previous comments ("Yes, I know what you mean. Last week I was....") or habitual turn-taking devices (e.g., pausing at the end of a sentence to give the other an opportunity to speak). Members of decision-making groups each have their own ideas and motivations, which are not always "in sync." For example, one member might be thinking about the solution of the problem the group faces, another about a personal need, and still another may be in the mood to joke. The following interchange might reflect this:

> Mbr. A: I think we should reduce our number of on-call office hours.
> Mbr. B: Yeah, and we should add filing cabinets to each office to store the order forms.
> Mbr. C: That's a great idea...I can keep my lunch in the bottom drawer!

These comments appear to be connected, but they really do not build on each other. This occurs in part because members are concentrating on working out what they are going to say and ignore the speaker (Brenner, 1973; Jablin & Seibold, 1978).

Of course, not all group interaction is like this, or groups would accomplish very little. There are also periods where members' thinking and motivations converge and the group works together. Looking at group interaction over time, we observe alternating periods of individual and group focus. Some meetings are disjointed, with members off in their own private worlds, whereas others maintain a common group focus throughout. Most are somewhere in between. Hewes and others (1986) have argued that the degree to which a group departs from the disjointed state is a good measure of its "groupness."

Groups consist of independent minds that work independently and then converge for various periods of time, after which one or more members withdraw again to their individual lines of thought. This alternation is useful, because the independent lines of thinking contribute additional ideas to the group, and the periods of convergence allow testing and cross-checking of individual ideas and thought-provoking interchanges.

Periods of convergence occur through members' active attempts to structure their discussion. The role GSS play in this structuring process is the subject of Adaptive Structuration Theory (DeSanctis & Poole, 1991; Poole & DeSanctis, 1990; Poole et al., 1986). Adaptive Structuration Theory (AST) can be integrated with Hewes's model to give a rounded picture of group interaction processes. Very simply, AST argues that advanced communication technologies such as GSS can be understood in terms of the structures (rules and resources) that they provide for group interaction. GSS provides both procedural rules (e.g., voting routines) and resources (e.g. public display screens, memory) for carrying out and organizing group activities. The effects of GSS on actual behavior depend on the design of technology structures and on the emergent (adaptive) structures that form in the group as members interact with the technology over time. Thus, from the design perspective, we can identify and develop structural capabilities that are likely to bring about desired group interaction processes. But outcomes from GSS use depend on precisely how these structures are brought into interaction, how they are combined with other available structures in the work environment, and how the structures are effectively "redesigned" by the group in the course of their appropriation for specific purposes. The process by which rules and resources are appropriated to organize and maintain social systems is termed structuration. Figure 15.1 summarizes the relationships in AST.

AST provides a dynamic view of GSS technology and group interaction, focusing on the emergence of new social orders through active use of technology structures. Independent variables such as task, group size, and organizational culture influence group use of technology through their impacts on the structurational process. Hence, AST attempts to explain how communication processes mediate and moderate input-output relationships (McGrath & Altman, 1966). Several studies have shed light on how structurational processes operate in laboratory and ongoing groups (Poole, Holmes, & DeSanctis, in press; Sambamurthy, DeSanctis, & Poole, 1991; Poole, DeSanctis, Kirsch, & Jackson, 1991b).

The integration of socioegocentric theory and AST provides a complete picture of the tensions that operate in groups. It also suggests a normative model to guide the design of GSS: An effective group must maintain a balance between independent thinking and structured, coordinated work. Too much independence shatters group cohesion and may encourage members to focus on individual needs. Too much synchronous, structured work is likely to regiment group thinking and stifle novel ideas. In terms of GSS design, this suggests that effective systems would be based on designs that (a) provide features to facilitate independent, private thinking, (b) provide features to focus members' attention and encourage convergent thinking, (c) give members autonomous control over features to enable them to "wander" by themselves through GSS procedures as they think independently, (d) keep records of group ideas and actions so that members who miss ongoing group discussion can inform themselves of what transpired, and (e) incorporate procedural structures that alternate between independent and group-centered foci and that synchronize members' alternations.

In addition to describing how groups define and organize themselves with GSS, AST allows researchers to tackle two additional issues. First, AST accounts

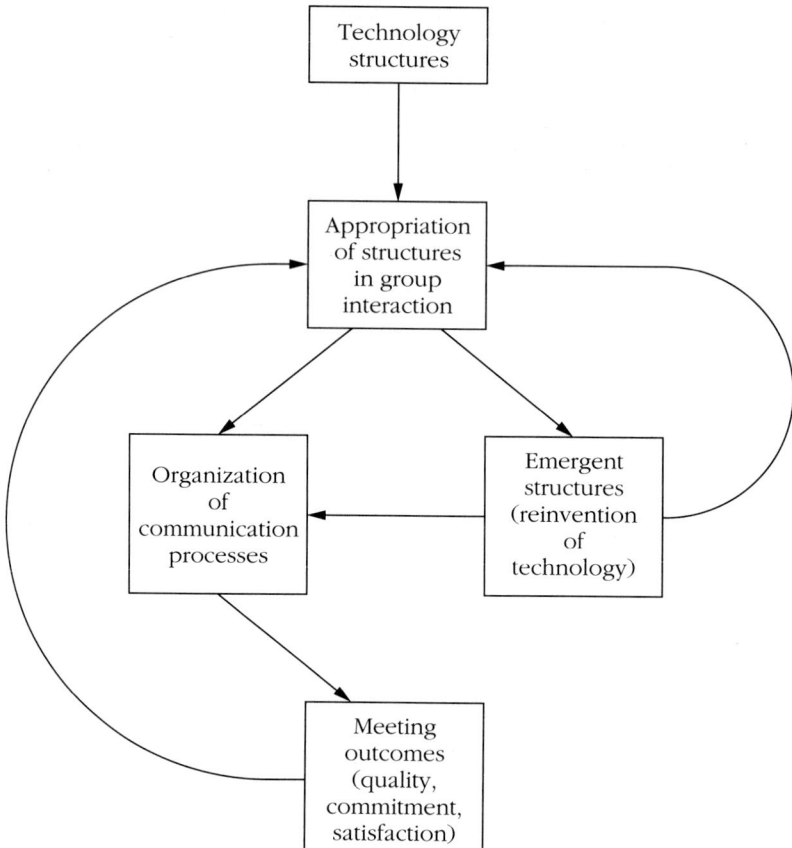

FIGURE 15.1 Relationships in Adaptive Structuration Theory.

for how reinvention of GSS occurs. Reinvention refers to the common practice of adapting and altering technological innovations during implementation (Johnson & Rice, 1987). AST posits that potential structures embodied within a GSS are activated through being appropriated by the group. Appropriation involves bringing the structure into action, adapting it to the situation (sometimes in ways inconsistent with design premises), and reproducing this adaptation by using it in a stable fashion over a period of time. This offers a picture of the process by which reinvention occurs.

AST also offers an explanation for the mixed results obtained in GSS research on questions such as whether GSS encourages greater equality of participation or whether GSS enhances group performance. Between-study discrepancies can be explained in several ways. Differences in study design, tasks, or instrumentation are possibilities. Diversity in GSS design across studies may also explain observed differences, although some replications with different GSS have yielded similar results (e.g., Watson et al., 1988 and Easton et al., 1989; see Chapter 3). Adaptive Structuration Theory argues that differences resulting from the process of structuration mediate the impact of GSS on group outcomes, resulting in different results both within and across types of GSS. The studies by DeSanctis, Poole, and colleagues cited above provide some evidence to support this explanation.

Much other communication research has been devoted to the effective management of group decision processes. Gouran and his colleagues have conducted a series of studies on orientation, communication that facilitates movement toward group goals (see Cragan & Wright, 1990, for complete references). Hirokawa (Hirokawa, 1985; Hirokawa & Scheerhorn, 1986; see also Cragan & Wright, 1990) has done a series of studies exploring communicative functions that promote effective and ineffective decision making. These studies define communication types that are effective in structuring group work and also carry insights for the facilitation of GSS.

Rationality and Argumentation

There is a long tradition of thought on how communication media influence thinking and reasoning. Plato ruminated at some length on the static nature of writing compared to the easy flight of spoken language. Ong (1982) extended this line of reasoning, arguing that successive transitions from oral to written to printed to electronically mediated communication brought about transformations in ways of thought. Heim (1987) has sought to extend Ong's reasoning to computer-mediated communication. He argues that word-processing technologies have changed the compositional process, rendering language less permanent and reducing the value of precise, permanent expression, ultimately changing the very phenomenology of thinking.

The complexity of argument as it unfolds in social contexts renders the application of traditional models of logic difficult and incomplete. Recognizing this difficulty, the speech communication field has been receptive to theories that stress multiple perspectives of argument. For example, the understanding of argument as both product (we construct arguments) and process (we engage *in* argument) is well established in the field (O'Keefe, 1977). Communication approaches are of value to GSS researchers in that they examine argument in both of these senses; further, the approaches are adapted to ordinary, everyday argument, or "practical reasoning" (Toulmin, 1969). When we focus on practical reasoning, we move away from the abstract concerns of logic and take into account the differences that individuals and characteristics of the situation introduce into arguments. Two approaches are presented in this section, the first developed by Joseph Wenzel and the second by Stephen Toulmin.

Wenzel's (1977; 1982) approach differentiates the ways that a researcher can *approach* and *evaluate* argument. He suggests that argument may be viewed from either a logical, dialectical, or rhetorical perspective. When operating from a logical perspective, research would analyze the truth or accuracy of evidence and the soundness of reasoning according to traditional standards of logic. A dialectical perspective shifts emphasis to the breadth of issues explored; it examines the extent to which all points of view and issues have been sought out and considered according to some standards or criteria and the best alternative chosen. Finally, the rhetorical perspective views arguments as appeals to an audience. Arguments are strategic. Group members are alternately rhetors, trying to persuade others through the uses of strategy and appeals, and auditors, responding to these efforts. Research from the rhetorical perspective focuses on argument as a strategic response to a particular context; the abstract elements of argument are less important than the characteristics of the situation and audience that produce particular strategies or make those strategies more or less successful.

Within this perspective, any particular argument may be understood and evaluated from three distinct vantage points. Wenzel's approach cautions us that an assessment of GSS impacts on reasoning may depend as much upon the view taken by researchers as upon the changes themselves. Further, the effects may be in tension with one another. For example, a GSS may provide structure to group discussion such that users produce arguments characterized by sound reasoning and truthful premises. Viewed from a rhetorical perspective, however, the argumentation practices fostered by this GSS are characterized by the dominance of a few individuals over others. Can such a change be characterized as an improvement in argumentation and rationality? GSS researchers should find Wenzel's approach useful for ascertaining effects in more detail and for probing the meaning of those effects in a larger context than is provided by traditional analytic models.

A second approach to the study of argument offers an alternative to traditional analytic models for characterizing the substance and structure of argument. Articulated in Toulmin, Rieke, & Janik (1984), the approach posits a general skeletal structure, or model, that is present in all arguments, and several recurring forms of reasoning, each of which is a variation on the substance or *content* of the model. The primary distinction between this model and an analytic model is the status given to context. The structural elements of the model are identified according to their *function* in the interaction. For example, *claims* are disputed statements advanced by a speaker with the desire of winning the adherence of others; *evidence*, or grounds, is the undisputed information advanced to support claims. The structure organizes the content of the argument into a general form, from which patterns may be recognized across time and contexts. These patterns are argument types. For example, a claim that makes a general statement about a class of things, supported by evidence consisting of several specific examples from that class, forms an argument by generalization. Patterns of argument emerge from combinations of structural elements; others include analogies, causal arguments, appeals to authority, and syllogisms (Toulmin, Rieke, & Janik, 1984).

Using this model, researchers would begin by identifying disputed statements, or *claims*, as starting points for arguments, and then would trace the development of the argument through supporting evidence. In this process, claims, at first disputed, will be accepted, and those statements will then be used as evidence. Evidence, at first accepted, will be disputed and will stand then as a claim. Statements will be offered as simple opinions or descriptions and drawn into argumentative status when challenged or when called upon to support some other statements in dispute. In this way, elements of argument will interconnect, forming a chain of reasoning across instances of argument (Warnick & Inch, 1989). These chains can then be analyzed in terms of how they unfold and the type of argumentation they represent.

The potential impacts of GSS upon rationality cannot be adequately captured by measures of group outcome or by analytic models of argument. The social context within which GSS and other groupware operate seems to allow even more room for impacts on thought and reasoning than does individualized software. The rationality expressed through group interaction is commonly made up of several lines of reasoning that evolve simultaneously, are interrupted and taken up again, and interweave in complex patterns. Studying the rationality supported by GSS in terms of standards of logical consistency or decision quality is useful, but this approach is inadequate for capturing the creation and recreation of arguments through social interaction (Seibold & Meyers, 1986). Technologies that rearrange the social processes of argumentation influence group rationality profoundly (Watson, DeSanctis, & Poole, 1988; Kraemer & Pinsonneault, 1989). To be complete, the assessment of this influence must address argumentation on the fundamental level of process.

Rhetorical Approaches

Rhetorical analysis concerns the understanding of humans as symbol-using beings (Burke, 1969; Campbell, 1982) and asks how symbols, or language, may be used "to alter perception, to explain, to change, reinforce, and channel belief, to initiate and maintain actions" (Campbell, 1982, p.15). Typically associated with analysis of formal public speech, the focus of rhetorical analysis has broadened to include organizational and group contexts as well—that is, contexts of GSS. Explorations of GSS use from a rhetorical perspective would pursue the ways in which GSS creates or alters among users the patterns and substance of language. Does GSS encourage distinct symbolic behavior in such forms as stories, arguments, or common themes? In what ways does a group seek to make sense of, or give meaning to, GSS? What effect does GSS have upon the perceptions and beliefs a group has about itself, technology, the larger organization, or society as a whole? We present several rhetorical approaches that may address these questions; one approach, fantasy theme analysis, is discussed in some detail, and we briefly suggest several others.

Fantasy theme analysis seeks to understand how groups create a shared reality through the use of stories or dramatizing messages (Bormann, 1972; 1980; 1982; 1986). In contrast to the term's common meaning of imaginary tales or dreams, fantasy, in this context, refers to a group's shared interpretations of events or experiences that are real and concrete. Fantasizing behavior, such as the telling of stories or jokes, enables the private, symbolic worlds of group members to overlap, or *converge*, into a shared symbolic reality that includes common values, beliefs, and understandings of events. Identification of a fantasy requires that two things be present: first, the members of the group must collectively participate and get caught up in the message; it must be "chained out" beyond the initial message. Second, the fantasy must deal with a specific incident or with a concrete theme that refers to events or experience located in *other than the here-and-now*, which may be either the past or the future. Research at the University of Minnesota is currently investigating the nature of fantasy chaining within GSS groups.

As an example of how this might be applied to GSS research, we might be interested in how groups adopt a GSS. Using fantasy theme analysis, we might look for stories members share with each other of how they used the GSS in the past or ways they might use it in the future. We might also look for references to the GSS as a person and what type of person it is. The nature of these stories will present a picture of the GSS that can help researchers to understand how some groups respond positively and others negatively to the same GSS technology. In other words, fantasies reflect the attitudes and bias with which the members interpret events and experience.

Further evidences of symbolic convergence are the presence of fantasy types and inside cues. A fantasy type is a general story line that encompasses a number of specific story lines. The classic spaghetti Western is an example of a fantasy type. Fantasy types tend to have archetypal or general personae that enact the group's experience or its bias. The characterization and experience of these personae reflect the motives of the group, how it sees itself in relation to the larger community. GSS may encourage particular fantasy types; for example, the group as pioneers, progressive and advanced, leaving behind the old, traditional ways that offer no challenge and no future. Or, if members resist the GSS, they may portray themselves as steadfast guardians, unwilling to bend in the face of dehumanizing technology. Inside cues are shorthand for previously shared and well-established fantasies. Inside cues allude to fantasies with abbreviated verbal or nonverbal cues—a specialized vocabulary, for example, or a reference to the GSS by personal name both "work" because they invoke a larger shared experience.

Fantasy theme analysis offers GSS researchers insight into the role of technology in shared group reality. Attempts made by the group to understand the technology on anything other than a technical level undoubtedly will involve fantasizing. Knowledge of the types of fantasies that groups develop to make sense of the technology might enable researchers to better understand the variation with which technology might be used or made more or less effective. The technology itself may affect the level of dramatizing in groups. According to symbolic convergence theory, fantasizing is essential to creating a common symbolic ground. Does GSS technology help or hinder that process, and, if so, in what way? Finally, consideration of a group's need to make sense of its experience through fantasies could be useful in guiding future technological developments.

A second rhetorical approach, narrative analysis, focuses specifically upon the stories people tell (Brown, 1990; Fisher, 1984, 1985; Pacanowsky & O'Donnell-Trujillo, 1983). Stories place events in time and furnish those events with characters, scenes, plot, and action. People use stories to sort happenings in the world into meaningful relationships. Fisher (1984) suggests that stories are a form of rationality, that within stories are the "good reasons" that inform people of the courses of action that are appropriate for a situation and justify their efforts. Narrative analysis would be useful for determining how users perceive and make sense of GSS. GSS may influence the nature of both stories and storytelling. GSS technology may appear in the substance of stories as a character, as setting, even as plot (for group support systems that have "built in" a particular sequencing of actions). Perhaps more significantly, GSS will alter the ways that stories are told. What are the differences between narrators using video conferencing, or electronic conferencing, when compared to non-GSS supported narratives? Who is the storyteller when the story is collectively written? Who is the audience? If narratives function as a type of rationality, it will be important to consider the influences of GSS in this area.

The final rhetorical approach we will suggest here is generic analysis, which seeks to identify and understand those *situations* that consistently provoke similar patterns of communication (Campbell & Jamieson, 1978, 1986; Black 1978; Harrel & Linkugel, 1978). Genre theory is a useful perspective for studying how situations influence or direct communication behaviors. Whether or not the situations of GSS use constitute a genre should be of immediate interest in current research. Chesebro and Bonsall (1989) have already suggested its existence. Although her study is limited to earlier communication technologies such as the memo or the report, Yates's (1989) research also provides evidence of the relevance of generic analysis for understanding the impact of GSS on organizational contexts. Genre provides a means by which researchers may explore the ways in which GSS may alter or shift social realities of participants and of larger cultures.

CONCLUSION

Many aspects of communication theory and research apply to GSS, because communication is a fundamental social process, the glue that holds groups together. Communication has been viewed as the "architechtonic art," that discipline and skill that makes possible and organizes all other human endeavors (McKeon, 1972). In this view, to understand GSS it is essential to grasp the communication processes they entail. The potential for heuristic interchanges between communication and GSS research seems great; to understand communication processes, which tend to become second nature, it is often useful to study them in novel contexts. GSS and other new technologies offer unusual contexts that force communication and other social processes to follow new paths. This may throw taken-for-granted practices into stark relief, generating new insights into the basic grounds of communication and into how to manage communication processes more effectively.

CHAPTER

16

Group Support Systems for Computer Assisted Language Learning: Of Evolution, Purpose, and Real-Time Interaction

Joy Egbert
University of Arizona

INTRODUCTION

Evidence of the ongoing "Computer Revolution" can be noted virtually everywhere; in journals, the popular press, newspapers, and on television, something can be seen or heard about the changes that technology supports. What looks like revolution in education, however, is just that—a circular process of reformatting the same traditions (Elmer-Dewitt, 1991). Technology can and should be employed to assist education on a path of evolution, to keep it moving forward and looking at the potential for change in the classroom rather than different but equal uses of existing materials and methods. In this way, there may be hope of arriving someday at improved classroom learning environments supported, in part, by technology.

Hampering the evolution of classrooms is the sheer amount of technological hardware and the speed with which it has been placed in the schools. It is fashionable to have computers in schools, and, indeed, there are over 3,300,000 in K-12 alone, or one for about every twenty learners (McCarthy, 1991). As many as 95 percent of our schools have at least one computer, and as of 1986 over

35,000 districts had at least one computer network (Maddux, 1989; Molnar, 1990). This growth is expected to explode in the next decade as the ratio of computers to learners increases to 1:5. Educational software products are churned out at a similarly frantic pace and are touted as being "just the thing" that will help math students learn algorithms or English as a Second Language (ESL) learners speak English fluently. In the race to be revolutionary, hardware is outpacing knowledge.

At the same time that the number of computers is increasing rapidly, changes in the purposes for which they are used in the curriculum in general are barely noticeable. Many educators assume that because computers have become so pervasive in education, the classroom environment (or "the social world in which [a] technology functions" [Newman, 1990]) and the process of learning have changed and will continue to change. Little is actually different in most cases (Bridwell, Nancarrow, & Ross, 1984; Hawisher, 1989; Jackson, 1986; Newman, 1990). This lack of change raises several questions: for example, what is being done with these computers, and why? What should schools look like and do in the highly technological future that they face? What theoretically sound, vital changes can and should be made? What types of systems are needed to affect these changes?

In this chapter, it is proposed that the goal for using computers in language learning should be to form effective classroom language-learning environments. Evidence is presented to support a general hypothesis concerning the appearance and functioning of such environments, and it is suggested that there are computer systems, in the form of simultaneous interaction systems, particularly Group Support Systems (GSS), that can assist in creating these environments.

A FRAMEWORK FOR LOOKING AT COMPUTERS AND THE ESL CLASSROOM

Bereiter and Scardamalia (1987) note that "methods cannot be judged except in relation to purposes" (p. 46). Unfortunately, educational computing research has found that, in many classrooms, methods of using computers are employed without specific goals in mind. Newman (1990) proposes a research scheme to counter this trend. In his framework, the first step is to set goals for the educational unit (the classroom, the school, the district, the college). After goals have been set, the technology is employed as part of the materials and organization that it takes to reach the goals. During the process, the goals and/or the means of attaining them can be changed or adapted. In this way, rather than throwing technology into the classroom to see what it will do, educators can make specific plans based in theory that may result in a desired reformulation of the classroom environment.

In this chapter, Newman's process approach will be applied to describe a relatively new type of computer system for English as a Second Language, the Group Support System (GSS). The framework for this paper includes four steps:

(1) discussing conditions and strategies that should lead to the goal of creating an effective language-learning environment, (2) analyzing ways in which technology supports these strategies, (3) examining simultaneous interaction technologies, particularly GSS, which create new opportunities for ESL classrooms, and (4) suggesting future research.

STRATEGIES FOR OPTIMAL LANGUAGE LEARNING

The goal of improving the learning environment in ESL classrooms is to ensure that learners have the opportunity to efficiently and effectively develop competence in English, including not only the skills of reading, writing, speaking, and listening, but also the use of paralinguistic and pragmatic features. The first step in determining how computers can be used to support language learning is to discuss strategies for creating an environment in which this type of learning can occur. In the framework of this paper, discussing strategies for the ESL classroom assists in the identification of the technological "material" needed to specifically support these strategies, and hence the goal of creating an optimal, or best possible, environment. The ESL, second language acquisition (SLA), educational technology, and learning theory literatures suggest many strategies/conditions that will help achieve this goal. Presented below is a summary of strategies that have been supported in one or more of the literatures listed above. It is important to note that these strategies/conditions are constrained by characteristics of both learners and the learning environment.

Strategy #1   Provide Opportunities for Learners to Interact

According to the literature, interaction is a necessary component of the learning environment in all content areas. In order to communicate and convey ideas, learners must be provided with one or more partners with whom to interact. Several different types of interaction are important to this discussion. The first is interaction between computers and humans, which has been conceived in many ways. Ahmad, Corbett, Rogers, and Sussex (1985) define computer interaction as the ability of the computer to assess answers and to provide somewhat subtle feedback to learners. Part of this interaction is also the learners' ability to move around inside the program; Levin and Boruta (1983) give examples of such "interactive" text programs for reading and writing. Suchman (1987) supports the view that computers are interactive due to their "reactive, linguistic, and internally opaque properties" (p. 7); that is, they can respond in a variety of ways using a variety of responses.

Many authors note, however, that computer use can cause learners to be isolated; Klobusicky-Mailander (1990) warns that the "constant 'communication' with the highlighted and prepolished products of his own mind fuse master and servant into a working unit that becomes increasingly walled off from its environment" (p. 2). This may be because interaction with computers does not involve true communication; Kelman (1990) notes that education is "first and foremost interaction between people (learner-teacher and learner-learner)" (p. 8). He laments the fact that often learners are relegated to a lab remote from the classroom and to activities that the teacher is aware of only through the printouts she receives of the progress learners make. If learning is a social process, as Vygotsky (1978) and others claim, then social interaction is necessary. This claim will be extended below.

Strategy #2   Provide an Authentic Audience and Opportunities to Negotiate Meaning

For most educators, "interaction" is more explicit than for human/computer interaction researchers (see Sullivan, 1989, for a discussion of this difference). It has already been noted that learning takes place during social interaction (Long & Porter, 1985; Vygotsky, 1978), and this is especially true for second language learners striving for communicative competence. In the ESL literature, interaction implies the negotiation of meaning. Therefore, the *type* of interaction is important for language learners. Pica (1987) notes that interactions that promote language learning include confirmation and comprehension checks and negotiated clarification requests. Webb (1982, 1985) found giving and receiving help to be productive interaction, and ESL research also claims positive effects for such interaction. Lake (1989) notes that learners must be involved in purposeful interaction, which includes a real audience that is actively involved with the learners, and Hainline (1987) agrees that language learners need such a "linguistically authentic environment" (p. 63). The implication, then, is that learners must be participants in social interactions.

In addition, some studies show that it is not only what *kind* of interaction takes place that is important, but *with whom* the interaction takes place. This implies that learners need an authentic audience, one that shares the schema behind the message being sent. Pica & Doughty (1985) note that when ESL learners "engage in genuine communication with each other" and when they "engage independently in group discussion" they are more involved and use their language for more purposes than when interacting with the teacher (p. 115).

One way to provide opportunities for learners to negotiate meaning is to use group work. The literature on all aspects of group work in education is expansive. For example, Daiute (1986) found that learners enjoy working in groups and that students learn from each other as they collaborate. Shlecter (1990) shows that small groups work quite efficiently on certain tasks, and Dickson & Vereen (1983) note research that found both cognitive and social benefits for learners working in groups. Maddison & Maddison (1987) suggest that learners work best in dyads or larger groups, and that this may help learners work at their optimal pace. Other studies have documented the gains learners working in groups around a computer have made due to the verbal peer interaction around the computer (Webb, 1982, and others). Benefits of group work include greater efficiency, greater learner achievement, more social modeling and peer reinforcement, and more attention to higher-level activities (Watson, 1990).

Of course, group work is not a panacea for the problems of education—individual learning styles and preferences and other variables can block group productivity or cause greater problems. However, interaction with and around the computer seem to be important aspects of an effective learning environment for most modes of language learning. Interaction in the ESL classroom, then, should be purposeful, authentic, peer-directed, and provide equal time and as much time as needed to negotiate meaning. In traditional computer programs/systems, the computer cannot negotiate meaning with the learner, and therefore true interaction does not take place with it.

The *how* of interaction for language learning is also very important. D. Johnson (1991) notes that cooperative interaction is more productive than competitive interaction—this implies that in the classroom, interaction, and therefore learning, may be a function of task.

Strategy #3 Create/Use Authentic Tasks

Authentic, in this context, implies something that learners know about and are interested in that has a real purpose behind it (for examples, see Carter, 1989; Reid, 1989; Roen, 1989). More specifically, authenticity implies that the task is transferable to real-life situations where the learner does not have the teacher or technology to rely on (Johns & Davies, 1983). By this definition, content provided by the learner is considered authentic. D. Johnson (1991) adds that the task must provide learners with a reason to share ideas and information, preferably within a system that allows problem solving, and studies have found that learners interact more when working on problem-solving tasks than on other activities.

Grammar drills, common to ESL classrooms and ESL software, are not authentic, and run counter to theories such as "students gain skills in critical thinking and writing more by the act of *writing* than by learning *about* writing" (McGinnis, 1989:p.15). McGinnis also notes research that suggests that discrete attention to mechanics does not have a significant impact on writing proficiency, and in some cases, could have a negative impact; this is also the case for other language skills. For ESL learners, attention to details may take away from the formulation of ideas. This is not to say that grammar teaching and learning should be ignored in the ESL classroom; rather, it implies that grammar study and the correction of errors must occur in authentic contexts.

Strategy #4 Promote Exposure to and Production of Varied and Creative Language

Being authentic is necessary but not sufficient—varied and creative language implies a diversity of tasks and "encouragement of meaningful language use" (Cummins, 1989:p.33). Language fluency is not supported by filling in the blanks of grammar exercises and completing other non-contextual, artificial drills (Krashen & Terrell, 1983); this may be because the input learners receive from such exercises is limited in many ways.

Researchers are not certain to what extent the quality and quantity of both input and production affect linguistic competence, but it appears that the relationship is strong. Teaching methods developed for ESL classrooms place a major emphasis on input (c.f. articles on methods by Asher, 1982; Curran, 1982; DiPietro, 1983; Gattegno, 1983; Lozanov, 1982, and summaries of theory and research in Chaudron, 1988; Ellis, 1984; McLaughlin, 1987). However, neither the methods nor the research testing their efficacy agree on the level, the form, or the content of input that is necessary for optimal language learning. Different theories of second language acquisition view input from very different perspectives; some see it as a "trigger," some as a "stimulus," and others as being involved in a complex partnership with innate language-learning mechanisms (Ellis, 1986). Many ESL researchers claim, as noted above, that the content of the message should be the focus of the input rather than its form (Burt & Dulay, 1983; Krashen, 1989), and that the receiver of the message should have some way of understanding the message.

Because there is "no unified theory" of second-language acquisition (Huebner, 1989), and because research shows that input is necessary for language learners, learners should be allowed to interact with a wide variety of input that is real and understandable. To both produce and receive a variety of language, learners should not be limited in the creativity with which they can respond. D. Johnson (1991) notes that situations that require learners to use rich and varied language must be planned carefully.

Strategy #5   Provide Learners Opportunities to Formulate Ideas and Thoughts

Learners need adequate time and feedback, both of which facilitate the formulation of ideas. Although learners can formulate ideas through interaction while participating in authentic tasks, the literature suggests that initial individual efforts, to be discussed by the group later, may also facilitate idea generation (Delbecq, Van de Ven, & Gustafson, 1975). If learners are encouraged to provide content, they must be given the opportunity to reflect on and communicate their ideas.

Strategy #6   Promote Intentional Cognition

Because learners are presented with opportunities to formulate ideas and thoughts does not imply that they will take the opportunities or make the best of them. During the learning process, learners must be "mindful" (Salomon, 1990), that is, they must be motivated to take the opportunities presented to them and to be cognitively engaged. Learners can be encouraged to be mindful through authentic, varied tasks, and through others of the strategies listed here.

Prompting or procedural facilitation may also be important. Vygotsky (1978) claims that students learn through the support of others, that assistance (prompting) with functions that learners cannot currently carry out individually can be internalized and become a part of the learner's repertoire. Zellermayer, Salomon, Globerson, & Givon (1990) have shown that prompting does make a difference in learner writing achievement and use of metacognitions, although the amount and type of prompting necessary for different learners varies. They found that learners using computers can overcome initial ability differences by being exposed to guidance as they need it.

A certain degree of guidance, whether from peers or others, is necessary to facilitate learning and promote mindfulness. In the ESL classroom, this guidance may be provided as feedback, as explicit instruction in language-learning strategies, or in any number of other ways depending on the learner's needs. Lipson & Fisher (1983) emphasize the need for students to learn procedural ("how-to") knowledge with the aid of the computer as a tool, rather than declarative (content) knowledge with the computer as teacher. Others claim that through procedural facilitation, with the computer or other supplying the guidance, learners will become more competent in the target language. Lesgold (1983) concludes that computer applications in education should promote learners to study their own ideas and to develop more complex ideas and plans. In order to internalize and perform these functions, the classroom environment must promote intentional cognition on the part of the learners.

Strategy #7 Create an Atmosphere with Optimal Stress/Anxiety

In order for learners to be mindfully engaged and to be willing to communicate and share their ideas, they must be at ease in the environment. McGinnis (1989) cites research that supports the theory that "students learn to write best within a social context and benefit from peer feedback in their writing, provided an atmosphere in which students feel comfortable with sharing their work is established from the beginning" (p.16). This optimal-stress atmosphere has been found beneficial for some language learners (Krashen & Terrell, 1983; Lozanov, 1978).

There are many aspects of classroom atmosphere; the use of computers can affect this atmosphere in different ways. Klobusicky-Mailander (1990) observes that "the computer's forbearance towards mistakes and abortive attempts reduce the fear of failure... With the mental and technical stumbling blocks removed, the group expectations help provoke in the individual a state of carefreeness and excitement" (p.7). However, even with drill and practice programs the teacher may keep count of what and how well the learner performed, thereby robbing the learner of some of her autonomy and creating stress. The teacher may indirectly be raising what Krashen & Terrell (1983) call the learner's "affective filter" and possibly inhibiting language acquisition, willingness to share or collaborate, and other classroom goals.

Strategy #8   Create a Learner-Centered Classroom

Creating a learner-centered classroom implies that learners should have some authority over their learning (Bereiter & Scardamalia, 1987; Kelman, 1990; Kreeft-Peyton, 1990; Kremers, 1990; Robinson, 1991; Sirc & Reynolds, 1990). Smagorinsky (1989) advocates a move away from teacher-centered classrooms and the memorization of formulas, because he agrees with the literature that suggests that too little control leads to frustration and a sense of imprisonment on the part of learners and may also take the creativity out of learning. Kreeft-Peyton (1990) suggests that giving more control to the learner removes the confounds of teacher, learner, and school personalities, styles, and goals and allows room for change.

Technology can play an important part in moving the locus of control in the classroom away from the teacher, but it can also hinder these efforts. According to Bereiter & Scardamalia (1987), computer use should not be so stimulating that it fails to allow learners to work at their own pace, in their own way—nor should it have such rigid control of the learners' thoughts that alternatives cannot be seen. Krendl & Lieberman (1988) propose that less-advanced learners need software control but that higher-aptitude learners should be allowed a greater degree of control over the system, whereas Bridwell & Ross (1984) suggest that the software should be seen by all learners as a tool over which they have control. Regardless of use problems, educational computing researchers agree that creating a learner-centered classroom is necessary to achieve an effective learning environment. Although consensus has not been reached over how much control over their learning students need, the research agrees that learners should have some degree of authority; this implies a change in the traditional conceptualization of what a classroom is and what its goals are.

Summary of Step One

The strategies drawn from the literature that support the goals of an effective ESL learning environment are listed in Table 16.1.

Gaies (1989) summarizes the main ideas of these strategies by stating that educators must: "acknowledge who our students are; we must understand and value their experiences and interests; we must offer tasks and challenges that create a genuine sense of urgency to communicate; and we must foster forms of interaction and collaboration... that stimulate thinking..." (p.xii).

These strategies do not speak to specific methods, techniques, or content, but rather to the creation (by learners and teachers) of an effective language-learning environment for ESL learners. If the attempt to reach the goals above succeeds, the teaching and learning of English as a Second Language will have evolved in important ways.

TABLE 16.1 Strategies for Creating an Effective Language Learning Environment

Strategy #1	Provide opportunities for learners to interact
	    One or more partners
	    Social interaction

Strategy #2	Provide an authentic audience and opportunities to negotiate meaning
	    Purposeful interaction with actively involved audience
	    Group work and collaboration

Strategy #3	Create/use authentic tasks
	    Transferable to real-life situations
	    Cooperative
	    Reason to share information/problem-solving

Strategy #4	Promote exposure to and production of rich and varied language
	    Diverse Tasks
	    Meaningful language use

Strategy #5	Provide learners opportunities to formulate ideas and thoughts
	    Adequate time on task
	    Adequate feedback

Strategy #6	Promote intentional cognition
	    Motivate and cognitively engage
	    Prompting and other assistance

Strategy #7	Create an atmosphere with optimal stress and anxiety Comfortable, sharing

Strategy #8	Create a learner-centered classroom
	    Learner authority over learning
	    Creative learning

EXAMINING COMPUTERS AS MATERIAL FOR SUPPORTING STRATEGIES

The second step in determining how computers can be used to support the learning and teaching of ESL is to examine how the technology fits with the strategies for creating an effective ESL environment. Educators in both first language (L1) and second language (L2) classrooms are employing computer technology in many ways in attempting to support these strategies. There have been some successes and some relative failures (see a study by Chapelle & Jamieson, 1986); technology can even exacerbate classroom problems (Holdstein, 1987). Ways in which computer technologies meet the goals for ESL classrooms are presented briefly below. Before this discussion, however, three general features of technology use that have an impact on its appropriateness for this environment must be addressed.

First, the technology must be adaptable (Bridwell & Ross, 1984). Langer (1986) suggests that teachers must be able to adapt the classroom environment—if a computer system is a part of this environment, the system must also be adaptable. Not only must the content be malleable, but so must the structure and other features of the system. Adaptability makes teachers more likely to welcome the system and also assures that the technology is not undermining or remote from the educational goals and that it can be integrated into the classroom.

This is not to say, however, that the technology should be fit into the unchanged, uncriticized, ongoing curriculum; rather, the technology must be integrated into the classroom as part of the effort to improve the environment for learning. According to Bracey (1990), this means using the technology as an integral part of the curriculum, not merely as an addition. Papert (1987) notes that integration does not mean that the technology should be used to "reinforce objectives already taught" (Bracey, 1990:p.20) or to support methods and content that are already a part of the curriculum. These researchers conceive of integration as change and envision the computer used for things that could not or would not be done without it. Lake (1989-90) provides as an example of computer integration a "learning circle" involving 250 learners and their teachers in which dispersed groups of learners worked on projects by gathering information from each other via a network. Learners' conceptions of what constituted a source of knowledge changed, as did their ideas about the definition of a classroom. The technology was an integral part of this change.

Finally, the technology must not be the focus of the lesson to the detriment of authentic content. Many teachers are confused about whether to teach about the computer or to teach other material via the technology (Bracey, 1990). Papert (1987) warns of technocentric thinking in education, noting that the computer alone is responsible for nothing—therefore, making it the focus of learning is questionable. Daiute (1985) agrees that, whereas the computer may act as catalyst for social and learning changes in the classroom, more important are factors such as the structure of activities, collaboration, and control. Although the debate over appropriate classroom content continues, most researchers agree that the content of the lesson should not be undermined by the technology.

Although many technological systems and programs do not meet these three criteria, Levy (1990) suggests caution in discarding any type of computer-assisted language-learning program, noting that "not enough is known about how language is learned to say categorically that a particular CALL program is not going to be of some value to a student in a particular circumstance" (p. 5). Although this may be true, it is neither practical nor useful to try to build a new classroom environment around a plethora of individual programs (for a similar argument, see Reid, 1987). In using the goals and strategies above as guidelines, educators must seek to create environments in which all students can learn.

In the following assessment of the use of computers to support effective learning environments, the technology will be critiqued according to how it meets these three criteria and may meet future changes in these criteria. This assessment includes stand-alone programs designed for use at a single terminal, local-area networks, and simultaneous interaction systems, including GSS.

Stand-Alone Programs

Drill and Practice. Many teachers use drill and practice programs, which have been found to be effective in certain language-learning contexts. For example, Holdstein (1986) notes that computer drills may be useful for remediation, and may be especially effective with groups of learners. However, instruction in grammar, which constitutes the majority of these programs for ESL learners, appears to have little or no effect on communicative competence. Use of these programs tends to isolate learners, and drills do not provide the true interaction that language learners need to develop communicative competence. In addition, teachers tend to use these programs as an addition to the curriculum, rather than an integral part of it. These programs do not permit users to input freely or creatively, making them useless for many important language learning processes. The use of drill and practice programs to support second-language learning is limited.

Simulations and Content-Free Programs. More recent advances in educational programming have produced a variety of basic simulation programs, but most are not appropriate for language learners due to the complexity of the language involved, the difficulty of using the program, and the specificity of the topics of the simulations. These programs do, however, promote a variety of interaction around them, and may be useful for providing the content of lessons.

Databases, spreadsheets, and other content-free programs have been used successfully in some circumstances, particularly because of the interaction that takes place around the computer (Phillips & Santoro, 1989; Henderson, 1990). Content-free systems or systems with an authoring component allow the content to be altered and adapted to the interests of those involved by those involved. Unfortunately, such programs are not used often in language-learning classes. These programs meet many of the goals because they allow learners to control content and pace (Strategy #8), they promote learner interaction (Strategies #1 and #2), they can be integrated into and promote a new classroom environment, and, because they meet these other goals, they may lower the amount of anxiety learners feel (Strategy #7). However, the amount of language used by each learner varies, and time on task can be controlled by one learner. Use of these programs for language learning should be investigated further.

Hypertext. Hypertext reading programs and systems offer some possibilities for learners to have more interaction with the computer, to be exposed to a "multi-directional association of ideas," and to take control over the learning process (Underwood, 1990). By using hypertext, learners are exposed to diverse uses of language and employ a variety of thinking skills; these programs may support the development of reading skills, which some researchers claim promotes the development of writing skills (see, for example, Galda, 1984). Although useful in their own right, hypertext programs as they exist may not add to the learner's repertoire of communication skills. Promising developments in this area are currently underway.

Word Processing.   Many ESL programs are using word processors (Berens, 1986), which have been found to encourage learners to revise more and so interact with the language to a greater extent. Robinson-Staveley & Cooper (1990) claim that use of a word processor can "foster more positive views of computers" and "improve the quality of the work produced" (p. 41). Benefits of word processing include the opportunity for students to understand the fluidity and versatility of text, and to produce longer works with fewer mechanical errors (Hawisher, 1988). These concepts are vital to language learners; word processing by itself, however, supports few of the strategies discussed above in that it is essentially an individualized process. There are logistical problems in working with word processors, such that group work and collaboration become subordinate to the sharing and placement of the hardware. The same problems occur with invention, prose analyzer, and other text editor programs, although programs such as the "Writing Partner" that provide guidance for learners and encourage a higher-level of thinking about written texts are an intriguing development in this area (see Zellermayer et al., 1990, for a description of this program).

Summary.   Few of the computer uses listed above fit all of the criteria for creating an effective ESL learning environment. The most obvious problem is that they are computer uses rather than parts of an environment in which computers are used. This is not to say that these technologies are not useful in the proper setting. There are ways to integrate this type of computer use or a combination of these programs into an effective language-learning environment; these ways may involve the use of computer networks.

Networks

Currently, local and wide area networks (LANs/WANs) in the schools serve mostly as an efficient way to allow multiple uses of one program. Where they have been employed to meet goals for effective learning, relative successes have been gained through their use in writing collective texts, conferencing, creating and publishing newspapers, and contacting other schools through E-mail activities (Thrush & Hardisty, 1990; Sayers, 1989). Databases on networks have been used to gather information and can be linked to other systems. Varied degrees of success have met programs that center on nonsynchronous messaging through E-mail systems, which authors feel is a more authentic form of interaction than computer/human. E-mail activities have allowed learners in isolated locations to become a part of "virtual" classrooms and given learners the opportunity to experience life in different areas of the earth. Learners have developed projects in cooperation with learners in other schools in other countries (see, for example, Sayers, 1989). Despite the fact that some schools have developed new learning environments through the use of networks, there are some drawbacks to these systems. McConnell's (1990) case study of graduate students using ICoSy found that, although the nonsynchronous messaging system was satisfactory for the more academic communications, it did not satisfy the students' desire for social interaction. In addition, barriers to collaboration, present with word processors, are still present in most educational LAN systems. Most of the E-mail and other functions do not occur simultaneously, and therefore, true negotiation does not take place via this system. Because of the time it takes to wait for a message, learner time on task is limited, and so is the amount of input the student receives. Although it is obvious that E-mail and other LAN functions can make exciting and valuable contributions to the language-learning classroom, programs that allow simultaneous interaction may support more of the strategies for developing an optimal environment.

EXPLORING NEW TECHNOLOGIES

Although developing rapidly, the computer technologies discussed above do not support all of the conditions and strategies for an improved ESL classroom environment. The next step, therefore, is to examine new, relatively unknown technologies to see whether they fit the criteria to a greater degree. Simultaneous interaction systems, particularly GSS, indeed show promise of doing so.

Interaction in Real time

Thrush & Hardisty (1990) observe that programs on networks are still relatively isolated from the social construction of knowledge that is needed. They suggest that the system should be designed to allow learners to "send a message to another student or the teacher to ask about puzzling points, or to discuss ideas... [at any point]" (p. 30). At the same time, Ahmad, et al. (1985) call for "software which is capable of semantic analysis of natural language" (p. 54); however, few if any such sophisticated systems are available to educators. In their vision of the future, these authors are looking for a system based on synchronous human interaction. Simultaneous interaction systems have the capability to support such interaction.

Most of the literature on synchronous interaction networks in education is based on the pioneering networked classrooms at Gallaudet University (DiMatteo, 1990; Hawisher & Selfe, 1990; Kreeft-Peyton & Mackinson-Smyth, 1989; Kreeft-Peyton, 1990; Kremers, 1990; Sirc & Reynolds, 1990), although a number of other institutions now have such networks. The ENFI network is used at Gallaudet with ESL learners whose first language is American Sign Language. Learners using the system are assigned to individual computers; the screen consists of three "windows"—at the top is the "teacher window," where a question might be posed or a statement made. At the bottom of the screen is a composing window, where participants compose their input. This input is sent to the center of the screen, where it is shared with all of the participants through a public window. Interaction is synchronous, or "real-time."

Use of the system has many benefits for learners and teachers. It allows learners to use authentic, comprehensible language with a real audience. In addition, teachers can set up carefully designed activities that are not under the teacher's direct control, what Batson (1988) calls an "environmental model" of teaching rather than the traditional "presentational model" (p. 8). In this way, learners can be given more control over what happens through the system (although some teachers are reluctant to give it [see DiMatteo, 1990; Kreeft-Peyton, 1990, for examples]). Learners receive immediate responses from peers and/or the teacher on content that is determined by individual learners, groups, or the teacher. Because responses can be immediate and human, learners can receive the guidance that they need and can be prompted to use higher-level thinking skills, something few other programs have achieved (Hofmeister, 1989). The system can also be broken into channels through which small groups can communicate privately. Kreeft-Peyton & Horowitz (1988) add to this list of benefits that: by writing conversations, learners see the spelling of words; when learners see others using the system and they use it themselves, they become more confident with its use, and experience less stress; use of the system forces learners to read and write rather than to rely solely on oral skills; system use provides a transition from "speaking" to writing due to the informal nature of the initial conversations and to activities to formalize these conversations, and it overcomes "different face-to-face communication modes" (p. 12). Researchers exploring the uses of this system have found that, not only has the use of this system supported many of the goals and strategies listed above, but also some of the conceptions about goals have changed (Kreeft-Peyton, 1990, and others).

Simultaneous interaction networks are clearly a step in the right direction; however, problems exist with current methods of using these systems. It is not clear from the literature whether and in what ways this system has been integrated into the curriculum at Gallaudet. Much of the traditional work, such as discussing what occurred via the computers, happens back in the classroom, and learners still write their papers individually. This implies that although some of the environment has changed, not all of it has. In addition, learners on the system may experience performance anxiety because their comments are always identified in one way or another (Sirc & Reynolds, 1990). Kreeft-Peyton & Horowitz (1988) also cite the lack of structure as a problem in that learners can and do easily deviate from the conversation being held on screen. They note that this system use causes learners to input short, unreflective thoughts because of the pressure to keep up with the conversation; while typing, learners may miss responses from others that continuously scroll off the screen.

To make this system even more productive for language learners, it must be used for activities with some kind of structure, and it also must have a mechanism that ensures that there will be freedom from bias, that learners will have an optimal-stress environment, and that the activity begun on the system can be completed in the same atmosphere and environment. Group Support Systems may be a technology that can overcome these deficiencies.

Group Support Systems

Group Support Systems (GSS) (for a discussion see Huber, 1984; DeSanctis & Gallupe, 1987), like the real-time network at Gallaudet, support simultaneous electronic conversation. Although GSS have been developed for organizational purposes, they may be ideal for language-learning classrooms, particularly because they are content free and activity based (see Egbert, Jessup, & Valacich, 1991, for a demonstration with ESL learners).

A GSS can be used to support a wide range of activities. Johansen (1988) provides examples of organizational activities supported by such systems, several of which have intriguing possibilities for ESL. Among them are presentation support, group-authoring, computer conferencing, conversational structuring, project management, screen-sharing, and the construction of content-based expert systems.

Unlike the communications emphasis of the real-time network, which allows learners to critique hard copies of essays or create a group document, a GSS is more task-based and centers on a task or problem. This is a very important difference, because although they are well-suited to such activities as brainstorming, they can also accommodate other educational activities. These systems "provide a means for a group to work on or complete a task, such as reaching a decision, conducting strategic planning, or solving problems" (Jessup, 1991, p. 4). GSS differ slightly from the real-time network in other ways, too. They afford opportunities for a variety of configurations of learner, teacher, and computer. In addition to allowing learners to send files directly to each other or to a central file, a GSS can also randomly assign files. A GSS can also be logically partitioned to allow student groups to work separately and then to collect all the information in a central file, to be worked with further. The systems not only aid initial communication, but also support follow-up activities such as ranking and voting. These systems also encourage "problem structuring, idea generation, idea organization, planning, creating, and even the elicitation of knowledge in the construction of expert systems" (Dennis, George, Jessup, Nunamaker, Vogel, 1988, p.593). In addition to adding task structure, an important difference between ENFI-type networks and GSS is that GSS have the capability to function in an identified or an unidentified condition. In the unidentified condition the user remains completely anonymous (no pseudonyms are attached as they are in the Gallaudet setting), which may work to lower learners' affective filter (see Connolly, Jessup, & Valacich, 1990; Jessup, Connolly, & Galegher, 1990; Jessup & Tansik, 1991, for studies of this phenomenon).

The advantages of GSS for language learning are clear—these systems can support most of the strategies for improving language-learning environments. For example, through their ability to sustain real-time interaction, GSS support the strategies of providing opportunities for learners to interact and negotiate meaning with an authentic audience (Strategies #1 and #2). In this situation, time on task is enhanced because learners can reply simultaneously. In addition, the relative freedom with which a system can be partitioned makes a variety of group configurations possible. GSS are content free, making the creation and use of authentic tasks limited only by the creativity and desire of the participants (Strategy #3). In addition, because GSS allow users to interact and negotiate through a variety of authentic tasks, they also promote learners' exposure to and production of rich and varied language (Strategy #4). Through its ability to support fun, motivating, real tasks, GSS may further promote intentional cognition in learners who are invested in the activity (Strategy #6). The combination of interesting, motivating tasks and potential learner anonymity may assist in creating an atmosphere with optimal stress and anxiety (Strategy #7). If the teacher is willing to give up control, GSS can be used to give more control to learners (Strategy #8). Because external information can be imported, a variety of other programs can be used in conjunction with activities on the GSS. More generally, GSS can be used as a tool to restructure ideas about what a classroom should be.

There are potential disadvantages to using GSS and simultaneous interaction systems in language learning, as Kreeft-Peyton (1990) and others have found. For example, time pressures may prohibit learners from taking time to reflect on their input (contrary to Strategy #5). The system can, however, be configured to provide learners with more time. In addition, learners may use abusive or very informal language when they see how much freedom they have, or, conversely, they may maintain the structure of traditional exercises for want of a different and better idea. This disadvantage may be overcome with proper activity structure or task construction. Also, as with any group, there exist social constraints to group achievement (Jessup & Tansik, 1991; Webb, 1982); the anonymity that the system affords may serve to lessen this problem. In addition, as with any technology, it is how it is used that will make a difference, and these programs can be used to propagate traditional classroom styles and locus of control (Kreeft-Peyton, 1990). It appears that GSS is one technology that is needed to assist in the creation of effective language-learning environments; it is clear that research is necessary to examine language-learning situations and the effects of technology use. Although research on GSS is growing quickly (Jessup, 1991), few empirical studies have observed GSS as part of an educational environment.

FUTURE RESEARCH

The fourth step in determining how computers can be used to support language learning is to test whether the technology chosen to support the strategies does so. In the framework of this chapter, it is necessary to discuss strategies and then to propose technology as part of the materials for achieving goals; "The mere fact, however, that advancements in technology have made new and different activities possible in the laboratory does not in itself justify these activities..." (Thrush & Hardisty, 1990: 24). Research must be conducted to see whether the strategies do promote the development of an effective learning environment, and it must examine whether learners using these systems accomplish the goals that have been set for them. Researchers in the field of Management Information Systems have begun to investigate GSS in organizational settings (see Chapter 2 in this text). However, these findings are potentially limited to the environments in which they were found, and it is therefore necessary to investigate these and other systems in their unique educational environments. Dennis et al. (1988) provide a research model for GSS that could be adapted to the classroom language-learning environment. This model suggests that group member and group characteristics, task features, the context or environment, and aspects of the technology affect group processes and outcomes. This research model can be used to ask questions suggested in the literature such as: In what ways do GSS promote the educational inertia of traditional methods and styles (Hawisher & Selfe, 1990)? How does the teacher presence on the system influence the interaction? Are the confounds to group achievement that Webb (1982) mentions overcome by the anonymity that the system affords? Is participation more equal using the system, or do aspects of the environment, such as anonymity, encourage learners to loaf or freeride? What strategies do learners use through the system to learn English as a Second Language (Chapelle & Jamieson, 1986)? What kinds of experiences do ESL learners have in GSS groups (Webb, 1982)? What is the link between talk elicited from learners working at computers and program design features (Levy & Hinckfuss, 1990)? How does interaction via a synchronous network relate to quality of language output, and how does the nature of the task affect the amount and variety of language used? Potential research questions cover a range from system to environmental characteristics, from cognitive to psychosocial processes and beyond.

SUMMARY

Language educators do not agree about which set of classroom goals is the most essential to attain nor what methods can be used to attain them most efficiently. It is clear, however, that even those goals that educators do agree upon are not currently being met. Formative research on GSS and other technologies may provide a better understanding of how students learn languages. The more we understand about the process of learning, the easier it may be to formulate new goals. This recursive process can lead to examination: examination of how schools are meeting these goals, which areas require more attention, and what changes must be made in order to provide learners with an optimal environment in which to learn. What seems like a circular ("revolutionary") process is actually the process of evolution.

CHAPTER

17

Future Directions and Challenges in the Evolution of Group Support Systems

Leonard M. Jessup
California State University, San Marcos

Joseph S. Valacich
Indiana University

INTRODUCTION

The computer increasingly provides feedback and organizes interrelated information while continuously expanding the frontiers of interrelation. It expands the range and the scope of designated participation. It awakens possibilities of creation among the many, rather than just the minorities of past ages. After all, most of human achievement has been the anonymous assembly of discoveries and insights, from proverbs to building techniques, and their equally anonymous loss. The individuals within the great faceless creating mass of the human race can now relate to one another directly in real time, rather than over trade routes and centuries. (LeeBaert & Dickinson, 1991, pp. 295–296)

The preceding forecast of future computing by LeeBaert and Dickinson is taken from an edited book by LeeBaert, *Technology 2001: The Future of Computing and Communications.* This passage characterizes a common theme in forecasts of future computing—*connection*. First, they speak of the possibility of connecting information—of bridging together and organizing interrelated information. With new networking technologies and mechanisms for exchanging and organizing information, we can more easily access diverse information from diverse places and make it available for timely, effective use. Second, they speak of the possibility of connecting people—of expanding the range and scope of human interaction. For example, computers now make it easier for creation to be a group phenomenon.

In this concluding chapter, we consider issues related to the future of GSS. We agree with Johansen (1991) and many others in this area that we are still in the "horseless carriage" stage in the development, deployment, and most important, *understanding* of GSS. Although there has been a lot of recent activity in this area in terms of empirical research, product development, and system adoption, it is safe to say that the field is still new. The technology is new and exploratory, certainly when compared to mature computer-based technologies such as the microchip or the electronic spreadsheet. Similarly, our understanding of GSS is new and exploratory. Our perspective of GSS use, as evidenced by our writings about GSS and by the GSS products available, is not significantly different than traditional notions of supporting group work. Most GSS technologies have not fundamentally changed the way groups work; most have focused on doing what groups have always done in the past, only better.

As we argued in the introductory chapter, to better understand GSS we need to expand, and in some cases change, our notions of what work groups do and of how and why they do it. In order to better imagine the research challenges that confront us, we will first discuss the motivation and evolution of GSS environments and speculate as to how they may change the nature of group work. In addition, we conclude the book by discussing several future GSS scenarios and related research challenges.

GSS in the Next Century: Anything, Anytime, Anywhere

There are numerous "motivations" and "enablers" for the evolution of GSS technologies to go beyond the horseless carriage stage. The motivations are a product of our increasingly competitive global economy. Huber and McDaniel (1986) refer to this as the "post-industrial" era, in which decisions must be made faster, more frequently, and in a much more complex and competitive environment. Johansen and his colleagues (1991) refer to this motivation as "pain relief"—relief from the faster business pace, increased competition, and the need to more easily communicate and organize group members, customers, and partners.

The enablers of change are also numerous and varied. Of course, two fundamental enablers of change for technology in general are our understanding and imagination. In particular, our understanding of computing technologies and our open-mindedness toward their application have enabled change. For example, our "no limits" attitude toward the better, smaller, less expensive central processing unit has lead to the proliferation of personal computers and workstations. If this trend continues, within 10 years these "low–cost micros" will exceed the raw processing capabilities of today's fastest mainframe computers (Gelsinger, Gargini, Parker, & Yu, 1991). The advances in networking and telecommunications are also numerous and impressive—higher bandwidth, greater transmission quality, and increased connectivity will result in a vast array of new possibilities (see W. R. Johnson, 1991). Finally, advances in the software component of these systems have enabled advantages such as modularity, which makes it easier to develop, repair, and tailor systems to particular applications. This has resulted in greater programmer productivity and more robust systems (*Business Week*, 1991).

If we are willing, we can adapt these technological advances in ways that may change the nature of GSS. Current organizational implementations of workgroup information systems are often limited to relatively "low-tech" solutions such as coordinated telephones, personal computers, and fax machines, or shared disk storage and printers on a local area network. Groupware applications, although one step more sophisticated than the applications just described, are still relatively routine automations of common group tasks such as scheduling, communication, and information sharing. Even GSS applications are often the result of automating, bundling, or repackaging existing workgroup techniques such as group idea generation and voting in the same time/same place dimension.

Fundamental change in GSS is, of course, limited not only by our imaginations but by what is technologically possible. For example, radical new technologies in the laboratory may not necessarily be economically or even technologically feasible in the field. In particular, as diverse new GSS technologies evolve, integration of those technologies becomes increasingly important. However, we suspect that with GSS, as with computing generally, the field will move toward compatibility, standardization, and openness, which will allow for a tighter bundling of these simpler, "Lego-like" pieces that are emerging. Our increased understanding should result in new forms of GSS, forms that have not yet been imagined, forms that will be more easily constructed and integrated, forms that enable new, and in some cases formerly impossible, methods of group work.

How we put these pieces together in the future to enhance group work was recently addressed by Johansen (1991) in a paper entitled *Teams for Tomorrow*. In this paper he presents several "scenarios" for the future in regards to the support of collaborative group work. Below, we revisit these scenarios and discuss several research challenges that lie ahead.

GSS Scenario 1: "Any Time/Any Place"

This scenario focuses on technologies that can be used to support distributed teams. Technologies such as lightweight notebook and pen-based computers, wireless local area networks, cellular modems and phones, and fax machines are identified as enablers for Scenario 1. Some sample applications would include variants of flexible, mobile GSSs for direct sales teams, field service and repair technicians, law enforcement and emergency services groups, and others where real-time communication and coordination is essential.

Challenges. This scenario challenges us to extend our growing theory base to include a much wider assortment of task, time, space, group, and technology dimensions. Most, if not all, of our evolving theories will need extension into this broader definition of GSS. Using the metaphor of Dennis and Gallupe in Chapter 3 on prior GSS research, this extension at the least may require that we "graft" several new branches of GSS research, or more likely, that we "plant" several new seeds.

Specifically, this broadening of the scope of GSS challenges the empirical researcher in terms of research methodology and theoretical foundations. For example, this research may be best approached as longitudinal field research, as it may be difficult and extremely costly to outfit and maintain an any time/any place laboratory. Zigurs, in Chapter 6, provides a useful discussion of the relevant methodological tradeoffs and recommendations for conducting such GSS research. In addition, DeSanctis, in Chapter 5, provides a discussion of several of the fundamental theories used in GSS research and suggests that a more expansive view of the role of GSS is needed. She argues that the development of more encompassing theories of organizations and organizational change are needed in order to address more encompassing questions. This theory development and refinement will be a substantial undertaking, especially as GSS evolves beyond the concept of supporting groups working at the same time and place.

Other challenges, very much related to theoretical foundations and methodology, are those regarding which research questions to address. Here, several of the issues discussed by McGrath and Hollingshead in Chapter 4, specifically their task/media fit hypotheses, are relevant to this scenario and any subsequent theory testing or building. Also, broader organizational issues, as discussed by Huber et al. (Chapter 13), are critical, as the deployment and use of any time/any place technologies will undoubtedly impact an organization's processes and structures.

GSS Scenario 2: "Orchestrated Workflow"

This scenario focuses primarily on process-oriented organizations in which the "coordination across teams of teams" is essential. Workflow automation is much like classic engineering and project management, where projects are defined as a series of steps performed by individuals or groups that may have some precedence ordering (see Limbaugh, Kapur, & Norguard, 1991 for a description of one collaborative workflow system). Technologies such as electronic data interchange, electronic mail, and on-line group and resource scheduling systems are fundamental to this coordination.

Challenges. A primary focus for research in this area will be on coordinating the differing tasks and needs that different groups have. Recent research by Connie Gersick (1988; 1989) on group evolution and development suggests that we need to change our antiquated notions of the structured, orderly ways that groups perform tasks and evolve over time. This view will be especially useful as new technologies enable more dynamic group configurations.

Also, issues discussed by Connolly in Chapter 14 on behavioral decision theory, specifically issues related to understanding the effect of the "efficient" process-oriented group activities on group perceptions, processes, and outcomes, is relevant from both a within-team and across-team perspective. This process structuring can have numerous effects beyond the group level, as a single workflow system could theoretically span several organizations (e.g., in a manner similar to a subcontractor and a manufacturer). This implies that the impact of workflow-type GSS may span not only teams, but may also span organizations and industries.

Much of the GSS research from the University of Arizona, discussed by Nunamaker et al. in Chapter 7, has taken an engineering approach for solving group problems. This approach has focused on designing "tools" to enhance group processes such that GSS-supported processes are more efficient than non-supported processes (i.e., GSS use improves the productivity of large groups for a given task). Their research has primarily focused on supporting single groups addressing multiple tasks during a given meeting. Research is needed to expand the scope of this efficient process approach to that of coordinating multiple distinct groups addressing interrelated tasks over numerous meetings. Designing a GSS to effectively support groups operating in a broadened, interrelated environment will clearly be a large technical challenge.

GSS Scenario 3: "Virtual Team Rooms"

In Chapter 2, Wagner, Wynne, and Mennecke provide us with several examples of existing GSS facilities, or team rooms. A team room can be thought of as a meeting room equipped with various resources, possibly customized to the specific needs of a particular team or group. The virtual team room scenario examines the possibility of combining aspects of the team room and virtual reality. In this scenario, Johansen (1991, p. 524) suggests that groups could "create a situation where a team designs its own *ideal* collaboration workspace, without the constraints of physical reality." Here, formal or informal teams could communicate using a mosaic of technologies regardless of any members' physical location.

Challenges. Research in this area will need to focus on the ergonomic aspects of GSS, both in terms of the facility and the GSS tools themselves. Issues pointed out by Polley and Stone in Chapter 9 concerning Flexspace—changing our preconceived notions on what the environment should look like—are clearly relevant. Also, in Chapter 10 concerning the user interface, Gray et al. highlight the interrelationships between the GSS tools, facility, and supporting technologies. Further, understanding how cognitive and cultural differences among GSS participants affect group processing and outcomes, in relation to all the other possible contingencies (e.g., tasks, situations), will be a large undertaking. It is clear that GSS designers and empirical researchers will need to work hand-in-hand in order to be successful. Group facilitation is also relevant in this scenario. Bostrom and his colleagues state in their chapter that the essential characteristic of facilitation is to help make an outcome easier to achieve. Will, or can, the role of the facilitator evolve such that we may see a nonhuman (e.g., an expert system) or "virtual" facilitator?

GSS Scenario 4: "Culture Bridging"

The focus of this scenario is on enhancing the performance of groups whose composition has members from different cultures and thus differ in terms of how they address a problem (see Walton, 1990). For example, the Japanese take a more process-focused approach when making a decision. Decision makers from the United States are often focused more on the decision outcomes than on the process. Thus, a GSS to support culture bridging will need to be flexible as to the process and presentation of group information.

Challenges. Research for this scenario may require that we focus on issues related to the group itself, independent of the technology. For example, research on group composition will need to extend beyond traditional studies of gender, age, education level, and so on, to focus on issues related to cultural norms, values, and processes. In Chapter 12, Weick and Meader suggest that GSS researchers need to focus on group "sensemaking"—the study of how and why people frame events as problems before they ever work together as a group. It seems reasonable to believe that sensemaking activities and the effective synchronization of differing processes will be especially important in multicultural teams, where baseline problem frames may be quite different.

The communications research will also be relevant here, as many aspects of communication theory and research apply to fundamental social processes. In Chapter 15, Poole and Jackson state that communication is the "glue" that holds groups together. It will be important to understand where and how this glue should be applied to most effectively support culture bridging. Also, Gray and his colleagues, in their chapter on the user interface (Chapter 10), discuss issues related to cultural differences, and how these differences are relevant from both a system design perspective and from an empirical one.

GSS Scenario 5: "Just-in-Time Learning"

The notion of just-in-time learning relates to the increased complexities of the business environment and the availability of more on-line repositories and memories. There is a need to quickly access prior relevant information (e.g., text, data, video) or generate new information (e.g., interactive simulations). This information can then be structured in a form most effective to the situation to enhance and focus the learning process, and ultimately the decision processes, of the group.

Challenges. Although this scenario may relate to virtually all aspects of GSS use and evaluation, it seems that there is a clear need for technical research in the areas of data storage and retrieval, and information manipulation, exchange, and presentation. The chapter by Hoffer and Valacich addressing the design of group memories as key components of group and organizational learning systems (Chapter 11) is applicable. Researchers will need to take a multi-disciplinary approach to this problem, as aspects of computer science, organizational science, and psychology are needed to evolve our understanding beyond its current state. Also, how GSS can be applied as a vehicle for learning can be found in Chapter 16, in which Egbert discusses how GSS can be applied to real-time learning for a specific population. Research to extend GSS as a more general-purpose learning vehicle is also needed. For example, a GSS may be helpful as a tool for group case analysis within the classroom, where subgroups could compete against each other in a real-time analysis that would allow greater and more equal participation, and possibly enhanced learning.

GSS Scenario 6: "Window to Anywhere"

This scenario is related to the "video wall" or "video window" research at Bell Communications Research or the "mirror project" at the University of Arizona. The objective of this "window to anywhere" scenario is to simulate the across-the-table feeling of being in the same room for groups that are physically distributed. The mirror project, for example, extends the concept of video conferencing by merging traditional GSS technologies and tools into the "window to anywhere" environment (see Chappell, Vogel, & Roberts, 1992).

Challenges. This scenario also has the capability of spanning most issues related to GSS research and design. McGrath and Hollingshead's work related to the fit of task to media is relevant. Specifically, how is a "windowed" meeting different from an across-the-table meeting? Further, which tasks need the added bandwidth provided by the video wall? These are relevant and important questions. How a "window to anywhere" meeting is conducted is also an important issue. Thus, aspects of meeting facilitation, group membership, communication processes, and so on are all related and should be addressed.

The "window to anywhere" form of GSS also poses a substantial technical challenge, requiring multidisciplinary research and design involving facilities designers, electrical and computer engineers, and GSS vendors and developers, as well as general infrastructure providers such as proprietors of wide-area networks, phone systems, or satellites. The application of this form of GSS will require a substantial investment, possibly limiting the opportunities for widespread deployment and examination.

CONCLUSION

Over the centuries, people have searched for technologies to help us do things better, faster, more accurately, more easily, more safely, more efficiently, and more precisely. With each significant advancement, there are numerous consequences—consequences that are anticipated and desired, consequences that are feared and detested, or more often, consequences that are misconceived and unforeseen. In this chapter we have discussed how GSS may evolve to extend the range and scope of human interaction. We have also presented several challenges that must be addressed in order to understand the numerous consequences of this advance. It is not yet clear that GSS technologies, as they currently exist, are a radically new technology. We do, however, believe that GSS and related technologies are rapidly evolving and that in many cases they are being readily adopted. Thus, we believe that GSS and related technologies have the potential to fundamentally change the way we work together.

We believe that this rapid evolution and adoption of GSS is appropriate. Indeed, we have argued that there is a large potential benefit, or motivation, to more effectively support communication and coordination of groups and teams. Furthermore, we have argued that our expectations of what we can do with GSS will largely be enabled by, and are limited mainly by, our imagination and understanding of GSS. However, blind acceptance and unthinking proliferation of any new technology are never appropriate. We hope that the chapters in this book provide a useful foundation from which to build and refine useful GSS theories and technologies.

As we discussed in Chapter 1, the primary objective of this book was to present a set of focused readings on several interrelated GSS issues. Each chapter in isolation represents an overview of our current understanding of GSS as it applies to a particular issue or set of issues. However, we hope that it is clear that no GSS topic can be viewed in isolation. Taken together, these chapters enable us to have a more complete understanding of the possible uses of GSS and of the possible effects GSS may have on the ways that we work together. We believe that the "new perspectives" provided in and prompted by the chapters in this book are critical to an intelligent, informed use of GSS.

REFERENCES

Abel, M. J. (1990). Experiences in an exploratory distributed organization. In J. Galegher, R. Kraut, & C. Egido (Eds.), *Intellectual teamwork: Social and technological foundations of cooperative work* (pp. 489–510). Hillsdale, NJ: Lawrence Erlbaum.

Abel, M. J., Corey, D., Bulick, S., Schmidt, J., & Coffin, S. (1992). The U.S. West advanced technologies telecollaboration research project. In G. Wagner (Ed.), *Computer augmented teamwork*. New York: Van Nostrand Reinhold.

Ackoff, R. L., Gupta, S. K., & Minas, J. S. 1962. *Scientific method*. New York: John Wiley & Sons.

Adelman, L. (1984). Real time computer support for decision analysis in a group setting. *Interfaces, 14*(2), 75–83.

Ahmad, K., Corbett, G., Rogers, M., & Sussex, R. (1985). *Computers, language learning, and language teaching*. Cambridge: Cambridge University Press.

Albanese, R., & Van Fleet, D. D. (1985). Rational behavior in groups: The free riding tendency. *Academy of Management Review, 10,* 244–255.

Alpert, A., & Raiffa, H. (1982). A progress report on the training of probability assessors. In D. Kahneman, P. Slovic, & A. Tversky (Eds.), *Judgment under uncertainty: heuristics and biases* (pp. 294–305). New York: Cambridge University Press.

Alter, S. A. (1975). *A study of computer-aided decision making in organizations*. Unpublished doctoral dissertation, Massachusetts Institute of Technology, Cambridge, MA.

Ancona, D. G., & Caldwell, D. F. (1990). Information technology and new product teams. In J. Galegher, R. Kraut, & C. Egido (Eds.), *Intellectual teamwork: Social and technological foundations of cooperative work.* (pp. 173–190). Hillsdale, NJ: Lawrence Erlbaum.

Ancona, D. G., & Caldwell, D. F. (1988). Beyond task and maintenance: External roles in groups. *Group and Organization Studies, 13,* 468–494.

Anson, R. (1990). *Effects of computer support and facilitator support on group processes and outcomes: An experimental assessment*. Unpublished doctoral dissertation, Indiana University, Bloomington.

Anson, R. & Heminger, A. (1991). An assessment of process facilitation in a Group Support System setting. Working paper, Boise State University, Boise, ID.

Anson, R. & Heminger, A. (1990). The effects of process facilitation in a Group Support System setting. Working paper, Indiana University, Bloomington.

Applegate, L. M. (1991). Technology support for cooperative work: A framework for studying introduction and assimilation in organizations. *Journal of Organizational Computing, 1*(1), 11–39.

Arbel, A., & Tong, R. M. (1982). On the generation of alternatives in decision analysis problems. *Journal of the Operational Research Society, 33* (4), 377–387.

Argyle, M., & Kendon, A. (1967). The experimental analysis of social performance. In L. Berkowitz (Ed.), *Advances in experimental social psychology* (Vol. 3). New York: Academic Press.

Argyris, C. (1971). Management information systems: The challenge to rationality and emotionality. *Management Science, 17*(6), B275–292.

Argyris, C., & Schon, D. A. (1978). *Organizational learning: A theory of action perspective*. Reading, MA: Addison-Wesley.

Arkes, H. R., & Hammond, K. R. (Eds.). (1986). *Judgment and decision making: An interdisciplinary reader*. New York: Cambridge University Press.

Asch, S. E. (1958). Effects of group pressure upon the modification and distortion of judgments. In E. E. Maccaby, T. M. Newcomb, & E. L. Hartley (Eds.), *Readings in social psychology* (3rd ed., pp. 2–10). New York: Holt, Rinehart & Winston.

Asch, S. E. (1955). Opinions and social pressures. *Scientific American, 193*(5), 31–35.

Asher, J. (1982). The total physical response approach. In R. Blair (Ed.), *Innovative approaches to language teaching* (pp. 54–66). Rowley, MA: Newbury House.

Austin, L. C., Liker, J. K., & McLeod, P. L. (1990). Determinants and patterns of control over technology in a computerized meeting room. *Proceedings of the Conference on Computer-Supported Cooperative Work* (pp. 39–51). New York: Association for Computing Machinery.

Bales, R. F. (1970). *Personality and interpersonal behavior.* New York: Holt, Rinehart & Winston.

Bales, R. F. & Cohen, S. P. (1979). *SYMLOG: A system for the multiple level observation of groups.* New York: The Free Press.

Ball, T. & Jones, S. (1977). The utilization of nominal groups as an aid in marketing organizations. In the *Proceedings of the Southeast American Institute for Decision Science,* (pp. 63–65).

Bariff, M. L., & Ginzberg, M. J. (1982, Fall). MIS and the behavioral sciences: Research patterns and prescriptions. *Data Base,* pp. 19–26.

Baroudi, J. J. & Orlikowski, W. J. (1989). The problem of statistical power in MIS research. *MIS Quarterly, 13*(1), 87–106.

Barley, S. R., & Tolbert, P. S. (1988, September). *Institutionalization as structuration: Methods and analytic strategies for studying links between action and structure.* Paper presented at the *Conference on Longitudinal Field Research Methods for Studying Organizational Processes,* Austin, TX.

Barnard, C. I. (1938). *The functions of the executive.* Cambridge, MA: Harvard University Press.

Barnlund, D. C. (1959). A comparative study of individual, majority, and group judgment. *Journal of Abnormal Social Psychology, 58,* 55–60.

Baron, R. S. (1986). Distraction-conflict theory: Progress and problems. In L. Berkowitz (Ed.), *Advances in experimental social psychology* (Vol. 19, pp. 1–40), New York: Academic Press.

Batson, T. (1988). The ENFI project: An update. *Teaching English to Deaf and Second Language Students, 6*(2), 5–8.

Beauclair, R. (1987). *An experimental study of the effects of group decision support system process support application on small group decision making.* Unpublished doctoral dissertation, Indiana University, Bloomington.

Benbasat, I. (1984). An analysis of research methodologies. In F. W. McFarlan (Ed.), *Proceedings of the Information Systems Research Challenge.* Harvard Business School Research Colloquium, (pp. 47–85). Boston, MA: Harvard Business School Press.

Benbasat, I., Goldstein, D. K., & Mead, M. (1987). The case research strategy in studies of information systems. *MIS Quarterly, 11*(3), 369–386.

Benbasat, I., & Nault, B. R. (1990). An evaluation of empirical research in managerial support systems. *Decision Support Systems, 6,* 203–226.

Benne, K., & Sheats, P. (1948). Functional roles of group members. *Journal of Social Issues, 4,* 41–49.

Bennett, J. L. (Ed.). (1983). *Building decision support systems ,* Reading, MA: Addison-Wesley.

Bereiter, C., & Scardamalia, M. (1987). *The psychology of written composition.* Hillsdale, NJ: Lawrence Erlbaum.

Berens, G. (1986). Using word processors in the EFL composition class. *TESOL Newsletter, 20 5,* 13.

Berlo, D. K. (1977). Communication as process: review and commentary. In B. D. Ruben (Ed.), *Communication yearbook* (Vol. 1). New Brunswick, NJ: Transaction Publishers.

Black, E. (1978). *Rhetorical criticism: A study in method* (2nd ed.). Madison, WI: University of Wisconsin Press.

Blair, D. C. (1990). *Brute facts, institutional facts, and large-scale computerized information systems.* Unpublished manuscript, School of Business Administration, University of Michigan, Ann Arbor.

References

Blumer, H. (1969). *Symbolic interactionism: Perspectives and method.* Englewood Cliffs, NJ: Prentice Hall.

Boorstin, D. J. (1985). *The discoverers: A history of man's search to know his world and himself.* New York: Vintage Books.

Bormann, E. G. (1972). Fantasy and rhetorical vision: The rhetorical criticism of social reality. *Quarterly Journal of Speech, 58,* 396–407.

Bormann, E. G. (1975). *Discussion and group methods: Theory and practice.* (2nd ed.). New York: Harper & Row.

Bormann, E. G. (1980). *Communication theory.* New York: Holt, Rinehart & Winston.

Bormann, E.G. (1982). Fantasy and rhetorical vision: Ten years later. *Quarterly Journal of Speech, 68,* 288–305.

Bormann, E. G. (1986). Symbolic convergence theory and communication in group decision-making. In R. Y. Hirokawa & M. S. Poole (Eds.), *Communication and group decision-making,* (pp. 219–236). Newbury Park, CA: Sage Publications, Inc.

Bostrom, R. P., & Anson, R. (1988). A case for collaborative work support systems. Working paper, University of Georgia; published in abbreviated form: CWS: A new member of your management team. *Information Executive, 1,* 43–46.

Bostrom, R. P. (1989). Successful application of communication techniques to improve the systems development process. *Information and Management, 16,* 279–295.

Bostrom, R. P., & Anson, R. (1991). Electronic meeting agenda design: mapping technology to tasks. Working paper, Department of Management, University of Georgia, Athens.

Bostrom, R. P., Clawson, V. K., & Anson, R. (1991). Training people to facilitate electronic environments. Working paper, Department of Management, University of Georgia, Athens.

Bracey, G. (1990). Education still not looking at the big picture. *Electronic Learning, 9*(8), 20–21.

Brehmer, B., & Joyce, C. R. B. (Eds.) (1988). *Human judgement: The SJT view.* Amsterdam: North-Holland.

Brenner, M. (1973). The next-in-line effect. *Journal of Verbal Learning and Verbal Behavior, 12,* 320–323.

Brickner, M. A., Harkins, S. G., & Ostrom, T. M. (1986). Effects of personal involvement: Thought-provoking implications for social loafing. *Journal of Personality and Social Psychology, 51*(4) 763–769.

Bridwell, L., & Ross, D. (1984). Integrating computers into a writing curriculum: Or, buying, begging, and building. In W. Wresch (Ed.), *The computer in composition instruction: A writer's tool* (pp. 107–119). Urbana, IL: National Council of Teachers of English.

Bridwell, L., Nancarrow, P., & Ross, D. (1984). The writing process and the writing machine: Current research on word processors relevant to the teaching of composition. In R. Beach & L. Bridwell (Eds.), *New directions in composition research* (pp. 381–398). New York: The Guilford Press.

Broome, B., & Keever, D. (1989). Next generation group facilitation: Proposed principles. *Management Communication Quarterly, 3*(1), 107–127.

Brown, Mary Helen (1990). Defining stories in organizations: Characteristic and functions. In S. Deetz (Ed.), *Communication Yearbook* (Vol. 13, pp. 162–190). Newbury Park, CA: Sage Publications, Inc.

Bui, T. X., & Jarke, M. (1984). A DSS for cooperative multiple criteria group decision making. *Proceedings of the 5th International Conference on Information Systems* (pp. 101–113).

Bui, T. X., & Jarke, M. (1986, April). Communications design for Co-oP: A group decision support system. *ACM Transactions on Office Information Systems, 4*(2), 81–103.

Bui, T. X., & Sivasankaran, T. R. (1990). Relation between GDSS use and group task complexity. *Proceedings of the Twenty-Third Annual Hawaii International Conference on System Sciences* (Vol. 3, pp. 69–78). Los Alamitos, CA: IEEE Computer Society Press.

Bukszar, E., & Connolly, T. (1988). Hindsight bias and strategic choice: Some problems in learning from experience. *Academy of Management Journal, 31,* 628–641.

Burke, K. (1969). *A grammar of motives.* Berkeley, CA: University of California Press.

Burt, M., & Dulay, H. (1983). Optimal language learning environments. In J. Oller & P. Richard-Amato (Eds.), *Methods that work: A smorgasbord of ideas for language teachers* (pp. 38–48). Rowley, MA: Newbury House.

Burton, G. (1987). The 'Clustering Effect': An idea-generation phenomenon during nominal grouping. *Small Group Behavior, 18*(2), 224–238.

Campbell, D. T., & Stanley, J. C. (1963). *Experimental and quasi-experimental designs for research*. Chicago: Rand McNally.

Campbell, K. K. (1982). *The rhetorical act*. Belmont, CA: Wadsworth.

Campbell, K. K., & Jamieson, K. H. (1986). Introduction. *Southern Speech Communication Journal, 51,* 293–299.

Campbell, K. K., & Jamieson K. H. (Eds.) (1978). *Form and genre: Shaping rhetorical action*. Falls Church, VA: Speech Communication Association.

Carlson, M., Charlin, V., & Miller, N. (1988). Positive mood and helping behavior: A test of six hypotheses. *Journal of Personal and Social Psychology, 55,* 211–29.

Carlson, David A., & Ram, Sudha (1990). Hyper intelligence: The next frontier. *Communication of the ACM, 33*(3), 311–321.

Carmel, E. (1991). *Supporting joint application development with electronic meeting systems: A field study.* Unpublished doctoral dissertation, University of Arizona, Tuscon.

Carter, K. (1989). Developing a sense of audience: The student to student handbook. *English Journal, 78*(1), 60–63.

Castore, C. H., & Murnighan, J. K. (1978). Determinants of support for group decisions. *Organizational Behavior and Human Performance, 22,* 75–92.

Chapanis, A. (1972). Studies in interactive communication: The effects of four communication modes on the behavior of teams during cooperative problem-solving. *Human Factors, 14,* 487–509.

Chapelle, C., & Jamieson, J. (1986). Computer-Assisted Language Learning as a predictor of success in acquiring English as a second language. *TESOL Quarterly, 20*(1), 27–46.

Chappell, D., Vogel, D., & Roberts, E. (1992). The Mirror Project: A virtual meeting place. *Proceedings of the Twenty-Fifth Annual Hawaii International Conference on System Sciences* (pp. 23–33). Los Alamitos, CA: IEEE Computer Society Press.

Chaudron, C. (1989). *Second language classrooms: Research on teaching and learning.* Cambridge: Cambridge University Press.

Cherwitz, R. A., & Hikins, J. W. (1986). *Communication and knowledge: An investigation in rhetorical epistemology.* Columbia, SC: University of South Carolina Press.

Chesebro, J. W., & Bonsall, D. G. (1989). *Computer-mediated communication: Human relationships in a computerized world.* Tuscaloosa: University of Alabama Press.

Chidambaram, L., Bostrom, R. P., & Wynne, B. E. (1991). An empirical investigation of the impact of computer support on group performance. *Journal of Management Information Systems, 7*(2), 7–26.

Chidambaram, L., Bostrom, R. P., & Wynne, B. E. (1990-1991). A longitudinal study of the impact of group decision support systems on group development. *Journal of Management Information Systems, 7*(3), 7–25.

Chilberg, J. (1989). A review of group process designs for facilitating communication in problem-solving groups. *Management Communication Quarterly, 3*(1), 51–70.

Clawson, V. K. (1990). Group facilitators: Research, issues, possibilities. Working paper, Walden University, Naples, FL.

Clement, A. (1990). Cooperative support for computer work: A social perspective on the empowering of end users. In *Proceedings of the Conference on Computer-Supported Cooperative Work* (pp. 223–236). New York: Association for Computing Machinery.

Connolly, T., & Bukszar, E. (1990). Hindsight bias: Self-flattery or cognitive error? *Journal of Behavioral Decision Making, 3,* 205-211.

Connolly, T., Jessup, L. M., & Valacich, J. S. (1990). Effects of anonymity and evaluative tone on idea generation in computer-mediated groups. *Management Science, 36*(6), 689–703.

References

Contractor, N., & Eisenberg, E. (1990). Communication networks and new media in organizations. In J. Fulk & C. Steinfield (Eds.), *Organizations and communication technology* (pp. 143–172). Newbury Park, CA: Sage Publications, Inc.

Cook, T. D., & Campbell, D. T. (1979). *Quasi-experimentation: Design & analysis issues for field settings*. Boston: Houghton Mifflin.

Cornell, P., & Luchetti, R. (1989). *Ergonomic and environmental aspects of computer supported cooperative work*. Paper presented at the Human Factors Society 33rd Annual Meeting, Denver, CO.

Courtright, J. A., Fairhurst, G. T., & Rogers, L. E. (1989). Interaction patterns in organic and mechanistic systems. *Academy of Management Journal, 32,* 773–802.

Cragan, J. F., & Wright, D. W. (1990). Small group communication research of the 1980s: A synthesis and critique. *Communication Studies, 41,* 212–236.

Crowston, K., & Malone, T. W. (1988). Information technology and work organization. In M. Helander (Ed.), *Handbook of human-computer interaction* (pp. 1051–1070). New York: Elsevier.

Cummins, J. (1989). The sanitized curriculum: Educational dispowerment in a nation at risk. In D. Johnson & D. Roen (Eds.), *Richness in writing: Empowering ESL students* (pp. 19–38). White Plains, NY: Longman Publishing Group.

Curran, C. (1982). Community language learning. In R. Blair (Ed.), *Innovative approaches to language teaching* (pp. 118–133). Rowley, MA: Newbury House.

Cyert, R. M., & March, J. G. (1963). *A behavioral theory of the firm*. Englewood Cliffs, NJ: Prentice Hall.

Czarniawska-Joerges, R., & Joerges, B. (1990). Linguistic artifacts of at service of organizational control. In P. Gagliardi (Ed.), *Symbols and artifacts: Views of the corporate landscape* (pp. 473–484). Norwood, NJ: Ablex Publishing Corp.

Daft, Richard L., & Huber, George P. (1987). How organizations learn: A communication framework. *Research in the Sociology of Organizations, 5,* 1–36.

Daft, R. L., & Lengel, R. (1986). Organizational information requirements, media richness, and structural design. *Management Science, 32*(5), 554–571.

Daft, R. L., & Macintosh, N. B. (1981). A tentative exploration into the amount and equivocality of information processing in organizational work units. *Administrative Science Quarterly, 26,* 207–224.

Daft, R. L., & Lewin, A. Y. (1990). Can organization studies begin to break out of the normal science straitjacket? An editorial essay. *Organization Science, 1*(1), 1–10.

Daft, R. L. & Weick, K. E. (1984). Toward a model of organizations as interpretation systems. *Academy of Management Review, 9,* 284–295.

Daiute, C. (1985). Issues in using computers to socialize the writing process. *Educational Communication and Technology, 33*(1), 41–50.

Daiute, C. (1986). Do 1 and 1 make 2?: Patterns of influence by co-authors. *Written Communication, 3,* 382–408.

Dalkey, N. C. (1969). *The delphi method: an experimental study of group opinion*. Santa Monica, CA: RAND Corp.

Dalkey, N., & Halmer, O. (1963). An experimental application of the delphi method to the use of experts. *Management Science, 6,* 458–467.

Daly, B. N. (1990). *The effects of computer-mediated communication on inductive learning by groups*. Unpublished doctoral dissertation, University of Illinois, Urbana-Champaign.

Daniels, R. (1991). *Enterprise analyzer: Automated support for business process re-engineering*. Unpublished doctoral dissertation, University of Arizona, Tuscon.

Davis, S. M., & Lawrence, P. R. (1977). *Matrix*. Reading, MA: Addison-Wesley.

Delbecq, A. L., & Van de Ven, A. H. (1971). A group process model for problem identification and program planning. *Journal of Applied Behavioral Science, 7,* 466–492.

Delbecq, A., Van de Ven, A., & Gustafson, D. (1975). *Group techniques for program planning*. Glenview, IL: Scott, Foresman.

Dennis, A. R. (1991). *Paralellism, anonymity, structure and group size in electronic meetings.* Unpublished doctoral dissertation, University of Arizona, Tucson.

Dennis, A. R., Briggs, R. O., and Nunamaker, J. F., Jr. (1991). Handwriting recognition and executive use of electronic meeting systems. Working paper, University of Arizona, Tucson.

Dennis, A. R., Briggs, R. O., and Nunamaker, J. F., Jr. (1990). A comparison of ad hoc and established groups in an electronic meeting system environment. *Proceedings of the Twenty-Third Annual Hawaii International Conference on System Sciences* (Vol. 3, pp. 23–29).

Dennis, A. R., George, J. F., Jessup, L. M., Nunamaker, J. F., & Vogel, D. R. (1988). Information technology to support electronic meetings. *MIS Quarterly, 12*(4), 591–624.

Dennis, A. R., Heminger, A. R., Nunamaker J. F., Jr., & Vogel, D. R. (1990). Bringing automated support to large groups: The Burr-Brown experience. *Information & Management, 18*(3), 111–121.

Dennis, A. R., Nunamaker J. F., Jr., & Paranka, D. (1991). Supporting the search for competitive advantage. *Journal of Management Information Systems, 18* (1), 5–36.

Dennis, A. R., Nunamaker, J. F., Jr., & Vogel, D. R. (1990–1991). A comparison of laboratory and field research in the study of electronic meeting systems. *Journal of Management Information Systems, 7*(2), 107–135.

Dennis, A. R., Tyran, C. K., Vogel, D. R., & Nunamaker, J. F., Jr. (1990). An evaluation of information technology to support strategic management. *Proceedings of the Eleventh International Conference of Information Systems,* (pp. 35–52).

Dennis, A. R., & Valacich, J. S. (1991). Electronic versus nominal group brainstorming. Working paper, University of Arizona, Tucson.

Dennis, A. R., Valacich, J. S., & Nunamaker, J. F., Jr. (1990). An experimental investigation of the effects of group size in an electronic meeting environment. *IEEE System, Man and Cybernetics, 25,* 1049–1057.

Dennis, A. R., Valacich, J. S., & Nunamaker, J. F., Jr. (1991). Group, sub-group and nominal group idea generation in an electronic meeting environment. In J. F. Nunamaker (Ed.), Proceedings of the Twenty-Fourth Annual Hawaii International Conference on System Sciences (Vol. 3, pp. 573–579). Los Alamitos, CA: IEEE Computer Society Press.

DeSanctis, G. (1989). Small group research in information systems: Theory and method. In I. Benbasat (Ed.), *The information systems research challenge: Experimental research methods* (pp. 53–82). Harvard Business School Research Colloquium, Boston, MA: Harvard Business School Press.

DeSanctis, G. L., Dickson, G. W., Jackson, B. M., & M. S. Poole. (1991, August). *Using computing in the face-to-face meeting: Some initial observations from the Texaco-Minnesota project.* Paper presented at the 51st Annual Meeting of the Academy of Management, Miami Beach, FL.

DeSanctis, G., D'Onofrio, M., Sambamurthy, V., & Poole, M. S. (1989). Comprehensiveness and restriction in group decision heuristics: Effects of computer support on consensus decision making. *Proceedings of the Tenth International Conference on Information Systems* (pp. 131–140).

DeSanctis, G., & Gallupe, R. B. (1987). A foundation for the study of group decision support systems. *Management Science, 33*(5), 589–609.

DeSanctis, G., & Poole, M. S. (1989). *Computer-supported meetings: A brief overview of the GDSS Research Project.* Minneapolis, MN: University of Minnesota.

DeSanctis, G., & Poole, M. S., (1991). Understanding the differences in collaborative system use through appropriation analysis. In J. F. Nunamaker, Jr. (Ed.), *Proceedings of the Twenty-Fourth Annual Hawaii International Conference on System Sciences* (Vol. 3, pp. 750–757). Los Alamitos, CA: IEEE Computer Society Press.

DeSanctis, G., Poole, M. S., Lewis, H., & Desharnais, G. (1991). Using computing to improve the quality team process: Some initial observations from the IRS-Minnesota project. In J. F. Nunamaker (Ed.), *Proceedings of the Twenty-Fourth Annual Hawaii International Conference on System Sciences* (p. 757). Los Alamitos, CA: IEEE Computer Society Press.

References

DeSanctis, G., Poole, M. S., Limayem, M., & Johnson, W. (1990, April). The GDSS research project: experimental materials summary and general questionnaires. Working Paper series, MISRC-WP-90-09, University of Minnesota, Management Information Systems Research Center, Minneapolis.

Dickson, G. W., DeSanctis, G., Poole, M. S., & Limayem, M. (1991). Multicriteria modeling and "what if" analysis as conflict management tools for group decision making. *Proceedings of the 11th International Decision Support Systems Conference,* San Diego, CA: The Institute of Management Sciences.

Dickson, G., Lee, J., Robinson, L., & Heath, R. (1989). Observations on GDSS interaction: chauffeured, facilitated, and user-driven systems. In J. F. Nunamaker, Jr. (Ed.), *Proceedings of the 22nd Annual Hawaii International Conference on System Sciences* (Vol. 3, pp. 337–343). Los Alamitos, CA: IEEE Computer Society Press.

Dickson, W., & Vereen, M. (1983). Two students at one microcomputer. *Theory into Practice, 22,* 296–300.

Diehl, M., & Stroebe, W. (1987). Productivity loss in brainstorming groups: Toward the solution of a riddle. *Journal of Personality and Social Psychology, 53*(3), 497–509.

DiMatteo, A. (1990). Under erasure: A theory for interactive writing in real time. *Computers and Composition, 7,* Special Issue, 71–83.

DiPietro, R. (1983). Scenarios, discourse, and real-life roles. In J. Oller & P. Richard-Amato (Eds.), *Methods that work: A smorgasbord of ideas for language teachers* (pp. 226–238). Rowley, MA: Newbury House.

Donoho, A. W., Donoho, D. L., & Gasko, M. (1988, July). MacSpin: Dynamic Graphics on a Desktop Computer. *IEEE Computer Graphics & Applications,* pp. 51–58.

Douglas, M. (1986). *How institutions think Syracuse.* New York: Syracuse University Press.

Doyle, M., & Straus, D. (1976). *How to make meetings work.* New York: Wyden.

Dreyfus, H. L. (1979). *What computers can't do.* New York: Harper Colophon Books.

Drucker, P. F. (1974). *Management: tasks, responsibilities, and practices.* New York: Harper & Row.

Dubrovsky, V. (1987). Social exchange in group consensus development: Face-to-face versus electronic mail. *Proceedings of the Human Factors Society, 31st Annual Meeting* (Vol. 2), pp. 701–705.

Durkheim, E. (1989). *The division of labor in society* (W. D. Hall, Trans.) New York: The Free Press.

Easterbrook, J. A. (1959). The effect of emotion on cure utilization and the organization of behavior. *Psychological Review, 66,* 183–201.

Easton, G. K., George, J. F., Nunamaker, J. F., Jr., & Pendergast, M. O. (1990). Using two different electronic meeting system tools for the same task: An experimental comparison. *Journal of Management Information Systems, 7*(1), 85–100.

Easton, A. C., Vogel, D. R., & Nunamaker, J. F., Jr. (1989). Stakeholder identification and assumption surfacing in small groups: An experimental study. In J. F. Nunamaker, Jr. (Ed.), *Proceedings of the Twenty-Second Hawaii International Conference on System Sciences* (Vol. 3, pp. 344–352). Los Alamitos, CA: IEEE Computer Society Press.

Egbert, J. L., Jessup, L. M., & Valacich, J. S. (1991). Interactive computer assisted language learning for groups: New technologies for English as a second language. *Computer Assisted English Language Learning (CAELL) Journal, 2*(1), 18–24.

Egido, C. (1990). Teleconferencing as a technology to support cooperative work: Its possibilities and limitations. In J. Galegher, R. Kraut, & C. Egido (Eds.), *Intellectual teamwork: social and technological foundations of cooperative work* (pp. 351–371). Hillsdale, NJ: Lawrence Erlbaum.

Einhorn, H. J., & Hogarth, R. M. (1981). Behavioral decision theory: Processes of judgment and choice. *Annual Review of Psychology, 32,* 53–88.

Eisenhardt, K. M. (1989). Making fast strategic decisions in high-velocity environments. *Academy of Management Journal, 32*(3), 543–576.

Eisenhardt, K. M. (1989). Building theories from case study research. *Academy of Management Review, 14*(4), 532–550.

Elam, J. J., Huber, G. P., & Hurt, M. E. (1986). An examination of the DSS literature (1975–1985). In E. R. McLean & H. G. Sol (Eds.), *Decision support systems: A decade in perspective* (pp. 1–17). Amsterdam: North-Holland.

Ellis, R. (1984). *Classroom second language development.* Oxford: Pergamon Press.

Ellis, R. (1986). *Understanding second language acquisition.* Oxford: Oxford University Press.

Ellis, C. A., Gibbs, S. J., & Rein, G. L. (1991). Groupware: Some issues and experiences. *Communications of the ACM, 34*(1), 39–58.

Ellis, C. A., Rein, G. L., & Jarvenpaa, S. L. (1989–1990). Nick experimentation: Selected results concerning effectiveness of meeting support technology. *Journal of Management Information Systems, 6*(3), 7–24.

Elmer-Dewitt. (1991). The Revolution that fizzled. *Time,* pp. 48–49. 20 May.

El Sawy, O. A., Gomes, G. M., & Gonzales, M. V. (1986). Preserving institutional memory: The management of history as an organizational resource. *Academy of Management Best Paper Proceedings, 37,* 118–122.

Esses, V. (1989). Mood as moderator of acceptance of interpersonal feedback. *Journal of Personal and Social Psychology, 57,* 769–81.

Etzioni, A. (1988). *The moral dimension: Toward a new economics.* New York: The Free Press.

Feldman, M. S., & March, J. G. (1981). Information in organizations as signal and symbol. *Administrative Science Quarterly, 26*(2), 171–186.

Fellers, J. W. (1989). *The effect of group size and computer support on group idea generation for creativity tasks: An experimental evaluation using a repeated measures design.* Unpublished doctoral thesis, Indiana University, Bloomington.

Festinger, L. (1954). A theory of social comparison processes. *Human Relations, 7,* 117–140.

Finholt, T., & Sproull, L. S. (1990). Electronic groups at work. *Organization Science, 1*(1), 41–64.

Finlay, M. (1987). *Powermatics.* London: Routledge and Kegan Paul.

Fiol, C. M., & Lyles, M. A. (1985). Organizational learning. *Academy of Management Review, 10,* 803–813.

Fischhoff, B. (1982). Debiasing. In D. Kahneman, P. Slovic, & A. Tversky (Eds.), *Judgment under uncertainty: Heuristics and biases.* New York: Cambridge University Press.

Fischhoff, B., Slovic, P., & Lichtenstein, S. (1977). Knowing with confidence: The appropriateness of extreme confidence. *Journal of Experimental Psychology: Human Perception and Performance, 3,* 552–564.

Fischhoff, B., Slovic, P., & Lichtenstein, S. (1978). Fault trees: Sensitivity of estimated failure probabilities to problem representation. *Journal of Experimental Psychology: Human Perception and Performance, 4,* 330–344.

Fisher, B. A. (1980). *Small group decision-making* (2nd ed.) New York: McGraw-Hill.

Fisher, W. R. (1984). Narration as human communication paradigm: The case of public moral argument. *Communication Monographs, 52,* 1–22.

Fisher, W. R. (1985). The narrative paradigm: An elaboration. *Communication Monographs, 52,* 347–367.

Flack, J. E., & Summers, D. A. (1971). Computer-aided conflict resolution in water resource planning: An illustration. *Water Resources Research, 7,* 1410–1414.

Forsyth, D. R. (1990). *Group Dynamics* (2nd ed.) Pacific Grove, CA: Brooks/Cole Publishing Co.

Franz, C. R., & Robey, D. (1987). Strategies for research on information systems in organizations: A critical analysis of research purpose and time frame. In R. J. Boland, Jr. & R. A. Hirschheim (Eds.), *Critical issues in information systems research* (pp. 205–225). Chichester, England: John Wiley & Sons.

Fulk, J., & Schmitz, J. (1988). *Rich or poor: It's how we see it.* Paper presented to the International Communication Association, New Orleans, LA.

Fulk, J., Schmitz, J., & Steinfield, C. (1990). A social influence model of technology use. In J. Fulk & C. Steinfield (Eds.). *Organizations and communication technology,* (pp. 117–140). Newbury Park, CA: Sage.

References

Gaies, S. (1989). Foreword. In D. Johnson & D. Roen (Eds.), *Richness in writing: Empowering ESL students* (pp. xi–xii). White Plains, NY: Longman.

Galbraith, J. R. (1973). *Designing complex organizations.* Reading, MA: Addison-Wesley.

Galbraith, J. R. (1977). *Organizational design.* Reading, MA: Addison-Wesley.

Galda, L. (1984). The relations between reading and writing in young children. In R. Beach & L. Bridwell (Eds.), *New directions in composition research* (pp. 191–204). New York: The Guilford Press.

Galegher, J., & Kraut, R. E. (1990). Computer-mediated communication for intellectual teamwork: A field experiment in group writing. *Proceedings of the Conference on Computer-Supported Cooperative Work* (pp. 65–78). New York: Association for Computing Machinery.

Galliers, R. D., & Land, F. F. (1987). Choosing appropriate information systems research methodologies. *Communications of the ACM, 39*(11), 900–902.

Gallupe, R. B. (1986). Experimental research into group decision support systems: Practical issues and problems. *Proceedings of the Nineteenth Annual Hawaii International Conference on System Sciences* (pp. 515–523). Los Alamitos, CA: IEEE Computer Society Press.

Gallupe, R. B. (1990). Suppressing the contribution of the group's best member: Is GDSS use appropriate for all group tasks? *Proceedings of the Twenty-Third Annual Hawaii International Conference on System Sciences* (Vol. 3, pp. 13–22). Los Alamitos, CA: IEEE Computer Society Press.

Gallupe, R. B., Bastianutti, L., & Cooper, W. H. (1991). Unblocking brainstorms. *Journal of Applied Psychology, 76* (1), 137–142.

Gallupe, R. B. and Cooper, W. (1991). Electronic brainstorming and production blocking. Working paper, Queen's University, Kingston, Ontario.

Gallupe, R. B., Cooper, W., and Bastianutti, L. (1990). Why is electronic brainstorming more productive than traditional brainstorming. *Proceedings of the 1990 Administrative Sciences Association of Canada Conference* (pp. 82–92). Whistler, British Columbia, Canada.

Gallupe, R. B., Dennis, A. R., Cooper, W. H., Valacich, J. S., Nunamaker Jr., J. F., & Bastianutti, L., (in press). Group size and electronic brainstorming, *Academy of Management Journal.*

Gallupe, R. B., DeSanctis, G., & Dickson, G. W. (1988). Computer-based support for group problem finding: An experimental investigation. *MIS Quarterly, 12*(2), 277–296.

Gallupe, R. B., & McKeen, J. D. (1988). Beyond computer-mediated communication: An experimental study into the use of a group decision support system for face-to-face versus remote meetings. *Proceedings of the 1988 Administrative Sciences Association of Canada Conference.* Halifax, Nova Scotia.

Gallupe, R. B., & McKeen, J. D. (1990). Enhancing computer-mediated communication: An experimental investigation into the use of a group decision support system for face-to-face versus remote meetings. *Information & Management, 18,* 1–13.

Gattegno, C. (1983). The silent way. In J. Oller & P. Richard-Amato (Eds.), *Methods that work: A smorgasbord of ideas for language teachers* (pp. 72–88). Rowley, MA: Newbury House.

Gelsinger, P., Gargini, P., Parker, G., & Yu, A. (1991). 2001: A microprocessor odyssey. In D. LeeBaert (Ed.), *Technology 2001: The future of computing and communication* (pp. 95–116). Cambridge, MA: The MIT Press.

George, J. (1990). Personality, affect, and behavior in groups. *Journal of Applied Psychology, 75,* 107–16.

George, J. F., Easton, G. K., Nunamaker, J. F., Jr., & Northcraft, G. B. (1990). A study of collaborative group work with and without computer based support. *Information Systems Research, 1*(4), 394–415.

George, J. F., Dennis, A. R., & Nunamaker, J. R., Jr. (1991). An experimental investigation of facilitation in an EMS decision room. Working paper, University of Arizona, Tucson.

George, J. F., & J. L. King. (1991). Examining computing and centralization debate. *Communications of the ACM, 34*(7), 62–72.

George, J. F., Valacich, J. S., & Nunamaker, J. F., Jr. (in press). Electronic meeting systems as innovation: A study of the innovation process. *Information and Management.*

Gersick, C. J. G. (1988). Time and transition in work teams: Toward a new model of group development. *Academy of Management Journal, 31,* 9–41.

Gersick, C. J. G. (1989). Marking time: Predictable transitions in task groups. *Academy of Management Journal, 32,* 274–309.

Gettys, C., & Fisher, G. (1979). Hypothesis plausibility and hypothesis generation. *Organizational Behavior and Human Performance, 24,* 137–142.

Glaser, B. G., & Strauss, A. L. (1967). *The discovery of grounded theory: Strategies for qualitative research.* Chicago: Aldine.

Glueck, W. F. (1979). Changing hours of work: A review and analysis of the research. *The Personnel Administrator, 24,* 44–47.

Goffman, E. (1959). *The presentation of self in everyday life.* New York: Doubleday Anchor.

Goodman, G. O., & Abel, M. J. (1987). Communication and collaboration: Facilitating cooperative work through communication. *Office: Technology and People, 3,* 129–145.

Gopal, A. (1991). *The effects of technology level and task type on group outcomes in a group decision support system environment.* Unpublished doctoral dissertation, University of Georgia, Athens.

Gouran, D. S. (1988). Group decision-making: An approach to integrative research. In C. H. Tardy (Ed.), *A handbook for the study of human communication: Methods and instruments for observing, measuring, and assessing communication processes* (pp. 247–267). Norwood, NJ: Ablex Publishing.

Gouran, D. S., Brown, C., & Henry, D. R. (1978). Behavioral correlates of perceptions of quality in decision-making discussions. *Communication Monographs, 45,* 51–63.

Gouran, D., & Hirokawa, R. (1983). The role of communication in decision making groups: A functional perspective. In M. Mander (Ed.), *Communications in transition* (pp. 168–185). New York: Praeger.

Gouran, D., & Hirokawa, R. (1986). Counteractive functions of communication in effective group decision-making. In R. Hirokawa & M. Poole (Eds.), *Communication and group decision-making* (pp. 81–92). Newbury Park, CA: Sage Publications, Inc.

Gray, P. (1983). Initial Observations from the Decision Room Project. *Proceedings of the Third International Conference on Decision Support Systems* (pp. 135–138).

Gray, P. (1987). Group decision support systems. *Decision Support Systems Journal, 3,* pp. 233–242.

Gray, P. (1988). The user interface in group decision support systems. *DSS-88 Transactions.* Providence, RI: The Institute of Management Sciences.

Gray, P., Olfman, L., & Park, H. (1988, January). *Decision of the human interface for international GSS.* Working Paper 88-1, Claremont Graduate School, Claremont, CA.

Gray, P., & Olfman, L. (1989). The user interface in group decision support systems. *Decision Support Systems, 5,* pp. 119–137.

Gray, P., Vogel, D. R., & Beauclair, R. (1990). Assessing GDSS Empirical Research. *European Journal of Operations Research, 49,* 162–176.

Green, S. G., & Taber, T. D. (1980). The effects of three social decision schemes on decision group process. *Organizational Behavior and Human Performance, 25,* 97–106.

Greif, Irene, & Sarin, Sunil. (1987). Data sharing in group work. *ACM Transactions on Office Information Systems, 5*(2), 187–211.

Grice, H. P. (1975). Logic and conversation. In P. Cole & J. Morgan (Eds.), *Syntax and semantics 3: Speech acts* (pp. 41–58). New York: Academic Press.

Grohowski, R., McGoff, C., Vogel, D., Martz, B., & Nunamaker, J. F., Jr. (1990). Implementing electronic meeting systems at IBM: Lessons learned and success factors. *MIS Quarterly, 14*(4), 369–384.

Gross, Andrew C. (1988). The information vending machine. *Business Horizons, 31,* 24–33.

Grudin, J. (1989). The case against user interface consistency. *Communications of the ACM, 32,* pp. 1164–1173.

Grudnitski, G. M. (1975). *A methodology for the design of decision-maker oriented information systems.* Unpublished doctoral dissertation, University of Massachusetts, Amherst.

Gutek, B. A. (1988). Work group structure and information technology: A structural contingency approach. In J. Galegher, R. E. Kraut, & C. Egido (Eds.), *Intellectual teamwork: The social and technical bases of cooperative work.* Hillsdale, NJ: Lawrence Erlbaum.

References

Hackman, J. R. (1987). The design of work teams. In J. Lorsch (Ed.), *Handbook of organizational behavior* (pp. 315–342). Englewood Cliffs, NJ: Prentice Hall.

Hackman, J. R. (1990). *Groups that work (and those that don't): creating conditions for effective teamwork.* San Francisco: Jossey-Bass.

Hackman, J. R., & Kaplan, R. (1974). Interventions into group process: An approach to improving the effectiveness of groups. *Decision Sciences, 5,* 459–480.

Hackman, J. R., & Morris, C. G. (1975). Group tasks, group interaction process, and group performance effectiveness: A review and proposed integration. In L. Berkowitz (Ed.), *Advances in experimental social psychology* (Vol. 8, pp. 47–99). New York: Academic Press.

Hainline, D. (1987). Computers in language instruction—Trends and possibilities. In D. Hainline (Ed.), *New developments in computer assisted language learning* (pp. 1–8). New York: Nichols Publishing Company.

Hall, E. (1966). *The hidden dimension.* Garden City, NY: Doubleday.

Hall, J., & Watson, W. (1970). The Effects of a normative intervention on group decision-making performance. *Human Relations, 23*(4), 299–317.

Hall, J., & Williams, M. (1970). Group dynamics training and improved decision making. *Journal of Applied Behavioral Science, 6*(1), 39–68.

Hamilton, E. E. 1988. The facilitation of organizational change: An empirical study of factors predicting change agents effectiveness. *Journal of Applied Behavioral Science, 24*(1), 37–59.

Hammond, K. R. (1971). Computer graphics as an aid to learning. *Science, 172,* 903–908.

Hammond, K. R., & Adelman, L. (1976). Science, values and human judgment. *Science, 194,* 389–396.

Harrel, J., & Linkugel, W. A. (1978). On rhetorical genre: An organizing perspective. *Philosophy and Rhetoric, 11,* 262–281.

Hawisher, G. (1988). *Research in computers and writing: Findings and implications.* Paper presented at the Annual Meeting of the American Educational Research Association. (ERIC Document, Reproduction Service No. ED 293 140).

Hawisher, G. (1989). Research and recommendations for computers and composition. In G. Hawisher & C. Selfe (Eds.), *Critical perspectives on computers and composition instruction* (pp. 44–74). New York: Teachers College Press.

Hawisher, G., & Selfe, C. (1990). Letter from the editors. *Computers and Composition, 7,* Special Issue, 5–14.

Hayes, G. (1991). *Group matrix: A collaborative modeling tool.* Unpublished doctoral dissertation, University of Arizona, Tucson.

Heim, M. (1987). *Electric language: A philosophical study of word processing.* New Haven: Yale University Press.

Heminger, A., & Valacich, J. S. (1991). Comments: A system to support distributed group meetings. *Proceedings of the Twenty-Second Annual Meeting of the Midwest Decision Sciences Institute* (pp. 45–47).

Henderson, K. (1990). Computer databases and critical inquiry. *CAELL Journal, 1*(3), 16–17.

Herniter, B. C. (1991). *Design and implementation of a negotiation support system.* Unpublished doctoral dissertation, University of Arizona, Tucson.

Hewes, D. E. (1986). A socioegocentric model of group decision-making. In R. Y. Hirokawa & M. S. Poole (Eds.), *Communication and group decision-making* (pp. 265–292). Newbury Park, CA: Sage Publications, Inc.

Hill, G.W. (1982). Group versus individual performance: Are N+1 heads better than one? *Psychological Bulletin, 91*(3), 517–39.

Hiltz, S. R. (1988). Productivity enhancement from computer-mediated communication: A systems contingency approach. *Communications of the ACM, 31*(12), 1438–1457.

Hiltz, S. R., Dufner, D., Holmes, M., & Poole S. (1991). Distributed group support systems: Social dynamics and design dilemmas. *Journal of Organizational Computing, 2*(1), 135–159.

Hiltz, S. R., & Johnson, K. (1990). User satisfaction with computer-mediated communication systems. *Management Science, 36*(6), 739–764.

Hiltz, S. R., Johnson, K., & Turoff, M. (1986). Experiments in group decision-making: Communication process and outcome in face-to-face versus computerized conferences. *Human Communication Research, 13*(2), 225–252.

Hiltz, S. R., Johnson, K. and Turoff, M. (1991). Group decision support: The effects of designated human leaders and statistical feedback in computerized conferences. *Journal of Management Information Systems, 8*(2), 81–108.

Hiltz, S. R., & Turoff, M. (1978). *The network nation: Human communication via computer.* Reading, MA: Addison-Wesley.

Hiltz, S. R., Turoff, M., & Johnson, K. (1989). Experiments in group decision making, 3: Disinhibition, deindividuation, and group process in pen name and real name computer conferences. *Decision Support Systems, 5*(2), 217–232.

Hirokawa, R. Y. (1982). Group communication and problem-solving effectiveness I: A critical review of inconsistent findings. *Communication Quarterly, 30*(2), 134–141.

Hirokawa, R. Y. (1985). Discussion procedures and decision-making performance: Test of a functional perspective. *Human Communication Research, 12,* 203–224.

Hirokawa, R. (1987). Why informed groups make faulty decisions: An investigation of possible interaction-based explanations. *Small Group Behavior, 18,* 3–29.

Hirokawa, R., & Gouran, D. (1989). Facilitation of group communication: A critique of prior research and an agenda for future research. *Management Communication Quarterly, 3*(1), 71–92.

Hirokawa, R., & Pace, R. (1983). A descriptive investigation of the possible communication-based reasons for effective and ineffective group decision making. *Communication Monographs, 50,* 363–79.

Hirokawa, R. Y., & Scheerhorn, D. R. (1986). Communication in faulty group decision-making. In R. Y. Hirokawa & M. S. Poole (Eds.), *Communication and group decision-making* (pp. 63–80). Newbury Park, CA: Sage Publications, Inc.

Hirschhorn, L. (1991). *Managing in the new team environment.* Reading, MA: Addison-Wesley.

Ho, T. H., Raman, K. S., & Watson, R. T. (1989). Group decision support systems: The cultural factor. In J. I. Gross, J. C. Henderson, & B. R. Konsynski (Eds.), *Proceedings of the Tenth International Conference of Information Systems* (pp. 119–129). Baltimore: ACM.

Hoffman, L. (1982). Improving the problem-solving process in managerial groups. In R. Guzzo (Ed.), *Improving group decision-making in organizations: Approaches from theory and research.* New York: Academic Press.

Hoffman, L. (1979). *The group problem-solving process.* New York: Praeger.

Hoffman, L., & Maier, N. (1959). The use of group decision to resolve a problem of fairness. *Personnel Psychology, 12,* 545–559.

Hofmeister, A. (1989). Teaching problem solving skills with technology. *Educational Technology, 29*(9), 26–29.

Hogarth, R. M. (1978). A note on aggregating opinions. *Organizational Behavior and Human Performance, 21,* 40–46.

Hogarth, R. M. (1987). *Judgment and choice: The psychology of decision* (2nd ed.). New York: Wiley.

Holdstein, D. (1987). *On composition and computers.* New York: The Modern Language Association of America.

Hollingshead, A. B., & McGrath, J. E. (in press). The whole is less than the sum of the parts: Interaction and performance in computer-assisted work groups. To appear in: R. Guzzo (Ed.), *Team decision making in organizations.*

Howell, J., Dorfman, P., & Kerr, S. (1986). Moderator variables in leadership research. *Academy of Management Review, 11*(1), 88–102.

Huber, G. P. (1984a, December). Issues in the design of group decision support systems. *MIS Quarterly, 8*(3), 195–204.

Huber, George P. (1984b). The nature and design of post-industrial organizations. *Management Science, 30,* 928–951.

Huber, G. P. (1990). A theory of the effects of advanced information technologies on organizational design, intelligence, and decision making. *Academy of Management Review, 15*(1), 47–71.

References

Huber, G. P. (1991). Organizational learning: The contributing processes and the literatures. *Organization Science, 2*(1), 1–28.

Huber, G. P., & McDaniel, R. R. (1986). The decision-making paradigm of organizational design. *Management Science, 32*(5), 572–589.

Huebner, T. (1989). SLA models and issues. *Annual Review of Applied Linguistics, 9,* 5–22.

Huff, A. S. (1981). Coping with social complexity: Multilectic methods of inquiry. *Human Systems Management, 2,* 83–94.

Innis, H. (1972). *Empire and communications.* Toronto: University of Toronto Press.

Isen, A., Daubman, K., & Nowicki, G. (1987). Positive affect facilitates creative problem solving. *Journal of Personal and Social Psychology, 52,* 1122–31.

Isen, A., Nygren, T., & Ashby, F. (1988). Influence of positive affect on the subjective utility of gains and losses: It is just not worth the risk. *Journal of Personal and Social Psychology, 55,* 710–17.

Isenberg, D. J. (1985). Some hows and whats of managerial thinking. In J. G. Hunt & J. D. Blair (Eds.), *Leadership on the future battlefield* (pp. 168-181). Pergamon-Brassey, International Defense Publishers.

Ives, B., Hamilton, S., & Davis, G. B. (1980). A framework for research in computer-based management information systems. *Management Science, 26*(9), 910–934.

Jablin, F. M., & Seibold, D. R. (1978). Implications for problem solving groups of empirical research on "Brainstorming": A critical review of the literature. *The Southern States Speech Communication Journal, 43,* 327–56.

Jackson, G. (1986). Technology and pedagogy: Making the right match is vital. *Change,* 18(3), 52–57.

Jamieson, J., & Chapelle, C. (1987). Working styles on computers as evidence of second language learning strategies. *Language Learning, 37,* 523–544.

Janis, I. L. (1972). *Victims of groupthink.* Boston: Houghton-Mifflin.

Janis, I. L. (1982). *Groupthink: Psychological studies of policy decisions and fiascoes.* Boston: Houghton Mifflin.

Jarvenpaa, S., Dickson, G. W., & DeSanctis, G. (1985). Methodological issues in experimental IS research: Experiences and recommendations. *MIS Quarterly, 9*(2), 141–156.

Jarvenpaa, S. L., Rao, V. S., & Huber, G. P. Computer support for meetings of medium-sized groups working on unstructured problems: A field experiment. *MIS Quarterly, 12*(4), 645–666.

Jelassi, M. T., & Foroughi, A. (1989). Negotiation support systems: An overview of design issues and existing software. *Decision Support Systems, 5,* 167–182.

Jessup, L. M. (1987). Group decision support systems: A need for behavioral research. *International Journal of Small Group Research, 3,* 139–158.

Jessup, L. (1991). On the study of group support systems: What was the question? Working paper series # 0020, California State University, College of Business Administration, San Marcos.

Jessup, L. M., Connolly, T., & Galegher, J. (1990). The effects of anonymity on group process in an idea-generating task. *MIS Quarterly, 14*(3), 313–321.

Jessup, L. M., & Tansik, D. A. (1991). Decision making in an automated environment: The effects of anonymity and proximity on group process and outcome with a group decision support system. *Decision Sciences, 22*(1), 266–279.

Jick, T. D. (1979). Mixing qualitative and quantitative methods: Triangulation in action. *Administrative Science Quarterly, 24*(4), 602–611.

Johansen, R. (1977). Social evaluations of teleconferencing. *Telecommunications Policy, 1,* 395–419.

Johansen, R. (1988). *Groupware: Computer support for business teams.* New York: The Free Press.

Johansen, R. (1991). Teams for tomorrow. In J. F. Nunamaker, Jr. (Ed.), *Proceedings of the Twenty-Fourth Annual Hawaii International Conference on System Sciences* (Vol. 3, pp. 521–534). Los Alamitos, CA: IEEE Computer Society Press.

Johansen, R., Sibbet, D., Benson, S., Martin, A., Mittman, R., & Saffo, P. (1991). *Leading business teams: How teams can use technology and process to enhance group performance.* Reading, MA: Addison-Wesley.

Johns, T., & Davies, F. (1983). Text as a vehicle for information: Classroom texts in teaching reading in a foreign language. *Reading in a Foreign Language, 1*(1), 1–19.

Johnson, B., & Rice, R. E. (1987). *Managing organizational innovation: The evolution from word processing to office information systems.* New York: Columbia University Press.

Johnson, D. (1991). Second language and content learning with computers: Research in the role of social factors. In P. Dunkel (Ed.), *Computer-assisted language learning and testing: Research issues and practice* (pp. 61–83). New York: Newbury House.

Johnson, W. R., Jr. (1991). Anything, anytime, anywhere: The future of networking. In D. LeeBaert (Ed.), *Technology 2001: The future of computing and communication* (pp. 150–175). Cambridge, MA: The MIT Press.

Kanter, R. M. (1989). *When giants learn to dance.* New York: Simon and Schuster.

Kayser, T. A. (1990). *Mining group gold.* El Segundo, CA: Serif Publishing.

Keen, P. G. W., & Scott-Morton, M. S. (1978). *Decision support systems: An organizational perspective.* Reading, MA.: Addison-Wesley.

Kelley, H. H., & Thibaut, J. W. (1968). Group problem solving. In G. Lindzey & E. Aronson (Eds.), *The Handbook of Social Psychology: Volume 4.* (pp. 1–101). Reading, MA: Addison-Wesley.

Kellogg, W. (1987). Conceptual consistency in the user interface: Effects on user performance. *Proceedings of INTERACT '87 Conference on Human-Computer Interaction.* Stuttgart.

Kelly, J. R., & McGrath, J. E. (1985). Effects of time limits and task types on task performance and interaction of four-person groups. *Journal of Personality and Social Psychology, 49*(2), 395–407.

Kelly, J. R., Futoran, G., & McGrath, J. E. (1990). Capacity and capability: Seven studies of entrainment of task performance rates. *Small Group Research, 21*(3), 283–314.

Kelman, P. (1990). Alternatives to integrated instructional systems. *CUE Newsletter, 13*(2), 7–9.

Kerr, N. L. (1983). Motivation losses in small groups: A social dilemma analysis. *Journal of Personality and Social Psychology, 45*(4), 819–828.

Kerr, S., & Jermier, J. (1978). Substitutes for leadership: Their meaning and measurement. *Organizational Behavior and Human Performance, 22,* 375–403.

Kiesler, S., Siegel, J., & McGuire, T. W. (1984). Social psychological aspects of computer-mediated communication. *American Psychologist, 39,* 1123–1134.

Kling, R. (1980). Social analysis of computing: Theoretical perspectives. *Computing Surveys, 12,* 61–110.

Klobusicky-Mailander, E. (1990). Putting the computer to work in your class. *English Teaching Forum, 28*(2), 2–7.

Knapp, M. L., & Miller, G. R. (Eds.). (1985). *Handbook of interpersonal communication.* Newbury Park, CA: Sage Publications.

Kraemer, K. L., & King, J. (1988). Computer-based systems for cooperative work and group decision making. *Computing Surveys, 20,* 115–146.

Kraemer, K. L., & Pinsonneault, A. (1989). The implications of group support technologies: An evaluation of the empirical research. In J. F. Nunamaker, Jr. (Ed.), *Proceedings of the Twenty-Second Annual Hawaii International Conference on System Sciences,* Vol. 3 (pp. 326–336). Los Alamitos, CA: IEEE Computer Society Press.

Kraemer, K. L., & Pinsonneault, A. (1990). Technology and groups: Assessment of the empirical research. In J. Galegher, R. Kraut, & C. Egido (Eds.), *Intellectual Teamwork: Social and technological foundations of cooperative work* (pp. 375–405). Hillsdale, NJ: Lawrence Erlbaum.

Krashen, S. (1989). We acquire vocabulary and spelling by reading: Additional evidence for the input hypothesis. *The Modern Language Journal, 73,* 440–464.

Krashen, S., & Terrell, T. (1983). *The natural approach: Language acquisition in the classroom.* Hayward, CA: Alemany Press.

Kraut, R. E., Fish, R. S., Root, R. W., & Chalfonte, B. L. (1990). Informal communication in organizations: Form, function, and technology. In S. Oskamp & S. Spacapan (Eds.), *People's reactions to technology in factories, offices, and aerospace.* Newbury Park, CA: Sage Publications.

Kraut, R. E., Galegher, J., & Egido, R. (1990). Pattern of contact and communication in scientific research collaborations. In J. Galegher, R. E. Kraut, & C. Egido (Eds.), *Intellectual teamwork: Social and technical foundations of cooperative work* (pp. 149–172). Hillsdale, NJ: Lawrence Erlbaum.

Kreeft-Peyton, J. (1990). Technological innovation meets institution: Birth of creativity or murder of a great idea? *Computers and Composition, 7,* Special Issue, 15–32.

Kreeft-Peyton, J., & Horowitz, D. (1988). Local area networks with deaf students: Some benefits and considerations. *Teaching English to Deaf and Second Language Students, 6*(2), 10–15.

Kreeft-Peyton, J., & Mackinson-Smyth, J. (1989). Writing and talking about writing: Computer networking with elementary students. In D. Johnson & D. Roen (Eds.), *Richness in writing: Empowering ESL students* (pp. 100–119). White Plains, NY: Longman Publishing Group.

Kremers, M. (1990). Sharing authority in a synchronous network: The case for riding the beast. *Computers and Composition, 7,* Special Issue, 33–44.

Krendl, K., & Lieberman, D. (1988). Computers and learning: A review of recent research. *Educational Computing, 4,* 367–389.

Kreps, G. L. (1990). *Organizational communication* (2nd ed.). White Plains, NY: Longman Publishing Group.

Krueger, G. P. (1976). *Teleconferencing in three communication modes as a function of the number of conferees.* Unpublished doctoral dissertation, Johns Hopkins University.

Kull, D. J. (1982, May). Group decision: Can computers help? *Computer Decisions,* p. 70.

Kutsko, J., & Smith, J. (1991). Effectiveness measures for distributed teams using electronic meeting technology: The Larsen/Lafasto instrument. In J. F. Nunamaker, Jr. (Ed.), *Proceedings of The Twenty-Fourth Annual Hawaii International Conference on System Sciences,* Vol. 3 (pp. 458–470). Los Alamitos, CA: IEEE Computer Society Press.

Lake, D. (1988–89, December/January). Two projects that worked: Using telecommunications as a resource in the classroom. *The Computing Teacher,* pp. 17–19.

Lamm, H., & Myers, D. G. (1978). Group induced polarization of attitudes and behavior. In L. Berkowitz (Ed.), *Advances in Experimental Social Psychology* (Vol. 11, pp. 145–195). New York: Academic Press.

Lamm, H., & Trommsdorff, G. (1973). Group versus individual performance on tasks requiring ideational proficiency (brainstorming): A review. *European Journal of Social Psychology, 3*(4), 361–388.

Landow, G. P. (1990). Hypertext and collaborative work: The example of intermedia. In J. Galegher, R. Kraut, & C. Egido (Eds.), *Intellectual teamwork: Social and technological foundations of cooperative work* (pp. 407–428). Hillsdale, NJ: Lawrence Erlbaum.

Langer, J. (1986). Computer technology and reading instruction: Perspectives and directions. In J. Orasanu (Ed.), *Reading comprehension: From research to practice* (pp. 189–202). Hillsdale, NJ: Lawrence Erlbaum.

Larson, C. E., & LaFasto, F. M. J. (1990). *Team Work: What must go right/what can go wrong.* Beverly Hills: Sage Publications.

Lee, A. (1989, March). A scientific methodology for MIS case studies. *MIS Quarterly, 13*(1), 33–50.

LeeBaert, D., & Dickinson, T. (1991). A world to understand: Technology and the awakening of human possibility. In D. LeeBaert (Ed.), *Technology 2001: The future of computing and communication* (pp. 293–321). Cambridge, MA: The MIT Press.

Lesgold, A. (1983). When can computers make a difference? *Theory into Practice, 22,* 247–252.

Levin, J., & Boruta, M. (1983). Writing with computers in classrooms: You get exactly the right amount of space! *Theory into Practice, 22,* 291–295.

Levine, J. M., & Moreland, R. L. (1990). Progress in small group research. *Annual Review of Psychology, 41,* 585–634.

Levitt, Barbara, & March, James G. (1988). Organizational learning. *Annual Review of Sociology, 14,* 319–340.

Levy, M., & Hinckfuss, J. (1990). Program design and student talk at computers. *CAELL Journal, 1*(4), 21–26.

Levy, M. (1990). Towards a theory of CALL. *CAELL Journal, 1*(4), 5–7.

Lewis, F. (1982). *Facilitator: A microcomputer decision support system for small groups.* Unpublished doctoral dissertation, University of Louisville.

Liang, T-P. (1988). Model management for group decision support. *MIS Quarterly, 12*(4), 667–680.

Lichtenstein, S., & Fischhoff, B. (1980). Training for calibration. *Organizational Behavior and Human Performance, 26,* 149–171.

Likert, R. (1961). *New patterns of management.* New York: McGraw-Hill.

Lim, L. H., Raman, K. S., & Wei, K. K. (1990). Does GDSS promote more democratic decision-making? *The Singapore Experiment, 23,* 59–68.

Limbaugh, M., Kapur, S., & Norguard, N. (1991). Workflow manager. *NCR Journal, 5*(1).

Lipson, J., & Fisher, K. (1983). Technology and the classroom: Promise or threat? *Theory into Practice, 22,* 253–259.

Long, M., & Porter, P. (1985). Group work, interlanguage talk, and second language acquisition. *TESOL Quarterly, 19,* 207–228.

Losada, M., Sanchez, P., & Noble, E. E. (1990). Collaborative technology and group process feedback: Their impact on interactive sequences in meetings. In *Proceedings of the Conference on Computer-Supported Cooperative Work* (pp. 53–64). New York: Association for Computing Machinery.

Lozanov, G. (1978). *Suggestology and outlines of suggestopedy.* New York: Gordon & Breach.

Lozanov, G. (1982). Suggestology and suggestopedia. In R. Blair (Ed.), *Innovative approaches to language teaching* (pp. 146–159). Rowley, MA: Newbury House.

Luthans, F., & Davis, T. R. V. (1982). An idiographic approach to organizational behavior research: The use of single case experimental designs and direct measures. *Academy of Management Review, 7*(3), 380–391.

Lynch, W. (1990, April). Social aspects of human-computer interaction. *Educational Technology,* pp. 26–30.

Maddison, P., & Maddison, A. (1987). The advantages of using microcomputers in language teaching. In D. Hainline (Ed.), *New developments in computer-assisted language learning* (pp. 20–31). New York: Nichols Publishing Company.

Maddux, C. (1989). Computer networking in education: The need for evaluation studies. *Computers in the Schools, 6*(1/2), 37–43.

Maidique, M.A. (1980). Entrepreneurs, champions, and technological innovations. *Sloan Management Review, 21*(2), 59–76.

Maier, N. R. F. (1963). *Problem-solving discussions and conferences: Leadership methods and skills.* New York: McGraw-Hill.

Maier, N. R. F. (1967). Assets and liabilities in group problem solving: The need for an integrative function. *Psychological Review, 74,* 239–249.

Maier, N. R. F. (1970). *Problem solving and creativity.* Pacific Grove, CA: Brooks/Cole.

Maier, N. R. F., & Hoffman, L. (1960). Using trained "developmental" discussion leaders to improve further the quality of group decisions. *Journal of Applied Psychology, 44,* 247–251.

Maier, N. R. F., & Maier, R. (1957). An experimental test of the effects of "developmental" vs. "free" discussions on the quality of group decisions. *Journal of Applied Psychology, 41*(5), 320–323.

Malone, T. W. (1986). Organizing information processing systems: Parallels between human organizations and computer systems. In W. Zachery, S. Robinson, & J. Black (Eds.), *Cognition, computation, and cooperation.* Norwood, NJ: Ablex Publishing Corp.

Malone, T. W. (1987). Modeling coordination in organizations and markets. *Management Science, 33,* 1317–1332.

Malone, T. W. (1988, February). *What is coordination theory?* Paper presented at the National Science Foundation Coordination Theory Workshop, Massachusetts Institute of Technology.

Malone, T. W., & Crowston, K. (1990). What is coordination theory and how can it help design cooperative work systems? In *Proceedings of the Conference on Computer-Supported Cooperative Work* (pp. 357–370). New York: Association for Computing Machinery.

Mandviwalla, M., Gray, P., Olfman, L., & Satzinger, J. (1991). The Claremont GDSS Support Environment. In J. R. Nunamaker, Jr. (Ed.), *Proceedings of the Twenty-Fourth Annual Hawaii International Conference on System Sciences,* Vol. 3 (pp. 600–607). Los Alamitos, CA: IEEE Computer Society Press.

Markoff, J. (1986, November). Computing in groups. *High Technology, 6,* pp. 56–57.

Markus, M. L., & Robey, D. (1988). Information technology and organizational change: Causal structure in theory and research. *Management Science, 34*(5), 583–598.

Martin, E. Wainright, DeHayes, Daniel W., Hoffer, Jeffrey A., & Perkins, William C. (1991). *Managing information technology: What managers need to know.* New York: Macmillan.

Martz, W. B., Vogel, D. R., & Nunamaker, J. F., Jr. (in press). Electronic meeting systems: Results from the field. *Decision Support Systems.*

Mason, R. O., & Mitroff, I. I. (1973). A program for research on management information systems. *Management Science, 19*(5), 475–485.

Mason, R. O., & Mitroff, I. I. (1981). *Challenging strategic planning assumptions.* New York: John Wiley & Sons.

McCarthy, R. (1991). The hardware industry: MS-DOS makes big strides. *Electronic Learning, 10*(7), 20–23.

McCartt, A. T., & Rohrbaugh, J. (1989). Evaluating group decision support system effectiveness: A performance study of decision conferencing. *Decision Support Systems, 5,* 243–254.

McConnell, D. (1990). Case study: The educational use of computer conferencing. *Educational and Training Technology International, 27,* 190–208.

McFadden, Fred R., & Hoffer, Jeffrey A. (1991). *Database management* (3rd. ed.). Redwood City, CA: Benjamin/Cummings.

McGinnis, J. (1989). *Computers in composition at the University of Arizona.* Doctoral dissertation, University of Arizona, Tucson.

McGoff, C. J., & Ambrose, L. (1991). Empirical information from the field: A practitioners' view of using GDSS in business. In J. R. Nunamaker, Jr. (Ed.), *Proceedings of The Twenty-Fourth Annual Hawaii International Conference on System Sciences,* Vol. 3 (pp. 805–811). Los Alamitos, CA: IEEE Computer Society Press.

McGoff, C. J., Hunt, A., Vogel, D., & Nunamaker, J. (1989). The role of the facilitator in the IBM decision support center process. Working paper, Department of MIS, College of Business and Public Administration, University of Arizona, Tucson.

McGrath, J. E. (1984). *Groups: Interaction and performance.* Englewood Cliffs, NJ: Prentice Hall.

McGrath, J. E. (1990). Time matters in groups. In J. Galegher, R. Kraut, & C. Egido (Eds.), *Intellectual teamwork: Social and technological foundations of cooperative work* (pp. 23–78). Hillsdale, NJ: Lawrence Erlbaum.

McGrath, J. E. (1991). Time, Interaction and Performance (TIP): A theory of groups. *Small Group Research, 22*(2), 147–174.

McGrath, J. E., & Altman, I. (1966). *Small group research: A synthesis and critique of the field.* New York: Holt, Rinehart & Winston.

McGrath, J. E., & Hollinghead, A. B. (1991, January). Interaction and performance in computer-assisted work groups. Paper presented at a conference on team decision making in organizations, University of Maryland.

McGrath, J. E., & Kelly, J. R. (1986). *Time and human interaction: Toward a social psychology of time.* New York: The Guilford Press.

McGrath, J. E., Martin, J., & Kulka, R. A. (Eds.). (1982). *Judgment calls in research.* Beverly Hills: Sage Publications.

McGregor, D. (1960). *The human side of enterprise.* New York: McGraw-Hill.

McKeon, R. (1972). The uses of rhetoric in a technological age: Architectonic productive arts. In L. Bitzer & E. Black (Eds.), *The prospect of rhetoric* (pp. 44–63). Englewood Cliffs, NJ: Prentice Hall.

McLaughlin, B. (1987). *Theories of second-language learning.* London: Edward Arnold.

McLeod, P. (1991, February). What we know, what we don't know, and what we think we know about GDSS: Results of a meta-analysis. Paper presented at the *Human Computer Interaction Consortium Workshop,* University of Michigan.

Meyer, A. D., & Goes, J. B. (1988). Organizational assimilation of innovations: A multilevel contextual analysis. *Academy of Management Journal, 31,* 897–923.

Meyers, R. A., & Seibold, D. R. (1990). Perspectives on group argument: A critical review of persuasive arguments theory and an alternative structurational view. In S. Deetz (Ed.), *Communication Yearbook,* (V. 1., 13 pp. 268–302). Beverly Hills: Sage Publications.

Miles, M. B., & Huberman, A. M. (1984). *Qualitative data analysis: A sourcebook of new methods.* Beverly Hills: Sage Publications.

Miles, R. (1975). *Theories of management implications for organizational behavior and development.* New York: McGraw-Hill.

Miller, C. R. (1984). Genre and social action. *Quarterly Journal of Speech, 70,* 151–167.

Miller, J. G. (1960, February). Information input overload and psychopathology. *American Journal of Psychiatry, 117,* 695–704.

Miller, J. G. (1978). *Living systems.* New York: McGraw-Hill.

Miller, P., & O'Leary, T. (1989). Hierarchies and American ideals, 1900–1940. *Academy of Management Review, 14*(2), 250–265.

Miner, F. C. (1979). A comparative analysis of three diverse decision making approaches. *Academy of Management Journal, 22,* 81–93.

Mintzberg, H. (1982). Comments on the Huber, Kunreuther and Schoemaker, and Chestnut, and Jacoby Papers. In G. R. Ungson & D. N. Braunstein (Eds.), *Decision making: An interdisciplinary inquiry* (pp. 280–287). Boston: Kent Publishing Co.

Mintzberg, H., Raisinghani, D., & Theoret, A. (1976). The structure of "unstructured" decision processes. *Administrative Science Quarterly, 21,* 246–275.

Mitchell, T. R., & Scott, W. G. (1990). America's problems and needed reforms: Confronting the ethic of personal advantage. *Academy of Management Executive, 4*(3), 23–34.

Mitroff, I. I., & Emsholf, J. R. (1979). On strategic assumption-making: A dialectical approach to policy and planning. *Academy of Management Review, 4,* 1–12.

Mitroff, I. I., & Mason, R. O. (1980). Structuring ill-structured policy issues: Further explorations in a methodology for messy problems. *Strategic Management Journal, 1,* 331–342.

Molnar, A. (1990, March). Information and communications technology: Today and in the future. *Educational Technology,* pp. 59–62.

Monge, P. R., McSween, C., & Wyer, J. (1989). A profile of meetings in corporate America: Results of the 3M Meeting Effectiveness Study. Available from 3M Meeting Management Institute, 3M Austin Center, Building A145-5N-01, P.O. Box 2963, Austin, TX 78769-2963.

Moran, T. (1981). An applied psychology of the user. *ACM Computer Surveys, 13,* 1–21.

Mosvick, R., & Nelson, R. (1987). *We've got to start meeting like this! A guide to successful business meeting management.* Glenview, IL: Scott, Foresman.

Murphy, A. L., & Winkler, R. L. (1974). Probability forecasts: A survey of National Weather Service forecasters. *Bulletin of the American Meteorological Society, 55,* 1449–1453.

Myers, D. G., & Lamm, H. (1976). The group polarization phenomenon. *Psychological Bulletin, 83,* 602–627.

Newman, D. (1990, April). Opportunities for research on the organizational impact of school computers. *Educational Researcher,* pp. 8–13.

Niederman, F. (1990). *Influence of computer-based support on group process and outcomes in problem formulation.* Unpublished doctoral dissertation, University of Minnesota.

Nielsen, J. (Ed.). (1989). *Coordinating user interfaces for consistency.* San Diego: Academic Press.

Noel, T., & Wynne, B. E. (1991). Grounding collaborative work support system research in theory: The case for procedural justice theory. In J. F. Nunamaker, Jr. (Ed.), *Proceedings of the Twenty-Fourth Annual Hawaii International Conference on System Sciences,* Vol. 3 (pp. 573–579). Los Alamitos, CA: IEEE Computer Society Press.

Nolan, R. L., & Wetherbe, J. C. (1980). Toward a comprehensive framework for MIS research. *MIS Quarterly, 4*(2), 1–19.

Nunamaker J. F., Jr., Applegate, L. M., & Konsynski, B. R. (1987). Facilitating group creativity with GDSS. *Journal of Management Information Systems, 3*(4), 5–19.

Nunamaker, J. F., Jr., Applegate, L. M., and Konsynski, B. R. (1988). Computer-aided deliberation: Model management and group decision support. *Journal of Operations Research, 36*(6), 826–848.

Nunamaker, J. F., Jr., Chen, M., & Purdin, T. (1990–91). Systems development in information systems research. *Journal of Management Information Systems, 7*(3), 89–106.

Nunamaker, J. F., Jr., Dennis, A. R., George, J. F., Valacich, J. S., & Vogel, D. R. (1991). Electronic meeting systems to support group work: Theory and practice at Arizona. *Communications of the ACM, 34*(7), 40–61.

Nunamaker J. F., Jr., Dennis, A. R., Valacich, J. S., & Vogel, D. R. (1991). Information technology for negotiating groups: Generating options for mutual gain. *Management Science, 37*(10), 1325–1346.

Nunamaker J. F., Jr., Vogel, D., Heminger, A., Martz, B., Grohowski, R., & McGoff, C. (1989). Experiences at IBM with Group Support Systems: A field study. *Decision Support Systems, 5*(2), 183–196.

Nunamaker, J. F., Jr., Vogel, D., & Konsynski, B. (1989). Interaction of task and technology to support large groups. *Decision Support Systems, 5*(2), 139–152.

Nutt, P. C. (1984). Types of organizational decision processes. *Administrative Science Quarterly, 29*(3), 414-450.

O'Keefe, D. J. (1977). Two concepts of argument. *Journal of the American Forensic Association, 13,* 121–28.

O'Reilly, C. (1991). Organizational behavior: Where we've been, where we're going. *Annual Review of Psychology, 42,* 427–58.

Ong, W. (1982). *Orality and literacy: The technologizing of the word.* London: Methuen, Inc.

Oppenheim, L. (1987). Making meetings matter: A report to the 3M Corporation. 3M Meeting Management Institute, Building A145-5N-01, P.O. Box 2963, Austin, TX 78769-2963.

Orlikowski, W. J. (in press). The duality of technology: Rethinking the concept of technology in organizations. *Organization Science.*

Osborn, A. F. (1957). *Applied imagination* (2nd ed.). New York: Charles Scribner's Sons.

Oskamp, S. (1967). Overconfidence in case-study judgments. *Journal of Consulting Psychology, 29,* 261–265.

Ouchi, W. (1981). *Theory Z.* Reading, MA: Addison-Wesley.

Pacanowsky, M. E., & O'Donnell-Trujillo, N. (1983). Organizational communication as cultural performance. *Communication Monographs, 50,* 126–147.

Papert, S. (1987). Computer criticism vs. technocentric thinking. *Educational Researcher, 17,* 22–30.

Parkinson, C. N. (1957). *Parkinson's Law and other studies in administration.* Boston: Houghton Mifflin.

Parsons, T. (1951). *The social system.* Glencoe, IL: The Free Press.

Pasmore, W. A. (1988). *Designing effective organizations: The social technical system perspective.* New York: John Wiley & Sons.

Perrow, C. (1986). *Complex organizations: A critical essay* (3rd ed.). New York: Random House.

Peters, T. J., & Waterman, R. H. (1982). *In search of excellence.* New York: Harper & Row.

Phillips, G., & Santoro, G. (1989). Teaching group discussion via computer-mediated communication. *Communication Education, 38,* 151–161.

Phillips, L. (1986, October). Computing to consensus. *Datamation—International,* pp. 68-2–68-6.

Phillips, L. D., & Phillips, M. C. (1990). On facilitating groups. Working paper, Decision Analysis Unis, London School of Economics and Political Science, London, England.

Pica, T., & Doughty, C. (1985). Input and interaction in the communicative language classroom: A comparison of teacher-fronted and group activities. In S. Gass & C. Madden (Eds.), *Input and second language acquisition* (pp. 115–132). New York: Newbury House.

Pica, T. (1987). Second language acquisition, social interaction, and the classroom. *Applied Linguistics, 8*(1), 3–21.

Pinsonneault, A., & Kraemer, K. L. (1990). The effects of electronic meetings on group processes and outcomes: An assessment of the empirical research. *European Journal of Operation Research, 46,* 143–161.

Pinsonneault, A., & Kraemer, K. L. (1989). The impact of technological support on groups: An Assessment of the empirical research. *Decision Support Systems, 5*(2), 197–216.

Pool, I. (1990). *Technologies without boundaries: On telecommunications in a global age.* Cambridge: Harvard University Press.

Poole, M. S. (1983). Decision development in small groups II: A study of multiple sequences of decision making. *Communication Monographs, 50,* 206–232.

Poole, M. S. (1990). Group decision support systems: Software architectures. In A. P. Sage (Ed.), *Concise encyclopedia of information processing in systems and organizations,* Oxford, England: Pergamon Press.

Poole, M. S. (1991). Procedures for managing meetings: Social and technological innovation. In R. A Swanson & B. O. Knapp (Eds.), *Innovative meeting management* (pp. 53–110). Austin, TX: 3M Meeting Management Institute.

Poole, M. S., & DeSanctis, G. (1987). Group decision making and group decision support systems: A 3-year plan for the GDSS research project. Working paper, Management Information Systems Research Center, School of Management, University of Minnesota.

Poole, M. S., & DeSanctis, G. (1990). Understanding the use of group decision support systems: The theory of adaptive structuration. In C. Steinfield and J. Fulk (Eds.), *Organizations and communication technology* (pp. 173–193). Beverly Hills: Sage Publications.

Poole, M. S., DeSanctis, G., Kirsch, L., & Jackson, M. (1991). *An observational study of everyday use of a group decision support system.* Presented at the Twenty-Fourth International Conference on System Sciences, Kauai, HI.

Poole, M. S., Holmes, M., & DeSanctis, G. (1991). Conflict management in a computer-supported meeting environment. *Management Science, 37*(8), 926–953.

Poole, M. S., Seibold, D. R., & McPhee, R. D. (1985). Group decision-making as a structurational process. *Quarterly Journal of Speech, 71,* 74–102.

Poole, M. S., Shannon, D., & DeSanctis, G. (forthcoming). Electronic modes of negotiation. In L. Putnam & M. Roloff (Eds.), *Communication perspectives on negotiation.* Newbury Park: Sage Publications.

Porter, M. E., & Millar, V. E. (1985, July-August). How information gives you competitive advantage. *Harvard Business Review,* pp. 149–160.

Post, B. Q. (1992). Building the business case for group support technology. In J. F. Nunamaker, Jr., & R. H. Sprague, Jr. (Eds.), *Proceedings of Twenty-Fifth Annual Hawaii International Conference on System Sciences* (pp. 34–45). Los Alamitos, CA: IEEE Computer Society Press.

Putnam, L. (1986). Conflict in group decision-making. In R. Hirokawa and M. Poole (Eds.), *Communication and group decision-making* (pp. 175–196). Beverly Hills: Sage Publications.

Quinn, Robert E. (1988). *Beyond Rational Management.* San Francisco, CA: Jossey-Bass.

Ralston, D. A., Anthony, W. P., & Gustafson, D. J. (1985). Employees may love flextime, but what does it do to the organization's productivity? *Journal of Applied Psychology, 70,* 272–279.

Rao, V. S., & Jarvenpaa, S. L. (1989). Computer support of groups: A search for theoretical models. In R. Blanning & D. King (Eds.), *Proceedings of the Twenty-Second Annual Hawaii International Conference on System Sciences* (pp. 310–320). Los Alamitos, CA: IEEE Computer Society Press.

Reder, S., & Schwab, R. G. (1988). The communicative economy of the workgroup: Multi-channel genres of communication. *Proceedings of the Conference on Computer-Supported Cooperative Work* (pp. 354–368). New York: Association for Computing Machinery.

Reid, J. (1987). The learning style preferences of ESL students. *TESOL Quarterly, 21*(1), 87–111.

Reid, J. (1989). English as a Second Language in higher education: The expectations of the academic audience. In D. Johnson & D. Roen (Eds.), *Richness in writing: Empowering ESL students* (pp. 220–234). White Plains, NY: Longman Publishing Group.

Rice, R. (1984). *The new media: Communication, research, and technology.* Beverly Hills: Sage Publications.

Rice, R. E., & Shook, D. E. (1990). Voice messaging, coordination and communication. In J. Galegher, R. Kraut, & C. Egido (Eds.), *Intellectual teamwork: Social and technological foundations of cooperative work* (pp. 327–350). Hillsdale, NJ: Lawrence Erlbaum Press.

Rifkin, J. (1987). *Time wars: The primary conflict in human history.* New York: Henry Holt and Co.

Robinson, G. (1991). Effective feedback strategies in CALL: Learning theory and empirical research. In P. Dunkel (Ed.), *Computer-assisted language learning and testing: Research issues and practice* (pp. 155–168). New York: Newbury House.

Robinson-Staveley, K., & Cooper, J. (1990). The use of computers for writing: Effects on an English composition class. *Journal of Educational Computing Research, 6*(1), 41–48.

Roen, D. (1989). Developing effective assignments for second language writers. In D. Johnson & D. Roen (Eds.), *Richness in writing: Empowering ESL students* (pp. 193–206). New York: Longman Publishing Group.

Rogers, E. M. (1983). *Diffusion of innovations.* New York: The Free Press.

Rorvig, M. (1989). The substitutability of images for textual description of archival materials in an MS-DOS environment. In K. D. Lehman & H. Strohl-Goebel (Eds.), *The application of micro-computers in information, documentation, and libraries* (pp. xx–yy). New York: North-Holland.

Ruble, M. R. (1984). *An empirical test of a decision support system in a group decision making environment.* Unpublished doctoral dissertation, Arizona State University.

Rule, J., & Attewell, P. (1989). What do computers do? *Social Problems, 36*(3), 225–241.

Rutter, D. R., & Robinson, B. (1981). An experimental analysis of teaching by telephone: Theoretical and practical implications for social psychology. In G. M. Stephenson & J. H. Davis (Eds.), *Progress in applied social psychology* (pp. xx–yy). New York and London: John Wiley & Sons.

Salancik, G. R. (1979). Field stimulations for organizational behavior research. *Administrative Science Quarterly, 24*(4), 638–649.

Salancik, G. R., & Pfeffer, J. (1978). A social information processing approach to job attitudes and task design. *Administrative Science Quarterly, 23,* 224–253.

Salomon, G. (1990). Cognitive effects with and of technology. *Communications Research, 17*(1), 26–44.

Salovey, P., & Birnbaum, D. (1991). Influence of mood on health-relevant cognitions. *Journal of Personality and Social Psychology, 57,* 539–551.

Sambamurthy, V., & DeSanctis, G. (1989). An experimental evaluation of GDSS effects on group performance during stakeholder analysis. In R. Blanning & D. King (Eds.), *Proceedings of the Twenty-Third Annual Hawaii International Conference on System Sciences* (Vol. 3, pp. 79–88). Los Alamitos, CA: IEEE Computer Society Press.

Sambamurthy, V., DeSanctis, G., & Poole, M. S. (1991). *The effects of alternative computer-based technologies on equivocality reduction during group decision-making.* Unpublished manuscript, School of Business, Florida State University, Tallahassee.

Sandelands, L. E., & Stablein, R. E. 1987. The concept of organization mind. *Research in the Sociology of Organizations, 5,* 135–162.

Satzinger, J. (1991). *User interface consistency across end-user application programs: Effect on learning and satisfaction.* Unpublished doctoral dissertation, Claremont Graduate School, Claremont, CA.

Sayers, D. (1989). Bilingual sister classes in computer writing networks. In D. Johnson & D. Roen (Eds.), *Richness in writing: Empowering ESL students* (pp. 120–133). White Plains, NY: Longman Publishing Group.

Schein, Edward H. (1984). Coming to a new awareness of organizational culture. *Sloan Management Review, 25,* 3–16.

Schlesinger, A. E. (1965). *A thousand days.* Boston: Houghton Mifflin.

Schramm, W. (1954). *The process and effects of mass communication.* Urbana, IL: University of Illinois Press.

Schwartzman, H. B. (1987). The significance of meetings in an American mental health center. *American Ethnologist, 14*(2), 271–294.

Schwartzman, H. B. (1989). *The meeting: Gatherings in organizations and communities.* New York: Plenum.

Schwenk, C., & Huff, A. S. (1986). Argumentation in strategic decision making. In R. Lamb and P. Shrivastrava (Eds.), *Advances in strategic management* (Vol. 4, pp. 189–202). Greenwich, CT: JAI Press.

Scott, R. L. (1967). On viewing rhetoric as epistemic. *Central States Speech Journal, 18,* 9–17.

Scott-Morton, M. S. (1984). The state of the art of research. In F. W. McFarlan (Ed.), *The information systems research challenge: Proceedings* (pp. 13–41). Harvard Business School Research Colloquium, Boston, MA: Harvard Business School Press.

Scott-Morton, M. S. (1970). Program management and interactive management decision systems. MIT Working paper, pp. 436–470.

Seely-Brown, J., & Duguid, P. (1989, September). Learning & improvisation: local sources of global innovation. Unpublished manuscript, Institute for Research on Learning, Palo Alto, CA.

Seibold, D. R., & Meyers, R. (1986). Communication and influence in group decision-making. In R. Y. Hirokawa & M. S. Poole (Eds.), *Communication and group decision-making* (pp. 133–156). Beverly Hills: Sage Publications.

Sengupta, K., & Te'eni, D. (1991). Reducing cognitive conflict through feedback in GDSS: An experiment in the formulation of group preferences. In J. F. Nunamaker, Jr. (Ed.), *Proceedings of the Twenty-Fourth Annual Hawaii International Conference on System Sciences,* Vol. 3 (pp. 631–640). Los Alamitos, CA: IEEE Computer Society Press.

Shannon, C. E., & Weaver, W. (1949). *The mathematical theory of communication.* Urbana, IL: University of Illinois Press.

Shaw, M. E. (1981). *Group dynamics: The psychology of small group behavior* (3rd ed.) New York: McGraw-Hill.

Shepherd, A., Mayer, N., & Kuchinsky, A. (1990). Strudel—An extensible electronic conversation toolkit. In *Proceedings of the Conference on Computer-Supported Cooperative Work* (pp. 93–104). New York: Association for Computing Machinery.

Shlecter, T. (1990). The relative instructional efficiency of small group computer-based training. *Journal of Educational Computing Research, 6,* 329–341.

Shor, R. (1988). The educational importance of local area networks in secondary schools. *Computers in Education, 13*(2), 129–134.

Short, J., Williams, E., & Christie, B. (1976). *The social psychology of telecommunication.* New York: John Wiley & Sons.

Shrivastava, P. 1983. A typology of organizational learning systems. *Journal of Management Studies, 20,* 1–28.

Shure, G. H., Rogers, M. S., Larsen, I. M., & Tassone, J. (1962). Group planning and task effectiveness. *Sociometry, 25,* 263–282.

Siegel, J., Dubrovsky, V., Kiesler, S., & McGuire, T. W. (1986). Group processes in computer mediated communication. *Organizational Behavior and Human Decision Processes, 37,* 157–187.

Silver, M. S. (1990). Decision support systems: Directed and non-directed change. *Information Systems Research, 1*(1), 47–70.

Simmel, G. (1950). *The sociology of Georg Simmel* (K. H. Wolff, Trans.). Glencoe, IL: The Free Press.

Simon, H. A. (1960). *The new science of management decision.* New York: Harper & Row.

Simon, H. A. (1976). *Administrative behavior* (3rd ed.). New York: Macmillan.

Simon, H. A. (1991). Individual learning and organizational routine. *Organization Science, 2*(1), 125–134.

Sinclair, R. (1988). Mood, categorization breadth, and performance appraisal: The effects of order of information acquisition and affective state on halo, accuracy, information retrieval, and evaluations. *Organizational Behavior and Human Decision Processes, 42,* 22–46.

Sirc, G., & Reynolds, T. (1990). The face of collaboration in the networked writing classroom. *Computers and Composition, 7,* Special Issue, 53–70.

Slovic, P., & Fischhoff, B. (1977). On the psychology of experimental surprises. *Journal of Experimental Psychology: Human Perception and Performance, 3,* 544–551.

Smagorinsky, P. (1989). Small groups: A new dimension in learning. *English Journal, 78*(2), 67–70.

Smith, G. F. (1988). Towards a heuristic theory of problem structuring. *Management Science, 34*(12), 1489–1506.

Smith, G. F. (1989). Defining managerial problems: A framework for prescriptive theorizing. *Management Science, 35*(8), 963–981.

Smith, J. Y., & Vanecek, M. T. (1990, Fall). Dispensed group decision making using nonsimultaneous computer conferencing: A report of research. *Journal of Management Information Systems, 7*(2), 71–92.

Sniezek, J., & Henry, R. A. (1989). Accuracy and confidence in group judgment. *Organizational Behavior and Human Decision Processes, 43,* 1–28.

Snyder, Joel M., & Lynch, Kevin J. (1990). *Technology to Support Groupware: The CARAT architecture.* Unpublished working paper. Tucson: University of Arizona.

Software made simple. (1991, September 30). *Business Week,* No. 3233, pp. 92–101.

Sommer, R. (1969). *Personal space: The behavioral basis of design.* Englewood Cliffs, NJ: Prentice Hall.

Sprague, R. H. (1980). A framework for the development of decision support systems. *MIS Quarterly, 4*(4), 1–26.

Sprague, R. H., & Watson, H. (1979). Bit by bit: Toward decision support systems. *California Management Review, 22*(1), 61–68.

Sproull, L., & Kiesler, S. (1986). Reducing social context cues: Electronic mail in organizational communication. *Management Science, 32*(11), 1492–1512.

Stabell, C. B. (1974). Individual differences in managerial decision making processes: A study of conversational computer usage. Doctoral dissertation, MIT.

Stasser, M. (1988). Computer simulation as a research tool: The DISCUSS method of group decision making. *Journal of Experimental Social Psychology, 24,* 393–422.

Steeb, R., & Johnston, S. C. (1981). A computer-based interactive system for group decision making. *IEEE Transactions on Systems, Man, and Cybernetics,* SMC-11, 544–552.

Stefik, M., & Brown J. S. (1989). Toward portable ideas. In M. Olsen (Ed.), *Technological support for group collaboration* (pp. 147–165). Hillsdale, NJ: Lawrence Erlbaum.

Stefik, M., Foster, G., Bobrow, D. G., Khan, K., Lanning, S., & Suchman, L. (1987, January). Beyond the chalkboard: Computer support for collaboration and problem solving in meetings. *Communications of the ACM, 30*(1), 32–47.

Steiner, I. D. (1966). Models for inferring relationships between group size and potential group productivity. *Behavioral Science, 11,* 273–283.

Steiner, I. D. (1972). *Group process and productivity.* New York: Academic Press.

Stone, P. J., & Luchetti, R. (1985). Your office is where you are. *Harvard Business Review, 63,* 102–117.

Straub, D. (1989, June). Validating instruments in MIS research. *MIS Quarterly, 13*(2), 147–169.

Suchman, L. (1987). *Plans and situated actions.* Cambridge: Cambridge University Press.

Sullivan, P. (1989). Human-computer interaction perspectives on word-processing issues. *Computers & Composition, 6*(3), 11–33.

Sundstrom, E., & Altman, I. (1989). Physical environments and work-group effectiveness. In L. Cummings and B. Staw (Eds.), *Research in Organizational Behavior* (Vol. 2, pp. 175–209). Greenwich, CT: JAI Press.

Tajfel, H., & Turner, J. C. (1986). The social identity theory of intergroup behavior. In S. Worchel & W. G. Austin (Eds.), *Psychology of intergroup relations, 2nd ed.* (pp. 7–24). Chicago: Nelson-Hall.

Tan, B. C. Y., Wei, K. K., & Raman, K. S. (1991). Effects of support and task type on group decision outcome: A study using SAMM. In J. F. Nunamaker, Jr. (Ed.), *Proceedings of the Twenty-Fourth Annual Hawaii International Conference on System Sciences* (Vol. 3, pp. 537–546). Los Alamitos, CA: IEEE Computer Society Press.

Taylor, F. W. (1947). Testimony before the special house committee, 1912. In F. W. Taylor (Ed.), *Scientific management* (pp. 5–287). New York: Harper & Row.

Thompson, J. D., & Tuden, A. (1959). Strategies, structure, and processes of organizational decision. In J. D. Thompson, P. B. Hammond, R. W. Hawkes, B. H. Junker, & A. Tuden (Eds.), *Comparative studies in administration* (pp. 195–216). Pittsburgh: University of Pittsburgh Press.

Thrush, E., & Hardisty, D. (1990). Computer networks for language learning: The creation of meaning through interaction. *CAELL Journal, 1*(1), 24–30.

Tobia, P. M., & Becker, M. C. (1990, August). Making the most of meeting time. *Training and Development Journal,* pp. 34–38.

Todd, P., & Benbasat, I. (1987). Process tracing methods in decision support systems research: Exploring the black box. *MIS Quarterly, 11*(4), 493–512.

Todd, P., & Benbasat, I. (1991). An experimental investigation of the impact of computer-based decision aids on decision making strategies. *Information Science, 2*(2), 87–115.

Tolcott, M. A., & Holt, V. E. (Eds.). (1987). *Impact and potential of decision research on decision aiding.* Technical Report, Decision Science Consortium Inc, Reston, VA.

Toulmin, S. E. (1969). *The uses of argument.* Cambridge: Cambridge University Press.

Toulmin, S. E., Rieke, R., & Janik, A. (1984). *An introduction to reasoning* (2nd ed.). New York: Macmillan.

Trevino, L. K., Daft, R. L., & Lengel, R. H. (1990). Understanding managers' media choices: A symbolic interactionist perspective. In J. Fulk & C. Steinfield (Eds.), *Organizations and communication technology* (pp. 71–94). Newbury Park, CA: Sage Publications.

Trevino, L., Lengel, R., & Daft, R. (1987). Media symbolism, media richness and media choice in organizations: A symbolic interactionist perspective. *Communication Research, 14*(5), 553–575.

Turoff, M., & Hiltz, S. R. (1982). Computer support for group versus individual decisions. *IEEE Transactions on Communications, 30*(1), 82–91.

Tversky, A., & Kahneman, D. (1974, September 24). Judgement under uncertainty: Heuristics and biases. *Science,* pp. 1124–1131.

Tyran, C. K., Dennis, A. R., Nunamaker, J. F., Jr., & Vogel, D. R. (1991). *Application and design of electronic meeting systems to support strategic management.* Working paper, University of Arizona.

Underwood, J. (1990). Research in hypertext: Desiderata. *CAELL Journal, 1*(4), 33–35.

Valacich, J. S. (1989). *Group size and proximity effects on computer mediated idea generation: A laboratory investigation.* Unpublished doctoral dissertation, University of Arizona.

Valacich, J. S., & Dennis, A. R. (1992). *A mathematical model of performance for computer-mediated group idea generation.* Working paper, Indiana University.

Valacich, J. S., Dennis, A. R., & Connolly, T. (in press). Idea generation in computer-based groups: A new ending to an old story. *Organizational Behavior and Human Decision Processes.*

Valacich, J. S., Dennis, A. R., & Nunamaker, J. F., Jr. (1991). Electronic meeting support: The Group Systems concept. *International Journal on Man-Machine Studies, 34,* 261–282.

Valacich, J. S., Dennis, A. R., & Nunamaker, J. F., Jr. (1992). Group size and anonymity effects on computer-mediated idea generation. *Small Group Research, 23*(1), 49–73.

Valacich, J. S., Vogel, D., & Nunamaker, J. F., Jr. (1989). Integrating information across sessions and between groups in group decision support systems. In R. Blanning & D. King (Eds.), *Proceedings of the Twenty-Second Annual Hawaii International Conference on System Sciences* (Vol. 3, pp. 291–299). Los Alamitos, CA: IEEE Computer Society Press.

Vancil, R. F., & Green, C. H. (1984, January/February). How CEOs use top management committees. *Harvard Business Review, 62,* 65–73.

Van de Ven, A. H., Angle, H. L., & Poole, M. S. (1989). *Research on the management of innovation: The Minnesota studies.* New York: Harper & Row.

Van de Ven, A. H., & Delbecq, A. (1974, December). The effectiveness of nominal, Delphi, and interacting group decision making processes. *Academy of Management Journal, 17,* 605–621.

Van Gundy, A. (1988). *Techniques of structured problem solving* (2nd ed.). New York: Van Nostrand Reinhold.

Varela, J. A. (1971). *Psychological solutions to social problems.* New York: Academic Press.

Venkatesh, M., & Wynne, B. E. (1991). Effects of problem formulation and process structures on performance and perceptions in a GDSS environment: An experiment. In J. F. Nunamaker, Jr. (Ed.), *Proceedings of the Twenty-Fourth Annual Hawaii International Conference on System Sciences* (Vol. 3, pp. 564–572). Los Alamitos, CA: IEEE Computer Society Press.

Venkatraman, N., & Grant, J. H. (1986). Construct measurement in organizational strategy research: A critique and proposal. *Academy of Management Review, 11*(1), 71–87.

References

Vinokur, A., & Burnstein, E. (1974). Effects of partially shared persuasive arguments on group induced shifts: A group problem solving approach. *Journal of Personality and Social Psychology, 29*(3), 305–315.

Vogel, D. R. (1988). The impact of "messy" data on group decision making. In *Proceedings of the Twenty-First Annual Hawaii International Conference on System Sciences* (Vol. 3, pp. 240–246). Los Alamitos, CA: IEEE Computer Society Press.

Vogel, D. R., & Nunamaker, J. F., Jr. (1990a). Design and assessment of a group decision support system. In J. Galegher, R. Kraut, & C. Egido (Eds.), *Intellectual teamwork: Social and technological foundations of cooperative work* (pp. 511–528). Hillsdale, NJ: Lawrence Erlbaum Press.

Vogel, D. R., & Nunamaker, J. F., Jr. (1990b). Group decision support system impact: Multi-methodological exploration. *Information & Management, 18,* 15–28.

Vogel, D. R., Nunamaker, J., George, J., & Dennis, A. (1988). Group decision support systems: Evolution and status at the University of Arizona. In R. M. Lee, A. M. McCosh, & P. Migliarese (Eds.), *Organizational decision support systems* (pp. 287–304). Elsevier Science Publishing Co.

Vogel, D. R., Nunamaker, J. F., Jr., Martz, W. B., Jr., Grohowski, R., & McGoff, C. (1989–90, Winter). Electronic meeting system experience at IBM. *Journal of Management Information Systems, 6*(3), 25–43.

Volkema, R. (1983). Problem formulation in planning and design. *Management Science, 28*(6), 639–652.

Von Winterfeldt, D., & Edwards, W. (1986). *Decision analysis and behavioral research.* New York: Cambridge University Press.

Vygotsky, L. (1978). *Mind in society.* Cambridge, MA: Harvard University Press.

Wagner, G. R. (1981, September–October). Decision support systems: Computerized mind support for executive problems. *Managerial Planning,* pp. 9–16.

Wagner, G., & Nagasunderam, M. (1988). Meeting process augmentation: Real substance of GDSS. In R. M. Lee, A. M. McCash, & P. Migliarese (Eds.), *Organizational Decision Support Systems* (pp. 305–316). New York: Elsevier Science Publishing Co.

Waldo, D. (1948). *The administrative state.* New York: Ronald Press.

Walsh, James P., & Ungson, Gerardo Rivera. (1991). Organizational memory. *Academy of Management Review, 16*(1), 57–91.

Walton, M. (1990). *Deming management at work.* New York: Putnam's Sons.

Warnick, B., & Inch, E. S. (1989). *Critical thinking and communication: The use of reason in argument.* New York: Macmillan.

Watson, J. (1990–91). Cooperative learning and computers: One way to address student differences. *The Computing Teacher, 18*(4), 9–12.

Watson, R., DeSanctis, G., & Poole, M. S. (1988, September). Using a GDSS to facilitate group consensus: Some intended and unintended consequences. *MIS Quarterly, 12*(3), 463–478.

Watson, R. T., Alexander, M., Pollard, C., & Bostrom, R. P. (1991). Use and adaptation: A key-pad based group decision support system. 3M Meeting Management Institute, Building A145-5N-01, P.O. Box 2963, Austin, TX 78769-2963.

Webb, N. (1982). Student interaction and learning in small groups. *Review of Educational Research, 52,* 421–445.

Webb, N. (1985). Verbal interaction and learning in peer-directed groups. *Theory into Practice, 24*(1), 32–39.

Weeks, G. D., & Chapanis, A. (1976). Cooperative and conflictive problem solving in three telecommunication modes. *Perceptual and Motor Skills, 42,* 879–917.

Weick, K. E. (1979). *The social psychology of organizing.* Reading, MA: Addison-Wesley.

Weick, K. E. (1984). Theoretical assumptions and research methodology selection. In F. W. McFarlan (Ed.), *The information systems research challenge: Proceedings* (pp. 111–132). Harvard Business School Research Colloquium, Boston, MA: Harvard Business School Press.

Weick, K. E. (1985). Cosmos vs. chaos: Sense and nonsense in electronic contexts. *Organizational Dynamics,* pp. 51–64.

Weill, P., & Olson, M. H. (1989, Summer). An assessment of the contingency theory of management information systems. *Journal of Management Information Systems, 6*(1), 59–85.

Weinberg, S., Rovinski, S., Weiman, L., & Beitman, M. (1981, February). Common group problems: A field study. *Small Group Behavior, 12*(1), pp. 81–92.

Weisband, S. (in press). Group discussion and first advocacy effects in computer-mediated and face-to-face decision making groups. *Organizational Behavior and Human Design Processes.*

Wenzel, J. W. (1977). Toward a rationale for value-centered argument. *Journal of the American Forensic Association, 13,* 150–158.

Wenzel, J. W. (1982). On fields of argument as propositional systems. *Journal of the American Forensic Association, 18,* 204–213.

White, S. E., Dittrich, J. E., & Lang, J. R. (1980). The effects of group decision-making process and problem-situation complexity on implementation attempts. *Administrative Science Quarterly, 25,* 428–440.

Williams, E. (1977). Experimental comparisons of face-to-face and meditated communication: A review. *Psychological Bulletin, 84,* 963–976.

Williams, F., Rice, R. E., & Rogers, E. M. (1988). *Research methods and the new media.* New York: The Free Press.

Williams, K., Harkins, S., & Latane, B. (1981). Identifiability as a deterrent to social loafing: Two cheering experiments. *Journal of Personality and Social Psychology, 40*(2), 303–311.

Winniford, M. A. (1989). *The effect of electronic meeting support on large and small decision-making groups.* Unpublished doctoral dissertation, University of Arizona.

Winniford, M. A. (1991). Issues in automated voting. In J. F. Nunamaker, Jr. (Ed.), *Proceedings of the Twenty-Fourth Annual Hawaii International Conference on System Sciences* (Vol. 3, pp. 621–630). Los Alamitos, CA: IEEE Computer Society Press.

Winston, P. H. (1977). *Artificial intelligence.* Reading, MA: Addison-Wesley.

Witte, E. 1972. Field research on complex decision-making processes: The phase theorem. *International Studies of Management and Organization, 2,* 156–182.

Yankelovich, N., Hann, B., Meyrowitz, N., & Drucker, (1988). Intermedia: The concept and the construction of a seamless information environment. *IEEE Computer, 21,* 81–92.

Yates, J. (1989). *Control through communication: The rise of system in American management.* Baltimore: The Johns Hopkins University Press.

Yates, J. F. (1990). *Judgment and decision making.* Englewood Cliffs, NJ: Prentice Hall.

Zack, M. H., & McKenney, J. L. (1989). Characteristics of organizational information domain: An organizational information processing perspective. Harvard Business School Working Paper 89-127.

Zajonc, R. B. (1968). Social facilitation theory. In D. Cartwright & A. Zander (Eds.), *Group dynamics: Research and theory* (pp. 63–73). New York: Harper & Row.

Zellermayer, M., Salomon, G., Globerson, T., & Givon, H. (1990). Enhancing writing-related metacognitions through a computerized writing partner. *American Educational Research Journal.*

Zigurs, I., DeSanctis, G., & Billingsley, J. (1989). Exploring attitudinal development in computer-supported groups. In R. Blanning & D. King (Eds.), *Proceedings of the Twenty-Second Annual Hawaii International Conference on System Sciences* (Vol. 3, pp. 353–358). Los Alamitos, CA: IEEE Computer Society Press.

Zigurs, I., DeSanctis, G., & Billingsley, J. (1991, Spring). Adoption patterns and attitudinal development in computer-supported meetings: An exploratory study with SAMM. *Journal of Management Information Systems, 7*(4), 1–20.

Zigurs, I., & Dickson, G. W. (1990). *Computer support for decision-making teams: The issue of outcome quality.* Faculty Working Paper Series, College of Business and Administration, University of Colorado.

Zigurs, I., Poole, M. S., & DeSanctis, G. (1988, December). A study of influence in computer-mediated group decision making. *MIS Quarterly, 12*(4), 625–644.

Zmud, R. W., Lind, M. R., & Young, F. W. (1990). An attribute space for organizational communication channels. *Information Systems Research, 1,* 440–457.

Zmud, R. W., & Boynton, A. C. (1989). *Survey measures and instruments in MIS: Inventory and appraisal.* Working paper, Florida State University, Tallahassee.

Zuboff, S. (1984). *In the age of the smart machine: The future of work and power.* New York: Basic Books, Inc.

Contributors

Leonard M. Jessup
College of Business Administration
California State University, San Marcos
820 West Los Vallecitos Boulevard
San Marcos, CA 92096
(619) 752-4233
FAX (619) 752-4030

Leonard M. Jessup is an Assistant Professor of Management Information Systems in the College of Business Administration at California State University, San Marcos. He received a Ph.D. in Organizational Behavior, with a minor in Management Information Systems, from the University of Arizona. He is a member of the Academy of Management and The Institute of Management Science. His research interests include individual and group problem solving and uses and effects of computer-based information systems for collaborative work. His instructional interests include teaching information systems and management courses and developing software to support problem solving. He has numerous research publications and has coauthored *Assignment One: City Guide,* an award-winning software application for language learning

Joseph S. Valacich
Decision and Information Systems Department
School of Business
Indiana University
10th and Fee Lane
Bloomington, IN 47405
(812) 855-3489
FAX (812) 855-8679

Joseph S. Valacich is an Assistant Professor of Decision and Information Systems at Indiana University. He received a bachelors degree in Computer Science and MBA from the University of Montana, and, in 1989, a Ph.D. from the University of Arizona. Dr. Valacich worked for several years in the information systems field as a programmer, analyst, and product manager. His research interests are in group decision behavior, focusing primarily on the design and investigation of group support technologies on group and organizational processes and performance. His publications on these and related topics include articles in *Management Science, Communications of the ACM, IEEE Transactions on Systems, Man, and Cybernetics,* and the *International Journal on Man-Machine Studies.*

Robert Anson
Computer Information Systems and
Production Management Department
Boise State University
1910 University Drive
Boise, ID 83725
(208) 385-3029
FAX (208) 385-3779
EMAIL RISANSON@IDBSU

Robert Anson is an Assistant Professor of Computer Information Systems at Boise State University. Rob holds a B.A. from the University of Washington, and an MBA and Ph.D. in Management Information Systems from Indiana University. His major research interests include group facilitation and facilitation in computer-supported environments.

Robert Paul Bostrom
Department of Management
University of Georgia
Athens, GA 30602
(404) 542-3559
FAX (404) 542-3743

Robert P. Bostrom is an Associate Professor of Management and the Program Director of the Collaborative Work Support Systems Research Project at the University of Georgia. He is also president of a small consulting company that provides consulting, training, and meeting facilitation services. Bob holds a B.A. in Chemistry and MBA from Michigan State University, an M.S. in Computer Science from SUNY at Albany, and a Ph.D. in MIS from the University of Minnesota. His overall research mission focuses on improving organizational systems through the effective integration of human/social and technological dimensions.

Victoria Kathleen Clawson
Walden University
Minneapolis, MN

103 West Parkway Drive
Columbia, MO 65203
(314) 442-4275
FAX (314) 442-4275

Victoria Clawson is an organizational and management consultant and trainer. Her interests and experience are in the areas of human behavior and performance, managing change, organizational design, and facilitation. Vikki holds a B.S. in Psychology and M.S. in Counseling and Education from Purdue University. She is currently working on a Ph.D. in Administration and Management at Walden University. Her major research interest is group facilitation in computer-supported environments.

Contributors

Terry Connolly
Department of Management and Policy
Eller School of Business
University of Arizona
Tucson, AZ 85721
(602) 621-5937
FAX (602) 621-7483

Terry Connolly is Professor of Management and Policy at the University of Arizona, where he also coordinates the Decision Behavior Laboratory. His academic background includes degrees in electrical engineering, sociology and organizational behavior, and he has held faculty appointments at Georgia Institute of Technology, University of Illinois, and University of Chicago. His primary research interests are in the cognitive processes underlying judgment and choice behavior in organizational settings, and the effects of information processing technologies on them. His publications on these and related topics include two books and over seventy journal papers and book chapters.

Alan R. Dennis
Department of Management
Terry College of Business
University of Georgia
Athens, GA 30602
(404) 542-3902
FAX (404) 542-3743

Alan R. Dennis is an Assistant Professor of Management Information Systems in the Terry College of Business at the University of Georgia. He received a Bachelor of Computer Science from Acadia University (Nova Scotia), an MBA from Queen's University (Ontario), and a Ph.D. in Management Information Systems from the University of Arizona. Prior to entering the Arizona doctoral program, he spent three years on the faculty of the Queen's School of Business and was a winner of the AACSB National Doctoral Fellowship. He has published articles in a variety of journals, including *Communications of the ACM, Academy of Management Journal, MIS Quarterly, Journal of MIS, Small Group Research,* and *IEEE Transactions on Systems, Man, and Cybernetics.* His current research interests include electronic meeting systems, systems analysis and design, and business process reengineering.

Gerardine DeSanctis
University of Minnesota
271 19th Avenue South
Minneapolis, MN 55455
(612) 624-8562
FAX (612) 626-1316

Gerardine DeSanctis is an Associate Professor of Information and Decision Sciences at the University of Minnesota. Since 1984 she has worked with an interdisciplinary team investigating the design and implementation of group support systems. Along with her

Minnesota colleagues, she has published numerous articles and monographs related to GSS. Her research in the GSS area is part of her larger research interests in decision support systems and information systems implementation. She currently serves as Associate Editor for *Management Science, Information Systems Research,* and *Organization Science.*

Joy Egbert
Center for the Study of Higher Education
College of Education
University of Arizona
Tucson, AZ 85721
(619) 752-1005

Joy Egbert is an Instructor in the Department of English as a Second Language at Palomar College in San Marcos, California. She has an M.A. in ESL from the University of Arizona and is currently ABD in Higher Education (emphasis in Teaching) at the same institution. Her dissertation focuses on the use of technology to support effective language learning environments. Her instructional interests include curriculum/materials development and teacher training. She has published numerous articles, has received grants to support the investigation of computer-assisted language learning, and has coauthored *Assignment One: City Guide,* an award-winning software application for language learning.

Brent Gallupe
School of Business
Queen's University
Dunning Hall, Room 131
Kingston, Ontario K7L 3NG Canada
(416) 545-2361
FAX (416) 545-2013

R. Brent Gallupe is an Associate Professor of Information Systems in the School of Business, Queen's University, Canada. His Ph.D. in Management Information Systems is from the University of Minnesota. His current research interests include group decision support systems, end-user computing, and the evaluation of information systems. His work has appeared in such journals as *Management Science, MIS Quarterly, Journal of Applied Psychology,* and *Information and Management.*

Joey F. George
Department of Management Information Systems
College of Business & Public Administration
University of Arizona
Tucson, AZ 85721
(602) 621-2748
FAX (602) 621-2433

Joey F. George is an Assistant Professor of MIS at the University of Arizona. He earned his bachelor's degree at Stanford University in 1979 and his Ph.D. in Management at the University of California at Irvine in 1986. His research focuses on information systems in the workplace. His current research investigates the effects of electronic meeting systems (EMS) use on the group work process and its outcomes, EMS use in non-American cultures, and the effects of extensive computerization in organizational work groups.

Paul Gray
Programs in Information Science
The Claremont Graduate School
Claremont, CA 91711-6190
(714) 621-8209
FAX (714) 621-8390

Paul Gray is Professor and Chairman of Information Science at The Claremont Graduate School, Claremont, CA. He has been involved in decision support systems, computer-based modeling, and simulation for many years in both research institutes and universities. He began his work in Group Support Systems in 1980. He received his Ph.D. in Operations Research from Stanford University, and holds degrees in mathematics and electrical engineering from New York University, The University of Michigan, and Purdue University. He spent most of the 1960s at SRI International. Since then he has been a professor at several universities, including Stanford, Georgia Tech, Southern California, and Southern Methodist. He became President-Elect of The Institute of Management Sciences in 1991 and President in September 1992. He was previous Secretary (1975–79) and Vice President-at-Large (1983–86) of The Institute of Management Sciences. In 1991 he became founding editor of *International Information Systems*, a research journal.

Jeffrey A. Hoffer
Decision and Information Systems Department
School of Business
Indiana University
10th & Fee Lane
Bloomington, IN 47405
(812) 855-9703
FAX (812) 855-8679

Jeffrey Hoffer received his Ph.D. in Operations Research from Cornell University. He was on the faculty of Case Western Reserve University (CWRU) until 1980, when he joined the IU School of Business. At CWRU he created the MIS course in the Executive MBA program and served for one year as Director of their MBA program. His research, writing, and consulting have been in the areas of database management, management of information systems, computer security management, and group decision support. He has written ten books, two monographs, and over thirty published papers in these fields. His database text (coauthored with Fred McFadden of the University of Colorado) is the leading book of its kind in North American business schools. Dr. Hoffer has also been active in executive education programs in both the United States and in Chile. He has served as an Associate Editor of three top research journals, and was General Chair of the 1985 International Conference on Information Systems. He is a cofounder of the College on Information Systems of The Institute of Management Sciences. He has consulted with a variety of organizations, including AT&T, NCR, FMC Corp., and the Indianapolis Symphony Orchestra.

Andrea B. Hollingshead
Psychology Department
University of Illinois
603 East Daniel Street
Champaign, IL 61820
(217) 333-4921
FAX (217) 244-5876

Andrea B. Hollingshead is a graduate student in social psychology at the University of Illinois. She received her Master's degree in Social Psychology from the University of Illinois in 1991. Her interests include small group processes, group decision making and intergroup relations. She is coauthor, with J. McGrath, of "The whole is less than the sum of the parts: Interaction and performance in computer-assisted work groups" to appear in M. Guzzo (Ed.) *Team Decision Making in Organizations,* in press.

George P. Huber
Department of Management
University of Texas
CBA 4.202
Austin, TX 78712
(512) 471-9609
FAX (512) 471-3937

George P. Huber is the Foundren Foundation Chaired Professor of Business at the University of Texas at Austin. His research focuses on organizational theory, design, and decision making. His 1984 *Management Science* article on the nature and design of postindustrial organizations was awarded First Prize in the International Prize competition sponsored by The Institute of Management Sciences. Since 1985, he and Dr. William H. Glick have been leading a multi-investigator study of changes in the design and effectiveness of over one hundred organizations.

Michele H. Jackson
Department of Speech-Communication
460 Folwell Hall
9 Pleasant Street S.E.
University of Minnesota
Minneapolis, MN 55455
(612) 624-5800
FAX (612) 624-6369

Michele H. Jackson (M.A., University of Minnesota) is a doctoral student in the Department of Speech-Communication at the University of Minnesota. Her research interests include rhetoric and knowledge, argumentation, and organizational communication. Currently she is investigating the implications of new communication technologies for rhetorical theory and models of rationality.

Contributors

Munir Mandviwalla
Programs in Information Science
The Claremont Graduate School
Claremont, CA 91711-6190
(714) 621-8209
FAX (714) 621-8390

Munir Mandviwalla is a doctoral candidate in MIS at the Claremont Graduate School Programs in Information Science. He has an MBA from the Drucker Management Center at Claremont Graduate School and a BSC from Boston University. He teaches part-time at California State Polytechnic University, Pomona, and has worked in systems-related jobs in Pakistan. He recently won first prize in the Zenith Masters of Innovation Business competition for the CGS Environment that is described in Exhibit 2 of this paper and is based on a design framework from his dissertation. He has presented papers on Group Support Systems, end-user training, interface design, and meeting memory at such conferences as the Hawaii International Conference on System Sciences (HICSS), International Conference on Information Systems (ICIS), and IFIP Working Group 8.2 on Desktop Information Technology.

Joseph E. McGrath
Psychology Department
University of Illinois
603 East Daniel Street
Champaign, IL 61820
(217) 333-4921
FAX (217) 244-5876

Joseph E. McGrath is a Professor of Psychology at the University of Illinois, Urbana. He received his Ph.D. in Social Psychology from the University of Michigan in 1955. His research interests include small group processes, methodology, gender issues, and the social psychology of time. He is coauthor, with A. Hollingshead, of "The whole is less than the sum of the parts: Interaction and performance in computer-assisted work groups" to appear in M. Guzzo (Ed.) *Team Decision Making in Organizations,* in press.

David Karl Meader
School of Business Administration
University of Michigan
Ann Arbor, MI 48109-1234
(313) 764-6715
FAX (313) 936-3168

David Meader is a doctoral candidate in Computer and Information Systems at the University of Michigan School of Business Administration. Meader's research applies organization theories to information systems problems. His work focuses on information equivocality, miscommunication, communication media, and new-product-development projects. Meader has worked as a marketing director and systems consultant for Teknekron Industries in Berkeley, a systems analyst for Chevron, and an end-user computing consultant for Bank of America. He holds a B.S. in Computer Science from the University of Michigan, and a MBA from the University of North Carolina at Chapel Hill.

Brian E. Mennecke
Decision and Information Systems Department
School of Business
Indiana University
10th and Fee Lane
Bloomington, IN 47405
(812) 855-9703
FAX (812) 855-8679

Brian E. Mennecke is a Ph.D. candidate at Indiana University and holds an MBA in Decision Science and Finance from Miami University in Oxford, Ohio. Prior to commencing his studies at Indiana, he was employed for three years as an MIS instructor at Miami University, for one and one half years as a consultant with Enviropact, Inc., of Miami, Florida, and for one year as an analyst with Allstate Insurance, Deerfield, Illinois. His areas of interest include group support systems, group and team development, organizational communications, organizational impacts of information system technology, and distributed systems. He is a member of The Institute of Management Science and the Association for Computing and Machinery.

Jay F. Nunamaker, Jr.
Department of Management Information Systems
College of Business & Public Administration
University of Arizona
Tucson, AZ 85721
(602) 621-2748
FAX (602) 621-2433

Jay F. Nunamaker, Jr. is Head of the Department of Management Information Systems and Professor of MIS and Computer Sciences at the University of Arizona. He received his Ph.D. from Case Institute of Technology in Systems Engineering and Operations Research. He was Associate Professor of Computer Science and Industrial Management at Purdue University before joining the University of Arizona in 1974 to develop the MIS program. He has authored numerous papers on group support systems, the automation of software construction, performance evaluation of computer systems, and decision support systems for systems analysis and design, and has lectured throughout Europe (including the USSR), Asia, and South America.

Lorne Olfman
Programs in Information Science
The Claremont Graduate School
Claremont, CA 91711-6190
(714) 621-8209
FAX (714) 621-8390

Lorne Olfman is Assistant Professor of Information Science at The Claremont Graduate School. He received his Ph.D. in Business-MIS from Indiana University where he first worked with Group Support Systems. The Decision Room at Claremont provided Lorne with ample opportunity to extend his research in this domain, including the design of Group Support Systems and the survey of attitudes of workers toward such systems.

Contributors

Lorne's other major research interests include end-user software training and evaluation of information systems. He has published articles in *MISQ, DSS Journal, Infor,* and the *Journal of Information Systems.* During winter and spring 1992 he was a Visiting Scholar at the College of Business, University of Hawaii at Manoa.

Richard Brian Polley
Business Administration
Lewis & Clark College
Portland, OR 97219
(503) 768-7602
FAX (503) 768-7379

Richard Brian Polley is Associate Professor of Business at Lewis & Clark College and Editor of *Small Group Research.* His recent publications on field theory, observational methods, leadership, and teambuilding have appeared in *Encyclopedia of Sociology, Group and Organizational Studies, Social Psychology Quarterly, Advances in Group Process,* and *Journal of Management.* He was senior editor of *The SYMLOG Practitioner: Applications of Small Group Research* (Praeger, 1988). His book, *Group Field Dynamics: Finding the Fulcrum* (Sage Publications), will appear in 1992.

Marshall Scott Poole
Department of Speech-Communication
460 Folwell Hall
9 Pleasant Street S.E.
University of Minnesota
Minneapolis, MN 55455
(612) 624-2808
FAX (612) 624-6369

Marshall Scott Poole (Ph.D., University of Wisconsin) is a Professor of Speech-Communication at the University of Minnesota. His research interests include group and organizational communication, organizational innovation, and social interaction analysis. For the past five years he has been a primary investigator on the Minnesota GDSS Research Project.

John Satzinger
Department of Management
Terry College of Business
University of Georgia
Athens, GA 30602
(404) 542-3746
FAX (404) 542-3743

John Satzinger is an Assistant Professor of Management at the University of Georgia. He received his Ph.D. in the Management of Information Systems at The Claremont Graduate School in 1991. Research interests include user interface design, Group Support Systems, and end-user training. He has held positions in industry at Carter Hawley Hale Information Services and The H. F. Ahnmanson Companies.

Philip J. Stone
Psychology Department
William James Hall
Harvard University
Cambridge, MA 02138
(617) 495-3847
FAX (617) 495-3728

Philip Stone completed undergraduate work at the University of Chicago and graduate studies at Harvard. A faculty member of Harvard for over thirty years, his research topics include group dynamics and environmental psychology. His work with architect Robert Luchetti on office design received an award from the French Ministry of Culture. He has consulted with manufacturers of office furnishings and with organizations seeking environments that support collaboration.

Douglas R. Vogel
Department of Management Information Systems
College of Business & Public Administration
University of Arizona
Tucson, AZ 85721
(602) 621-2748
FAX (602) 621-2433

Douglas R. Vogel is an Assistant Professor of MIS at the University of Arizona. He has been involved with computers and computer systems in various capacities for over twenty years. He received his M.S. in Computer Science from U.C.L.A. in 1972 and his Ph.D. in Business Administration from the University of Minnesota in 1986 where he was also research coordinator for the MIS Research Center. His current research interests bridge the business and academic communities in addressing questions of the impact of management information systems on aspects of interpersonal communication, group decision making, and organizational productivity.

Gerald R. Wagner
16009 Avenue de la Fontaine
Austin, TX 78734
(512) 794-8858
FAX (512) 794-8861

Dr. Wagner is presently with Collaborative Technologies Corporation, Austin, Texas, which he founded in 1988. Previously he founded Execucom Systems Corporation, which was the leading DSS software corporation prior to its acquisition in 1984. From 1978 until 1979 he was Professor and Head of the Operations Research Group, University of Texas, College of Engineering. Wagner founded the DSS International Conference in 1981 and the TEAMS conference in 1991. His academic research associated with human judgment modeling led to his interest in DSS and Group DSS in the mid-1970s. He had the first working prototype of a GDSS in an electronic decision room in 1978.

Its functionality and appearance were very similar to most of the "decision centers" that exist today.

Karl Edward Weick, Jr.
School of Business Administration
University of Michigan
Ann Arbor, MI 48109-1234
(313) 996-1716
FAX (313) 763-5688

Karl E. Weick, who is the Rensis Likert Collegiate Professor of Organizational Behavior and Psychology at the University of Michigan, is also the former Editor of *Administrative Science Quarterly,* the leading research journal in the field of organizational studies. Dr. Weick studies and writes about such topics as how people make sense of confusing events, the effects of stress on thinking and imagination, techniques for observing complicated events, self-fulfilling prophecies, the consequences of indeterminacy in social systems, the craft of applying social science, substitutes for rationality, determinants of effective managerial performance, high-reliability organizations, and the management of professionals. Weick's writing about these topics is collected in four books, one of which—*The Social Psychology of Organizing*—is cited as furnishing significant background for Peters and Waterman's *In Search of Excellence,* and one of which—the co-authored *Managerial Behavior, Performance and Effectiveness*—won the 1972 Book of the Year award from the American College of Hospital Administration. In addition to the four books, Weick's writing appears in 40 journal articles, 35 chapters in edited books, 61 book reviews, and 127 speeches presented to academic and practitioner audiences.

Bayard E. Wynne
Decision & Information Systems Department
School of Business
Indiana University
10th and Fee Lane
Bloomington, IN 47405
(812) 855-9703
FAX (812) 855-8679

Bayard E. Wynne is a Professor of Decision & Information Systems in the Graduate School of Business Administration at Indiana University and a former corporate officer of several Fortune 500 firms. Wynne's research focuses on management issues and the practice of management by individuals and groups in the context of interacting organization and information systems. Business strategy, innovation, technology transfer, team development, and problem solving and decision making are areas of active interest to him. Active internationally, Wynne researches, teaches or trains doctoral students, publishes, and consults in these areas. His professional activities as founder, officer, or merely participating member of societies span engineering, psychology, management, planning, and the management sciences.

Ilze Zigurs
University of Colorado, Boulder
College of Business and Administration
Campus Box 419
Boulder, CO 80309-0419
FAX (303) 492-5962

Ilze Zigurs completed her Ph.D. in Management Information Systems at the University of Minnesota in 1987. She is currently an Assistant Professor of Information Systems at the University of Colorado, Boulder, where she is continuing her research interests in group support systems and the behavioral and managerial issues associated with the development and use of information technology. Professor Zigurs' work has been published in the *MIS Quarterly, Decision Support Systems,* and the *Journal of Management Information Systems.*

Index

Action, 235
    aided, 238–41
    unaided, 237–40
Activity setting, 170, 172-77
Adaptability, of computers to classroom, 303
Adaptive Structuration Theory (AST), 9–11, 17, 162–63, 259, 285–89
    relationships in, 288
Affect/emotions, 157
Affiliation, 235, 243
    aided, 245–46
    unaided, 244–45
American Sign Language, 306–7
Analysis, unit of, 119
Anonymity, 66, 69–70, 74, 75–76, 132–33, 142–44, 145, 226, 274
Argument, 289–91
Argumentation, 289–91
Arizona, University of, 9, 64, 69, 88, 193, 194, 195, 198, 273
    administrative use, 15
    Boardroom 2000, 44
    curriculum, 15
    development, 13–14
    DIC Laboratory, 45
    Distributed GSS Laboratory, 45–46
    Enterprise Room, 46
    facilities, 14–15
    GSS program, 13–15
    inception, 13
    personnel, 14
    research, 15
    software, 14
    3rd Generation Room, 43–44
Aspects, 27
AST. *See* Adaptive Structure Theory
Aukland, University of, 46–47
Authenticity, in learning tasks, 298

Back-channel information, 82
Behavioral decision theory, GSS and, 270–80
Bindingness, 283–84
Boise State University, 34
Bootstrap Institute, 8
Boundary control, 184
Brainstorming, 69, 308
    electronic. *See* Electronic brainstorming
    group, 272–73
Bridge Toolkit, 205

CAD programs, 204
Calgary, University of, 47
California, University of, Irvine, 47–48
California State University, San Marcos, 34–35
CAM (Computer Aided Meeting), 16
Carleton University, 35
Case Western Reserve University, 35–36
Causal linkages, 233–35
Change, response to, 223
Claremont Graduate School, 13, 193, 194, 195, 198, 199
    administrative use, 30
    curriculum, 30
    development, 28–29
    facilities, 29–30
    GSS program, 28
    inception, 28
    personnel, 29
    research, 30
    software, 29
Claremont GSS Support Environment (CGSE), 205–11
    background, 205–6
    user environment, 206–10
        group interaction, 209–10
        information, 207–9

Claremont GSS Support Environment
  (CGSE), (*continued*)
    meeting, 207–208
    personal, 210
    tools, 210
Close-Up Lan, 31
Cocktail party syndrome, 286
Cognition, intentional, in learning, 299–300
Cognitive Science & Machine Intelligence
  Lab, 36
Cognitive style, 200
Collaboration, 185–86
  assumptions, 181–85
Collaboration Technology Suite (CTS), 27
Collaborative environments, 180
Collaborative Management Room, 14–15
Collaborative Systems Laboratory, 23
Collaborative work, 169, 170
  communication in, 79–80
  flexspace designs for, 185–86
  mistaken premises of, 179–85
Collaborative Work Lab, 21
Collectivism, 100–101, 106–7
Colorado, University of, 48
Comments, 20–21, 31
Communication, 79
  among participants, 200
Communication media, 91–92
  research, 282–85
Communication space, 165
Communication theories, 105–6
  and GSS, 281–93
Comparisons, problem of appropriate,
  118–19
Computer(s)
  adaptability to classroom, 303
  ESL classroom and, 295–96
  as material for supporting strategies,
    302–6
Computer-aided groups, difference between
  face-to-face and, 84
Computer Aided Team (CATeam) room, 30
Computer-assisted communication, 255–56
Computer assisted language learning,
  294–310
Computer-based heuristics, 71
Computer-based information systems, 5
Computer-based meeting support systems, 9
Computer conferences
  asynchronous, 84–85
  synchronous, 83–84
Computer messaging, 60–61
Conference and training centers, 186–88

Conference room, future, 19
Confusion, 232–33
Connection, 311
Consensus, 73, 228, 245
Consistency, 202
Content facilitation, 158–59
Context characteristics, 127
Contextualization, 235, 249–50
  aided, 250–51
  unaided, 250
Cooperative Group Decision Support System,
  63–64
Coordination theory, 107
Coordinator, 31
COPE, 18
Cultural differences, 200–201
Culture bridging, 316
Curtin University, 36–37
Customization, 206

Daft-Lengel hypothesis, 92
Database(s), 215
  on networks, 305–6
Database management, 216
  relationship to group memory
    management, 224–28
Database system
  capabilities for group memory
    management, 224–28
  limitations for group memory
    management, 228–29
Data management, 216
DECAID1 group software, 24
Decision-aiding software, 270–71
Decision-aiding technologies, 255–56
Decision and Information Systems (D&IS),
  21
Decision behavior research, 272–72
Decision heuristics, 70–71
Decision laboratories, 9
Decision making, 270. *See also* Group
  decision making
  strategies, 233
  theories of, 103–4
  theory of effects of GSS on, 258
Decision-making rooms, 180
Decision quality, 89, 118
Decision room, 63, 88, 171
Decision support systems (DSS), 60, 63,
  192–93
  computer-based, 88
  individual-based, 60

Index

Deliberation, 235, 246–47
    aided, 248
    unaided, 247–48
Delphi Technique, 63–64
Denver, University of, 49
Dependent variable, 116–17
Diamond/Slate, 27
Distributed group, support for, 223
Distributed networks, 260
Distributed teams, 313–14
Dramaturgical analysis, 184
Drill down information, 203

EIES (Electronic Information Exchange System), 23
EIES 2, 23, 24
ELECTRE, 64
Electronically mediated systems (EMS), 9–10, 80
Electronic blackboard, 135–36
Electronic brainstorming (EBS), 25, 139, 273, 274
Electronic bulletin board (EBB), 84
Electronic Data Systems, 37
Electronic Discussion System (EDS), 139
Electronic mail (E-mail), 84, 200
    in schools, 305–6
Electronic systems, 89
ELMER (Electronic Meeting Room), 178
    units, 186
E-mail. *See* Electronic mail
Empirical research, GSS. *See also* Research
    early experiences, 60, 64–66
    field studies, 60, 66–68
    history of, 59–77
    in-depth studies, 60, 68–73
    initial explorations, 60, 62–64
    roots, 60, 61–62
ENFI network, 306–7
Engelbart, Doug, 8–9
English as a Second Language. *See* ESL
Equivocality, 142, 245
ESL (English as a Second Language), 295–306, 308–09
Established groups, 72
Evaluation apprehension, 273
Execucom, 9
Exploration, 142
EXPRES, 26
External facilitator (EF), 159

Facilitating, in different GSS environments, 164–66
Facilitation
    framework, 157, 165
    functions, 160
    future research issues, 162–68
    group, 146–68
    in GSS effectiveness, 155
    procedural, 300
    process, 71, 158–59
    review of research literature, 152–56
    sources, 159–60
    targets, 158–59
    theoretical perspective of, 162–63
Facilitation activities, meeting stage, 150–52
Facilitation skills, developing, 166–67
"Facilitator," 63
Facilitators, 75, 160–61
    in GSS environments, 163–64
    training program for, 166–67
Facilities, 8–55
Fantasy theme analysis, 291–92
Flexspace, 169–91, 315
    designs for collaborative work, 185–86
    implications of, for future research on groups, 188
    questions for structured interview on, 189–91
Flextime, 170
Foundation Task, 70–71
Free riding, 273

Gallaudet University, 306–7
GCSS (Group (Internal) Communication Support Systems), 80–85
    asynchronous, 83
    synchronous, 83
    types, 81–85
Generate-and-choose task, 72
Generic analysis, 293
Genre theory, 293
Geographic Information Systems (GIS), 204
George Mason University, 37–38
Georgia, University of, 11–12
    administrative use, 20
    curriculum, 19–20
    development, 18
    facilities, 19
    GSS program, 18–20
    inception, 18

Georgia, University of, (*continued*)
    PC Research Laboratory, 49–50
    personnel, 18–19
    research, 19
    Smart Office, 50
    software, 18
GISS (Group Information Support Systems), 80, 86–88
Good calibration, 275
GPSS (Group Performance Support Systems), 80, 88–89
Groups, 257
    characteristics, 90, 127
Groups, (*continued*)
    cohesiveness, 72–73
    consensus of, 155
    functions, 93–94
    idea generation, 271–72
    implications of flexspace for future research on, 188
    large, 133
    member support, 93–94
    natural, 180
    production, 93–94
    satisfaction of, 155
    systems for technological enhancements of, 79–89
    well-being, 93–94
Group and organizational design, theory of effects of GSS on, 258
GroupJox, 200, 209–10
Group coordination, work flow management and, 223
Group Decision Aid, 62
Group decision making, 63. *See also* Decision making
    communication processes, 285–89
    computer-based support on, 62
    role of group memory and, 221–24
    socioegocentric model, 285
Group Decision Support Systems (GDSS), 256
    foundations for, 99
Group development, 72–73
Group dynamics, 170, 180, 185
    theoretical issues, 78–96
Group dynamics/process interventions research, 153–54
Group environment, 197
Group facilitation, GSS and, 146–68
Group interaction, 164–65, 286
Group members, education of, 222
    satisfaction, 73

Group memory, 132–33, 145, 215, 248
    creation of, 224
    group decision making and, 221–24
    in GSS, 214–29
    management capabilities, 225
    security and restrictiveness, 227
    support for the design of, 224–28
Group memory management, capabilities, 225
    database system capabilities for, 224–28
    database system limitations for, 228–29
    relationship to database management, 224–28
Group process, 4, 201, 255
    gains, 128
    intervention studies, 154
    losses, 129
    theories, 104–5
Group-process tasks, 13
Group productivity, 89
Group sensemaking in meetings
    potential negative contributions, 239
    potential positive contributions, 238
Group size, 4, 70, 75, 140–41
Group space, shared, 165
Group support software, 185
Group Support Systems (GSS)
    assumptions of, 101–11
    behavioral decision theory and, 270–80
    challenges in the evolution of, 311–18
    communication theory and, 281–93
    conceptual theory and, 257–68
    critique of facilities, 170–79
    design, 133–36
    in education, 308–9
    future directions of, 311–18
    group facilitation and 146–68
    interface in, 193
    issues in design, 194–205
    in language learning, 309–10
    nature of, 256–57
    in next century, 312–13
    potential effects, 130
    in practice, 136–45
    research and development on, 5–7
    research sites, 13
    role in organizations, 98–101
    sensemaking and, 230–52
    theories of, 101–11, 255–69
    use over time, 72
    user interface in, 192–213

Index

GroupSystems, 13–15, 16, 18, 20, 24, 25, 29, 31, 64, 66, 67, 69, 70, 71, 72–73, 135
Group tasks, classification system for, 90–91
Group theories, 93–95, 179–80
Groupthink, 184, 245
Group/user interface, 76
Group work, 221
    in learning, 297–98
Groupware, 7, 189, 291, 313
GROVE, 27
GXSS (Group External Communication Support System), 80, 85–86

Harvard Business School Advanced Management Program, 187
Hawaii, Unversity of, 50–51
Hawaii International Conference on System Sciences (HICSS), 6
Hindsight, 274–77
    bias, 272, 275–76
Hohenheim, University of, 43
    administrative use, 32
    curriculum, 32
    development, 30–31
    facilities, 31
    GSS program, 30
    inception, 30
    personnel, 31
    research, 32
    software, 31
H-P New Wave, 31
Human-computer interaction laboratory, 178
Human-computer interactions, 192–93
Hypermedia, 83
Hypertext, 203

IBM, 6, 67–68, 138, 155, 258
Idea generation, 142, 272–74
    group, 271–72
    in learning, 299
    process, 64, 69
Ignorance, 232–33
Indiana University, 11–12, 20–22, 38, 65
    administrative use, 22
    Collaborative Work Laboratory, 20, 38–39
    curriculum, 22
    development, 20
    facilities, 21
    inception, 20
    Institute for the Study of Developmental Disabilities (ISDD), 20
    personnel, 21
    research, 21–22
    software, 20–21
Individual decision maker, 271
Individualism, 98–100
Individual screen, interaction with public screen, 196–97
Individual workstation, design in the work environment, 197–99
Informating, 4
Information
    distribution, 216
    integration, 87
    interpretation, 216
    overload, 87–88
    processing, 87, 215
    sharing of, 87
Informational, external, 222
Information input and output
    database, 204
    numeric, 203–4
    object orientation, 204–5
    sources, extragroup, 86
    textual, 202–3
    visual, 204
Information-intensive work, use of computers in, 87
Information package, 207, 209
Information richness, 91–93, 94, 95, 283–84
Input devices, 197–98
Input-process-output model, 60, 116
Institute for Research on the Management of Information Systems (IRMIS), 11, 20
Institutional theories, 106–7
Instituto Tecnologico de Monterrey, 39
Integration, 202, 303
Interaction
    among participants, 199–200
    of the individual with the system, 198–99
    in learning, 296–97
    in real time, 306–8
    type of, 297–98
Interaction networks, synchronous, in education, 306–8
Interface, 192–213
    consistency, types of, 211–12

Interface, (*continued*)
  in a GSS, 193
  issues in design, 194–205
International Association of Conference Centers (IACC), 186–87
International Business Machines. *See* IBM
Interpretive perspective, 218
ISDOS, 13

Joint application development (JAD), 17
Joint Application Design, 67
Judgments, externalizing, 277–80
Just-in-time learning, 316–17

Knowledge acquisition, 216
Knowledge-based systems, 76

Language learning environment, strategies for creating an effective, 302
Language translation systems, 201
Leadership, 182–83
Learner-centered classroom, creating, 301
Learning circle, 303
Learning strategies
  computers as material for supporting, 302–6
  for optimal language, 296–302
Lighting, 178
Local area network (LAN), educational, 305–6
London School of Economics & Political Science, 40
Lotus Notes, 31

Management Priorities, 31
Measurement instruments, development of, 117–8
Meeting(s), 236–51
  administration, 202
  agenda, 72
  content specific to, 201–2
  cycle model, 151
  environments, 165
  facilitation framework, 156–62
  goal/outcome-directed, 148
  leader/facilitator, 134, 139
  memory, 202
  model, 148–52
  process, 65, 156–57
  relationships, 156–57
  research, 152–53
  task outcomes, 156–57
Member
  characteristics, 90
  satisfaction, 73
Memory, 202, 214
Michigan, University of, 12
  administrative use, 28
  curriculum, 28
  development, 26
  facilities, 27
  GSS program, 26–28
  inception, 26
  personnel, 27
  research, 27–28
  software, 27
Microsoft Windows. *See* Windows
Mindsight, 8–9, 16, 63, 211
Minnesota, University of, 9, 10–11, 51, 64–65, 88
  administrative use, 18
  curriculum, 18
  development, 16
  facilities, 17
  GSS program, 16–18
  inception, 16
  personnel, 17
  research, 17
  software, 16–17
Modes of activity, 93–94
Montana, University of, 51–52
Mosel, 31

Narrative analysis, 292–93
Networks, in schools, 305–6
New Jersey Institute of Technology (NJIT), 12, 22–24, 41
  administrative use, 24
  curriculum, 24
  development, 23
  facilities, 23
  inception, 22
  personnel, 23

Index

research, 23–24
software, 23
New York University, 41–42
Nominal Group Technique, 63–64
Nonverbal cues, 84
North Carolina, University of, at Greensboro, 52
Northern Colorado, University of, 53–54
North Texas, University of, 53
NUCLEUS, 212–13

Object Works, 31
Office tensions, 185
Optimal-stress atmosphere, in learning, 300
OptionFinder, 18, 19
Organizational change
    mechanisms, 101–11
    opposing perspectives of technology and, 102
Organizational information, 222
Organizational learning, 216–21
Organizational memory, 214, 216–17, 219–21
    creation of, 224
    retention and memory processing, 219–20
    role of, 220–21
Ottawa, University of, 54
Outcome preferences, 233–35
Overconfidence, 272, 274–77

Parallel communication, 132–33, 145
Parallelism, 69, 74–76
Paraverbal cues, 84
Participants
    interaction among, 199–200
    communication among, 200
PC Research Laboratory, 19
Performance, 73, 73
PIPELINE, 212–13
Planning laboratories, 9
Planning process, 181
PlexCenter, 13, 14–15, 171
PLEXSYS, 13, 14, 18, 20, 24, 64
Polarization processes, 245
Policy capturing, 277–80

Private screen, 198
Procedural facilitation, in learning, 300
Process facilitation, 71, 158–59
Process gains and losses, 126–33, 141
Process structure, 70–72, 128, 145
    in practice, 138–39
    in theory, 131–32
Process support, 128
    chauffeured style, 135–36
    interactive style, 135–136
    in practice, 140–44
    supported style, 135–36
    in theory, 132–33
Production blocking, 69, 84, 273, 274
Prompting, in learning, 300
Public screen, 194–96
    interaction with individual screen, 196–97

Queen's-Arizona Group Size Study, 70
Queen's Executive Decision Center (QEDC), 25
Queen's University, 12–13, 24–26, 42, 69
    administrative use, 26
    curriculum, 26
    development, 24
    facilities, 25
    inception, 24
    personnel, 25
    research, 25–26
    software, 24–25

Rationality, 289–91
Real-time network, 308
Reference disciplines, role in GSS research, 115–16
Research. *See also* Empirical research
    choosing an appropriate method, 114–15
    competing theories for, 103–7
    data issues within, 120
    development of measurement instruments, 117–18
    future, 76–77
    implications, 75–76
    method and measurement recommendations for, 121
    method issues within, 115–22
    methodological and measurement issues, 112–22
    methods, 112–13

Research, (*continued*)
  recommendations, 120–22
  role of reference disciplines, 115–16
  shifting foundations, 109-11
  summary of findings, 73–75
  theoretical foundations, 126–33
Research facilities, GSS, 33–55
Research model, 127
Research sites, capsule descriptions, 13–32
Responses, tone of, 274
Retention facilities, 220
Rhetorical analysis, 291

SAGE, 16, 18, 24–25
Same time/same place GSS, 193
SAMM (Software-Aided Meeting Management), 16, 18, 25, 65, 66, 68, 69, 71, 72, 203
San Diego State University, 42–43
Second language acquisition(SLA), 296
  theories of, 299
Sensemaking
  activities of, 235–36
  in equivocal contexts, 231–35
  GSS and , 230–52
  in meetings, 236–51
Session continuity support, 222–23
Shared screens, 199–200
Singapore, National University of, 40–4
SMALLTALK, 23
Smart Office, 18
Social presence, 283–84
Socioegocentric model, 285
Sociofugal, 169
Sociopital, 169
Soft determinism, 182
Software, 6, 14, 16–17, 18, 20–23, 27, 29, 31, 185
  development, 10
  GSS, 8–55
  toolkit, 134–36
Southern California, University of, 54–55
Stakeholder Identification and Assumption Surfacing tool (SIAS), 137
Stand-alone programs
  drill and practice, 304
  hypertext, 304–5
  simulation and content-free programs, 304
  word processing, 305

Strategic planning, 66–67
  groups, 64
  processes, 67
Structure, 74–75
  facilitator, 160–61
Structuring modules, 89
Structuring processes, 285
Studies over time, 72–73
Subgroups, 188
Support, facilitator, 161–62
Symbolic convergence, 292
Symbolic meaning, 283–84
System
  development process, 67
  usage, 117–18
Systems-structural perspective, 218

Task characteristics, 127, 134
Task circumplex, 90–91
Task complexity, 74
Task information, 141–42
Task-media combinations, 93
Task-media fit, 92–93
  on information richness, 95
Task performance processes, 91
Task quadrants, 91
Task structure, 128, 134, 308
  in practice, 137–38
  in theory, 131
Task support, 128, 134, 145
  in practice, 138
  in theory, 131
Task types, 90–91
Teamfocus, 27
Team rooms, 315–16
Teams, 181, 184
Technological diffusion, research on, 259
Technology, organizational change and, 102
Telephone conferences, 83
Temporal issues in group communication, 84
Theory of Adaptive Structuration. *See* Adaptive Structuration Theory
THINX, 204–5
Time and space, 170
Time Interaction and Performance (TIP) theory, 93–95
Total meeting environment, 187
Toulmin, S., 289–91
Trainers, 187–88

Index

Training centers, 186–88
Triangulation, 235, 241–42
    aided, 242–43
    unaided, 242
Typing, 73

User interface, in GSS, 192–213.
    See also Interface
Video conferencing, 260
Video phones, 82
Video systems
    asynchronous, 83
    synchronous, 82–83
Video wall, 82, 317
Video window, 82, 317
Virtual Classroom, 23, 24
VisionQuest, 18, 20, 24, 29
Voice messaging, 83

Wagner, Gerald R., 9
Western Washington University, 55
Wide area network (WAN), 305
WINDOWS™, 13, 29, 31, 183, 202, 204–5
Work flow
    automation, 314–15
    management and group coordination, 223
Work groups, 214–15
Work teams, 181–82
Writing Partner, 305
WYSIWIS (What You See Is What I See), 199, 246
XEROX PARC, 193, 194, 195, 196, 198, 199

MISQ Dec '90-14(4) Grohowski et al. 369-383
Sept '92-16(3) Tyran et al. 313-34 *

27^R